DI034287

WITHDRAWN FROM
MACALESTER COLLEGE
LIBRARY

Hitler and the Quest for World Dominion

Geoffrey Stoakes

Hitler
and the Quest for
World Dominion

BERG
Leamington Spa / Hamburg / New York
Distributed exclusively in the US and Canada by
ST. MARTIN'S PRESS   New York

Berg Publishers Limited
24 Binswood Avenue, Leamington Spa, CV32 5SQ, UK
Schenefelder Landstr. 14K, 2000 Hamburg 55, W.-Germany
175 Fifth Avenue (Room 400), New York, NY 10010, USA

Copyright © Geoffrey Stoakes 1986

All right reserved

British Library Cataloguing in Publication Data

Stoakes, Geoffrey
 Hitler's changing conception of foreign policy
 in the 1920s.
 1. Hitler, Adolf   2. Germany—Foreign relations
 —1933–1945
 I. Title
 327.43′0092′4   DD240

 ISBN 0–907582–56–7

Library of Congress Cataloging-in-Publication Data

Stoakes, Geoffrey.
  Hitler and the quest for world domination.

  Bibliography: p.
  Includes index.
  1. Hitler, Adolf, 1889-1945--Views on foreign
relations. 2. Germany--Foreign relations--1918-1933.
I. Title.
DD247.H5S7768 1986   327.43   86-31740
ISBN 0-907582-56-7

Printed in Great Britain by Billings of Worcester

Contents

For Carolyn and our Parents

Preface

I have accumulated a considerable number of debts of gratitude to institutions and individuals over the many years in which this project has been researched. The staff of the following institutions were always courteous and helpful: the Bundesarchiv in Coblenz; the Bavarian State Archives and Institut für Zeitgeschichte in Munich; and the Foreign Office Library and Public Record Office in London. Deserving of special acknowledgement, however, are the marvellous staff at the Wiener Library in London, especially Mrs G. Johnson, Miss J. Langmaid and Mrs C. Wichmann, who provided a stimulating environment in which to work as well as, at times, almost a second home.

Of the individuals who have guided my research I should like to record a special word of thanks to Professor Heinz Haushofer for a highly memorable and informative visit to the family home at Hartschimmelhof, Bavaria, and to Herr Fabian von Schlabrendorff, who provided useful information about Heinrich Class's unpublished second volume of memoirs. My indebtedness to several West German historians for their pioneering works in this field will become evident as the text unfolds. Fritz Stern, Hans Koch and Robert Cecil directed me to sources which I might otherwise have overlooked. Professor Francis Carsten made a number of thought-provoking comments on my original thesis. However, my main intellectual debt is to Professor William Carr, who first fired my enthusiasm for the Third Reich, and whose erudition, unfailing support and above all patience have helped to see this project through to its completion.

I am very grateful also to 'long-suffering' Elizabeth Swainston for the efficient way in which she typed — without visible signs of irritation — the seemingly unending drafts of this book and the original thesis. I would also like to thank Janet Langmaid for her second contribution to this book as a highly perceptive and acute sub-editor and Marion Berghahn for her confidence in the project.

My greatest debt, though, is to Carolyn, who provided both constant encouragement and merciful distraction in the hope of a 'normal life' in the future.

College of Ripon and York, St John
September 1985*   _Geoffrey Stoakes_

*The author would like to acknowledge the financial assistance of the College of Ripon and York, St. John, in the final stages of the preparation of this book.

Abbreviations

ADV	Alldeutscher Verband
Agd	*Auf gut deutsch*
A.Bl.	*Alldeutsche Blätter*
BAK	Bundesarchiv (Koblenz)
BHStA	Bayerisches Hauptstaatsarchiv
BO	Bund 'Oberland'
DAP	Deutsche Arbeiterpartei
DGFP	*Documents on German Foreign Policy*
DVFP	Deutschvölkische Freiheitspartei
HA	Hauptarchiv der NSDAP (National Archives Microfilm)
IfZ	Institut für Zeitgeschichte (Munich)
LA	*Letzte Aufzeichnungen* (Rosenberg's memoirs)
MK	*Mein Kampf*
MNN	*Münchener Neueste Nachrichten*
NS 26	Hauptarchiv der NSDAP (BAK Documentation)
NSDAP	Nationalsozialistische Deutsche Arbeiterpartei
PRO	Public Record Office (London)
VB	*Völkischer Beobachter*
VfZG	*Vierteljahrshefte für Zeitgeschichte*
VK	*Völkischer Kurier*
WPA	*Wirtschaftspolitische Aufbau-Korrespondenz*
ZfG	Zeitschrift für Geopolitik

Introduction

In view of the enormous outpouring of literature since the 1960s on the history of the Nazi Party and on the life of Adolf Hitler in particular, any new work on the subject needs to justify itself. This book has been written primarily as an attempt to remedy a serious, if understandable, imbalance in previous studies of the Nazi foreign policy programme,* namely the tendency to concentrate unduly on the ideas of Adolf Hitler to the consequent neglect of those of other Nazi theorists.[1] This tendency undoubtedly derives, in part, from the projection backwards into the 1920s of the belief (current for a long period) that the Third Reich was a monolithic, totalitarian entity, in which the only views that mattered were Hitler's.[2] The relative neglect of men such as Dietrich Eckart and Alfred Rosenberg is probably due also to the conviction that their ideological ruminations in the 1920s had little impact on decisions taken by the Nazis once they were in power.[3]

Adolf Hitler has therefore been portrayed as the prime mover in the development of a Nazi foreign policy programme in the 1920s. However, since the main sources for Hitler's ideas before 1923 are frequently short police or newspaper reports on speeches lasting between two and three hours, one cannot be entirely confident about

---

*The term 'programme' is used to distinguish the party's conceptual views on foreign affairs from the actual policy of the Third Reich after 1933.

1. W. Michalka has called for further examination of Nazi foreign goals and their impact on Hitler; 'Die nationalsozialistische Aussenpolitik im Zeichen eines "Konzeptionen-Pluralismus"'. Fragestellungen und Forschungsaufgaben' in M. Funke (ed.), *Hitler, Deutschland und die Mächte* (Dusseldorf, 1976), p. 62.

2. Ibid., pp. 55–6. See also K. Hildebrand, *The Foreign Policy of the Third Reich* (London, 1973), pp. 12–13.

3. B. M. Lane agrees; 'Nazi Ideology: Some Unfinished Business', *Central European History*, vol. 7 (1974), pp. 3–30.

conclusions based on this evidence.[4] By examining Hitler's ideas within the context of the views expressed by a broad cross-section of prominent party members, it should be possible to clarify Hitler's ideas, to assess the influence which other Nazi propagandists may have had on the evolution of a foreign policy programme, and, therefore, to estimate more precisely the extent of Hitler's authorship of it.

Some attempt has to be made also to relate Nazi ideas to the main theories about foreign affairs prevalent in early postwar Germany. By comparing the Nazi Party's emerging outlook on foreign affairs with those of influential individuals and groups, such as the Pan-German League and the geopoliticians, with whom the party came into contact in the early 1920s, it may be possible to determine their contribution — conscious or otherwise — to the party's developing strategies. Examining the Nazi Party's reaction to the diplomatic initiatives of successive Weimar governments should also throw its view of world affairs into clearer relief.[5]

Since the publication of Eberhard Jäckel's excellent analysis of Hitler's *Weltanschauung*, it has been customary to pay lip-service to the influence of ideological factors on the formulation of the Nazi foreign policy programme.[6] It is now usual for historians to note how neatly Hitler's self-proclaimed crusade against 'Jewish' Bolshevism dovetailed with his desire for an empire in Eastern Europe. However, there has been no systematic evaluation of the extent to which ideological preconceptions may have shaped initial Nazi approaches to foreign affairs. Hence, this study also attempts to provide the further analysis, which some historians have called for, of the crucial question of 'whether it was considerations of racist ideology or pure power politics which decisively influenced Hitler'.[7]

This study also confronts the continuing debate over whether Hitler's expansionist ambitions were limited to the acquisition of territory in Europe or whether he envisaged — however distantly —

---

4. Most of these reports have recently been published in E. Jäckel and A. Kuhn, *Hitler. Sämtliche Aufzeichnungen, 1905–1924*. With the publication of fuller accounts of Hitler's speeches in the *Völkischer Beobachter* after 1922 and in E. Boepple's collection, *Adolf Hitlers Reden* (Munich, 1925), one can argue with greater authority.

5. J. Hiden has recently argued that there has been no sustained analysis of the relationship between early Nazi views and Weimar foreign policies; 'National Socialism and Foreign Policy, 1919–33' in P. D. Stachura (ed.), *The Nazi Machtergreifung* (London, 1983), p. 151. The present study has by no means completely filled this gap.

6. E. Jäckel, *Hitlers Weltanschauung. Entwurf einer Herrschaft* (Tübingen, 1969). See also G. Schubert, *Anfänge nationalsozialistischer Aussenpolitik* (Cologne, 1963).

7. Hildebrand, *Foreign Policy*, pp. 19–20.

German world domination. Did Hitler conceive in the 1920s a *Stufenplan* — a stage-by-stage strategy by which Germany might realise this grandiose vision?[8]

No attempt has been made to relate the party's philosophy to long-term trends in German intellectual history or to investigate in any great detail Hitler's general intellectual development before 1914, since these tasks have already been accomplished by more capable hands.[9] The first chapter examines the ideas which were current in Munich in 1918 and 1919 amongst the men who provided the youthful German Workers' Party with the bare bones of a political philosophy before Adolf Hitler arrived on the scene. The second chapter investigates the extent to which Hitler brought with him, and sustained, a Pan-German outlook on foreign affairs. The third chapter assesses the impact of an emerging antisemitic and anti-Bolshevik ideology on his outlook. The fourth chapter scrutinises the motivations behind Hitler's evolving alliance strategy and the different conceptions of foreign policy with which he came into contact. The fifth chapter attempts to lay bare the nature and extent of Hitler's territorial ambitions for Germany and the degree to which they can be fairly attributed to geopolitical inspiration. The sixth chapter shows how Hitler's foreign policy programme was challenged from within the Nazi Party and how it was refined by the time Hitler wrote his second book in 1928.

By clarifying the exact nature of Hitler's views in the 1920s and his part in the formulation of a Nazi foreign policy programme, it is hoped that this book as a whole will help to illuminate the wider historiographical debate on Nazi foreign policy in the 1930s. Was it the execution of 'long established priorities' or the product of 'pure opportunism' or merely the result of the 'internal dynamics' of the Nazi régime?

8. The major work on Hitler's programme in the 1920s rather neglects this issue; A. Kuhn, *Hitlers aussenpolitisches Programm. Entstehung und Entwicklung 1919–1939* (Stuttgart, 1970). On this debate, see principally G. Moltmann, 'Weltherrschaftsideen Hitlers', O. Brunner and D. Gerhard, *Europa und Übersee. Festschrift für Egmont Zechlin* (Hamburg, 1961), pp. 197–240; A. Hillgruber, *Hitlers Strategie. Politik und Kriegführung 1940–1941* (Frankfurt/Main, 1965); K. Hildebrand, *Vom Reich zum Weltreich. Hitler, N.S.D.A.P. und koloniale Fragen, 1919–1945* (Munich, 1969).

9. On Hitler's youth, see F. Jetzinger, *Hitler's Youth* (London, 1958); W. A. Jenks, *Vienna and the Young Hitler* (New York, 1960); and B. F. Smith, *Adolf Hitler: His Family, Childhood and Youth* (Stanford, 1967). On the intellectual background, see for example G. Mosse, *The Crisis of German Ideology* (New York, 1964); F. Stern, *The Politics of Cultural Despair* (Berkeley, 1961).

1

Before Hitler: Ideology and Foreign Policy in the German Workers' Party

It is impossible to present a coherent picture of the evolution of Nazi attitudes on foreign policy without an understanding of the rudiments of Nazi ideology. In the immediate postwar period, the German Workers' Party under the initial direction of journalist Karl Harrer, like most other *völkisch* organisations, was not really interested in articulating a carefully worked out foreign policy. What interested the party was the unmasking of those responsible for the outbreak of the First World War and for Germany's ultimate defeat. Predictably, the Jews were found to have been the main culprits.[1] It was on the basis of this antisemitic platform, designed initially to explain Germany's internal collapse, that the framework of Nazi foreign policy was slowly to emerge. It is necessary, therefore, to analyse the ideology absorbed by the Germany Workers' Party from a rich vein of antisemitic propaganda circulating in Germany and, indeed, in most of Central and Eastern Europe at the end of the First World War and to examine how those ideas might have influenced Nazi attitudes towards foreign affairs.

Crucial to such an investigation is the work of the three earliest 'theorists' of the incipient Nazi movement, Dietrich Eckart, Alfred Rosenberg and Gottfried Feder. In the spring of 1919, the German Workers' Party was still a small, insignificant political group with vague anti-capitalist and antisemitic leanings but without a clearly defined programme of any kind. During the summer of 1919, how-

---

1. At an early meeting of the DAP, Harrer described the Jew as 'Germany's worst enemy'; the next worst was England, G. Franz-Willing, *Die Hitlerbewegung — Der Ursprung, 1919–22* (Hamburg, 1962), p. 64.

ever, it attracted the support of Dietrich Eckart, the editor since December 1918 of a virulently antisemitic periodical, *Auf gut deutsch* (*Agd*), Alfred Rosenberg, a Baltic German émigré who became a regular contributor to *Agd* after February 1919, and Gottfried Feder, an outspoken opponent of finance capitalism. This seems to have been a turning-point in the party's development. On 14 August Eckart addressed an audience of thirty-eight people at a meeting held under its auspices and by 12 September when Feder, standing in for Eckart who was ill, spoke to an audience of about forty people, the party had attracted the attention of the Bavarian Reichswehr, who sent along Adolf Hitler to report on its political complexion.[2] These three men — Eckart, Rosenberg and Feder — who had met almost certainly through the good offices of a Pan-German-influenced patriotic association, the Thule Society (*Thulegesellschaft*),[3] were thus already helping to fashion the political outlook of the German Workers' Party before Hitler's fateful first encounter with it on 12 September 1919.

All three were also to exercise some influence over the new recruit, a fact noted by contemporary observers as well as by Hitler himself. Ernst Hanfstängl, an early party recruit, believed that in the early 1920s Hitler was 'deeply under the spell of Rosenberg'. Konrad Heiden, the author of the first major analysis of the Nazi Party, wrote of Rosenberg and Eckart that 'Hitler was little more than their mouthpiece for some years to come. Rosenberg taught him facts. Eckart polished his style.' In May 1921 Hitler referred publicly to Rosenberg and Eckart as 'leaders of the antisemitic movement'. At the end of *Mein Kampf*, of course, Hitler paid homage to Eckart as 'that man, one of the best, who devoted his life to the awakening of his, our people, in his writings and his thoughts finally in his deeds'.[4] But in his autobiography, Hitler also acknowledged the impact on him of Feder's disquisition on the 'breaking of the slavery of interest', which he first encountered during a political indoctrination course organised by the Reichswehr in June 1919: 'I knew at once

2. For details of the meeting, see *Hauptarchiv der NSDAP* (hereafter HA), roll 3, folder 80; A. Hitler, *Mein Kampf* (London, 1969), pp. 197–9; Rosenberg later revealed that he and Eckart had met Anton Drexler in May 1919 and that he had asked Eckart to deliver a talk on Bolshevism to the German Workers' Party, A. Rosenberg, 'Meine erste Begegnung mit dem Führer' (1934), *Bundesarchiv Koblenz* (hereafter BA) *NS 8 (Kanzlei Rosenberg), folder 177*.

3. R. Cecil, *The Myth of the Master Race. Alfred Rosenberg and Nazi Ideology* (London, 1972), pp. 22–4.

4. E. Hanfstängl, *The Missing Years* (London, 1957), p. 41; K. Heiden, *The History of National Socialism* (London, 1971), p. 94; A. Hitler, 'Sie kennen ihre Pappenheimer', *Völkischer Beobachter* (hereafter VB), 12 May 1921; Hitler, *Mein Kampf*, p. 627.

that this was a theoretical truth, which would be of immense importance to the future of the German people.'[5]

In view of these remarks, it may seem surprising that Eckart, Rosenberg and Feder have until recently been poorly served by historians.[6] However, there are a number of possible reasons for this relative neglect. The most obvious is the fact that these three men were rapidly eclipsed by Adolf Hitler's meteoric rise to prominence. Eckart's premature death in 1923 — very early in the Nazi Party's history — has limited his appeal to prospective biographers. Feder slipped into obscurity once his anti-capitalist ideas proved inconvenient when Hitler was trying to attract the support of powerful industrialists in 1932.[7] And Rosenberg's rather inconspicuous later career in the Third Reich has perhaps encouraged the belief that he possessed only limited intelligence and that therefore his contribution to Hitler's intellectual development can only have been marginal.[8] Another reason may be an understandable reluctance to analyse abhorrent and irrational prejudice in a systematic way for fear of endowing Nazi ideology with an unwarranted intellectual veneer. A further impediment for some historians is their conviction that that ideology is largely irrelevant to an understanding of the Third Reich which, in their view, was motivated solely by the pursuit and exercise of power.[9]

However, these qualms can no longer be allowed to impede serious discussion of the ideological roots of Nazi attitudes towards foreign affairs. What were the ideas about the Jews which Rosenberg and Eckart helped to propagate in Nazi circles and how did these ideological concepts relate to concrete issues of foreign policy?

Rosenberg, Eckart and the Jews

A native of the Baltic city of Reval and a product of a middle class family, Alfred Rosenberg had fled to Germany at the end of 1918 in

5. Hitler, *Mein Kampf*, p. 194.

6. This has been corrected by two recent biographies: R. Cecil, *The Myth of the Master Race* and M. Plewnia, *Auf den Weg zu Hitler. Der 'völkische' Publizist Dietrich Eckart* (Bremen, 1970). Feder still awaits a biographer, though there is an informative essay: A. Tyrell, 'Gottfried Feder and the NSDAP' in P. Stachura (ed.), *The Shaping of the Nazi State* (London, 1978), pp. 48–87.

7. Tyrell, in Stachura, *The Shaping of the Nazi State*, pp. 77–9.

8. See N. Cohn, *Warrant for Genocide. The Myth of the Jewish World Conspiracy and the Protocols of the Elders of Zion* (Harmondsworth, 1967), p. 217; W. Maser, *Die Frühgeschichte der NSDAP* (Frankfurt am Main, 1965), pp. 181–5.

9. On this tendency, see B. M. Lane, 'Nazi Ideology: Some Unfinished Business' in B. M. Lane and L. Rupp (eds.), *Nazi Ideology before 1933* (Manchester, 1978), p. ix.

the face of the Soviet Red Army's drive through the Baltic Provinces. He was already a committed antisemite.[10] In an essay entitled *Der Jude*, written on 10 July 1918 but not published until 1943, he had argued that Europe was currently witnessing a struggle 'for and against the Jewish idea'. Germany, he believed, was in the forefront of this struggle and the Jews were seeking to denigrate her achievements and her individuality and to create 'chaos' in the country.[11]

He went on to describe three characteristics of the Jews which, if unchecked, would surely realise these ambitions. Firstly the Jews were parasitic; they always lived off other people, living in houses which they had not built and eating food grown in fields which they had not cultivated. Whilst Aryan peoples were concerned with matters of art and science, the Jews were preoccupied with 'trade and usury'; the Jewish spirit itself thus reflected a 'passion for exploitation'. This alien, parasitic spirit inside German society, Rosenberg believed, had to be 'exorcised'.

The second characteristic with which Rosenberg endowed the Jews was religious intolerance; 'the Jew', he maintained, 'was the father of all religious hatred and fanaticism'. This intolerance was rooted in the Jews' belief in their own exclusiveness, in the conviction that they were God's chosen people and that they would eventually rule the world. This desire for world dominion (*Weltherrschaft*) of course clashed with the interests of every nation in the world. The Jews, therefore, had concocted the doctrine of international socialism to subvert national unity. The ultimate effect of socialist ideas would, in Rosenberg's opinion, be a 'racial catastrophe', leaving the Jews triumphant. Jewish intolerance, therefore, bred political radicalism and would result in racial disintegration.

The Russian Revolution illustrated the Jew's third major trait — his destructiveness. After the overthrow of the Czar in February

---

10. B. M. Lane has recently suggested that Rosenberg's antisemitism may have been 'a cynical concoction used whenever he found a favourable market', Lane in Lane and Rupp, *Nazi Ideology*, p. xv. This challenges the generally accepted view that Rosenberg 'took his principles and ideas seriously', M. H. Boehm, 'Baltische Einflüsse auf die Anfänge der Nationalsozialismus', *Jahrbuch des Baltischen Deutschtums*, vol. 14 (1967) p. 65; Cohn, *Warrant for Genocide*, p. 217. However, whilst it is true that antisemitism did provide Rosenberg with an entrée into Munich society and ultimately into the Nazi government, three overtly antisemitic essays — 'Staat, Sozialismus und Persönlichkeit', 'Eine ernste Frage' and 'Der Jude' — written between May and July 1918 when he was a teacher in Reval, and later published in *Schriften und Reden* vol. 1 (Munich, 1943), suggest that his adoption of antisemitism was not motivated primarily by materialistic considerations. Rosenberg later claimed that he had delivered a speech about Bolshevism and the Jewish question in Reval on 30 November 1918 immediately prior to his departure for Germany; letter to his lawyer Lorenz Roder, 17 March 1931, NS 8/120.

11. Rosenberg, *Schriften*, vol. 1, pp. 89–90.

1917, the Jews, according to Rosenberg, had orchestrated the socialist agitation against the provisional government of Kerensky and hence, following the October Revolution, Jews such as Trotsky, Zinoviev and Stecklov had taken leading positions in the new Bolshevik regime. However, instead of showing sympathy towards the Russian people, who had suffered as much as, if not more than, themselves from Czarist oppression, and who had indeed carried out the original revolution, the Jews led a movement which 'aimed consistently — either consciously or instinctively — at the destruction of Russia as a state'.

All this forced Rosenberg to conclude that 'wherever one allows the Jews to come to power, the most relentless exploitation, the most relentless intolerance towards other ideas and customs, and the most relentless destructive frenzy . . . grips everything'.[12] This combination of exploitation, intolerance and destructiveness, to Rosenberg's mind, now threatened Germany.

Der Jude is noteworthy in that it provides early evidence of many of the arguments which Rosenberg was to repeat so often in the 1920s and 1930s. The use of the term 'Aryan' as a counterpoint to the 'Jew' reveals that even at this early stage Rosenberg's view of the Jews was overwhelmingly biological; 'Jewishness' denoted not simply a different religion or philosophy but a distinctive racial characteristic, ideas almost certainly picked up whilst reading the works of the British antisemite, Houston Stewart Chamberlain.[13] Furthermore the conspiratorial world-view later adopted by the Nazi Party was clearly present in outline in Rosenberg's early tract; the association of international socialism with Jewry and the 'revelation' of the leading role played by the Jews in the Bolshevik Revolution were already articles of faith.

It is, therefore, difficult to accept without reservation the view of Werner Maser that 'unlike Hitler, in the year 1918 Rosenberg did not yet have at his disposal concrete political notions'. He may have been a novice as a political activist when he arrived in Germany at the end of 1918 but he had already formulated the basis of a political philosophy, one perhaps fashioned by his experience at first hand of the Russian Revolution, as he put it in his memoirs:

So I came to the Reich. Originally a man devoted completely to art,

12. Ibid., pp. 111–14, pp. 105–11, p. 95.
13. Rosenberg later described H. S. Chamberlain's *Die Grundlagen des neunzehnten Jahrhunderts* as 'the greatest impetus I received'; A Rosenberg, *Letzte Aufzeichnungen: Ideale und Idole der nationalsozialistischen Revolution* (Göttingen, 1955), p. 274; see also pp. 275–85.

philosophy and history, who had never thought of getting involved in politics at any time. But I had observed the present; it too would be history and tradition one day. I had seen many forces pushing their way in to positions of leadership and had been able to witness the course of a revolution.[14]

Committed to the propagation of these ideas in Germany, in January 1919 Rosenberg sought out Dietrich Eckart, whom, as he was later to explain in his biography of Eckart, 'had already begun . . . a similar struggle to the one I had before me'.[15] A month before, Eckart, a playwright and sometime literary critic, already possessing a certain notoriety for a rather eccentric translation of *Peer Gynt*, had launched the journal *Auf gut deutsch* to publicise his literary skills and antisemitic views.

Though he shared Rosenberg's intellectual rather than physical abhorrence of Jewry, Eckart's antisemitic views were seemingly quite different, if again not entirely original. For Eckart, 'Jewishness' was a spiritual rather than a racial characteristic. Jewishness, which he defined as the preoccupation with worldly or material considerations, born of a religious denial of immortality, was not the preserve of one race — the Jews — but was visible in all races. In essence, Eckart's antisemitism, unlike Rosenberg's, was metaphysical rather than biological and at first glance it seemed to bear little relation to policies of persecution or expulsion, let alone extermination, of the Jews as a race. As he wrote in 1919, 'it is not a question of fighting the Jew as a person, but of fighting the Jewish spirit'.[16]

What motivated Eckart's antisemitism was, he claimed, 'the desire for self-knowledge' since everybody has 'Jewishness' inside him. Early in a long-running series in *Agd*, significantly entitled 'Das Judentum in und ausser uns' ('Jewishness in and around us'), he used a simple analogy to elucidate his views: 'Jewishness belongs to the organism of mankind like . . . certain bacteria on the human body, and indeed just as essentially as these. . . . Our body contains, as we know, a mass of tiny lifeforms without which, despite the fact that they feed on it, it must perish.'[17] 'Jewishness' was thus a

14. Ibid., p. 65; W. Maser believes that Rosenberg was a political novice in 1918, *Die Frühgeschichte*, pp. 183–4.
15. A. Rosenberg, *Dietrich Eckart. Ein Vermächtnis* (Munich, 1935), p. 45.
16. Quoted in Plewnia, *Auf dem Weg zu Hitler*, p. 57.
17. D. Eckart, 'Das Judentum in und ausser uns' (hereafter 'Das Judentum'), *Auf gut deutsch* (hereafter *Agd*), 7 February 1919, p. 95. This series began on 10 January 1919 and was never completed. It is uncertain whether Hitler's later references to the Jews as bacteria were borrowed from Eckart.

necessary evil. Such views seemed to have been derived from the works of the antisemitic theorist Otto Weininger, in particular his *Geschlecht und Charakter* (published in 1903), which Eckart cited in his series of articles.[18]

However, it should not be overlooked that Eckart's view of 'Jewishness' as a state of mind did not prevent him from treating the Jews as an identifiable racial group when he reviewed Germany's contemporary political situation. In January 1919 he laid the blame for Germany's defeat squarely at their door: 'Whichever way an empire is destroyed, whether [it be] by means of Christianity as with Ancient Rome, or by means of Bolshevism as with the German state, matters little to the Jew'.[19] The Jews had supported the Entente powers during the war; 'behind Wilson's policy, behind the entire Entente policy', he wrote, 'stands no other than Jewry, not just literally but *in spirit* also'[20] [emphasis added]. He also claimed that the ultimate aim of Jewry was world dominion; St. Paul, who never, according to Eckart, fully freed himself of his 'Jewishness', worked instinctively to 'unseat the Roman Empire, the overmighty rival of his people for world dominion'.[21]

Recent attempts to distance Eckart from the Nazi Party's more rabid antisemites by dwelling on his musings about Jewishness should, therefore, be treated with caution; in fact, he endorsed propaganda about the Jewish community that was designed to encourage discrimination, if not pogroms, against the Jews.[22] He evidently possessed in outline an antisemitic conspiratorial world-view similar to Rosenberg's before the two men met in January 1919.

What attracted Eckart to his rather earnest young recruit was the latter's 'expert' knowledge of the Russian Revolution. Eckart had already identified the hand of Jewry at work behind German 'Bolshevism', but Rosenberg could supply him with detailed information about Jewish manipulation of the Russian Revolution. Introducing Rosenberg's first article in *Agd*, 'Die russisch-jüdische Revolution' in February 1919 Eckart wrote: 'Whoever reads the report on the Russian Revolution will realise what the final goals (hidden from us)

---

18. Eckart referred specifically to Weininger's chapter on Jewry, *ibid.*, *Agd*, 17 January 1919, pp. 45–8. See also Lane and Rupp, *Nazi Ideology*, p. 17.

19. Eckart, 'Das Judentum', *Agd*, 10 January 1919, p. 31.

20. D. Eckart, 'Immer lächeln, und doch eine Schurke', *Agd*, 7 February 1919, pp. 83–4.

21. Eckart, 'Das Judentum', *Agd*, 17 January 1919, p. 46.

22. M. Plewnia, in particular, has tried to rehabilitate Eckart, *Auf dem Weg zu Hitler*, p. 57. It is true that Eckart was not a Jew-baiter in the mould of Julius Streicher.

of Jewish-Asiatic blood are. . . . The conformity of revolutionary developments in Russia with those here no longer leaves anything to be desired as far as clarity is concerned.'[23] Rosenberg's interpretation of events in Russia was his most distinctive contribution to the development of a Nazi *Weltanschauung* and this article established the central lines of argument.

What emerges most clearly from Rosenberg's account of the February Revolution was his opposition to Czarism and his sympathy for the Russian people. In his view, Czarist government had deprived Russia of all its vitality and 'the rule of the corrupt bureaucracy was oppressive'. The February Revolution — described elsewhere by Rosenberg as a 'liberation'[24] — raised great hopes, which were to be cruelly dashed when the Jews took over the workers' and soldiers' councils and organised (with foreign assistance) the Bolshevik seizure of power. His sympathy for the Russian people — a stark contrast to the Russophobia so often attributed to him because of his Baltic German background — seems genuine enough.[25]

The Bolshevik government, on the other hand, was portrayed by Rosenberg as an aberration in Russian history; it introduced a censorship far stricter than anything known under the Czars; it fostered class conflict and perpetrated a campaign of extermination against the Russian 'intelligentsia'; and the National Assembly — 'the long-cherished aim of all Russian patriots' — was dispersed by the Red Guards. In short, the October Revolution was at odds with Russia's traditions and current aspirations. However, its success was not yet assured, in Rosenberg's view, because antisemitism was growing apace in Russia: 'The most weak-willed and the most tolerant Russians are now as imbued with it as any former Czarist officials. If the present regime falls, then no Jew would remain alive in Russia.'[26]

This account of events in Russia, though by no means entirely original,[27] does appear to have been Rosenberg's passport into antisemitic circles and eventually into the young Nazi Party. By the

23. Eckart's introduction to A. Rosenberg, 'Die russisch-jüdische Revolution', *Agd*. 21 February 1919, p. 114.

24. A. Rosenberg, 'Russe und Deutscher', *Agd*, 4 April 1919, p. 187.

25. W. Laqueur, on the other hand, stresses Rosenberg's 'dislike of Russians', *Russia and Germany. A Century of Conflict*, (London, 1965), pp. 68–78.

26. Rosenberg, 'Die russisch-jüdische Revolution', pp. 122–3.

27. For a very similar account, see H. Reinl, 'Die rassenpolitischen Ursachen des Zusammenbruchs', *Neue Tiroler Stimmen*, 9, 10, 30 December 1918. I am very grateful to Professor F. L. Carsten for bringing this series to my attention.

early months of 1919, before either came into contact with the German Workers' Party, Eckart and Rosenberg had already acquired an antisemitic world-view; to Eckart's belief that the Jews were manipulating the capitalist West, Rosenberg added evidence of their abetting of Bolshevism in Eastern Europe. As yet, no evidence was presented to prove that the two activities were directly connected in a coordinated, clandestine conspiracy to achieve the Jewish goal of world dominion. By 1921, however, a vast web of Jewish intrigue had been 'unearthed'; the suspected collaboration between the Jewish capitalists and Jewish Bolshevism had been substantiated; and three other links in the chain of conspiracy — namely Zionism, Freemasonry and Jesuitism — had been established to the satisfaction of the Nazis.

The Development of the Conspiracy Theory

Much of the credit for the propagation of the conspiracy theory in the Nazi Party must go to Alfred Rosenberg. This is not to say that his ideas were at all original in themselves; Karl Harrer, the first chairman of the German Workers' Party, had already claimed that the Jews controlled the press and that they were in collusion with the Freemasons.[28] It was Rosenberg who investigated these claims further by ransacking antisemitic literature both past and present for incriminating evidence of Jewish subversion, and it was he who synthesised the various strands of argument to build up a composite picture of the secret machinations of World Jewry. Eckart acknowledged Rosenberg's growing expertise by quoting him extensively.[29]

In June 1919, however, Rosenberg published in *Agd* his first detailed examination of the role of the Jews in politics, entitled *Judenheit und Politik*. He argued that the Jews could affect foreign policy at two levels. Firstly they could advise foreign policy makers in their host nations. Because of the Jewish diaspora and their extensive involvement in international trade, the Jews were considered to be peculiarly well-informed about world affairs. However, the advice of the Jews was not always to be relied upon; if the interests of the host nation coincided with those of the Jews then they were advanced; 'if not, they were abandoned without

28. See R. H. Phelps, 'Anton Drexler — Der Gründer der NSDAP', *Deutsche Rundschau*, vol. 87 (1961), p. 1136.

29. D. Eckart, 'Heine als Prophet', *Agd*, 25 July 1919, p. 356.

scruple'.[30] In seeking to advance their own interests, therefore, the Jews could either render a state valuable service or act as a 'fifth column' undermining its national security.

The Jews could also influence foreign affairs at international level. They could construct and lead an international alliance against the nations who opposed Jewish ambitions. At that time, Rosenberg believed, such a vendetta was being directed against Russia and Germany. The reasons for Jewish antagonism towards Germany (the Russian case will be dealt with later) were to him self-evident. Firstly, the German Empire opposed the creation of a Jewish state in Palestine; the Entente powers, and in particular Britain, did not. So, although initially Jewish opinion had been divided over whom to support in the First World War, eventually 'all Jews gradually came to agree with the English orientation'. The second reason for the Jewish opposition to Germany was, he claimed, that the leading statesmen of the Entente nations, including Poincaré, Briand, Clemenceau, Lloyd George, Balfour and Orlando were all Freemasons, as were many influential Jews. Thus the Freemasonic lodges had, in Rosenberg's view, facilitated the anti-German coalition.[31] Hence, in this early article on the Jewish question in June 1919,[32] he identified Zionism and Freemasonry as two major instruments of Jewish influence giving the Jews the ability to manipulate international opinion to further their own ends.

While the role of the Freemasons in this Judeo-Masonic conspiracy remained largely unexplored at this point, Rosenberg was already trying to demonstrate convincingly what many antisemites already accepted as an article of faith, that the Zionist movement was indeed part of the worldwide Jewish conspiracy to dominate the world.[33]

The task was not an easy one. The Zionists were, as he was forced to admit, 'Jewish nationalists' (Nationaljuden) who wanted to create a national home in Palestine.[34] So how could this nationalistic endeavour be compatible with the internationalist aspirations (world revolution, world dominion) allegedly at the heart of the

30. A. Rosenberg, 'Judenheit und Politik' (hereafter 'Judenheit'), *Agd*, 13 June 1919, pp. 263–6. This article was later republished in A. Rosenberg, *Die Spur des Juden im Wandel der Zeiten* (Munich, 1920).

31. Rosenberg, 'Judenheit', pp. 266–7.

32. Much earlier than hitherto suspected; see Lane in Lane and Rupp, *Nazi Ideology*, p. 161, note 41.

33. For a review of antisemitic literature on Zionism, see Cohn, *Warrant for Genocide*, pp. 74–85.

34. A Rosenberg, 'Jüdische Zeitfragen', *Agd*, 23 October 1919, p. 533.

Jewish conspiracy? In 1920, seemingly aware of this apparent inconsistency, Rosenberg claimed in his pamphlet, *Die Spur des Juden*, that the Jews only pretended to be nationalistic; in fact, they harboured internationalist ambitions because in the last resort, 'Jewish internationalism is anti-national . . . the call for internationalism in the sense of anti-nationalism is the call of national Jewry'.[35]

Rosenberg was driven to similar obfuscation when examining Soviet policy towards Zionism. He found that the 'Jewish-led' Soviet regime had not only 'predictably' condemned antisemitism as 'counter-revolutionary' but had also criticised the Zionist movement as nationalistic and sponsored by capitalist forces. This seemed to contradict the argument that Bolshevism and Zionism were two strands of a Jewish world conspiracy. Perceiving this flaw in his argument, Rosenberg maintained that, whilst Zionism had been denounced by Marxist–Leninist theorists, the Zionist organisation had not been declared counter-revolutionary 'by any single decree of the Russian government'.[36] Hence the Bolshevik Jews were managing to prevent the implementation of any anti-Zionist campaign called for by the party ideologues.

Despite the difficulty of disguising the incompatibility of its nationalistic impulse with the internationalism of the supposed Jewish world conspiracy, the Zionist movement produced a rich vein of propaganda for Rosenberg. The fact that it had supporters in all the major states was evidence enough of an international Jewish menace which cut across national frontiers. It should not be forgotten, of course, that the famous antisemitic tract, *The Protocols of the Elders of Zion* (of which more later), which purported to prove the existence of a Jewish plot to achieve world domination, allegedly drew on the proceedings of the first Zionist conference in Basle in 1897.

Despite suggestions that Eckart may have inspired Rosenberg's early anti-Zionist tracts, there can be little doubt that Rosenberg was responsible for incorporating Zionism into the Nazi Party's antisemitic philosophy.[37] In fact, Eckart's views on Zionism differed markedly from Rosenberg's. Since he regarded 'Jewishness' as a metaphysical rather than a racial attribute, and as a necessary counterweight to more favourable features, he opposed the creation of a separate Jewish state. Indeed, in *Das Judentum in und außer uns*, Eckart prophesied that 'if . . . the Jewish people perished, there

35. Rosenberg, *Die Spur des Juden*, pp. 158–9.
36. A. Rosenberg, 'Unter Jacobsstern', *Agd*, 30 December 1919, pp. 703–4.
37. Lane in Lane and Rupp, *Nazi Ideology*, p. xiv.

would be no more nations . . . the end of all time would come', and added that 'this would also be the case if the Zionist idea were to be realised, that is, if the whole of Jewry amalgamated into one unified state, whether it be in Palestine or elsewhere'. This was because the Jews had, he explained, always been dispersed, living amongst the Gentiles and it was precisely this coexistence between Jews and Gentiles which maintained the natural balance: 'The world could not exist, if the Jews lived alone by themselves'.[38] Rosenberg would certainly not have endorsed this argument. Indeed, he later argued that 'Zionism must be supported in order to get rid of a certain number of Jews each year to Palestine or beyond our frontiers'.[39] Significantly it was recommendations of the type made by Rosenberg that the Jews be treated as aliens inside Germany which later commended themselves to the Nazi Party leadership.[40] So it seems fair to credit Rosenberg with the incorporation of Zionism into the emerging antisemitic *Weltanschauung* which the party absorbed.

Later in 1919, Rosenberg began to explore more fully the case for Masonic complicity in Jewish plans. Again, he was not the first to suggest links between Jews and Freemasons; as he readily admitted, previous writers had investigated this relationship. Rosenberg quoted often from *Weltfreimaurerei, Weltrevolution, Weltrepublik* by Dr. F. Wichtl, published in 1919, and in 1923 he was to translate into German Gougenot des Mousseaux's classic indictment of the Jews and Freemasons, *Le Juif, le judaïsme et la judaïsation des peuples chrétiens* (1869). Two prominent members of the German Workers' Party — Karl Harrer and Paul Tafel — were also keen to establish such a connection.[41] However, Rosenberg appears to have done most of the spadework, digging out information from often obscure secondary sources to support the claim that the Jews had infiltrated the ranks of the Freemasons. Eckart cited Rosenberg in *Agd* as an expert on

---

38. Eckart, 'Das Judentum', *Agd*, 31 January 1919, pp. 79–80.

39. Rosenberg, *Die Spur des Juden*, p. 161.

40. The Nazi Party Programme of February 1920 does include the call to combat 'the Jewish-materialistic spirit in and around us' but the theme of the 'Twenty-Five Points' is the treatment of the Jews as aliens. Rosenberg's proposals are laid out in *Die Spur des Juden*, pp. 160–1. These ideas, however, were popular among the leadership, so one cannot conclude that Rosenberg influenced the programme directly himself.

41. For Harrer's views, see Phelps, 'Anton Drexler', p. 1136: Paul Tafel, chairman of the anti-republican *Bayerische Ordnungsblock* and later a member of the German Workers' Party held views very similar to Rosenberg's: P. Tafel, *Das Neue Deutschland. Ein Rätestaat auf nationaler Grundlage* (Munich, 1920), pp. 39–42. Rosenberg was attracted to des Mousseaux's work because it predicted 'the present events . . . with peculiar confidence': A. Rosenberg, 'Börsenjuden und Revolution', *VB*, 22 February 1921.

Freemasonry, referring to the 'many books' which he latter had collected on the subject and exhorting his readers to follow the traces of Judeo-Masonic subversion 'with the sure hand of Alfred Rosenberg'.[42]

In 1920 Rosenberg defined Freemasonry in his pamphlet, *Die Spur des Juden im Wandel der Zeiten*, as 'a secret order with the aim of erecting an anti-religious World Republic'.[43] The similarity between this goal and the global ambitions of the Jews was probably, in Rosenberg's view, the main reason for Judeo-Masonic collaboration. The Freemasons and the Jews, via the Socialist International, had also, in his view, formed two wings of the anti-monarchical movement since the middle of the nineteenth century.[44] Rosenberg claimed that the Freemasons were behind every revolution and major assassination since 1789. Even Archduke Franz Ferdinand of Austria had been a victim of a Freemasonic plot — a claim which enabled Rosenberg to argue that the First World War had been unleashed by the Jews and Freemasons as the first stage towards the creation of a New Jerusalem: 'world war, world revolution, world republic, this is the Freemasonic programme', he concluded.[45] Though the vast majority of Masons were unaware of it, Freemasonry, like Zionism was being manipulated by the Jews to advance the cause of their own world dominion.[46]

Rosenberg's series of articles on Freemasonry, *Das Verbrechen der Freimaurerei*, published in *Agd* during 1920 and 1921 added little of substance on the Jewish-Masonic conspiracy but did unmask another unwitting agent of Jewish intrigue: Jesuitism. The suggestion that the Freemasons and Jesuits were collaborating — albeit in a league organised by the Jews — appeared at first sight patently absurd even to Alfred Rosenberg. The Jesuits and the Freemasons were rivals 'for one and the same prize: world rule'; the Jesuits sought a universal spiritual monarchy, the Freemasons a 'social, theocratic world republic'.[47]

Rosenberg, however, side-stepped these apparently conflicting ambitions by identifying a common characteristic which made the Jesuits and Freemasons real, if unlikely, bedfellows in the Jewish

42. D. Eckart, 'Das fressende Feuer', *Agd*, 22 August 1919, pp. 402–05.

43. Rosenberg, *Die Spur des Juden*, p. 89.

44. Ibid., p. 99.

45. Rosenberg, *Die Spur des Juden*, p. 106.

46. Eckart had told his readers that 'our Baltic friend Rosenberg . . . advises us not to condemn the Masons as a whole': D. Eckart, 'Wer nicht mit uns ist . . .', *Agd*, 31 October 1919, p. 554.

47. Rosenberg, 'Das Verbrechen der Freimaurerei', *Agd*, 15 January 1921, p. 30.

world conspiracy. The majority of Jesuits, like most Freemasons, were kept in ignorance of the order's real ambitions by its leadership: 'Just as the Jesuit order strives for world tyranny from a despotic base, so in the same way the league of Freemasons strives for a world republic from a despotic base'. It was the absolutism of the two very different orders which made it possible for the Jews to infiltrate them and to distort their outlook: 'Jesuitism (like Judaism) aimed directly at subjugation — spiritual as well as physical — and held the picture of Christ before one's face and preached "humility"; Freemasonary originated in a generous and thoroughly un-Jewish movement which had nonetheless become, because of its immoderation and foggy notions, a tool of intriguers. It symbolised freedom and brotherhood. The more the Jews penetrated it, the more the practices, the goals of Freemasonry approached not only the Semitic–Basque methods and goals of the Jesuits but also the principles of the Talmud.'[48] The sleight of hand was quite perceptible to any discerning reader. All that Rosenberg offered as proof of Jesuit collusion in Jewish plans was the assertion that the Roman Catholic Centre Party in Germany under the leadership of Matthias Erzberger had collaborated during the First World War with the 'enemies of Germandom: the judaicised Democrats and Social Democrats'.[49]

Once again, the 'credit' for the assimilation of the Jesuits into the conspiracy theory must go to Rosenberg; the rather desperate attempt to persuade his readers to ignore the evidence of perennial hostility between the Freemasons and the Roman Catholic Church seems original. This is not to say that he was the first to dream up such notions — the secrecy which surrounded the activities of the Jesuits naturally aroused the suspicions of antisemitic bloodhounds trained to sniff out any whiffs of complicity in Jewish plans.[50] But it was Rosenberg who attempted to provide a plausible explanation for Jesuit involvement in such schemes.

For Rosenberg, the capitalists of the Western world provided the final link in the chain of conspiracy engineered by the Jews. Exactly how this particular element evolved in what became the Nazi *Weltanschauung* is difficult to establish with any certainty because it was very common, in view of American financial assistance to the Entente powers, for Germans in 1918–19 to hold Western capitalism responsible for Germany's defeat in the First World War. As

48. Ibid., 15 February 1921, p. 80.
49. Ibid., pp. 31–2; 31 January 1921, pp. 39–49, 60–3.
50. Eckart wrote in 1919 that 'Rome and Jerusalem had found each other once again' in common vengeance against Germany: D. Eckart, 'Erzberger', *Agd*, 17 July 1919, p. 348.

early as December 1918, Dietrich Eckart had referred to the perni-
cious influence of the 'Princes of Gold', exploiting nations by playing
one off against another, 'creating Empires here, Republics there,
chaos with us, as its suits them'.[51] The activities of the stock
exchanges and the banks were already, therefore, the object of
vilification in right-wing (let alone left-wing) propaganda.

However, also significant in the evolution of later Nazi attitudes
towards capitalism were the views of Gottfried Feder, the third of
the early theorists who were in contact with the German Workers'
Party during 1919. In that year Feder, a thirty-six-year-old civil
engineer and manager of a small firm of building contractors,
launched a campaign against the system of high interest rates on
loans, which he held to be largely responsible for Germany's near-
bankruptcy in 1918.[52]

Feder's aim was, as he put it in his pamphlet *Manifest zur Brechung
der Zinsknechtschaft des Geldes*, to break 'interest-slavery'. In effect, he
wanted state socialism; he wanted the state to extend its control over
the system of banking and transportation and into private enterprise; he wanted the state to own land and to regulate rents, and, in
some cases, to abolish mortgages. In the financial field, he wanted
the abolition of non-productive 'finance capital' — that is, capital
devoted to interest-gathering — and the lifting of restrictions on
'industrial capital', which was used to produce goods.[53]

These demands coloured Feder's approach to foreign affairs. For
example, on one occasion, he referred optimistically to Bolshevism
as an 'acute reaction against this mammonistic enslavement
[interest-slavery]'. He had hoped, he said, that the German Revolution of November 1918 would lead the new German state to a similar
rejection of Western values but he had been disappointed. Feder's
endorsement (albeit limited) of the Bolshevik Revolution — in stark
contrast to Rosenberg's response — should be noted as an early
indication of divergent views on foreign policy amongst the theorists
of the German Workers' Party.[54] Furthermore, Feder did not identify the great evil of finance capitalism — pure monetary speculation
— with the Jewish community. Indeed, he explicitly denied that it

51. D. Eckart, 'Der grosse Krumme', *Agd*, 7 December 1918.

52. Tyrell, in Stachura, *The Shaping of the Nazi State*, p. 49.

53. G. Feder, 'Innere Geschichte der Brechung der Zinsknechtschaft', *VB*, 12 August 1920.

54. G. Feder, 'Der soziale Staat', *Agd*, 24 May 1919, pp. 219–20. Eckart, perhaps in an
attempt to deflect Feder's pro-Bolshevik stance, called the renunciation of interest (of which he
too approved) 'German Bolshevism' as opposed to 'Jewish Bolshevism': D. Eckart, 'Deutscher
und jüdischer Bolschewismus', *Agd*, 16 August 1919, p. 389.

could be associated with any particular section of the community.[55] It would seem therefore that, for Feder at least, Bolshevism was a praiseworthy attempt to liberate the world from the bondage of the capitalist and that he did not consider that capitalism was being used by world Jewry.

Rosenberg, on the other hand, believed fervently, as did many others, that the Jews were manipulating the world's financial markets and it was he who was eventually to claim that the Jews were utilising both capitalist and anti-capitalist forces (such as Bolshevism) in an orchestrated operation designed to realise their global ambitions. Although Rosenberg was initially cautious about Feder's ideas on interest-slavery, perhaps out of jealousy since Eckart had 'picked up the ideas in a spirited fashion' or out of the genuine conviction that Feder had mistaken a symptom of the disease for its cause, he did recognise the propaganda potential of the attack on finance capitalism. It provided, as Rosenberg admitted in his memoirs, 'an additional piece of verification for so many a theory'.[56]

It was thus Rosenberg who mixed Eckart's bitterness about capitalism and Feder's phobia about interest-slavery together with the prevailing antisemitism into the heady brew which Hitler was to find so appealing. In October 1919, Rosenberg duly revealed that 'everywhere the Jew is the master of interest (*Zinsherr*)', adding a month later that 'whoever knows the Jewish nature knows that the Golden International [international capitalism] will move mountains to bring empires to ruin'.[57]

The key to an understanding of the Jewish world conspiracy was that the 'Jewish stock exchange capitalists' like the Rothschilds had financed revolutions inspired by Jewish Socialists, for example in Paris in 1870–1 and in Russia in 1917.[58] The Soviet regime was, in fact, being supported by the Jews of the capitalist West because Bolshevism was, in Rosenberg's eyes, 'the continuation of Jewish usury by other, more savage, means'.[59] In short, political radicalism and high finance capitalism were merely two devices by which the Jews sought to undermine the nation-states of the world and to lay the foundations of their own world dominion.

55. G. Feder, *Manifest zur Brechung der Zinsknechtschaft des Geldes* (Munich, 1919), pp. 34–5.

56. Rosenberg, *Letzte Aufzeichnungen*, p. 76. Rosenberg regarded Feder as his chief rival for the position of party philosopher. In his memoirs he criticized Feder for having demanded large advance payments for his lectures and for having plagiarised Theodore Fritsch's 'Hammer' publications of 1917; ibid., pp. 76–7.

57. A. Rosenberg, 'Jüdische Zeitfragen', *Agd*, 23 October 1919, p. 541.

58. A. Rosenberg, 'Börsenjuden und Revolution', *VB*, 22 February 1921.

59. A. Rosenberg, *Pest in Russland*, 2nd edn (Munich, 1924), p. 85.

Barbara Miller Lane is perfectly correct, therefore, when she maintains that 'the equation between the Jews, bankers and Bolsheviks, which appears in *Mein Kampf*, stems from combined influence upon Hitler of Feder, Eckart and Rosenberg'.[60] Nevertheless, this summation underestimates the importance of Rosenberg's role in the development of an overall synthesis of their various contributions. Eckart and Feder had their own *idées fixes* which produced impressive-looking slogans calling for the combatting of 'the Jewishness in and around us' or 'the breaking of interest-slavery', but it is Rosenberg who has the dubious distinction of having incorporated the gist of their ideas into a self-contained and, given the insane premise on which it rested, reasonably coherent philosophy which became the stock-in-trade of the Nazi movement.

A discussion of the evolution of Nazi conspiracy theories would not be complete without an assessment of the impact of *The Protocols of the Elders of Zion*, the famous tract which purported to provide detailed evidence of the Jewish direction of a vast subterranean conspiracy.

Generally historians have attached considerable importance to the 'Protocols' in the political education of Alfred Rosenberg; indeed, his most recent biographer repeats a colourful, but unsubstantiated, account of how a book by Sergei Nilus, one of the Russian purveyors of the 'Protocols', was left on Rosenberg's desk by a mysterious visitor in the summer of 1917 and how it made a great impression upon the immature young man.[61] This account is far from convincing. There is, for example, no concrete evidence in Rosenberg's articles in 1918 and 1919 to suggest that he was acquainted with the text of the 'Protocols'. Also, if the 'Protocols' had made a great impact on Rosenberg, it is strange that he never mentioned the source of his inspiration, particularly since he was in the habit of disclosing his sources. Doubts about the authenticity of the 'Protocols' are unlikely to have deterred him since they were not proved to be a forgery until 1921 and even then this did not prevent him from publishing his own commentary on them, *Die Protokolle der Weisen von Zion und die jüdische Weltpolitik*, two years later. It would appear therefore that Rosenberg may in fact have been unaware of

60. Lane, in Lane and Rupp, *Nazi Ideology*, p. 159.
61. The story can be traced to K. Heiden, *Der Führer*, (London, 1944), p. 9. Robert Cecil has recently repeated it, *The Myth of the Master Race*, p. 17.

the existence of this particular antisemitic tract when he arrived in Germany.

The case for Rosenberg's ignorance of the 'Protocols' is further strengthened by his article *Judenheit und Politik*, published in June 1919, in which he referred to the 'world conspiracy to secure a Jewish cosmopolitan world empire' and also to the first Zionist conference at Basle in 1897 but made no connection between the two. This would be very surprising if Rosenberg had been familiar with either the Russian version of the 'Protocols' produced by Nilus in 1917 or the German version to be published at the end of 1919, since both claimed that the 'Protocols' were a record of the proceedings of the conference at Basle at which the Jewish plot was hatched. In fact, Rosenberg mentioned the conference merely to highlight the programme of the Zionist movement formulated there and its goal — the creation of a Jewish state in Palestine.[62] The most likely explanation of his failure to make use of 'evidence' that the plot had originated in Basle was that he had no detailed knowledge of either version of *The Protocols of the Elders of Zion* at the time.

It is also worth stressing that, as has been seen, the belief in the existence of a Jewish plot was commonplace in antisemitic circles before the 'Protocols' were published, and the evidence about a conspiracy to which Rosenberg drew attention in 1919 was, in all probability, culled from other sources. In his commentary on the 'Protocols' written in 1922, Rosenberg argued that it was impossible to prove whether or not they were a forgery, but that this was irrelevant since he could, he claimed, produce documents which conveyed the same message as the alleged forgery. 'The "Protocols" signified nothing unprecedented in Jewish history, but can be illustrated in Jewish literature throughout the centuries up to the present day', wrote Rosenberg.[63] He had been engaged since 1919 in collecting just such illustrations so that even if the 'Protocols' themselves were discredited, his belief in a Jewish conspiracy would remain unshaken.

So the impact of *The Protocols of the Elders of Zion*, at least in the forms published in 1917 in Russia and in 1919 in Germany, has been exaggerated. This tract merely reinforced what Rosenberg (and

---

62. Rosenberg, 'Judenheit', pp. 272–4. That he did later appreciate the deeper significance of the meeting at Basle is shown by his pamphlet on the subject, *Der Weltverschwörerkongress zu Basel* (Munich, 1927).

63. A. Rosenberg, *Die Protokolle der Weisen von Zion und die jüdische Weltpolitik* (Munich, 1923), reprinted in Rosenberg, *Schriften*, vol. 2, pp. 255, 258. Eckart published a similar document in 'Tagebuch', *Agd*, 10 October 1919, p. 512.

other convinced antisemites) had believed for some time — that a Jewish conspiracy to achieve world dominion really did exist.

The Conspiracy Theory and Foreign Policy

How far did this antisemitic ideology colour the way in which Rosenberg and Eckart (Feder showed little interest in antisemitism and even less in foreign affairs) assessed the major powers? Given the Jewish diaspora and the all-embracing nature of the supposed world conspiracy, the Jewish question potentially affected all nations. As Rosenberg argued in his article *Judenheit und Politik*, in every nation the Jews formed a 'state within a state' or, as he preferred it, a 'state *above* the state',[64] and pursued their own interests. In every country, therefore, there ought to be evidence of two probably, but not necessarily, divergent foreign policies — one reflecting the ambitions of the Jews and one reflecting the priorities of the host nation. If the host nation's priorities coincided with Jewish ambitions, the Jews would offer assistance; if they clashed, the Jews would attempt to alter that nation's political course, either by influencing the process of domestic decision-making in foreign affairs or by constructing a combination of hostile powers against it. If Rosenberg genuinely believed all this, or at least if he was consistent, then one would expect that his appraisal of each nation would emphasise either the degree of perceived compatibility between its national interests and those of the Jews or the extent of perceived Jewish infiltration of its government circles.

Rosenberg's assessment of 'England' (he rarely referred to 'Great Britain')[65] appears to confirm these expectations. In *Judenheit und Politik* he argued that London had during the First World War become the focal point for Jewish activities: 'here lay, and lies even today, the kernel of the Jewish question.' The main reason for this was that, in Rosenberg's view, 'the internationally-led national goals of Jewry are to be regarded as coinciding with those of the English empire'. The compatibility of British and Jewish aspirations had led to the British Empire being acclaimed as 'the protector (*Schutzpatron*) of the Jewish people'. These observations persuaded Rosenberg of the existence of an 'Anglo-Jewish world dominion (*Weltherrschaft*)'.[66]

64. Rosenberg, 'Judenheit', p. 269.

65. Many Germans (including Hitler) use 'England' to refer to Great Britain. The present author has preserved this convention when basing his writing on German sources.

66. Rosenberg, 'Judenheit', p. 268–70.

The main area where British and Jewish interests coincided was Palestine. The support of a major power was required if the Zionist dream of a Jewish state in Palestine was to be realised and if the new state was to enjoy 'the maximum of national security'. Fortunately it suited both Britain's imperial strategy and wartime diplomacy to give such support, according to Rosenberg: 'At that time England possessed Egypt, India, and footholds on the Persian coast; [but] lacked a territorial connection between these lands, and there Palestine fell into place excellently as a link in the chain. . . . Turkey was the enemy and to promise her land to the Jewish people as national territory meant acquiring their sympathies.'[67] This community of interest resulted, he declared, in the Balfour Declaration of 2 November 1917 affirming the British government's support for the creation of a Jewish state in Palestine.

Rosenberg's evaluation of England in *Judenheit und Politik* also stressed the extent of Jewish influence over policy-making. He noted, in particular, the near-monopoly of the British press enjoyed by the 'Jewish' newspaper magnate and wartime Propaganda Minister, Lord Northcliffe, to whom, he claimed, 'three-quarters of the most influential English newspapers belong'. Jewish power was not restricted to newspapers; 'besides Northcliffe', Rosenberg insisted, 'a dozen ennobled Jews of the Upper House steer the ship of English politics'.[68] Hence, Rosenberg appears to have been saying that, even if the imperial argument over Palestine had not carried the day, the Jews were well placed to sway a wavering cabinet.

The obvious inference to be drawn from this analysis was that Britain was not considered to be a suitable ally for Germany because she was assisting the Jewish cause and Jews held influential positions within the state. However, it is possible, of course, that Rosenberg's antipathy towards Britain had entirely different origins, the product merely of his hostility towards an intractable, and lately victorious, opponent of Germany. There is no evidence to substantiate this view, however. It may also have been the result of racial prejudice and there is certainly a hint of this in *Judenheit und Politik*:

The Jew has always hated the German people. Indeed, he does not exactly love the French or Anglo-Saxon either but he feels closer to them,

---

67. Ibid., p. 275. Later Rosenberg claimed that the British and the Jews were also collaborating over Russia, wishing to create the maximum chaos: a passage by Rosenberg entitled 'Die bolschewistische Gefahr'; quoted in D. Eckart, 'Zwischen den Schächern', *Agd.* 5 March 1920, pp. 106–9.

68. Rosenberg, 'Judenheit', p. 269.

and they provide him with far more points of contact than the Germans. The vain and ever more superficial Frenchman, the Anglo-Saxon, sensible and at the same time prone to bigoted superstition, both increasingly divorced from their original race, can at any time become far more approachable characters for the Jews than the Germans.[69]

It should be noted, of course, that this isolated racist remark seems indistinguishable from Rosenberg's antisemitic world-view; the declining racial quality of the Anglo-Saxons was seen as making the British more susceptible to Jewish blandishments. In the final analysis, it is impossible to know for certain what prompted Rosenberg's animosity towards Britain; what is clear is that, in his early published works, he gave a great deal of prominence to British support for Zionism.

Rosenberg was much more positive in his appraisal of Russia as a potential ally for Germany. The Germans and the Russians had proved far more resistant to Jewish enticements; they represented, in Rosenberg's opinion, 'the spiritual antithesis of the Jews'.[70] This polarity manifested itself in opposition to Zionism and in burgeoning antisemitism in both countries. Furthermore, Jewish ambitions frequently clashed with the national interests of Germany and Russia. Rosenberg suspected, for example, that a number of German Jews had initially perceived the First World War 'as a struggle conducted against the antisemitic Russian government' and some Zionists 'believed that they could identify their interests with those of a German Eastern policy'. Such illusions could not be sustained for long, he explained, since the Turkish Empire, which controlled Palestine, remained Germany's ally.[71]

Germany and Russia were, therefore, arch-enemies of the Jews, and this was the reason, in Rosenberg's eyes, for the Judeo-Bolshevik Revolution. The Jews were determined to destroy Russia and, accordingly, once in power they had unleashed a 'pogrom' against the Russian people. Tens of thousands of Russians — even those who had opposed the old regime — were simply being murdered or forced into exile. No state had ever been laid so low. And the Jews were, in Rosenberg's view, longing 'to assist Germany . . . to a similar fate'.[72]

Since Germany and Russia were perceived as being in the fore-

69. Ibid., p. 267.
70. Ibid., pp. 266–7.
71. Ibid., pp. 274–5.
72. A. Rosenberg 'Jüdische Zeitfragen', *Agd*, 23 October 1919, p. 539.

front of the battle against World Jewry, it is not surprising that as early as March 1919 Rosenberg was talking of a future alliance: 'German policy has scarcely any alternative than to make an alliance with the new Russia after the elimination of the Bolshevik government, and no indication of a possible approach ought to pass unutilised.'[73] His belief in the need for a Russo-German alliance — seemingly on the basis of the two countries' hostility to the Jews — and his rejection of any such collaboration between Germany and Bolshevik Russia on the grounds that the latter was controlled by the Jews seem to testify unequivocally to the formative influence of ideological considerations on foreign policy attitudes.

However, strategic concerns were also evident in Rosenberg's writings about a future Russo-German alliance. In March 1919 he voiced his concern that the 'Entente powers' were about to curtail their intervention in the Russian civil war, thus abandoning the anti-Bolshevik cause. The result of such a withdrawal, in his view, would be that Germany would have 'to share the role of outcast Cinderella with Russia and the same fate must lead both empires together'. The balance of power in Europe in 1919 was, therefore, also pushing Russia into the German orbit. Even here, however, such observations on the current state of international diplomacy were accompanied by an ideologically-based explanation, namely that the policy of the Entente powers was being decided by the Jews of the London and New York stock exchanges, whose profits rose 'in direct proportion to the degree of Russian bankruptcy'.[74] On another occasion, Rosenberg claimed that Jewish politicians were supporting the new Polish state in order to 'build her into a breakwater between Russia and Germany'.[75] So it would seem that diplomatic manoeuvrings may have affected his judgement on the question of Russia, but these too were inseparable in his mind from the ideological struggle.

Another factor, which cannot be ignored when examining Rosenberg's attitude towards Russia, is the possible influence exerted by racial considerations. In other words, his views on Russia may have been inspired by a predilection for the Russian people, or at least by the feeling that Russians and Germans shared some kind of spiritual affinity.

The latter thought was one which exercised Rosenberg's mind regularly. In a brief essay written before the Bolshevik Revolution,

73. A. Rosenberg, 'Russische Stimmen', *Agd*, 28 March 1919, p. 146.
74. Ibid., p. 146.
75. Rosenberg, 'Judenheit', p. 268.

for example, he compared the two national characters as follows: 'One attributes to the first [the Germans] as good qualities fidelity, sincerity, honesty, perseverance (leaving aside intellectual qualities), as bad, coarseness and arrogance; to the latter [the Russians], friendliness and humanity on the one side, insincerity, inconsistency and inactivity on the other.' The Russians definitely fare worse in Rosenberg's thumbnail sketch, particularly when he identified the source from which these traits of character sprang: whilst those of the Germans derived from a 'physical, intellectual and moral strength', those of the Russians were found to stem from a 'physical and intellectual strength and moral frailty'. 'In a nutshell', Rosenberg concluded, 'the German has character, the Russian is characterless'.[76]

In April 1919, in an article entitled *Russe und Deutscher*, Rosenberg set out to discover whether the 'similar fate' of the two countries at the end of the First World War was the result of similarities in national character. In fact, he argued, the Russian and German psyches were very different; whilst the German could be characterised as a 'man of action', the Russian displayed a marked propensity for a 'brooding preoccupation with the infinite' which resulted in 'the most unproductive musings and doubts'.[77]

There can be little doubt that these two articles reveal Rosenberg's conviction that the Russians were inferior to the Germans. Nevertheless one should not assume that he regarded the Slavs as subhumans; in both articles, he was concerned merely to refute the case made by Dostoevski that the Slavs had a special mission to revitalise Christianity. It would seem unlikely, however, that it was any special predilection for the Russians which provoked his interest in a Russo-German alliance. Indeed, when Rosenberg did in *Russe und Deutscher* isolate a shared characteristic, which might explain the current state of both Russia and Germany, it was the 'toleration of foreigners', which, in his view, enabled the Jews to create chaos in their adopted countries.[78] In other words, it would appear to have been the Jewish menace — as revealed by the Bolshevik Revolution — rather than any feelings of close racial or cultural affinity, which persuaded him that Germany and Russia were being drawn together.[79]

76. A. Rosenberg, 'Gedanken über die Persönlichkeit' (dated 1 September 1917) in *Schriften*, vol. 1, p. 20.

77. A. Rosenberg, 'Russe und Deutscher', *Agd*, 4 April 1919, p. 185.

78. Ibid., pp. 187–90.

79. Later Rosenberg did say that the Russian soul was 'closely related to the German' but

So, once again, Rosenberg's antisemitic ideology seems to have dictated his approach to foreign affairs. It is possible, however, that this was merely what he wanted his readers to believe and that his ideological assertions disguised convictions actually based on power policy or racial prejudice. Nevertheless, all the available evidence, including essays dating from 1917 and 1918 and probably not intended for publication, would suggest that ideological considerations were of paramount importance to Rosenberg.

In assessing the impact of ideology on Rosenberg's outlook on foreign policy, one must tentatively conclude, firstly that the degree of Jewish predominance in a particular country and the extent to which its natural interests seemed to coincide with those of the Jews did appear to determine his appraisal. Britain's involvement with Zionism and Judeo-Bolshevik rule in Russia made an alliance with either country out of the question in the short term; but the nationalist and anti-Bolshevik forces in the Russian civil war offered a better prospect in the long run. Secondly, it seems unlikely that strong racial prejudice (of which there is little trace at this time) decisively coloured Rosenberg's attitude to any particular country. Thirdly, strategic and diplomatic considerations, though evident in his writings, were difficult to separate from his ideological frame of reference. Perhaps for him a clear distinction between a conspiratorial *vision* of world politics and the *realities* of world politics did not exist. His ideological flights of fancy, after all, do seem to have been stimulated by one or two concrete facts, that is, the Balfour Declaration by the British government and the prominent role played by a number of Jews in the Russian Revolution. These facts (albeit exaggerated) are almost certain to have prejudiced the response of an already committed antisemite to Britain and Russia.

Despite the world-wide ramifications of the Jewish question, Rosenberg's interest in foreign affairs was restricted essentially to the European continent at that time. America received only passing mention.[80] Dietrich Eckart, on the other hand, did occasionally comment on American affairs, perhaps because of his preoccupation with the power of capitalism. In his view, America was Germany's deadly enemy. She had at no time been neutral during the First World War; in fact, she had worked for Germany's defeat throughout, because, he believed, America was very much the tool of

---

again this was in the context of their mutual antipathy towards the Jew: Rosenberg, 'Judenheit', pp. 266–7.

80. Rosenberg, 'Jüdische Zeitfragen', p. 534.

'Anglo-Jewish world capitalism'. On the other hand, he also felt that Woodrow Wilson had prevented the complete destruction of Germany in order to forestall French ambitions to become 'master of the continent'; for this purpose, Germany had to retain 'at least the semblance of a certain dangerousness'.[81] Eckart's interpretation of American foreign policy in 1919 clearly combined both power politics and ideology.

In general Eckart rarely referred to foreign affairs but there is nothing to suggest that his views differed markedly from Rosenberg's. He was, perhaps, a little more outspokenly racist than Rosenberg, describing Britain, for example, as 'the arch-Pharisee amongst the Aryan people' and France as 'the Gallic Jezebel, this embodiment of feminine vanity and vindictiveness'.[82] Nevertheless he agreed with Rosenberg that Britain was Germany's chief enemy inside the Entente and that Russia and Germany would be natural allies once the 'Jewish' regime in Russia had been removed.[83]

Conclusion

This chapter has, it is hoped, shown that between the end of 1918 and the autumn of 1919 — before Adolf Hitler emerged on the political stage — Rosenberg, Eckart and Feder were publicising a number of ideas (none of them particularly original), which would eventually form part of the *Weltanschauung* of the German Workers' Party. Eckart expounded on the nature of 'Jewishness'; Feder warned about the excesses of 'interest-slavery' and Rosenberg revealed the 'Jewish' manipulation of the Bolshevik Revolution. It was Rosenberg, however, who felt the need to weave these and other fairly disparate ideas into a coherent antisemitic philosophy — in effect, to substantiate a world conspiracy theory by reference to backstage intrigue in the twilight world of Freemasonry, Jesuitism and Zionism, and behind the closed doors of the world's stock exchanges. The resulting *Weltanschauung* appears largely to have predetermined Rosenberg's and Eckart's approach to foreign affairs. How far Hitler and the Nazi Party would adopt this approach is a

---

81. D. Eckart, 'Immer lächeln, und doch eine Schurke', pp. 82–83.
82. D. Eckart, 'Die Schönheitsfehler der bayerischen Volkspartei', *Agd*, 7 December 1918, p. 13.
83. D. Eckart, introducing an anti-British diatribe by Rosenberg in Eckart, 'Zwischen den Schächern', p. 106; on Russia, D. Eckart, 'Die Schlacht auf den katalaunischen Feldern', *Agd*, 20 February 1920, p. 87.

question which will be discussed later, but Rosenberg gave his own account of what happened as early as 1928; the German Workers' Party of 1919 was, he said, acquiring 'deeper insights into the character of the competing forces in world politics' and 'these insights developed into principles and ideologies when Adolf Hitler entered the circle of this little troop'.[84]

84. A. Rosenberg, *Dietrich Eckart*, p. 51.

2

Hitler and the Pan-German
Legacy

What was the political outlook of the young Adolf Hitler when he attended the meeting of the German Worker's Party on 12 September 1919? The generally accepted answer is that Hitler espoused a 'Pan-German' philosophy; that is, his ideas were gleaned, in general, from the prewar propaganda of the Pan-German movement and, in particular, from the publications of the Berlin-based *Alldeutscher Verband* (ADV) or Pan-German League.[1] In the area of foreign policy especially, he seems at this time to have been influenced by Pan-German goals; indeed, according to one historian, Hitler only abandoned his Pan-German heritage in 1924 when he began to write *Mein Kampf* and to lay down his own anti-Russian *Lebensraum* ideology.[2]

These claims need careful re-examination. To decide whether Hitler was merely reiterating Pan-German notions on foreign affairs at the beginning of his political career, one needs not only a detailed comparison of the Pan-German outlook and Hitler's early comments on foreign policy but also a clear understanding of the relationship between the ADV and the DAP in the early 1920s. One historian has suggested that a 'special relationship' existed between the two movements at this time which came to an end only with the Munich putsch of November 1923, when the Nazis 'upstaged' the ADV, and with Hitler's attempt at his ensuing trial to implicate Heinrich Class, the chairman of the ADV, in the treasonous plot against the

---

1. H. Auerbach, 'Hitler's politische Lehrjahre und die Münchener Gesellschaft, 1919–1923, *VfZG*, vol. 25 (1977), p. 14. See also Franz-Willing, *Die Hitlerbewegung*, p. 80; W. Maser, *Hitler's Mein Kampf*, (Munich, 1966), p. 66, Maser, *Die Frühgeschichte*, p. 208.
2. A. Kuhn, *Hitlers aussenpolitisches Programm*, pp. 119–20, 56.

state.[3] If such a relationship did exist, then it is more than likely that the ADV did exert a decisive influence on Hitler's (and indeed the Nazi Party's) developing outlook on foreign policy. Fortunately, now that Class's second and unpublished volume of memoirs — dealing with the period 1912–1933 — is available for scrutiny, it is possible to assess whether a special relationship did exist by placing the ADV's dealings with the DAP in the wider context of Pan-German machinations with other *völkisch* groups.[4]

The Pan-German League and the Nazi Party

The ADV was one of the most significant and durable extra-parliamentary political associations in recent German history. Between the dismissal of its mentor, Bismarck, as chancellor in 1890 and the outbreak of the Second World War in 1939, the ADV constituted a kind of unofficial 'National Opposition' to governmental policy. Under the leadership of first Ernst Hasse, a professor of statistics from Leipzig, and after 1908 of Heinrich Class, a solicitor from Mainz,[5] the ADV's vociferous advocacy of German imperialism encouraged German commercial and naval rivalry with Britain.[6] According to one recent authority, there is no doubt that the ADV managed to 'influence a considerable portion of the German

---

3. A. Kruck, *Geschichte des Alldeutschen Verbandes 1890–1939* (Wiesbaden, 1954), pp. 193, 197–9.

4. The first volume of Class's memoirs was published in 1932 as *Wider den Strom. Vom Werden und Wachsen der Nationalen Opposition im alten Reich* (Leipzig, 1932). The second volume (henceforth 'Wider den Strom, vol. 2'), a 955-page typescript dating from 1936, is one of the two manuscripts in the Class *Nachlass* now in the Bundesarchiv in Coblenz. The other is a 63-page account of Class's contacts with the Nazi Party (of which pages 1 to 7 are missing) and was written, according to marginal notes, between 29 October and 17 November 1936 (henceforth 'Class und die NSDAP'). Extracts from the latter were published in F. von Schlabrendorff, *The Secret War against Hitler* (London, 1966). I am grateful to Herr von Schlabrendorff for his assistance in locating this document and for the details of its provenance. Both documents, it seems, were deposited in a Swiss bank vault by Class during the Second World War and retrieved by von Schlabrendorff at the request of Class's daughter. On her death in 1973, they were deposited in the Bundesarchiv and, in accordance with her will, became available to historians in 1977; letters from von Schlabrendorff to the author, 2 January and 7 February 1974.

5. Ernst Hasse was chairman of the ADV from 1894 until his death in 1908. Heinrich Class was born in Rheinhessen in 1868 and studied in Berlin, Freiburg and Giessen before becoming a solicitor. He attended lectures by von Treitschke, whom he later described as his 'master, the man who guided my whole life', *Wider den Strom*, vol. 1, pp. 15–16. He had been an antisemite ever since.

6. Kruck, *Geschichte des ADV*, pp. 24–30. The ADV's support for naval expansion led it into collaboration on occasion with the Naval Office; see R. Chickering, *We Men Who Feel Most German, A Study of the Pan-German League 1886–1914* (London, 1984), pp. 59–62.

iddle class in an anti-English direction and indeed to stir up
feelings of hatred in times of national excitement during the Boer
War (1899–1902) and the Agadir crisis (1911)'.[7]

During the First World War the ADV's Executive Committee
drew up a memorandum on German war aims, later published by
Class under the title *Zum deutschen Kriegsziel*. Its proposals for German territorial aggrandisement in Europe went far beyond those
which Chancellor Bethmann Hollweg had included in his secret
'September Programme' of 1914.[8] In 1915 Class organised a War
Aims Movement which urged that Germany take the opportunity
offered by the war to establish her pre-eminence in Central Europe
and to achieve economic self-sufficiency.[9] The ADV undoubtedly
helped to fashion public opinion and, perhaps, even influenced
governmental policy on foreign affairs during the war.

In domestic affairs, Class had consistently criticised the trend
towards parliamentary democracy. In the delightfully entitled *Wenn
ich der Kaiser wär* (If I were Kaiser) published in 1912, Class
enumerated the faults of the Reichstag and called for a dictatorship.[10] During the war he tried and failed to convince both the
Kaiser and General Ludendorff of the need for a fully-fledged
military dictatorship.[11] Defeat and Revolution in 1918 were taken as
confirming the correctness of the ADV's stand and radicalised the
movement further. Antisemitism, long espoused by Class, was endorsed officially by the ADV's Bamberg Declaration of 16 February
1919 as part of its programme of reform.[12] As a result, the ADV
sponsored the establishment of the *Deutschvölkische Schutz- und Trutzbund*, an organisation designed to promote a more popular and rabid
antisemitism.[13] The Revolution also removed the ADV's last qualm
about radical change, its loyalty to the Kaiser. The ADV became a
subversive force working in secret to overthrow the Weimar Republic.

In 1920 Class began to establish contact with other counter-
revolutionary forces in Germany. In 1920 he collaborated briefly

7. D. Aigner, *Das Ringen um England* (Munich, 1969), p. 15.

8. H. Class, *Zum deutschen Kriegsziel* (Munich, 1917); on this see F. Fischer, *Germany's Aims in the First World War* (London, 1967), pp. 186–8.

9. Fischer, *Germany's Aims*, pp. 166–7.

10. D. Frymann, (alias Class), *Wenn Ich der Kaiser wär*, 4th edn. (Leipzig, 1913).

11. For details see G. Stoakes, 'The Evolution of Nazi Ideas on Foreign Policy, 1919–1928', doctoral dissertation, University of Sheffield, 1984, pp. 61–62.

12. W. Jochmann (ed.), *Nationalsozialismus und Revolution. Ursprung und Geschichte der NSDAP in Hamburg 1922–1933. Dokumente* (Frankfurt, 1963), p. 17; see also Kruck, *Geschichte des ADV* pp. 130–1.

13. Class, *Wider den Strom*, vol. 2, pp. 451–2.

with the Bavarian extremist Georg Escherich. In 1922 he worked for a short time with *Organisation Consul* (this successor to the more famous counter-revolutionary group *Brigade Ehrhardt*) and *Bund Bayern und Reich* which was striving to reinstate the Wittelsbachs, the Bavarian royal house.[14] In the wake of the Franco-Belgian invasion of the Ruhr in 1923, Class made two attempts to enlist the support of General von Seeckt, head of the Reichswehr, for a military engagement with the occupying forces and in the establishment of a military dictatorship.[15] In October 1923 Class planned a national uprising with Bavarian Minister-President and later State Commissioner Gustav von Kahr and Munich Police President Ernst Pöhner.[16] Their plans were apparently thwarted by the actions of the Hitler-Ludendorff group on the night of 8–9 November 1923. But Class's clandestine attempts to coordinate the counter-revolutionary forces in Germany had brought the Nazi Party to Class's attention long before Hitler's pre-emptive strike in November 1923.

Eckart Kehr once described the ADV as a 'sort of political ideological holding company, which delivered intellectual armaments to other pressure groups'. That the young German Workers' Party was one of the recipients of the ADV's ideological guidance is in little doubt. For example, when Hitler delivered a speech to the DAP on 16 October 1919, the main speaker that evening was Dr. Erich Kühn, editor of the ADV's journal *Deutschlands Erneuerung*.[17] The full extent of the ideological indebtedness of Nazism to the ADV is, however, difficult to establish since, as has been seen, the ADV patronised at different times a wide range of rightwing political causes. Nevertheless, a closer investigation of the political and financial contacts between the ADV and the DAP is now possible on the basis of Heinrich Class's account of his relationship with the Nazis before 1933, written in October–November 1936 and only recently made available in full to historians.[18]

This account has to be treated with caution for several reasons.

14. Ibid., 498–508. See also B.S. Chamberlin, 'The Enemy on the Right. The Alldeutsche Verband, 1918–26', unpublished Ph.D. thesis, University of Maryland, 1972, pp. 142–8.

15. Class, *Wider den Strom*, pp. 644–8, see also G. Franz-Willing, *Krisenjahr der Hitlerbewegung 1923* (Oldendorf, 1975), pp. 101–2.

16. Class, *Wider den Strom*, vol. 2, p. 715.

17. E. Kehr, 'Die Grundlagen der Tirpitzischen Flottenpropaganda', *Die Gesellschaft*, vol. 2 (1928), p. 225, quoted in Chamberlin, 'Enemy on the Right', p. 21. For further links between the ADV and the DAP, ibid., pp. 215–217.

18. 'Class und die NSDAP', see note 4 above.

Firstly, it is known that Class, along with many Pan-Germans, felt that the debt of gratitude owed by the Nazi Party to the ADV had never been adequately acknowledged.[19] It is quite possible that in trying, as he saw it, to set the record straight for posterity, he may have exaggerated his own and the ADV's contribution to the success of the Nazis. Secondly, as the account was written in 1936, some sixteen years after the earliest events which it describes, allowance has to be made for errors in recollection; these are evident in Class's account of his first conversations with Hitler, which includes observations obviously made only later.[20] The third reason for caution is the difficulty in locating corrobative evidence for Class's version of these meetings, at which quite often no-one else was present. Despite these important limitations, the document does provide a fascinating, if largely unsubstantiated, account of the financial and political assistance given by the ADV to the Nazi party.

It seems likely that Class met Hitler first in March 1920 and then on at least two further occasions that year.[21] His impression was, to say the least, mixed. After being addressed like a public meeting — a fate shared by many of Hitler's visitors — Class labelled the future dictator 'a political savage' and 'a pronounced hysteric'. Nonetheless Class recognised that if Hitler could 'manage to make contact with Marxist elements, it seemed probable that he could be capable of, at least, loosening the bonds that tied them to that party [the KPD]' and for this reason — the prospect of a more popularly-based 'National Opposition' — Class decided to keep in touch with him.[22] The ADV helped to publicise the party in the Pan-German press and facilitated contacts between the Nazis and Austrian Pan-Germans.[23] Following the meeting of Austrian and German völkisch groups in Salzburg in August 1920, Hitler undertook a speaking tour of Austria, almost certainly paid for by the ADV.[24]

19. See, for example, an ADV situation report, dated 3 February 1934, quoted in H. A. Jacobsen and W. Jochmann (eds.), *Ausgewählte Dokumente zur Geschichte des Nationalsozialismus* (Bielefeld, 1960), vol. 2, p. 3.

20. See the comments on the earlier published extracts in A. Tyrell, *Vom 'Trommler' zum 'Führer'* (Munich, 1975), p. 224.

21. Their first meeting almost certainly took place in Berlin during the Kapp putsch (13–17 March) and was arranged by Eckart who was already in contact with ADV members, K. A von Müller, *Im Wandel einer Welt. Erinnerungen. Bd. 3, 1919–32* (Munich, 1966), p. 143. The missing first 7 pages of Class's account probably describes this meeting. A second meeting took place when Hitler was on a fund-raising trip in North Germany in December 1920; Chamberlain, 'Enemy on the Right', pp. 222–3.

22. 'Class und die NSDAP', pp. 8–9.

23. Ibid., pp. 9–11; see also M. Maurenbrecher, 'Adolf Hitler', *Deutsche Zeitung*, 10 November 1923.

24. Chamberlin, 'Enemy on the Right', p. 216.

Whether this was the first occasion on which the ADV rendered financial assistance to the Nazi cause is a matter of some debate. It has been claimed that it helped to finance several Nazi projects including the purchase of the *Völkischer Beobachter* (VB).[25] No solid evidence has been presented to substantiate these claims, but in his memoirs Class claimed that he intervened reluctantly in 1922 to save the *VB* from bankruptcy by raising two instalments of 15,000 marks to pay off the paper's creditors. He complained that he had received no thanks whatsoever from the newspaper or from the party for his assistance.[26] Though this story was intended to substantiate Class's claim for greater credit in the rise of the Nazis, probably this incident (or one like it) did occur. The fact is that in 1923 Hitler privately acknowledged his financial indebtedness to the ADV; when Bruno Wenzel, the founder of the party cell in Hanover, asked whether he should accept an offer of over a million Reichsmarks from the ADV as an inducement to support the League against the *Deutschvölkische Freiheitspartei* (DVFP), its rival for the leadership of the völkisch movement, Hitler replied: 'If you can get 10 million, so much the better. Those are the sources which I am tapping also'.[27] Evidently the ADV did give financial succour to a party which might attract the mass support which it could not attract itself and which might be a useful ally in the völkisch movement.

However, in view of the ADV's patronage of a multiplicity of rightwing causes, perhaps an analysis of the organisational contacts between the Nazi Party and the ADV will provide a better clue to the exact relationship between the two movements. It is true, for example, that leading members of the former, including Rosenberg, Eckart and Hitler himself, attended meetings of the ADV-sponsored *Deutschvölkische Schutz- und Trutzbund* (DVSTB). However, since Rosenberg and Eckart had long-established contacts with the Pan-German movement via the Thule Society in Munich and since the DVSTB shared the DAP's antisemitic outlook, this contact should not be regarded as especially significant. It is also true that when the DVSTB was banned in 1922, the ADV advised its members to join

25. On the *VB* story, see ibid., p. 218. Those who have suggested that the NSDAP was financed by the ADV include Kruck, *Geschichte des ADV*, p. 193, W. Görlitz and H. Quint, *Adolf Hitler. Eine Biographie* (Stuttgart, 1952), pp. 143, 158 and von Müller, *Im Wandel einer Welt*, p. 143. Franz-Willing is sceptical about all these claims, *Die Hitlerbewegung*, p. 185.

26. 'Class und die NSDAP', p. 11.

27. Quoted in Franz-Willing, *Krisenjahr*, p. 204. Class was hoping to discredit his two opponents in the DVFP, Albrecht von Graefe, its leader and Reinhold Wulle, former editor of the Pan-German *Deutsche Zeitung*, who were attacking him in the völkisch press; Class, 'Wider den Strom', vol. 2, pp. 603–21.

the NSDAP.[28] However, this might be interpreted as another illustration of the cynical pragmatism of Class's dealings with counter-revolutionary groups rather than as a firm endorsement of the Nazi Party; certainly in view of their ideological similarities, the NSDAP was a natural successor to the DVSTB.[29]

Though the financial and political contribution of the ADV to the NSDAP is clear and undeniable, the decisive consideration was, probably, Hitler's attitude towards the ADV. In general one might say that he had no qualms about accepting its political and financial assistance, provided that his party leadership and freedom of manoeuvre remained unimpaired. In 1923, for example, when Class was attempting to coordinate the counter-revolutionary forces of Northern and Southern Germany, he was reluctant to approach Hitler, since the latter, as Class recalled later, 'had lost contact and gone his own way'.[30] When he did meet the Nazi leader on Whit-Sunday 1923 in Berlin to brief him on a projected national uprising, Hitler promised to go with Class 'through thick and thin'. However, only two days later, Hitler failed to attend an important meeting of the counter-revolutionary leaders in Munich, sending Hermann Göring instead. Class suspected that either Hitler's attitude towards the ADV leadership had been poisoned by his own enemies in the DVFP or that Hitler considered the contact to be 'politically useless'.[31] A more likely explanation, since he had sent Göring and therefore had not completely abandoned the project, might be that Hitler was merely maintaining his freedom of action. Later, as Class himself revealed, Hitler learned of everything discussed at the meeting but 'committed himself to nothing'.[32] Thus, even before the abortive Munich putsch of 8–9 November 1923 — Hitler's attempt to pre-empt the counter-revolution plotted by von Kahr and Class — he had displayed what the Pan-German *Deutsche Zeitung* was later to call 'the vanity of a prima donna'.[33]

Class's account of his dealings with Hitler certainly does not suggest that the ADV and the NSDAP were collaborating closely.

28. Kruck, *Geschichte des ADV*, p. 195. The DVSTB was banned after its leader, Alfred Roth, had made a speech praising the murder of Walter Rathenau; U. Lohalm, *Völkischer Radikalismus, Die Geschichte des Deutschvölkischen Schutz- und Trutzbundes 1919–23* (Hamburg, 1970), p. 274; see also W. Krebs, 'Der Alldeutsche Verband in den Jahren 1918 bis 1939', unpublished D. Phil. thesis, Humboldt Universität zu Berlin 1970, p. 124. For Hitler's participation in a DVSTB discussion on 7 January 1920, see PND report BHSTA I/1477.

29. Class, 'Wider den Strom', vol. 2, pp. 458–9.

30. 'Class und die NSDAP', p. 15.

31. Ibid., pp. 17–21. See note 27 above.

32. 'Class und die NSDAP', p. 23.

33. M. Maurenbrecher, 'Adolf Hitler', *Deutsche Zeitung*, 10 November 1923.

Their political goals may have been compatible, but the ambitions of their leaders were not. At his trial following the putsch, Hitler did his best to implicate Class and the ADV in the piot to overthrow the Weimar Republic, a ploy which, Class believed, could do nothing to help his own case but would undoubtedly damage the reputation of the ADV. Class was not indicted but his relationship with Hitler was permanently embittered; he felt justified in describing Hitler was a *homo afidelis*, a man incapable of keeping his word.[34]

However, whilst Hitler's actions in the early 1920s did not imply any gratitude towards the ADV leadership, from isolated references in his speeches and letters it is evident that he fully appreciated the political and historical significance of the ADV. Indeed he was very much inclined to spring to the defence of the ADV, which was the subject of frequent attack in the early years of the Weimar Republic. The most common criticisms were that it had helped to cause the First World War and then to prolong it by its virulent propaganda. On several occasions, Hitler defended the ADV specifically on both charges, blaming 'the Jews who controlled German foreign policy in 1914' for starting the war and the opponents of an increased military budget for the duration of the conflict.[35]

Nevertheless, Hitler's appraisal of the ADV's postwar position was rather different; whilst he recognised its pioneering efforts before 1914, he felt that it had had its chance and failed to take it. Hence, in 1923, he remarked: 'Politically we all depend on the Pan-German League, of which we can only complain that, despite its correct analysis and the long existence of such an influential organisation, up to now it has done no practical work. But we can make up for that by using its resources.'[36] Thus, whilst prepared to draw on the League's funds, he was reluctant to tie the NSDAP too closely to the ADV (or any other organisation); in March 1924, following the Munich putsch, Bruno Wenzel, in Hanover, received the following unequivocal statement from party headquarters: 'In order to prevent continued misunderstandings, it is once again reiterated that all kinds of special alliances with the "Deutschnationale Volkspartei", with the "Bund Wiking" and with the "Alldeutscher Ver-

34. 'Class und die NSDAP', pp. 32–6; Schlabrendorff, *Secret War*, p. 353. Hitler was trying to implicate Class and through him von Kahr, and thus discredit the chief witness for the prosecution.

35. Speech by Hitler on 17 April 1920, report in R. H. Phelps, 'Hitler als Parteiredner in Jahre 1920', *VfZG*, vol. 11 (1963), p. 298; speech on 13 April 1923, report by Munich police to the Bavarian Ministry of the Interior in BHStA Sonderabgabe I Folder 1755 (I/1755).

36. Hitler to Bruno Wenzel quoted in J. Noakes, *The Nazi Party in Lower Saxony, 1921–33* (London, 1971), p. 32.

band", with the "Vereinigten Vaterländischen Verbände" are out of the question.'[37] Hitler may have been sensitive to the threat represented by the ADV (amongst others) to his leadership of the völkisch movement, but his overt criticism of the ADV related to its continued failure to put principle into practice by means of a seizure of power.[38]

In short, the organisational links between the ADV and the NSDAP, and the personal contacts between their leaders in the early 1920s, do not point to the existence of a 'special relationship' but rather one born of political convenience and marred by suspicion and personal ambition. Contact between the two organisations was intermittent, if at times financially beneficial to the Nazis. The Munich putsch proved to be the occasion, not the cause, of the final rupture; it confirmed Class's worst fears about Hitler's unreliability; it proved to Hitler that he, unlike Class, was a man of action. Nevertheless, despite his growing disillusionment with the Pan-German League in the mid-1920s, Hitler clearly embarked on his political career full of veneration for its prewar achievements, in particular in the field of propaganda. And the Nazi Party as a whole may have been enormously indebted to the Pan-Germans on an ideological level. During their meeting on Whit-Sunday 1923, for example, Hitler took time to request Class's view on the international impact of the Franco-Belgian occupation of the Ruhr.[39] Whatever their personal differences, Hitler still respected Class's opinions on foreign affairs in 1923 and this raises the crucial question of how far his outlook on foreign affairs had been fashioned by Pan-German influences.

Pan-German Foreign Policy

At his trial in 1924 Hitler claimed that he had left Vienna in 1913 'as an absolute antisemitic, as a deadly enemy of the whole Marxist outlook and as a Pan-German in my political persuasion'.[40] It must be emphasised at this point that the ADV was only part of the

37. Rolf Eidhalt (anagram of 'Adolf Hitler' used by Alfred Rosenberg in 1924 during Hitler's imprisonment) to Wenzel, 18 March 1924, *HA 42/843*.
38. On 22 May 1926 Hitler was particularly sarcastic about the 'frightful danger' posed by the recently uncovered plot by the 'bloodthirsty society of the Pan-German Leagues and Class' to murder von Seeckt and overthrow the government, speech reported in *VB*, 26 May 1926.
39. 'Class und die NSDAP', pp. 17–18.
40. Report in the *Grossdeutsche Zeitung* (the paper of the banned Nazi Party in 1924–5), 27 February 1924.

Pan-German movement in Central Europe and it is clear from Hitler's fulsome praise of the Austrian Pan-Germans in *Mein Kampf* that they, as much as the Berlin-based ADV, were responsible for his early (prewar) political education.[41] However, as will be seen, Hitler was well-acquainted at the end of the First World War with the major publications of the ADV leadership. So what ideas did the Pan-Germans propagate before, during and immediately after the First World War?

The basic aim of the Pan-German movement was the defence and fortification of the German *Volk* throughout the world. Inside Germany, this meant the reanimation of national consciousness and the curbing of threats to it within the country. Abroad, it entailed, firstly, the protection of the Germanism of German communities in foreign lands (with their eventual reunification with German Reich as a long-term objective) and, secondly, the expansion of German influence abroad.[42]

Heinrich Class, in the most famous Pan-German publication, *Wenn ich der Kaiser wär*, written in 1912, gave the clearest exposition of the thinking behind these principles. In order to preserve Germanism at home, Class recommended, for example, the expropriation of Polish property to limit Polish influence in Upper Silesia, Posen and West Prussia. Similar measures were envisaged for the population of Alsace-Lorraine, which remained 'curiously' pro-French and anti-German, though, he admitted, measures to limit French influence there might have to follow another war with France.[43]

In foreign affairs the Pan-German creed was expansion. If ever a state had cause to increase its sphere of influence, Class argued, it was the German Empire 'because her population figures are rising so quickly, her industry needs new markets, her whole economy [needs] land for the production of tropical and semi-tropical products of all kinds, the supply of which has brought us into an unbearable dependence on others'.[44] Hence, German expansionism was justified by the need to avert demographic catastrophe and to promote economic self-sufficiency.

Anticipating that his claims for Germany's overpopulation would be questioned, Class also acknowledged the need for internal coloni-

41. Adolf Hitler, *Mein Kampf* (London, 1969), pp. 89–112 (henceforth *MK*). Many Austrian Pan-Germans were also members of the ADV; Kruck, *Geschichte des ADV*; p. 108.

42. See the original programme of the ADV, quoted in Kruck, *Geschichte des ADV*, p. 10.

43. Frymann, *Wenn ich*, pp. 88, 81–2.

44. Ibid., p. 5.

sation: 'the correct colonial policy lies in the east of the Empire', he wrote, but this was 'not sufficient argument against overseas colonisation. It means doing one and not neglecting the other.' The government, in his view, was neglecting both. There was no disguising Class's preference for overseas colonies, however; they would provide not only markets for German industry and vital raw materials, but also a reservoir of 'land for the settlement of Germans, for whom some day the fatherland will have no more room'.[45] Behind this fear of future overpopulation lies his horror of Germans emigrating and his determination never again to allow a 'loss of people through emigration to foreign states'.[46]

Class did not disguise his interest in colonial expansion in Europe however. European locations were climatically more suitable for settlement by Germans than territories in Africa.[47] Nevertheless Class did recognise the difficulties involved in expansion in Europe, not the least of which was that such a scheme could, in his words, 'only be brought about by successful wars, since neither France nor Russia will be so humanitarian as to cede parts of their countries to us'. And even if land were acquired by warfare, there was still the problem of what to do with the indigenous population; 'evacuation' was one solution but Class admitted that this contravened the laws of 'historical development and modern rights of citizenship'. German expansion to the east and the west was, therefore, in his opinion, only to be adopted as an expedient in extreme necessity.[48]

He also considered the possibility of German expansion into Southeastern Europe. The settlement of the Slav-populated areas of the Austro-Hungarian Empire and the Balkans would have been a 'sound solution' to Germany's problems but only on two conditions: firstly, that 'an eternal alliance' were signed between Germany and Austria–Hungary to ensure 'a complete and lasting harmony of interest between the two states' and, secondly, that the Hapsburg Empire should assume a form which secured for all time 'the cultural and political leadership of the Germans within it'.[49]

Since expansion at French and Russian expense was impossible without war and since the preconditions for German penetration of Southeastern Europe did not yet exist, Class concluded in the 'Kaiserbuch' that the only realistic option available to an increas-

45. Ibid., pp. 8–9.
46. Ibid., p. 144.
47. Ibid., p. 12–14.
48. Ibid. p. 140.
49. Ibid. p. 141.

ingly overpopulated Germany was 'settlement overseas'. It should be stressed, of course, that this conclusion did not imply any real commitment to the territorial status quo in Europe; his stated preference for overseas colonies was merely an attempt to avoid giving the public the impression that the ADV leadership was warmongering. In private, few qualms were expressed about German expansion in Europe and, in effect, the creation of a German-dominated *Mitteleuropa*.[50]

Whether such foreign policy objectives determined or derived from the ADV's assessment of the major powers is difficult to establish. In the 'Kaiserbuch' Class showed that he was fully aware that a German overseas empire would cause problems with 'England'. England already regarded the development of Germany's economic and naval potential as a direct threat to her security and more generally 'feared for the basis of her own position as a world power (Weltmachtstellung)'; Germany's interest in overseas colonies would exacerbate this fear.[51] In Class's view such fears were unfounded: 'We have no political plans that will be dangerous to England . . . [there are therefore] no grounds for rivalry, even less for enmity, if only England were willing to recognise that 65 million people can live in Germany proper, perhaps even 75 if necessary, but not 80 or 90 million.' In short, if England were to accept the demographic argument in favour of German colonial expansion, the 'two Germanic blood cousins' could 'shape the fate of the world together'.[52] So, whilst he hoped for Anglo-German collaboration, realistically Class anticipated a struggle with Britain to establish an overseas empire.

The second power with whom Germany was likely to have trouble was France. The problem here, to Class's mind, was not Germany's ambitions but the French desire to avenge the defeat of 1871 and to recover Alsace-Lorraine; this drive had led the French into the English and Russian camps. If France were to provoke another war, she 'would have to be destroyed', part of her homeland would have to be taken as 'lasting security', and her colonial possessions taken to help to meet Germany's needs.[53] This analysis seems to confirm

50. On the ADV's interest in *Mitteleuropa*, see Chickering, *We Men*, pp. 77–9. On the view of Pan-Germans expressed privately, see General von Gebsattel's letter to Class of 23 July 1914, quoted in F. Fischer, *The War of Illusions, German Policies from 1911 to 1914* (London, 1975), p. 456.

51. Frymann, *Wenn ich*, p. 144.

52. Ibid., pp. 145–7.

53. Ibid., pp. 149–52.

Class's belief that Germany should seize territory in Europe if war broke out.

As far as Russia was concerned, Class believed that 'viewed from the German standpoint, no sensible reasons are to be found which ought to alienate the two [powers]'. The Russians, he felt, saw things very differently: 'the Russian hates the German with the instinctive hatred of one who is an absolute inferior in face of his superior.' Hatred of Germany was the driving force behind Pan-Slavism, and Russia was likely to go to war to protect the Slavs in the Balkans. Class saw 'nothing tempting, but also nothing to be feared' in such a war, even with Russia allied to France, since the enormous potential of the Russian army was more than offset by the indiscipline of the Slavs. If Russia were defeated in such a conflict, she would be required to make territorial concessions which would give Germany 'a better frontier as well as land for settlement, a process in which evacuation cannot be avoided'.[54] So, once again, Class seems to have been arguing that Germany would not seek war in Europe but, if one broke out, she should take the opportunity to acquire territory there.

In effect, therefore, in 1912 Class was already elaborating Pan-German war aims in *Wenn ich der Kaiser wär*. These plans also included Belgium and the Netherlands, towards whom Class believed his Pan-German colleagues had been too patient. The law of the jungle applied here, he said: 'such small states have already lost their right to exist: for only that state which can carry it through sword in hand can assert its right to independence.' Should war occur, they would be presented with a choice between limited national independence in alliance with the German Empire or cooperation with England and France, in which case 'they would be annexed'.[55] So the ADV's leader made no secret of the fact that in the event of war possible opponents would be neutralised either by agreement or by conquest.

How then did the ADV regard Germany's allies in the Triple Alliance? Class's views on both Austria–Hungary and Italy, as set out in the 'Kaiserbuch', were equivocal. On the whole, he supported the Austro-Hungarian alliance 'because it corresponded to the needs of both allied powers and carried with it the security of permanence'.[56] He did have doubts about the internal strength of a state

---

54. Ibid., pp. 168–70. Class refused to recognise that difficulties experienced by Baltic Germans at the hands of Czarist officials were sufficient causes for hostility towards Russia.

55. Ibid., pp. 152–5.

56. Ibid., p. 157.

in which the two halves were mutually antagonistic, but ultimately the strength of the Austrian army was, for him, the decisive consideration: 'the alliance with Austria–Hungary has value for us only if her army is strong and efficient; should the army decay because of the further internal disintegration of the state, then any interest in this alliance will disappear.'[57] In brief, Class felt that Germany should continue to aid Austria–Hungary in maintaining her great power status.

It should be stressed at this point that Class's views were not shared by the Austrian Pan-Germans, whom Hitler admired so much, or even by all members of the ADV inside Germany. The Austrian Pan-Germans were very critical of the Austro-Hungarian Empire as a racial conglomeration in which German influence was declining. In 1906, their leader Georg von Schönerer published the *Alldeutsches Zukunftprogramm*, which called for preparations for a 'German-Austrian' *Anschluss* with Germany.[58] This was to be accompanied by a German-Russian alliance. This anti-Habsburg and pro-Russian stance became the object of considerable controversy after 1912 with the emergence after the Balkan Wars of a Russian-backed Serbia as a direct challenge to the security of the Austro-Hungarian Empire. Class, though dubious about its internal cohesion, reiterated his support for the Habsburg Empire but was criticised from within his own ranks by Theodor Reismann-Grone, who argued that 'if we were tied to this cadaver [Austria–Hungary] any longer, it would bring us to ruin'.[59] Within the ADV the pro-Habsburg line ultimately carried the day, but it is important to remember that the young Adolf Hitler was undoubtedly exposed to the anti-Habsburg propaganda of Schönerer's Austrian Pan-German movement in the years leading up to the outbreak of the First World War.

Of Germany's other ally, Italy, Class was more critical. From her, he argued in the 'Kaiserbuch', 'we may expect nothing and we have nothing to fear' because she lacked weight in the power-political sense. Furthermore, Class surmised, she was already essentially in the Anglo-French camp: 'she is not our ally but plays at being

57. Ibid., p. 165.

58. For further details, A. G. Whiteside, *The Socialism of Fools. Georg von Schönerer and Austrian Pan-Germanism* (Berkeley, 1975), p. 295. Kruck, *Geschichte des ADV*: p. 112.

59. Ibid., pp. 110–11. In 1919 Reismann-Grone, in *Der Erdenkrieg und die Alldeutschen* (Mühlheim-Ruhr, 1919), criticised Class for having encouraged Habsburg expansionist ambitions, thereby spoiling Russo-German relations. Class defended himself in a review of the book, arguing that he would have preferred to return to the Bismarckian policy of alliance with Russia but the Russians' attitude prevented this, *Alldeutsche Blätter* (A.Bl.), 22 November 1919.

one'.[60] He predicted that, in the event of war with Britain and France, Italy would not fulfil her duties as Germany's ally.

Despite his qualms about Austria–Hungary and his outright scepticism concerning Italy, Class did not appear unduly alarmed by the prospect of war between Germany and the Triple Entente. Perhaps this was because he was firmly convinced that America, despite her overt hostility towards Germany, would remain neutral in any such conflict, since her interests would not be in jeopardy. However, he was rather afraid that she would exploit all the economic and political advantages accruing from a European imbroglio. He was already perturbed by Germany's economic dependence for certain imports on the United States, and one reason for his interest in overseas colonisation was his desire to secure Germany's access to those goods in order to 'liberate' her from American suppliers.[61] Hence Classs attitude towards America was, it seems, determined more by his interest in German economic self-sufficiency than by fears of US interventionism.

It is interesting to note the criteria by which Class appeared to judge the major powers. At first sight, considerations of power politics seem to have been predominant, with the emphasis on England's fear of German commercial and imperial rivalry, France's desire for revenge on her powerful neighbour and America's growing economic strength. However, there is evidence of racial motivation behind some of Class's observations. At root, of course, the whole Pan-German credo was racially inspired; it aimed at the preservation and extension of the influence of the Germanic race. Furthermore, Class's sympathy with the British seems to have been coloured by a belief in the natural alignment of the two 'Germanic cousins'. His attitude towards Russia and the Austro-Hungarian Empire was seemingly affected by his anti-Slav prejudices.

In the final analysis, it is difficult to assess the relative contribution of race and *Realpolitik* to Class's evaluation of the powers concerned. For example, in the case of the Dutch and Belgians, he cautioned Germans not to 'become sentimental' and not to expect the allegiance of 'racial comrades of lower German blood': 'selfish interests, not blood relations, would have to bring Holland and Belgium to our side.'[62] On the other hand, in the case of Japan, racial factors were, by Class's own admission, of decisive significance. Despite admiring the 'heroic patriotism' of its people, Class

60. Frymann, *Wenn ich*, pp. 177–8.
61. Ibid., pp. 173–5.
62. Ibid., p. 153.

rejected the suggestion that Germany should exploit Russo-Japanese tensions in the Far East because this would 'contradict the German racial conscience (*Rassegewissen*)'; for if, he explained, 'we want to build our whole internal policy on race and want to make [the country] sound again by establishing the rule of the racial idea, then external policy must be subordinated to the law of race'. This law prevented Germany 'from joining with a coloured race against a white race . . . from joining with any other race against a white race'. On these grounds alone, an alliance between Germany and Japan was out of the question, a decision, which Class himself acknowledged, would cause a 'so-called *Realpolitiker*' to smile.[63] It is difficult not to accept Class's words at their face value since Russo-Japanese friction certainly created tactical grounds for cooperation between Germany and Japan.

It should, perhaps, be added that Class did not appear to associate the Jewish question with foreign policy at this time. Whilst he identified the Jews as a force at work behind social democratic ideas and behind the press in Germany, he did not seem to perceive any international coordination behind Jewish policy.[64]

Such then was the Pan-German outlook on foreign affairs which Hitler had absorbed before the outbreak of the First World War. The ADV ostensibly advocated expansion overseas rather than in Europe; it recognised British, French and Russian hostility to German ambitions, though it acknowledged no real conflict of interest between Germany and Britain, or Germany and Russia. The Austrian Pan-Germans opposed the alliance between Germany and Austria–Hungary and called for an immediate *Anschluss*, but the majority of German members of the ADV accepted the alliance and regarded the *Anschluss* as a distant objective.

Once war broke out in 1914, a war which Class predictably welcomed as 'the greatest piece of luck that could have happened to us',[65] the ADV's executive rapidly produced in September 1914 a programme of German war aims — published in May 1917 by Class as *Zum deutschen Kriegsziel*. This revealed the League in its true colours. Germany was expected to expand both overseas and in Europe. Overseas colonial territory acquired from her defeated

63. Ibid., pp. 176–7.

64. Ibid., pp 71–2, 38.

65. Quoted in E. Hartwig. 'Der Alldeutsche Verband 1890–1939 in D. Fricke et. al., (eds.), *Die bürgerlichen Parteien in Deutschland* (Leipzig, 1968), p. 14.

enemies, principally the Belgian Congo, was to contribute to making her self-sufficient; the colonies, by supplying her with much-needed raw materials, as well as markets for finished goods, would reduce her reliance on foreign powers, in particular Britain, whose 'world domination' (*Weltherrschaft*) Class was determined to destroy.[66]

In Europe, Germany was to acquire territory from her defeated opponents primarily in order to improve her strategic security. In the west, Belgium, large areas of Eastern France and possibly Luxembourg and Holland were to be annexed; possession of the North Sea coast would secure German 'freedom of the seas' against Britain.[67] In the east, Russia was to be weakened by the annexation of Courland, Livonia and Estonia and by the detachment of Finland, the Ukraine and Poland, the latter to be a German protectorate with frontiers in line with those of 'Congress Poland'.[68] These territorial changes would also advance the cause of German autarky as the land taken from Belgium and France would supply coal and iron ore, and land in the east would be settled by German farmers.

Hence Germany's overseas empire would remove Britain's pre-eminence in world affairs and the creation of a *Mitteleuropa* under German rule would ensure her economic and strategic invulnerability in Europe. Clearly, therefore, the outbreak of the First World War freed the ADV from peacetime restraints; but its war aims programme only made explicit what was implied in Class's 'Kaiserbuch' in 1912.

But did the outcome of the First World War alter the ADV's outlook on foreign affairs? Certainly its approach to foreign affairs did not appear to change. Events appeared (or could be made to appear) to have confirmed Class's predictions; Germany had stood by Austria –Hungary and Italy had let down both her allies. Germany's defeat, which Class had not predicted, was attributed to the subversive activities of the Jews and Socialists, about whom he had warned in the 'Kaiserbuch'. Because he believed that defeat had come, not on the battlefield but on the home front because of the socialists' propaganda, the ADV set itself the goal of improving the political education of the German people. The Bamberg Declaration of 16 February 1919, which marked the ADV's return to active political life, stressed that 'the explanation of the fundamental

66. H. Class, *Zum deutschen Kriegsziel* (Munich, 1917), pp. 60–2, p. 41.
67. On Belgium, ibid., pp. 29–34; on France, ibid., pp. 35–9; on Britain ibid., pp. 41–2.
68. Ibid., pp. 55–8; on Russia, ibid., pp. 44–8.

questions of external policy' was 'the most significant way' of achieving that goal.[69]

Hence the outcome of the war put an even greater premium on what the ADV had always regarded as its prime directive — to publicise the needs of German foreign policy. However, Europe had, of course, been transformed by the war, and the ADV's goals for German foreign policy could not remain unaffected by the collapse of the Russian and Austro-Hungarian empires or by the Versailles settlement. For example, the re-emergence of a Polish state meant the loss of West Prussian territory acquired at the time of the partition of Poland; this the ADV was not prepared to accept, as its Bamberg Declaration showed: 'The Imperial region in the East, as far as it encompasses portions of the earlier Polish state, belongs because of the facts of history to Germany; also the parts settled by Poles have become through German endeavour the genuine possession of the German people which can never be renounced.' The same applied to Alsace-Lorraine; this was German land and its recovery was for the ADV a major priority. The collapse of the Austro-Hungarian Empire removed the ADV's former caution about the *Anschluss*; the Bamberg Declaration, accordingly, demanded that 'the whole of German-Austria including the German western area of Hungary . . . be taken into the National Federation'. In addition, of course, the Versailles settlement had deprived Germany of her overseas colonies and, not surprisingly, the ADV called for the return of these 'stolen' territories.[70]

As well as changes brought about by the defeat of Germany and her allies, the Pan-Germans had to adjust to changed circumstances in Russia. The two revolutions of 1917 had been unexpected but, in the short term, helped to realise Pan-German ambitions. The Treaty of Brest-Litovsk, signed by Germany and the new Bolshevik government in March 1918, seemed to satisfy the requirements laid down by Class in the 'Kaiserbuch' and again in his pamphlet on Pan-German war aims in 1917. The *Alldeutsche Blätter* wrote in March 1918 of the treaty:

If we compare what the German sword has gained for us in the east with the war aims of the *Alldeutscher Verband*, as our League's chairman Heinrich Class has presented them in the belief of a German victory in his pamphlet 'Zum deutschen Kriegsziel', then it shows that the armistice

69. Jochmann, *Nationalsozialismus*, pp. 14–17.
70. Ibid., pp. 19–22.

has in the main realised what we hoped for from the fates. . . . In the east our goals have become facts.[71]

Class himself, speaking at an ADV conference in Berlin on 14 April 1918, expressed his satisfaction with the Brest-Litovsk peace; in 1912 he had wanted, he said, the greatest possible weakening of Russia, so long a threat to Germany's eastern frontier, and the war had to be waged 'until Russia's alien border states had been detached and she was divorced from her economically productive areas . . . . this goal had been reached. The eastern flank is relieved, Russia is destroyed and will not in the foreseeable future pursue a policy of conquest'.[72] Of course, Germany was very rapidly deprived of the fruits of victory. But it seems likely that the ADV kept the 'solution' of March 1918 in mind as it looked to the future; the Bamberg Declaration, indeed, demanded the incorporation of 'the ancient German colonial area of the Baltic lands' into Germany.[73]

The German defeat in the First World War, therefore, provided the ADV with some new short-term goals, but the old ones were not forgotten. In view of this, it would seem unlikely that the ADV's appraisal of the major powers had altered significantly. The emergence of Bolshevism in Russia — the most dramatic change in Europe — was regarded by Heinrich Class as having eliminated Russia as a serious threat to Germany; in a speech at the ADV conference in Frankfurt in September 1920, he suggested that 'of Russia [it] need only be said that it is languishing in frightful decay . . . dangerous for our fatherland only if it succeeds in assisting Bolshevism to victory on German soil'. Class's 'discovery' that the leaders of the Bolshevik Revolution were Jews did not significantly alter his already anti-Russian outlook; it merely reinforced it.[74]

Class's attitude towards the Western powers remained unchanged. He placed no faith in the League of Nations and was gravely concerned about Germany's future, dependent as she was 'on the goodwill of her enemies, of whom the strongest at present, like France and England, want our complete destruction or, like the United States who watches our fate with heartfelt indifference; of

71. 'J. D.', *A.Bl.*, 16 March 1918.

72. Speech reported in *A.Bl*, 20 April 1918. 'V' (probably von Vietinghoff-Scheel, the ADV's business manager) agreed, *A.Bl.*, 30 March 1918.

73. Jochmann, *Nationalsozialismus*, p. 19.

74. Report in *A.Bl.*, 2 October 1920. Class identified the 'Jewish rulers of Russian Bolshevism' in postwar editions of Einhart's *Deutsche Geschichte* (Leipzig, 1921), p. 662.

whom the basest, like the Poles, pursue a policy of naked robbery, which conforms to their character and their history'.[75] In short, though the political constellation of Europe had been transformed by the First World War, the Pan-German outlook had changed very little. Indeed the loss of Germany's navy, her overseas colonies and territory in Europe merely strengthened Pan-German arguments about her overpopulation. Moreover the ADV's assessment of the major powers remained essentially the same; the Bolshevik Revolution reinforced a prewar tendency not to take the Russian threat seriously and America's retreat into isolation was seen as a return to her prewar lack of interest in European affairs. But however much the Pan-Germans tried to pretend that Germany faced an external situation similar to that of 1912, they could not ignore the changes that had occurred. The country was now defeated, weakened and isolated — facts as unpalatable to the ADV as to a young Austrian-born orator just beginning his political career in 1919.

Hitler's Views on Foreign Policy, 1919–20

How far was Hitler's political outlook fashioned by Pan-German propaganda? This is a difficult question since relatively little is known in any detail about the early, and politically formative, years of Hitler's life in Linz, Vienna and Munich before 1914. Unimpeachable sources for Hitler's early political development are few in number and limited in content. Among them, the recollections of August Kubizek of a youthful friendship in Linz and Vienna, *The Young Hitler I Knew*, and a few letters and postcards from Hitler to friends stand out and act as an essential corrective to his own, idiosyncratic, account of his early life in *Mein Kampf*.[76]

As noted above, in 1924 Hitler claimed that he had been a Pan-German before he left Vienna for Munich in 1913. In *Mein Kampf* he went even further, suggesting that when he arrived in Vienna from Linz in 1907, his 'sympathies were fully and wholly on the side of the Pan-German tendency'. It should be stressed that it was the Austrian Pan-German movement, led by Georg von

75. Report of Class's speech, *A.Bl.*, 2 October 1920.
76. Though written after *Mein Kampf*, it is unlikely that Kubizek's account was influenced by Hitler's since the two clash on many occasions; *The Young Hitler I Knew* (New York, no date) — citations below are from the paperback edition. Some of Hitler's letters and notes were published in W. Maser (ed.), *Hitler's Letters and Notes* (New York, 1976) but this has been superseded by E. Jäckel and A. Kuhn, *Hitler. Sämtliche Aufzeichnungen 1905–1924*.

Schönerer, whose political ideas elicited Hitler's endorsement, though not an unqualified endorsement, in *Mein Kampf*: 'The Pan-German movement was right in its theoretical view about the aim of a German renascence but unfortunate in its choice of methods. It was nationalistic, but unhappily not socialistic enough to win the masses. But its antisemitism was based on a correct understanding of the importance of the racial problems, and not on religious ideas'.[77] Kubizek's recollections confirm both that Hitler supported Pan-Germanism — in fact, he suggests that Hitler was influenced by his history teacher at school, Leopold Pötsch — and that he did so with some reservations: 'The Schönerer movement would have needed much stronger socialistic tendencies to capture Adolf fully'.[78]

Nevertheless, there is evidence that Hitler may have absorbed Austrian Pan-German propaganda, in particular its marked hostility towards the Habsburg Empire. When Kubizek received his call-up papers for Austrian national service, Hitler apparently urged his friend, if he was passed as fit, to cross into Germany secretly to avoid the draft because, in his view, 'this moribund Habsburg Empire did not deserve a single soldier'.[79] Hitler, like the Austrian Pan-Germans, despised Austria–Hungary as a racial menagerie which was no longer really German. 'Was this Vienna, into which streamed from all sides Czechs, Magyars, Croats, Poles, Italians, Slovaks, Ruthenians and, above all, Galician Jews, still indeed a German city?', Hitler asked on one occasion. As Kubizek recalled later, 'in the state of affairs in Vienna, my friend saw a symbol of the struggle of the Germans in the Habsburg Empire. . . . He hated this state which ruined Germanism'.[80]

Hitler, therefore, almost certainly opposed the Dual Alliance because of Pan-German propaganda. Indeed, in a speech on 17 April 1923 Hitler described Germany's commitment to Austria–Hungary as the great mistake of prewar German diplomacy and pointed out that 'the Pan-Germans alone' (the Austrian Pan-Germans, that is) had warned against this policy.[81] Without doubt Hitler, even before the war, would have preferred the incorporation of German Austria in a Greater Germany; Kubizek recalled Hitler in a typical tirade demanding the creation of a 'Reich for all the Germans' which would put the 'guest nations' of the Habsburg

77. *MK*, pp. 111–12, 90.
78. Kubizek, *Young Hitler*, pp. 223, 75.
79. Ibid., p. 195.
80. Ibid., p. 224.
81. Report by the Munich police to the Bavarian Ministry of the Interior, BHStA I/1755.

Empire 'where they belonged'.[82] Clearly Hitler's views on his homeland mirrored quite faithfully those of the Austrian Pan-Germans.

The other assertion about Hitler's politics before 1914 that can be made with some confidence is that he was already a confirmed antisemite. Whether his antisemitism was another product of Pan-Germanism is difficult to say; a great deal of controversy and speculation, of course, surrounds the question of the origins of Hitler's antisemitism.[83] In *Mein Kampf* Hitler claimed that he had not really noticed the Jewish problem before he arrived in Vienna in 1907; there had been few Jews in Linz and they were so assimilated that he did not realise that they were not Germans. However, Kubizek recalled later that when he first met Hitler in Linz in 1904, 'his antisemitism was already pronounced'.[84] On this issue there seems less reason to doubt Kubizek's account than Hitler's. In *Mein Kampf*, Hitler was suggesting that the large number of Jews in Vienna led to his conversion to antisemitism — a version which lent more justification as well as drama to the story of his political awakening. If Hitler was an antisemite whilst still in Linz, it would strengthen the case for antisemitic Pan-German literature as the crucial influence, rather than actual contact with large numbers of Jews in Vienna.[85] However, in the final resort, it is impossible to say whether Hitler's antisemitism derived from Austrian Pan-German literature, or from parental influences, or from the social environment in which he grew up. All that one can conclude is that his views on the corrosive effect of the Jews on German life, which Kubizek later recollected, were in line with the propaganda in favour of the removal of Jewish influence which the Austrian Pan-German movement had been disseminating since 1885.[86]

It is very probable however that Hitler was acquainted before 1914 not just with Austrian Pan-German propaganda, but also with the major publications of the ADV in Germany, especially those of Heinrich Class. It is difficult to establish for certain which books

82. Kubizek, *Young Hitler*, p. 221.

83. R. Binion has recently claimed that Hitler's antisemitism derived from two traumas: the death of his mother whilst being treated by a Jewish doctor in 1907 and his own gassing in the trenches in 1918; 'Hitler's concept of Lebensraum: The Psychological Basis', *History of Childhood Quarterly. The Journal of Psycho-History*, vol. 1 (1973), pp. 189–90.

84. Kubizek, *Young Hitler*, pp. 78–9; Hitler, *MK*, p. 48.

85. Hitler claimed in 1921 that he came from a cosmopolitan family, but there are indications that his father may in fact have been a follower of Schönerer's antisemitic Pan-German movement: see W. Maser, *Adolf Hitler* (London, 1974), pp. 164–6.

86. Kubizek, *Young Hitler*, pp. 224–6; Whiteside, *Socialism of Fools*, pp. 118–19.

Hitler had read, since he very rarely quoted his sources; in private, however, Hitler did acknowledge his indebtedness to Class. According to one account, when they met for the first time, Hitler kissed Class's hand and declared himself to be his 'faithful pupil'.[87] In his memoirs Class recalled a meeting of the executive committee of the ADV in Potsdam on 18 May 1930 at which one of the committee members (identified only as 'State Director of Law R') who knew Hitler well stated that he 'knew from many conversations how highly Hitler valued the work of the ADV, my *Deutsche Geschichte* and the *Kaiserbuch*; he followed the *Deutsche Zeitung* and the *Alldeutsche Blätter* [the ADV's journals] closely.' However, when Hitler was asked why he did not express his debt to the ADV publicly and attract Pan-German support, he had evidently replied: 'That I cannot do. A *Führer* can never admit that what he advocates he got from others.'[88] This story, if true, and one has to remember that Class was hardly the most objective chronicler where Hitler was concerned, would suggest that the ADV's major publications were a formative influence on Hitler's political development.

If Hitler's indebtedness to Pan-Germanism cannot be fully established because of a lack of evidence in the period before he embarked on a political career in 1919, it is somewhat easier to do so afterwards. Hitler's earliest speeches in 1919 and 1920, recorded by police or Reichswehr observers and local reporters, reveal his thoughts on the *goals* of a future German foreign policy as well as *his impressions of the major powers*; both suggest a more than passing acquaintance with Pan-German literature, especially Class's 'Kaiserbuch' and *Deutsche Geschichte*.

The foreign policy *goals* advocated by Adolf Hitler at the start of his political career were, in effect, those summarised in the first three points of the DAP programme in February 1920: that is, firstly, 'the unification of all Germans in a Greater Germany on the grounds of the rights of national self-determination', secondly 'equal status for the German people with regard to the other nations, the abrogation of the peace treaties of Versailles and St. Germain' and thirdly 'land and soil (colonies) for the sustenance of our people and the settlement of our surplus population'.[89]

87. Kruck, *Geschichte des ADV*, p. 192. This fawning deference was inflicted on others at this time; on Houston Stewart Chamberlain, see. H. Heiber (ed.), *The Early Goebbels Diaries. The Journal of Joseph Goebbels from 1925–1926* (London, 1962), p. 83; on Moeller van den Bruck, see below, p. 118.

88. 'Class und die NSDAP', p. 41.

89. W. Hofer (ed.), *Der Nationalsozialismus. Dokumente 1933–1945* (Frankfurt, 1957), p. 28.

The initial step towards the realisation of the first goal — the creation of a *Grossdeutschland* — was the *Anschluss* with Austria. In a speech on 6 July 1920 Hitler argued that 'Austria belongs to Germany and wants and ought to join the German Empire.'[90] In August 1920 he delivered a series of speeches in a similar vein on a visit to Austria. But the *Anschluss* was only part of the task of uniting all Germans in one empire. Hitler's concept of *Grossdeutschland* seems to have been linguistic, not racial, in inspiration; it was to contain all German-speaking peoples rather than all those of Germanic stock: as he put it in a speech on 5 September 1920, 'as far as the German tongue is heard, we want to strengthen continually the feeling of belonging together'.[91] These views clearly were comparable with those of the ADV; it is true that some members of the ADV favoured a racial vision of an empire which included Anglo-Saxons and Scandinavians, but this conception was less popular in the ADV after 1900.[92]

Hitler's linguistic vision of a Greater Germany was, of course, very closely related to the second demand of the DAP's programme, the abrogation of the peace treaties of Versailles and St. Germain, which, in addition to forbidding an *Anschluss*, deprived Germany and Austria of areas with German-speaking populations. In his earliest speeches for the DAP, Hitler called specifically for the protection and eventual return of German-speakers in the South Tyrol, which had been ceded to Italy, in the Sudeten area of the newly created Czechoslovak state, and in Upper Silesia, whose ultimate fate awaited a League of Nations plebiscite.[93] Such speeches were, of course, very much in line with ADV propaganda and, indeed, folkish propaganda as a whole, at the time.

However, it is often forgotten that Hitler opposed the Versailles settlement on economic as well as *völkisch* grounds. On 24 September 1920, he put his case most succinctly: 'the shameful and humiliating peace of Versailles has robbed us of all our economic strength. The three main supports, coal, iron and potash, have for the most part been taken from us.' As a result Germany, he claimed, had a 55,000

90. Report in *VB*, 11 July 1920.

91. Report in R. H. Phelps. 'Parteiredner', p. 316.

92. Chickering, *We Men*, p. 78. Class himself wanted to encourage Scandinavian, German-Swiss and German-Austrian workers to settle in Germany to provide an increased workforce, Frymann, *Wenn ich*, pp. 90–2.

93. Hitler's speeches on 19 November, reported in *VB*, 25 November, on 14 August, account in E. Deuerlein, 'Hitlers Eintritt in die Politik und die Reichswehr', *VfZG*, vol. 7 (1959), p. 214, and on 20 September 1920, ibid., p. 216.

million mark trade deficit in 1920, and next year this would be increased by interest payments on loans to 70,000 million marks; if Germany's creditors insisted on payment, then her economy might follow Austria's into collapse. In short, Germany was being economically enslaved by the Versailles Settlement. These arguments, especially those concerned with the role of interest payments, suggest that Hitler may already have been influenced in his analysis by the view of Gottfried Feder.[94]

The needs of Germany's economy also lay behind the third point of the DAP's programme — the demand for 'land and soil (colonies)' to feed the German people and to settle its excess population. The confiscation of German colonies at Versailles was described by Hitler in an early speech as 'an irreparable loss': 'we are compelled to take our raw materials from the Allies and, indeed, at so high a price that we are eliminated as competitors on the world markets'.[95] Hitler, like Class, was clearly aware that colonies could help to make Germany more self-sufficient in terms of raw materials. He also recognised the value of colonial markets for German exports; on 1 August 1920 he pointed out that 'because of the loss of our colonies, our industry stands on the point of collapse. Either we get back market outlets or 20 million Germans must emigrate'.[96] It would appear from these comments that, again, like Class, Hitler saw the return of colonies primarily as a way of boosting the German economy, creating more jobs and thereby averting large scale emigration and, in fact, sustaining a German population of 90 million in Europe.[97] The settlement of a surplus German population seems to have been only a secondary attraction.

These pro-colonial sentiments appear to be very similar to those expressed by Class in *Wenn ich der Kaiser wär*. One wonders whether Hitler in 1920, despite his public advocacy of overseas colonies was actually dreaming, like Class in 1912, of a large continental empire in Europe. The available evidence, which is fairly limited and related almost entirely to his comments in public in 1919 and 1920, is inconclusive. On 19 November 1920 Hitler appeared to hint at German expansion in Eastern Europe; after prescribing measures

---

94. Report in Deuerlein, 'Hitlers Eintritt', p. 218. He had already publicly attacked 'Zinsknechtschaft'; see his speeches on 9 April 1920, PND report in BHStA I/1478 and on 11 May 1920, reported in *MNN*, 12 May 1920.

95. Speech on 10 December 1919, report in Deuerlein, 'Hitlers Eintritt', p. 209; see also ibid., p. 206.

96. Hitler's speech in Rosenau, account in H. Preiss (ed.), *Adolf Hitler in Franken. Reden aus der Kampfzeit* (Nuremberg, 1939), p. 10.

97. Speech on 20 September 1920, report in Duerlein, 'Hitlers Eintritt', p. 216.

designed to restore German internally, he declared that 'when we are strengthened internally, we can also turn towards the East'.[98] Other accounts of the same speech, however, give the impression that Hitler was referring to the liberation of German-speaking areas lost by Germany and Austria–Hungary in the Versailles Settlement, rather than the conquest of territory without large German-speaking populations.[99] As he put it on 27 April 1920: 'we are hoping that a united German Reich may soon arise again, which reaches from Memel to Bratislava and from Königsburg to Strasbourg.' This would involve the recovery of Alsace-Lorraine and the elimination of the Polish Corridor as well as the incorporation of former Habsburg territories in Czechoslovakia and Poland. Hitler, therefore, was advocating more than the resurrection of Germany's 1914 frontiers but not the conquest of large areas of French and Russian territory.[100]

Thus Hitler was not prepared — in public at least — to go as far as Class had done in his pamphlet on German war aims in 1917; whether at this time he privately harboured similar dreams of a large German empire in Europe is impossible to say. But it is important to note that his public ambitions for Germany in 1920 were almost identical to those published by the ADV in its Bamberg Declaration the previous year.[101]

However, the clearest evidence of Hitler's indebtedness to the ideas of the Pan-Germans and especially those of Heinrich Class can be found in his discussion of how Germany might feed her growing population. By comparing his early speeches with Class's observations in the 'Kaiserbuch', striking similarities immediately appear.[102] On the problem of overpopulation, Hitler identified the same four alternative solutions which Class had outlined in 1912. The first was a policy of internal colonisation — increasing the food output of existing German land. Hitler questioned, however, whether it was possible 'to increase the yield of the land indefinitely'. Like Class, he believed that this was only a temporary solution;

98. Report in Phelps, 'Parteiredner', p. 327.

99. The *VB* for example reported Hitler referring to 'the emancipation [of Germans] from foreign servitude', *VB*, 25 November 1920; another report referred to 'external liberation', *MNN*, 23 November 1920. See also Kuhn, *Programm*, pp. 58–9.

100. Report in Phelps, 'Parteiredner', p. 300. Hitler did ask on 10 December 1919 whether it was right that 18 times more land is available to each Russian than to every German', but whether he was advocating the redistribution of European territory is not clear, ibid., p. 289.

101. See above, pp. 46–49.

102. A. Kuhn compares the 'Kaiserbuch' to *Mein Kampf* — a comparison which tends to show how far Hitler had moved by 1925 from Pan-German aims rather than how close they were earlier; Kuhn, *Programm*, pp. 118–21.

Germany, in fact, had to acquire more land.[103]

This second solution, of course, raised the question of whether land ought to be sought in Europe or overseas. Since in 1920 Hitler did not publicly discuss the possibility of territorial expansion in Eastern Europe, there are no indications whether or not he shared Class's views on the need to 'evacuate' the indigenous inhabitants of land acquired in this way. Like Class in 1912, Hitler publicly endorsed the policy of overseas colonial expansion.[104]

If this second option was not chosen, in Hitlers view there remained (apart from birth control) only emigration and 'world trade' as possible solutions to Germany's demographic problems. Hitler shared Class's concern about 'the export of people' as a solution, believing that Germans who emigrated to other countries lost their Germanness: 'which nation wants to sacrifice its children as cultural fertilizer (*Kulturdünger*) for other nations?' — the term *Kulturdünger* was popularised by the Pan-Germans.[105] The fourth alternative — 'world trade' in Hitler's shorthand — was, he believed, that which had been followed by the German government before the war: Germany could pursue a policy of commercial expansion enabling her to import more food. This policy, in Class's view, ignored overseas colonisation and resulted in Germany's being reliant on imports from abroad.[106]

It would seem, therefore, that Hitler's publicised *goals* for a future German foreign policy were largely the same as those published by the ADV before 1914. That this was not a pure coincidence is proved by his close knowledge of the arguments and terminology used by the ADV and, in particular, Heinrich Class to justify selection of those goals. But were his *impressions of the major world powers* derived from the same sources?

Britain, or as he preferred it, 'England', was portrayed by Hitler in one of his earliest public speeches as one of Germany's 'absolute enemies'. The reason for this was the challenge posed by Germany to England's position as the leading world power. For centuries, according to Hitler, England had been ' *the* world power (*Weltmacht*)': however 'after the Englishman first had sent out his own trading

103. Notes for a speech entitled 'Versailles und der deutsche Arbeiter', reprinted in Maser, *Hitler's Letters*, p. 253. The speech was delivered on 31 May 1921; the report in *VB*, 5 June 1921, makes no reference to internal colonisation. For Class's views on Germany's choices, Frymann, *Wenn ich*, pp. 139–42.

104. *VB*, 5 June 1921.

105. Ibid. Class referred to German emigrants as 'Kulturdünger', *Deutsche Geschichte*, pp. 368, 377. Hitler had used the word in 18 January, report in *VB*, 20 January 1920.

106. Frymann, *Wenn ich* p. 5; Maser, *Hitler's Letters*, p. 253.

ships around the whole world, we later succeeded in making ourselves independent of him and in competing with him. Germany had gained a footing on every continent and was about to emerge as the leader of the world powers. That was also the reason for the English to make war on us'.[107] Hence, in Hitler's view, Germany's economic rivalry and her overseas empire constituted a threat to Britain's pre-eminence amongst the world powers, leading to British hostility towards Germany.

This was precisely the explanation offered by Heinrich Class in the 'Kaiserbuch' and, like Class, Hitler evidently admired the British; 'the English', he observed on 10 December 1919, 'have, as a people, reason to be proud'.[108] The reasons for Hitler's admiration were revealed in a speech in April 1920: 'England with a few million [people] rules practically one-fifth of the whole earth. English naval power! English colonial power, the greatest in the world! England controls world trade'. Clearly on the basis of her naval, colonial and commercial achievement, Britain was a model state, whom Germany would do well to emulate. But Hitler was also impressed by what he regarded as the reasons for Britain's success: the strength of the British national feeling, her racial purity and the 'extraordinary geniality', which enabled her to turn conquered enemies into friends.[109] Above all, it was the successful exercise of power politics through the centuries which appealed to Hitler. British history was, in his view, filled with examples of 'might making right', of attacks on the rights of other people. He referred, for example, to the British 'destruction of the native inhabitants of North America with whisky, the attempt to do the same to the Chinese with opium', the use of concentration camps against the Boers as well as 'the destruction of Spain with the help of Holland, the latter's destruction with the help of France, the latter's destruction in 22 years with the help of other nations and, recently, the destruction of Germany'.[110]

Hitler's respect for the British and the reasons for it mirrored those of Heinrich Class and the Pan-Germans almost exactly; indeed, his description of how cynical British diplomacy defeated Spain, Holland and France is very reminiscent of Class's own

---

107. Speech on 10 December 1919, report in Deuerlein, 'Hitler's Eintritt', p. 209; cf. Phelps, 'Parteiredner', p. 290.

108. Phelps, 'Parteiredner', p. 290. For Class's views, see above p. 41.

109. Speech on 17 April 1920, report in Phelps, 'Parteiredner', p. 297. The report uses the term 'Rasseneinheit' but this is almost certainly a spelling error; Hitler used the term 'Rassenreinheit' in a speech on 26 May; reported in Süddeutsche Zeitung, 29 May 1920, Jäckel and Kuhn, *Hitler*, p. 135.

110. Speech on 20 September 1920, report in Deuerlein, 'Hitlers Entritt', pp. 215–16.

account in his *Deutsche Geschichte*.[111] This, however, was not Hitler's only source of inspiration; his evidence was, in all probability, drawn from a number of different sources. However, despite his admiration for the British, there is no doubt that he would have endorsed Class's assertion in a public address in September 1920 that Britain (along with France) 'wants our complete destruction'.[112] Britain was one of the architects of the hated Versailles Settlement and was committed to its defence; she could be expected, therefore, to oppose Hitler's foreign policy plans for Germany. If in 1920 he did harbour secret designs for a future Anglo-German alliance (as he later claimed), it was not yet the time to make a public avowal of this policy.[13]

Such dissimulation (if such it was) did not arise in the case of France, towards whom Hitler was unremittingly hostile. Here, in his eyes, was the hereditary enemy, traditionally seeking to annex the left bank of the Rhine and thus to establish a 'natural' frontier with Germany.[114] France's Rhenish aspirations must have been common knowledge at the time of the Versailles peacemaking, so it would be unwise to suggest that Hitler's views should be traced simply to Pan-German literature on the subject.[115] The French desire to implement the Versailles Settlement to the letter probably reinforced Hitler's contempt. He would, he said, have supported a war of revenge against the French at any time: 'even if we were defenceless, we would not avoid a war with France.'[116] The extent of his hatred can be gauged from his comment on the idea of a Danubian Confederation, which he felt would make Bavaria dependent on French and Czechoslovakian coal: 'rather a Bolshevik Greater Germany than a South Germany dependent on the French and the Czechs.'[117]

111. Einhart, *Deutsche Geschichte*, p. 149.

112. Class's speech reported in *A.Bl.*, 2 October 1920.

113. In 1928 Hitler claimed that he had viewed England as a possible alliance partner in 1920, T. Taylor (ed.), *Hitler's Secret Book* (New York, 1961), p. 166.

114. Speech by Hitler on 20 September 1920, reports in Phelps, 'Parteiredner', p. 318 and in Deuerlein, 'Hitlers Eintritt', p. 216; see also his speech on 27 July 1920, Phelps, 'Parteiredner', p. 308.

115. Class certainly made this point, Einhart, *Deutsche Geschichte*, pp. 191, 265. He also referred to France as an 'Erz- und Erbfeind', a phrase often used by Hitler; Class, *Zum deutschen Kriegsziel*, p. 35.

116. Speech on 5 September 1920, report in Phelps, 'Parteiredner', p. 314.

117. Speech by Hitler at the Salzburg meeting of German and Austrian National Socialists on 5 August 1920, reported in *MNN*, 11 August 1920. The different versions of this speech indicate the unreliability of the press and police reporting; one police account reported Hitler as saying it was better to be a 'German vagabond than French counts', Phelps, 'Parteiredner', p. 314, another refers to 'French slaves', ibid., p. 316.

In contrast, Hitler seems to have been quite well disposed towards Russia, if one can rely on his comments concerning prewar foreign policy. In speeches of 1919 and early 1920 he placed Russia in the category, not of Germany's absolute enemies; but of those nations 'which as a result of their own unfortunate situation or as a result of special circumstances became our enemies'.[118] He seems to have believed that war between Germany and Russia could have been avoided since there had been no real conflict of interests between the two countries — probably because he considered Russia was pursuing a predominantly 'Asiatic policy of conquest'.[119]

Hitler did admit, however, that Russia's traditional desire for an 'outlet to the sea' (the Baltic or the Mediterranean) had brought her into conflict 'with various nations', including Germany. That he did not consider Russia's drive towards the Baltic incompatible with German interests in the Baltic provinces clearly requires some explanation. The key perhaps lies in the Pan-German approach to foreign policy. Indeed, Class's assessment of Russian ambitions in the postwar edition of *Deutsche Geschichte* may have provided the framework of Hitler's own analysis. Class argued that the Russian desire for access to the Baltic (as well as to the Mediterranean) provided no reason for Russo-German opposition since it did not constitute a threat to the *Reichsdeutsche* (Germans living within the Empire) but only to the *Volksdeutsche*, Germans living outside the Empire, in this case those in the Baltic provinces. Hence he concluded that 'the *Reichsdeutsch* and Russian national interests ran nowhere contrary to one another but rather coincided in many places'. Class was arguing in 1919, as he had in 1912, that the harassed Baltic Germans in the Russian Empire could not be allowed to damage Russo-German relations, a line of argument probably accepted by Hitler at this stage.[120]

What ultimately had spoilt Russo-German relations and led to confrontation in the First World War was, in Hitler's view, the German diplomats' failure to renew Bismarck's Reinsurance Treaty with the Russians. 'Since Bismarck' Hitler explained on 10 December 1919, 'we have pursued a Poland policy [*Polen-Politik*]. The so-called Reinsurance Treaty ran out in 1892 [sic], it was not renewed'; the Franco-Russian alliance of 1893 resulted and led ultimately to the outbreak of war in 1914.[121] What Hitler meant was

---

118. Speech on 10 December 1919, report in Phelps, 'Parteiredner', p. 290.
119. Speech on 17 April 1920, ibid., p. 297.
120. Einhart, *Deutsche Geschichte*, pp. 436–7; Frymann, *Wenn ich*, pp. 168–9.
121. Report in Phelps, 'Parteiredner', p. 290.

that, after Bismarck's fall from power, Germany decided to support Austria–Hungary at the expense of Russian friendship, 'Russia . . . became our enemy only because of Austria'.[122] Significantly this was precisely the argument used in the 1919 edition of *Deutsche Geschichte* and, what is more, Class also identified Germany's support for Austria–Hungary's *Polen-Politik* — that is the policy of stirring up Polish demands for independence within the Russian Empire — as the key element in Russia's alienation.[123] There is, therefore, strong evidence to support the conclusion that Hitler's opinions on Russia were derived primarily from the works of the ADV, though it must, of course, be remembered that before the war Class had supported the German government's pro-Habsburg line and had revised his views after 1918. It may be, then, that Hitler's favourable view of Russia derived originally from the pro-Russian propaganda of the prewar Austrian Pan-German movement.

Italy also belonged to Hitler's second category of powers, those not absolute enemies of Germany but who had fought against her in the First World War. Once again, in the Italian case, the reason for Italy's belligerency was Austria–Hungary; hatred of Austria, Hitler argued on 10 December 1919, had been inculcated in Italian schools for 50 years before it erupted.[124] He also stressed that leading German politicians had recognised before the war that Italy was an unreliable ally; 'men like Höltzendorf [sic], Bismarck and Ludendorff', he explained, 'had long seen that Italy would not be on Germany's side if she took an active part in the war'. Once again, Hitler's retrospective analysis reflected the anti-Habsburg stance of Austrian Pan-Germanism as well as the critical attitude of the ADV towards Italy — in his 'Kaiserbuch' Class, it will be recalled, had in 1912 questioned the reliability of Italy as an ally.[125]

Axel Kuhn has argued that the idea of an alliance between Italy and Germany emerged in Hitler's programme in 1920.[126] This is certainly possible. On 6 July 1920, Hitler indicated that Germany's enemy lay on the other side of the Rhine and not in Italy.[127] This rather backhanded compliment soon received positive reinforce-

122. Hitler's speech on 13 April 1923, PND report No. 406, BHStA I/1755.

123. Einhart, *Deutsche Geschichte*, pp. 301. Class wrote that 'only the . . . need to protect the Austro-Hungarian empire stood between Russia and our fatherland. Over that, it finally came to the breach.', ibid., p. 437.

124. Report in Deuerlein, 'Hitlers Eintritt', p. 209.

125. Report of the same speech in Phelps, 'Parteiredner', p. 290; Frymann, *Wenn ich*, pp. 177–8.

126. Kuhn, *Programm*, p. 42–5.

127. Report in Phelps. 'Parteiredner'. p. 305.

ment. On 1 August, knowing that France and Italy were at that moment in dispute over the port of Fiume, which Italy had been denied at Versailles, Hitler declared: 'Away with the peace treaty! To this end we must use all means at our disposal: chiefly to make use of the conflicts between France and Italy so that we can get Italy on our side.'[128] Evidently Hitler saw that Italy could be useful in helping to destroy the Versailles Settlement. But did this mean that an Italian alliance was now part of his own foreign policy programme? Or was he simply giving contemporary politicians a piece of advice, that is, to exploit Italo-French tensions? No certainty is possible here.

However, if, as Kuhn suggests, such an alliance was indeed now part of Hitler's programme on foreign affairs, it must be emphasised that Hitler had not yet fully thought out his attitude towards Italy. The knotty problem of the large German-speaking population under Italian rule in the South Tyrol had certainly not been resolved. In November 1920, Hitler referred to a comment by the then German foreign minister, Dr. Simons, disclaiming any desire on Germany's part to relieve the South Tyrolean Germans of Italian rule, as 'proof of national incompetence'; 'the German state', he went on, 'ought to intervene every time for every single German'.[129] This desire to 'recover' the South Tyrol was clearly an obstacle to future Italo-German friendship and plainly Hitler had not fully examined the political implications of such an alliance.

It is often said that Hitler was too narrowly European in his outlook on foreign affairs and in his first year as a political speaker a relative neglect of extra-European powers is certainly noticeable. Japan, for example, received very short shrift. In the prewar period, she had been, in Hitler's view, one of the powers with no conflict of interest with Germany; she had merely tried 'to keep the whites out of East Asia'.[130] There are no indications as to whether he was contemplating a future alliance with Japan or whether he shared Class's racial qualms about an alliance with a non-white nation.

Hitler was a little more forthcoming about the United States. 'America', along with Britain and France was labelled one of Germany's 'absolute enemies' in his speech on 10 December 1919. Her prime preoccupation, however, was business and she had had to intervene in the First World War, according to Hitler, in order not

128. Report in Preiss, *Adolf Hitler in Franken*, p. 11.
129. Speech on 19 November, reported in *VB*, 25 November 1920.
130. Speech on 26 May, reported in *Süddeutsche Zeitung*, 29 May 1920; cf. Hitler's speech on 10 December 1919, report in Phelps, 'Parteiredner', p. 290.

to lose her loans to the Entente powers. It should be noted that this interpretation of American intervention though also popular with left-wing opinion was the same as that given by Class in the postwar editions of *Deutsche Geschichte*.[131]

In his speeches of 1920 Hitler displayed a curious mixture of hatred and respect for President Woodrow Wilson. He despised Wilson because of the great disparity between his 'Fourteen Points' (which encouraged the German people to expect a negotiated peace) and the resulting Versailles Settlement: 'the Versailles treaty . . . is the work of the vilest secret diplomacy'.[132] On the other hand, he seemed to admire what Wilson achieved for his nation: 'although this criminal Wilson was a great rascal, one has to respect him because, by these means, he acquired advantages for his people'.[133] Nevertheless, it was his words after the Senate's rejection of Wilson's great *tour de force*, the Versailles Settlement and the Covenant of the League of Nations, that revealed Hitler's awareness of America's real potential; 'she is mighty enough and does not need the help of others . . . and she feels restricted in her freedom of action'.[134]

Conclusion

In conclusion, it can be said that, during his first year as a member of the German Workers' Party, Hitler's approach to foreign affairs seems to have been largely derived from Pan-German literature. One must, of course, be wary of too glibly assuming that, because he expressed ideas similar to those of the Pan-German leaders, Hitler therefore took his ideas exclusively from them; other men in other right-wing circles were saying similar things. Nevertheless, the degree of similarity between Hitler's goals and the arguments he used to justify them, and those expounded in particular by Heinrich Class before the war, is often too remarkable to be ignored.

Hitler seemed to endorse the ADV's main goal of a *Grossdeutschland* with his talk of a German Reich stretching from Memel to Bratislava and from Königsberg to Strasbourg. If he harboured

131. Hitler's speech on 10 December 1919, reports in Phelps, 'Parteiredner', pp. 290–91, and in Deuerlein, 'Hitlers Eintritt', p. 209; for Class's views see Einhart, *Deutsche Geschichte*, p. 509.

132. Speech on 6 July 1920, report in Phelps, 'Parteiredner', p. 305; cf. speeches on 5 September, ibid., pp. 315–16 and 24 November 1920, ibid., p. 329.

133. Speech on 24 November 1920, report in Deuerlein, 'Hitlers Eintritt', p. 226.

134. Speech on 10 December 1919, report in Phelps, 'Parteiredner', p. 290. Hitler was commenting on the treaty's initial failure to achieve the necessary two-thirds majority in the Senate on 19 November 1919.

designs on more territory in Western and Eastern Europe (as the ADV did), these were certainly not aired in public. Like the ADV also, Hitler publicly advocated the pursuit of an empire overseas. Generally, his assessments of the major world powers, glimpsed occasionally in his retrospective analysis of the diplomatic origins of the First World War, also closely resemble Class's prewar prognosis in the 'Kaiserbuch' — a prognosis seemingly confirmed by the events of 1914–1918.

Britain, France and America were seen as Germany's 'deadly enemies' since they opposed her ambition of becoming a major world power — Britain because she feared the loss of her own pre-eminence amongst the world powers; France out of a desire to avenge past defeats; and America in order to protect her investments in the Entente nations. Where Hitler differed from Class was in his total lack of respect for the old Austro-Hungarian Empire and a corresponding belief that Germany and Russia had no conflicting interests in 1914. These differences were almost certainly attributable to Hitler's exposure to Austrian Pan-German anti-Habsburg propaganda before 1914, though it should be noted that after 1918 Class had propagated the same line.

In short, Hitler does appear to have been profoundly influenced by Pan-Germanism in the formative stages of his political development. Indeed, it may be that he regarded the emerging Nazi Party as assuming the mantle of the ADV. As early as November 1919, he appeared to acknowledge the need for a kind of 'National Opposition' and was clearly aware of the Pan-German precedent when he declared that 'the present government cannot govern because it has not the faintest idea how to govern. When people criticise . . . they are called Pan-Germans. We want to inculcate defiance among the people'.[135] However, as shown by his postwar dealings with the ADV leadership and also perhaps by his comments in 1920 on Italy, Hitler intended to go his own way.

---

135. Speech on 26 November 1919, report in Deuerlein, 'Hitlers Eintritt', p. 208.

3

The Impact of Ideology on Hitler's Outlook on Foreign Affairs, 1919–20

During the first few months of his collaboration with the German Workers' Party, Adolf Hitler's comments on foreign affairs seemed largely to reflect Pan-German convictions, probably acquired before the First World War. The Versailles Settlement, by depriving Germany both of German-speaking lands in Europe and of her colonial possessions overseas, appeared once again to legitimise Pan-German demands for the unification of all Germans in one state and the creation of an overseas empire. Furthermore, the attitude of the major powers to the Versailles Treaty seemed to confirm the correctness of Hitler's diagnosis of foreign affairs, mainly derived from prewar Pan-German propaganda. Britain and France, the two powers most hostile to Germany before the war, were the settlement's chief defenders; America, rather uninterested in German affairs before 1914, proved unwilling to sign the treaty; Italy and Russia, whose enmity, Hitler believed, could have been averted by more skilful German diplomacy before 1914, opposed it; the former was dissatisfied with her share of the spoils, the latter had not been consulted despite the disposal of Russian territory.

However, it was not long before Hitler's analysis both of the prewar diplomatic scene and the postwar settlement began to show a subtle change. In his early speeches, for example, he had argued that Russia and Germany had come into conflict only because of Germany's failure to renew Bismarck's Reinsurance Treaty with Russia and because of Germany's commitment to Austria–Hungary. By April 1920, he was saying that before the war only 'the international Jewish press concern' had prevented an alliance between the two powers.[1] This comment, implying as it did that the Jews had been undermining Germany's international position before the First World War, represents the first modification of Hitler's outlook on foreign affairs. Deeply rooted antisemitic prejudices were seemingly beginning to colour his assessment of world affairs.

Historians have been preoccupied, quite understandably in view of later events, with the timing and inspiration behind Hitler's 'conversion' to antisemitism. It could be argued, however, that almost as important is the date when he adopted an antisemitic *world-view*, that is, when he ceased to regard the Jewish question solely as an internal problem for Germany and began to accept its international ramifications. At this point, it might be suggested, Hitler began to look beyond the mere expulsion of the Jews from Germany towards a global solution to the 'Jewish question'; the road to Auschwitz and the policy of extermination would then be clear. However that may be, the emergence of an international dimension to his antisemitism is clearly of relevance in the evolution of Nazi attitudes towards foreign policy and this chapter will attempt first to explain its origins and, secondly, to assess its impact on his approach to foreign affairs.

Hitler and the Internationalisation of the Jewish Menace

It has been argued that Hitler's ideas underwent an ideological transformation in the early months of 1920. Both Günther Schubert and Fritz Dickmann have tried to establish a causal connection between the emergence of a Jewish dimension in his references to foreign affairs and the publication in Germany of *The Protocols of the Elders of Zion*.[2] However, since the 'Protocols' were published in Germany in December 1919 and there is no evidence of an international dimension in Hitler's attacks on the Jews before April 1920, some have found this interpretation unconvincing.[3] Certainly such a time-lapse needs to be explained.

Schubert and Dickmann both suggest that Hitler was ignorant of

1. Speech on 17 April 1920, Phelps, 'Parteiredner', p. 297.
2. Schubert, *Anfänge*, p. 27; F. Dickmann, 'Machtwille und Ideologie in Hitlers aussenpolitischen Zielsetzungen vor 1933' in K. Repgen and St. Skalwert (eds.), *Spiegel der Geschichte, Festgabe für Max Braubach* (Münster, 1964), p. 934.
3. In particular, W. Horn, 'Ein unbekannter Aufsatz Hitlers aus dem Frühjahr 1924', *VfZG*, vol. 16, (1968), p. 287. The *VB* reviewed the 'Protocols' only on 22 April 1920.

the supposed world Jewish conspiracy until the publication of the 'Protocols' but that the book's revelations gradually transformed his antisemitic outlook in the early months of 1920.[4] It is, however, difficult to accept that Hitler was totally unaware of the conspiracy theory until the 'Protocols' were published at the end of 1919. Their existence was well-known in antisemitic circles as early as April 1919 when the antisemitic journal *Auf Vorposten* referred for the first time to the 'Secrets of the Elders of Zion'.[5] As has been seen, Dietrich Eckart had published extracts from a document very similar to the 'Protocols' in October 1919, and throughout 1919 Alfred Rosenberg had been propounding in *Agd* his views on World Jewry's involvement in domestic and international politics, especially its manipulation of the Russian Revolution. Furthermore, Rosenberg revealed later that at the end of 1919 Hitler had told him that he had 'already read Dietrich Eckart's periodical' and knew of his own articles in it.[6]

It would therefore appear likely that Hitler was well aware, before the publication of the 'Protocols', of the claims that the Jews practised subversion on a worldwide scale. Why then did his early speeches not make use of this potent propaganda material in attacking the Jews? Perhaps they did. It is worth noting that the reports of Hitler's early speeches drawn up by the Munich Police, Reichswehr observers or local journalists are very incomplete records of the actual content; they are short accounts of speeches lasting between one and two hours and what was recorded often depended on the interests of the chronicler.[7] This argument should perhaps not be pressed too far. The police observer at the DAP meeting on 24 February 1920 noted on a speech by Dr. Johannes Dingfelder, a physician and racist, that 'the word Jew never came into his mouth', which might suggest that the authorities were on the lookout for expressions of antisemitic prejudice.[8] Also it should be remembered that, after April 1920, references to the role of international Jewry were recorded in reports of a similar length and style. Even so, the nature of the available evidence as to Hitler's earliest public speeches prevents confident assertions about what he did not say.

Nevertheless, it still seems likely that Hitler did know of the

4. Schubert, *Anfänge*, p. 27, Dickmann, 'Machtwille', p. 935.

5. Cohn, *Warrant for Genocide*, pp. 146–67.

6. A. Rosenberg, untitled and undated memoir, BAK, NS 8/20; for Eckart's review see above, p. 21. W. Horn argues that Karl Harrer referred to the ultimate Jewish goal of 'Pan-Jewish world rule' in January 1919, Horn, 'Ein unbekannter Aufsatz', p. 287.

7. Kuhn, *Programm*, pp. 31–2.

8. Report in Phelps, 'Parteiredner', p. 295.

international ramifications of the Jewish question before April 1920 and chose not to exploit the issue publicly. From a private letter to Adolf Gemlich, written in September 1919, it is quite evident that he believed that the effects of Jewish influence were felt around the world. The activities of Jews, he wrote, 'produce a racial tuberculosis among nations': their methods varied from one state to another depending upon the differing political complexions: 'In an autocratically governed state, he whines for the favour of the 'Majesty' of the prince and abuses it to batten on his subjects like a leech. In a democracy, he courts the favour of the masses, grovels before the 'majesty of the people' and yet knows only the majesty of money.'[9]

Since Hitler seemingly acknowledged in private that the Jews represented a worldwide menace, why then did he not present this international dimension of the Jewish question in his early public speeches? One possible explanation is that he was primarily concerned at this time with explaining *Germany's* problems and calling for a *German* national revival, and perhaps felt that propaganda about an *international* Jewish threat would divert attention from the task in hand — a *national* resurgence. This revival, Hitler told Gemlich, would not be achieved by the 'political leadership of irresponsible majorities under the influence of particular party dogmas [or] of an irresponsible press, not by phrases and slogans of international coinage, but only through the ruthless actions of personalities with the capacity for national leadership and an inner sense of responsibility'.[10] In other words, Hitler may have preferred to play down the international aspect of the Jewish problem lest it reinforce the tendency to look for international solutions, a trend which he had long abhorred.[11]

The DAP's preoccupation with the question of 'German communism' may also reflect this self-denying ordinance. On 5 February 1920, Eckart spoke on this subject to members of the DAP, arguing that 'the links between the Germany type of communism and the desires of the Jews for world-rule through capitalism are so clearly evident that it is impossible to avoid referring to them'.[12] This

9. Deuerlein, 'Hitlers Eintritt', p. 204.

10. Ibid.

11. On 5 February 1915, writing from the western front to his friend Ernst Hepp, Hitler had expressed the hope that 'our domestic internationalism will collapse. This will be worth much more than any gain in territory.' Maser, *Hitler's Letters*, pp. 88–9. See also the reports of his speeches on 24 February 1920, Phelps, 'Parteiredner', p. 295 and on 24 September 1920, Deuerlein, 'Hitlers Eintritt', p. 218.

12. Report on the meeting, drawn up on 8 February 1920 by Ferdinand Wiegand, who was for a time a member of the DAP's executive committee, HA 4/11, p. 1. Hitler argued that German

speech shows that the DAP was being exposed to propaganda about the Jewish world conspiracy — alleged collaboration between 'Jewish' communism and 'Jewish' capitalism was the major pivot of the theory — over two months before Hitler's first recorded and unequivocal reference to the Jewish factor in international diplomacy. However, Eckart was undoubtedly emphasising the threat to the German state from 'German communism' rather than from international communism. So perhaps he, like Hitler, refrained at this stage from dwelling on the international ramifications of the Jewish question for fear of reinforcing those very internationalist trends which he regarded as responsible for Germany's present difficulties.[13]

It may be, therefore, that it was the widespread interest generated by the publication of the 'Protocols' and their serialisation by several rightwing journals which convinced Hitler after April 1920 that more political capital would accrue than be lost by exploiting such an all-embracing conspiracy theory. However, it would appear that the appearance of the 'Protocols' merely helped to determine the timing of the emergence of an international dimension in his antisemitic propaganda. To identify the reasons for the development of this new dimension, the nature of Hitler's revised antisemitic philosophy needs to be examined.

It should be noted again that the fragmentary records of many of Hitler's 1920 speeches do not permit a full analysis of the change in his outlook. However, a detailed account of a speech entitled 'Why are we antisemites?', delivered on 13 August 1920, has survived and illustrates the evolution of Hitler's antisemitic rhetoric since the letter to Gemlich in September 1919.

He began by contrasting the Aryan and the Jew; the Aryan was hardworking, racially pure, spiritually and culturally creative, whilst the Jew was workshy, racially weak, lacking in all spiritual and cultural creativity, and, above all, instinctively driven to destroy other states. Conflict between the Aryan and the Jew was, by implication, inevitable. Whilst the emphasis on Aryan qualities was a novel departure for Hitler, at least compared to the letter to Gemlich, the list of Jewish characteristics was familiar.[14] However,

Communists did not know that they were serving the interests of high finance, speech on 16 January 1920, PND report, BHStA I/1478.

13. Any improvement in Germany's position, according to Eckart, 'must come from our own selves', HA 4/11, p. 2.

14. R. H. Phelps, 'Hitlers "grundlegende" Rede über den Antisemitismus', *VfZG*, vol. 16 (1968), pp. 400–6.

his discussion of the weapons and tactics allegedly used by the Jews to destroy other states, highlighted his acceptance of the need to present the Jews as an international threat.

The first major weapon in the Jewish armoury was international capitalism, whose aim, according to Hitler on 13 August 1920, was to undermine the work ethic and to destroy national economics: 'The Jews had learned how to acquire wealth without lifting a finger, without sweat and blood, by means of money-lending at huge rates of interest and by the manipulation of stock .exchanges. In short, they accumulated loan and stock exchange capital.'[15] In his letter to Gemlich, Hitler had mentioned interest payments as the source of Jewish wealth and power and as the means by which 'a most dangerous yoke' was imposed upon other nations. He had, in other words, already picked up the idea of 'interest-slavery' from Gottfried Feder, whom he had heard lecture in June 1919, and identified it (though Feder had not) as an exclusively Jewish phenomenon.[16] The main difference in Hitler's 'fundamental' speech on antisemitism on 13 August 1920 was the emphasis on 'loan' or 'finance' capitalism. He drew the distinction — which had been carefully elaborated by Feder in 1919 in his manifesto on the breaking of interest-slavery — between 'industrial' capital and 'loan' (or 'finance') capital. 'Industrial' capital — money invested in equipment and factories and as working capital to tide a business through bad times — was, in Hitler's view, indispensable to production and a sound economy, and therefore was not to be attacked. 'Loan' (or 'finance') capital was not productive and was the real enemy because it worked to 'destroy whole states, annihilate whole cultures, to neutralise national industries, not in order to socialise them but to throw everything into the jaws of international capitalism'.[17]

Hence in August 1920 Hitler was presenting in public a more carefully considered indictment of international capitalism than that contained in the letter to Gemlich. Significantly, he stressed that the international capitalist menace did not require an *international* response; this would be foolhardy since the Jews monopolised international movements; as Hitler put it: 'fire cannot be put out with fire but only with water . . . international capital, which belongs to the

15. Ibid., pp. 409–10.

16. Deuerlein, 'Hitlers Eintritt', p. 204. Hitler wrote in his autobiography that after hearing Feder lecture, 'the thought ran through my head that I had now found the way to one of the most essential premises for the foundation of a new party', *MK*, pp. 189–91.

17. Phelps, 'Hitlers "grundlegende" Rede', pp. 409–10.

international Jew, will only be broken by national strength'.[18]
Though now publicly espoused, the international dimension to the
party's antisemitic platform was evidently not to be allowed to dilute
the demand for a national revival; clearly Hitler remained vigilant
about the danger of encouraging discussion of internationalist solutions.

Hitler's speech on 13 August, however, also 'revealed' that making nations the slaves of international capitalism by means of
financial extortion was only one tactic in an orchestrated Jewish
conspiracy to take over the world. The other main strategy was to
subvert states from within. In his letter to Gemlich, Hitler had
alluded briefly to this second subversive tactic, referring to the Jews
as 'the motive force of revolution'. But, by August 1920, he was
delivering a detailed explanation of their activities: 'in order to be
able to organise, erect and maintain his definitive world-rule', the
Jew needed 'the lowering of the racial level of other peoples so that
he, as the only racially pure [one], is able in the last resort to rule
over all others'. The methods used to achieve this were many and
varied: the Jews held back food supplies to cause famine; they
encouraged moral laxity in others and 'the destruction of pro-
ductivity and . . . when necessary, of the people's means of production as well'. Furthermore, they attempted to destroy national
culture by eliminating the intelligentsia and ultimately, in order to
destroy national unity, they fostered class conflict. Hitler illustrated
all these tactics by reference to events inside Russia since the
Bolshevik Revolution.[19]

In short, therefore, the two main weapons in the Jewish armoury
were loan capitalism and worldwide revolution; to use Hitler's own
words: 'the revolutionary Jew makes the revolution and destroys
everything; the bank Jew then rebuilds in order to fill his pockets'.[20]
By the summer of 1920, therefore, Hitler was propagating the idea of
a Jewish world conspiracy. It is certainly true that many of his
notions about the Jews — their lack of creativity, their materialistic
spirit, their destructiveness — can be traced back to the antisemitic
writings of Heinrich Class, Theodor Fritsch and others, but his
acceptance of the idea of a conspiracy between international capitalism and international socialism may have been the result of
influences closer to home.[21]

18. Ibid., p. 410.
19. Ibid., pp. 411–15; Deuerlein, 'Hitlers Eintritt', p. 204.
20. Speech on 18 October 1920, Phelps, 'Parteiredner', p. 323; see also speech on 19 November
1920, ibid., p. 329.

It is interesting to note that Heinrich Class's first reaction on reading the antisemitic sections of the DAP's programme in 1920 was to suspect that 'Dietrich Eckart's influence had been decisive'.[22] Indeed point 24 seemed explicitly to endorse the brand of antisemitism publicised by Eckart, when it spoke of combating 'the Jewish materialistic spirit in and around us'.[23] One historian has objected that, according to Eckart's own account, his relationship with Hitler grew closer only during the Kapp putsch of March 1920 and that therefore he could not have influenced Hitler's antisemitism.[24] However, this ignores the fact that Hitler knew of Eckart's work in *Agd* and, indeed, knew Eckart well enough at the end of 1919 for the latter to arrange an introduction for Alfred Rosenberg in his home. Whilst it would be wrong to suggest, as has Eckart's biographer, that he 'pushed' Hitler into antisemitism (Hitler did not need to be pushed in that direction), it is very probable that Eckart exerted some influence over Hitler and Anton Drexler, the two main authors of the party programme. He had, after all, spoken at two DAP meetings before the publication of the programme on 24 February 1920.[25]

However, whilst Eckart's influence on the party's antisemitic outlook should not be discounted, other evidence suggests that Hitler's views on the international machinations of the Jews derived mainly from Alfred Rosenberg. Rosenberg, as has already been shown, took a particular interest in uncovering 'traces' of Jewish

---

21. For example, referring to the unholy alliance of Freemasonry, Socialism and high finance, Hitler used the phrase, 'the black-red-gold government', a phrase almost certainly coined by the Pan-Germans, see Hitler's speech on 6 July, *VB*, 11 July 1920 and Frymann, *Wenn ich*, pp. 192–3.

22. 'Class und die NSDAP', p. 8. Class claimed that the antisemitic portions of the party programme came as a shock to him since Hitler had, in private, given him to understand that the Jewish question would not feature prominently in it. This incident is, perhaps, explained by DAP's resolution on 5 February 1920 not to be a narrowly antisemitic party but to commit itself to a wider platform of 'Resistance to Anti-Germanism', see report by Wiegand, HA 4/111. This resolution had obviously been overturned by 24 February 1920.

23. Hofer, *Der Nationalsozialismus*, p. 30. Eckart did not, of course, have a monopoly on the term, see for example R. J. Gorsleben's essay on 'Die Überwindung des Judentums in uns und ausser uns' in Paul Tafel (ed.), *Das neue Deutschland* or A. Drexler, *Mein politisches Erwachen* (Munich, 1919).

24. Tyrell, *Trommler*, p. 85.

25. M. Plewnia in her biography of Eckart attributed the increased aggressiveness of Hitler's antisemitism to Ekcart, *Auf dem Weg zu Hitler*, pp. 55, 66. Anton Drexler later denied that anyone other than Hitler and himself was responsible for the party programme, though he admits that they included Feder's point about 'breaking the slavery of interest' because it was 'so useful'; letter from Drexler to the party archives, 24 February 1940; HA 4/10. However, Eckart's views were bound to be common knowledge in DAP circles after his speeches on 14 August 1919 and 5 February 1920.

conspiratorial activity and it is certainly very likely that Hitler drew on his revelations about the 'Jewish-Bolshevik' Revolution and the involvement of the Freemasons in Zionist plans; indeed his view of Zionism might have been partly coloured by Rosenberg's approach.

In June 1920 Hitler was arguing that Bolshevism was 'entirely a Jewish affair' and that the Jews were directly responsible for the famine and misery currently endured by the Russian people.[26] Almost certainly, he relied for information about Russia on the detailed reports written by Rosenberg for *Agd* in 1919 and 1920.[27] By the middle of 1920, Hitler had also accepted Rosenberg's explanation of how events in Russia were being manipulated from outside the country. He argued in his 'fundamental' speech on antisemitism that behind the few Jewish millionaires who were running Russia stood 'another organisation, which is not even inside the state: the "Alliance israélite" and its grandiose propaganda organisation and driving force . . . Freemasonry'. Although Rosenberg was by no means the only antisemite to investigate these organisations and indeed, the *Protocols of the Elders of Zion* declared that they were in collaboration, it is nonetheless likely that Hitler, given his regular contact with Rosenberg in 1920 and his knowledge of the latter's writing, utilised Rosenberg's revelations about Russian conditions.[28]

It was also quite commonplace for antisemites to express support for Zionist ambitions. The idea of a Jewish state in Palestine was attractive to them as one way of encouraging Jews to leave Germany. Hitler felt that the Jew 'belongs in his own state in Palestine'.[29] There are no indications that he shared Eckart's rather more esoteric view that Zionism had to be combatted since the cohabitation of Jews and Gentiles was necessary to preserve the natural order. However, Hitler's attempt to explain the apparent contradiction between the clear evidence of Jewish nationalism in the Zionist movement and the alleged Jewish commitment to internationalism bears the imprint of Alfred Rosenberg: 'the Jew exists as a state within a state. . .and nevertheless represents the most nationalistic race. Nationalism and religion complement one another and push

---

26. Speech on 2 June 1920, report in BHStA, Abt. IV, 48/8, reprinted in Jäckel and Kuhn, *Hitler*, p. 140; see also speech on 11 June, Deuerlein, 'Hitlers Eintritt', p. 214.

27. These were republished in Rosenberg *Die Spur des Juden*, pp. 82–4, 115–22.

28. Phelps, 'Hitlers "grundlegende" Rede', pp. 414–15. Paul Tafel also wrote about the Freemasons and the Jews but he stressed their differences rather than their similarities, Tafel, *Das neue Deutschland*, pp. 39–42.

29. Speech on 6 July 1920, Phelps, 'Parteiredner', p. 305. Class, for example, made the same point in *Zum deutschen Kriegsziel*, pp. 50–1.

him towards world-rule'.[30] Like Rosenberg, Hitler sidestepped the issue by arguing that Zionism was merely a cover for aspirations of a more international, if not global, nature.

It seems probable, therefore, that the international dimension to Hitler's antisemitism may have derived as much from the writings of Alfred Rosenberg as from the publication of *The Protocols of the Elders of Zion*. Indeed, Rosenberg's contribution to the evolution of the entire Nazi *Weltanschauung* seems to have been seriously underestimated by recent historians.[31] Though his later career in the Third Reich may have been relatively inconspicuous — he failed in his ambition to become German Foreign Minister in the 1930s and was not a particularly successful Governor-General of the Eastern Occupied Territories during the war — this does not necessarily mean that, in the earliest years of the party's existence, he was merely a 'disciple' of Hitler.

Indeed, such an assessment flatly contradicts the view of well-informed contemporaries, whether friendly, hostile or indifferent. Kurt Lüdecke, who joined the party in 1922 and later became a friend of Rosenberg, was advised by Hitler to get to know him better; 'he is the only man to whom I always listen. He is a thinker. His large conception of foreign policy will interest you'.[32] At the other extreme, Ernst Hanfstängl, a vituperative and vindictive critic of Rosenberg in party circles, in his memoirs repeatedly bemoaned the fact that 'Rosenberg wielded tremendous influence over Hitler and his associates when it came to propagating this anti-Bolshevik, anti-Russian line'.[33] In 1931, even the Berlin Police-President, investigating allegations by Rosenberg's own party colleagues that he had been a Western spy during the last months of the First World War, found that he was 'said to exert a strong influence on Hitler'. The investigation concluded that the allegations had been concocted by party rivals envious of Rosenberg's position, but the fact that colleagues should stoop so low to try to undermine his credibility indicates the apparent strength of his hold over Hitler during the *Kampfzeit*.[34] The relationship between the two men, therefore, merits closer investigation.

30. Phelps, 'Hitlers "grundlegende" Rede', p. 405.

31. See, for example, Maser, *Die Frühgeschichte*, pp. 181–4 and J. Fest, *The Face of the Third Reich* (London, 1972), p. 248. R. Cecil's recent biography goes some way towards righting the balance, *The Myth of the Master Race*, passim.

32. K. Lüdecke, *I Knew Hitler* (London, 1938), p. 83.

33. E. Hanfstängl, *The Missing Years* (London, 1957), pp. 64, 41. Hanfstängl was particularly worried about Rosenberg's neglect of extra-European affairs and saw it as his duty to educate Hitler about America, *ibid.*, pp. 32, 36.

Rosenberg first seems to have heard Hitler speak on 10 December 1919 at the 'Zum deutschen Reich' tavern in Munich. 'Shortly afterwards' he met Hitler for the first time with a small circle of party colleagues at Dietrich Eckart's house and in the same month decided to join Hitler's cause. The two encounters in December 1919 constituted, Rosenberg wrote in 1934, 'the decisive turning point in my political and intellectual life, the concrete affirmation of that which had once driven me thousands of kilometers from my home'.[35]

What precisely attracted Rosenberg to Hitler is not clear. In his memoirs, written under the shadow of the gallows at Nuremberg, he revealed that he had not been very impressed by his first discussion with him at Eckart's house. Nevertheless, they did have 'a not very detailed conversation about the Bolshevik danger'.[36] Perhaps it was Hitler's endorsement of Rosenberg's reading of events in Russia which proved decisive. Comments in Rosenberg's memoirs, however, seem to suggest that there was a meeting of minds on a wider range of subjects: 'it only needed a few words to discover that in a most remarkable way [our] entire outlooks coincided so much that there were really no problems of substance.'[37] Even in 1945, Rosenberg was still surprised by the degree of agreement between Hitler and himself; they had, he admitted, had their 'small controversies' but it was 'uncanny' how similar their opinions had frequently been.[38] After reading Rosenberg's notes for a speech at a party conference, Hitler remarked that 'this is as much like mine as if we had compared notes beforehand'.[39] A cynic might attribute the coincidence to mutual intellectual impoverishment but it was almost

---

34. Letter from Berlin Police-President to the Munich police, dated 9 June 1931, HA 53/1259. Rosenberg had, in fact, spent the period in question working as a German teacher with the German Government in Estonia, as the Munich police reported on 19 December 1931, *ibid*. A summary of the controversy prompted by allegations made by Hanfstängl, Hermann Göring and Otto Strasser is given in *Vorwärts*, 14 November 1931; see also *VB*, 29 June 1932.

35. A. Rosenberg, 'Meine erste Begegnung mit dem Führer' (1934) in BAK, NS 8/177. On the timing of the meeting, see Rosenberg, *Letzte Aufzeichnungen*, p. 80.

36. Rosenberg, *Letzte Aufzeichnungen*, p. 91.

37. An untitled and undated memoir by Rosenberg in NS 8/20; see also Rosenberg, 'Meine erste Begegnung'.

38. Rosenberg cited, as an example of the 'small controversies', an argument over whether the trees planted in the Odeonsplatz in Munich spoilt the view of the monument, *Letzte Aufzeichnungen*, p. 22.

39. Ibid., p. 325. He recalled that both he and Hitler had once written articles on alcoholism for the *VB* without each other's knowledge and that they were so similar that Rosenberg decided not to publish his own. Hitler, however, insisted that they both be published in the same issue. See

certainly this ideological compatibility which forged the relationship between the two men in the 1920s.

Ideological affinity, however, did not generate intimate friendship or personal warmth, probably because Rosenberg was too serious and introverted for Hitler's taste (possibly, he was too much like Hitler in some ways). Hitler seemed to prefer the company of more lighthearted and boisterous acquaintances, men of the mould of Eckart or Max-Erwin von Scheubner-Richter, a soldier of fortune, who entered Nazi circles in 1921. Hence, as Rosenberg remarked rather bitterly in 1945, Hitler 'valued me highly, but he did not love me'.[40]

Hitler's respect for Rosenberg was the result of the latter's tireless contribution to the ideology of the party, which he chose to join late in 1919. During 1920, Rosenberg was busy publishing his first pamphlet and writing two more. At the same time, he was contributing articles to Eckart's *Auf gut deutsch* and producing the journal himself 'whenever the idleness of the poet came over Eckart and he felt incapable of political work'.[41] When the DAP managed to purchase its own newspaper at the end of 1920, Rosenberg initially contributed only an occasional article (the first being in February 1921) because of his work for *Agd*.[42] However, once Eckart abandoned his own journal, recommending its readership to transfer their allegiance to the *VB*, where he became editor in chief with Rosenberg working as an assistant, very soon the cycle of events on *Agd* repeated itself: Eckart found himself incapable of sustained periods of regular work and Rosenberg 'relieved him, in practice, of the entire editorial workload'.[43] During 1923, Eckart's attendance at the paper's offices in Munich's Schellingstrasse became so intermittent that Hitler declared that since Rosenberg was doing all the work he should get all the credit; accordingly on 10 March 1923, he became political editor of the *VB*.

As Rosenberg was deeply involved in the day-to-day running of the *VB*, he was particularly well placed to exert considerable influ-

---

A. Hitler, 'Zur Frage der Trockenbewegung' and A. Rosenberg, 'Alcoholverbot', *VB*, 31 March 1926.

40. Rosenberg, *Letzte Aufzeichnungen*, p. 325.

41. Undated memoir, NS 8/20; Rosenberg, *Dietrich Eckart*, pp. 45, 55. Rosenberg's publications in 1920–1 were *Die Spur des Juden, Unmoral im Talmud* (Munich, 1920) and *Das Verbrechen der Freimaurerei* (Munich, 1921).

42. Rosenberg, *Letzte Aufzeichnungen*, p. 99. His first article, 'Der Zionismus' appeared in *VB*, 17 February 1921.

43. Rosenberg, *Letzte Aufzeichnungen*, p. 100.

ence on Nazi interpretation of current events. He did not shirk his responsibilities, accepting regular punishment in the form of fines or imprisonment meted out by the local courts for libellous articles published in the paper.[44] It has, of course, to be admitted that there were limits to Rosenberg's value to the party. He delivered relatively few speeches to Nazi gatherings, since he evidently lacked Hitler's ability to sense the mood of his audience; his first talk at the Rosenheim *Ortsgruppe* taught him that religion (and in particular Jesuitism) was far too sensitive an issue to discuss in Catholic Bavaria.[45] Also he was not a rousing public speaker in the style of Hitler or Hermann Esser. In June 1922 the *VB* reported on several speeches by party officials but tactfully commented that Rosenberg's was 'a longer, tactical lecture dealing with the fundamentals'.[46] Another possible reason for his reluctance to speak in public was his desire to keep a low profile until he gained German citizenship; as he commented in his memoirs, 'until then [February 1923] I could easily have been deported as an "undesirable alien"'. How serious a threat this was is difficult to establish, but in retrospect Rosenberg made a lot of it, claiming that on receiving German citizenship he 'called Eckart and told him that . . . all our former caution was now superfluous'.[47] Whatever the truth of this claim, his talent evidently did not lie in oratory but rather in the day-to-day political editorship of the *VB* and in the painstaking culling of useful snippets of antisemitic information from folkish literature and current affairs.

Nevertheless, on the eve of his arrest following the failure of the Munich putsch, Hitler sent Rosenberg a note which read quite simply: 'Dear Rosenberg, lead the movement from now on.'[48] The reasons for his selection as party leader have intrigued historians ever since. Many have assumed that Rosenberg was chosen because he would not be a serious rival to Hitler when the latter returned after a short imprisonment.[49] However, Robert Cecil, Rosenberg's latest biographer, has argued that, since Hitler could not have anticipated a prison sentence of barely a year, the choice may have been made on merit; admittedly the Munich putsch had narrowed Hitler's options considerably.[50] Though it has to be conceded that

44. Details of his impressive record of convictions can be found in HA 53/1259.
45. Rosenberg, *Letzte Aufzeichnungen*, p. 102.
46. *VB*, 21 June 1922.
47. A. Rosenberg, *The Memoirs of Alfred Rosenberg*, (New York, 1949), pp. 70, 49.
48. A. Rosenberg, *Grossdeutschland: Traum und Tragödie*, (Munich, 1970), p. 69; see also *Letzte Aufzeichnungen*, p. 107.
49. Schubert, *Anfänge*, p. 116; J. Fest, *Hitler. Eine Biographie* (Frankfurt a. M., 1973), p. 331.
50. Cecil, *Myth of the Master Race*, pp. 42–3.

Hitler could not have predicted how leniently he would be treated by the German courts, the idea that Rosenberg was selected on merit to lead the rump of the Nazi Party is difficult to accept. Hitler had little alternative; Eckart's health was deteriorating rapidly; Scheubner-Richter had been killed during the putsch; Ernst Röhm was in hiding; and Hermann Esser and Hermann Göring had fled the country.[51] Furthermore, he must have realised that Rosenberg had in Esser and Ernst Hanfstängl strong and jealous critics within the party. Finally, and perhaps most importantly, Hitler must have appreciated that his nominee did not possess the qualities of leadership; his undoubted achievements as political editor of the *VB* and his status as resident party philosopher did not equip him for party leadership. Rosenberg was aloof and uncharismatic and, what is more, as he himself acknowledged later, totally ignorant of 'questions of an organisational nature'.[52]

Hitler's appointment of Rosenberg was therefore largely the product of necessity; there was little choice but to commit the movement to a solid, competent, but inspired leadership and hope it might survive his own imprisonment. Rosenberg proved unequal to the task of keeping the banned party together. This was partly because Hitler undermined his position, receiving and· encouraging visits from Rosenberg's rivals in Landsberg gaol and denouncing his decision to contest the Landtag and Reichstag elections in 1924 and the suggested fusion of the rump of the Nazi Party with the *Deutschvölkische Freiheitspartei*; this finally led to Rosenberg's relinquishing the party leadership.[53] Nevertheless, Hitler still valued his collaboration, writing to him in April 1925 to persuade him not to proceed with libel actions against his two rivals, Esser and Hanfstängl. Though Hitler did have this ulterior motive for flattering Rosenberg, the letter is worth quoting at length:

> I know you, Herr Rosenberg, and regard you not only as one of the most valuable collaborators with our movement, chief editor of my former *VB*, to whom was due the main share in developing the paper so far as content was concerned, but also as a man of whose integrity of personal intention I am absolutely convinced. In the difficult period in which, unexpectedly and without explanation, you took over the leadership of the movement, you tried to advance the cause of the movement as much as possible — with me, this conviction goes without saying; in the process, mistakes

51. On the fate of the Nazis after the failure of the putsch, see Fest, *Hitler*, pp. 204–5.

52. Rosenberg, *Letzte Aufzeichnungen*, p. 107.

53. Ibid., pp. 107–8. On this subject, see W. Horn, *Führerideologie und Parteiorganisation in der NSDAP* (Düsseldorf, 1972).

have crept in, as can happen with you as with anyone else. But it is not my object to give an opinion on mistakes, but solely on intentions and goodwill. For this I must give you the highest credit in everything.[54]

For a man ever grudging in his praise of others, this letter bears witness to the contribution which Hitler felt Rosenberg had made to the party in the period 1921–5. Evident in the letter, also, is a certain coolness and formality which characterised their relationship. Hitler needed Rosenberg's collaboration but did not have to make a friend of him. Rosenberg's contribution to the Nazi Party was, therefore, limited to the development of its ideology. The full extent of Hitler's personal indebtedness to Rosenberg in matters of ideology will become clearer if the impact of the ideological transformation of 1920 on Nazi thinking on foreign affairs is now examined (and later when the development of Hitler's alliance strategy is considered).

The Initial Impact of the World Jewish Conspiracy on Hitler's Outlook on Foreign Affairs

The usefulness of the alleged world-wide Jewish conspiracy to Nazi propaganda should not be underestimated. It enabled Hitler and others to utilise current events abroad in their antisemitic campaign; it enabled them to criticise the diplomacy of successive Weimar governments; and, finally and perhaps most important, it enabled them to interpret foreign affairs for their followers. Put another way, Nazi propagandists were able to give the impression that the Nazi Party had a foreign policy of its own (even when it had not). Pan-German analyses of prewar diplomatic change were of limited use in formulating a day-to-day response to postwar developments; the Jewish world conspiracy provided an adaptable frame of reference.

Jewish influence in foreign affairs could, as Rosenberg had explained in 1919, be traced at several different points and, as 1920 wore on, Hitler began, consciously or otherwise, to illustrate these in his speeches. Inside Germany, the Jews were shown to be impeding foreign policies dictated by national interest and the popular will; for example, on 6 July Hitler claimed that 'all Germans want the *Anschluss*, only the Jews do not because otherwise too many

---

54. Quoted in Cecil, *Myth of the Master Race*, p. 51.

antisemites would come into the Reichstag'. In the same speech Hitler complained bitterly about the Jews who were currently representing Germany at the international conference in Spa.[55] Outside Germany, the Jews were manipulating internationalist ideas to their own advantage: 'the League of Nations', Hitler claimed in June, 'is there only to guarantee the relentless execution of this "peace" which means the enslavement of the German people under the authority of international world capitalism.[56]

But did such observations bring about any real change in Hitler's outlook? Were the goals of his foreign policy or his view of the major powers fundamentally altered by the revelation of the hidden hand of international Jewry in world affairs?

Turning firstly to his foreign policy goals, it has been suggested recently that Hitler began to harbour dreams of eventual German world conquest in 1920 'as a reaction against Jewry's presumed goal of world-rule'. In other words, his own dreams of German 'world-rule' were fired by the propaganda about similar Jewish ambitions and he hid them 'behind the fight against Jewry with its supposed striving for world-rule'.[57] This is a neat and attractive theory, which acknowledges the significance of the antisemitic ideology to Hitler's foreign policy. Unfortunately it cannot be proved.

There is in fact no hard evidence to suggest that in 1920 Hitler's crusade against Jewish imperialism concealed his own dreams of world conquest. In his 'fundamental speech' on antisemitism of 13 August 1920, Hitler certainly gave the impression that antisemitism was a universal crusade but not that it would result in German world domination; 'should we succeed [in the struggle against Jewry], as we are convinced we shall, then though we may perish wholly destitute — we shall nevertheless have assisted in the greatest movement, which will stretch over Europe and the whole world'.[58] The talk of Germany perishing should, of course, be taken for the rhetoric which it was, and there may have been a hidden subtextual message, impossible to prove from the available evidence. The evidence does suggest, however, that Hitler's long-term goal at this stage was the re-emergence of Germany as a 'world

55. Speech on 6 July 1920, report in Phelps, 'Parteiredner' p. 305.

56. Speech on 9 June, report in *Münchener Zeitung*, 15 June 1920, BHStA I/1478. For Rosenberg's views, see above, pp. 12–14.

57. J. Thies, *Architekt der Weltherrschaft. Die 'Endziele' Hitlers* (Düsseldorf, 1972), pp. 44, 60. At this point (p. 44), Thies seems to be arguing that the global dimensions entered Hitler's vision of a struggle between Aryans and Jews in 1922, but his conclusion dates it from 1920. He quotes no evidence to support such a conclusion.

58. Phelps, 'Hitlers "grundlegende" Rede', p. 416.

power' amongst other 'world powers' rather than German world domination.[59]

But did the internationalisation of the Jewish menace affect the more immediate foreign policy goals laid down in the Nazi Party programme? It would appear not. On the contrary, those same goals were treated after the spring of 1920 as part and parcel of the ideological struggle against the Jews, who were now portrayed as hostile to the creation of a *Grossdeutschland*. For example, the Jews in Germany, as has been seen, were viewed as opponents of the *Anschluss* with Austria, and because, in Hitler's view, Austria was 'almost completely in the hands of international high finance', the need to effect the *Anschluss* was even more pressing.[60] Furthermore, Hitler now labelled the various separatist schemes mooted in 1920 such as the creation of a Danubian Confederation as 'Jewish humbug', that is, they were in reality Jewish attempts to destroy Germany's internal unity.[61] Clearly, the adoption of an antisemitic world-view did not alter but merely complemented Hitler's Pan-German inclinations.

Likewise, Hitler's demands for the dismantling of the Versailles Settlement and the return of Germany's colonies now acquired ideological bite. The hated postwar settlement was part of the Jewish campaign against Germany; reparations payments were designed to keep Germany in debt. As he explained, 'international capitalism only wants to use us as a source of interest, and to make us slaves'.[62]

The introduction of an international dimension to Hitler's antisemitism, though pregnant with possibilities, did not therefore significantly change his basic foreign policy goals. Rather the realisation of those goals was thereafter seen as vital in the battle against World Jewry. But if the antisemitic crusade was here being used to sanctify the Nazi Party's goals in foreign policy, the reverse was also true. Conflict with the Jews was justified by the drive to improve Germany's international fortunes; as Hitler put it in May 1920: 'The precondition for any German recovery is . . . [the] revision of the peace, [the] precondition for this is [the] recognition of our internal national solidarity. [This] can only be achieved by the struggle

---

59. See above, pp. 52–5; see also Tyrell, *Trommler*, pp. 47–8. See also chapter 5 for a fuller discussion.
60. Speech on 26 October 1920, Phelps, 'Parteiredner', p. 324.
61. Speech on 20 September 1920, ibid., p. 300.
62. Speech on 22 September 1920, ibid., p. 320–1.

against the destroyers (Jews)'.[63] Hence, as early as May 1920, the struggle against the Jews was considered an integral part of Hitler's scheme to resurrect Germany as a force in world affairs.

Wolfgang Horn has argued that the influx of ideas about an international Jewish conspiracy caused not just a revision of Hitler's attitude towards foreign affairs, but a complete volte-face. Ideology now took precedence over power politics in Hitler's assessment of foreign relations.[64] This claim can best be examined by tracing the impact of ideological considerations on Hitler's appraisal of individual nations. It is clear, though, that he did apply the conspiracy theory to his division of the major world powers into 'absolute enemies' and potential friends. On 13 August 1920 he argued that Britain, France and America — Germany's 'deadly enemies' — were already 'practically ruled' by international loan capitalism.[65] On the other hand, the First World War had been, Hitler asserted on 22 September 1920, 'nothing more than an endeavour on the part of international loan capitalism to destroy the national economy in Germany, Russia and Austria–Hungary, in order to make these countries colonies of international interest-capital'.[66]

But did the identification of a world-wide Jewish 'threat' seriously modify Hitler's appraisal of foreign powers or did he again merely adapt the conspiracy theory to reinforce his earlier convictions, which were based on his, or rather the Pan-Germans', reading of the power political situation? Despite his references to the power exerted by finance capitalism over Britain, France and America, there is little evidence to suggest that Hitler's view of Germany's 'deadly enemies' had altered in fact.

Hitler still combined an implacable hostility towards Britain with a sneaking respect for her empire. The quality which he most admired and feared about the British Empire was that its strength was built on the ruthless destruction of other nations: as the Chinese, the Indians and the Boers had found to their cost, Britain was 'the expert destroyer of the health of nations' and the Versailles Settlement, in Hitler's view, made it clear that the object of the First World War from the British perspective had been 'the economic and political annihilation of Germany'.[67] Whilst continuing to cite Bri-

63. Speech on 31 May 1920, report in NS 26/1929–2698.
64. W. Horn, 'Ein unbekannter Aufsatz Hitlers aus dem Frühjahr 1924', p. 287; Schubert does not agree, *Anfänge*, pp. 35–6.
65. Phelps, 'Hitlers "grundlegende" Rede', p. 420.
66. Report in *VB*, 26 September 1920.
67. Speech on 24 November, report of *MNN*, 26 November 1920.

tain's record approvingly as evidence of her conviction that 'might makes right', he did observe on one occasion that the destructiveness of the British mirrored that of the Jews: they were 'almost a second Jewry'.[68] This, of course, was the worst possible insult and indicated the depth of his hostility towards 'England' at this time. Nevertheless, Hitler's attitude towards England seems still to have been based primarily on a power political analysis of prewar Anglo-German rivalry; the main reason for British enmity towards Germany was the latter's emergence as a commercial and imperial rival to Britain.[69]

Hitler's attitude to France also remained unaffected by the ideological revision of 1920. France and Germany were 'eternal' enemies for purely tactical reasons: the French wanted to control the left bank of the Rhine and were willing to espouse any cause, for example that of separatist movements inside Germany, to achieve this goal; on 9 September 1920 Hitler claimed that the French Chamber of Deputies had raised 300 million francs to finance German separatists.[70] On the other occasions, he ascribed precisely the same tactics of 'divide and rule' to the Jews, but he did not at this stage attribute French policy to Jewish influence in Paris, but simply and solely to French *Weltpolitik*, which aimed to destroy Germany.[71]

Furthermore, the 'uncovering' of a Jewish world conspiracy had little impact on Hitler's assessment of America, the third of Germany's deadly enemies, since American foreign policy had long been associated in folkish circles with the power of high finance. Like the Pan-Germans before him, Hitler had argued in December 1919 that America had intervened in the First World War not because of Germany's resumption of unrestricted submarine warfare but, 'as the land of money', in order not to lose her loans to the Entente nations.[72] It was a small step further to lambast President Wilson as 'the representative of high finance', whose conciliatory Fourteen Points had been deliberately designed to deceive the German people.[73] After the war, Germany's need for American loans to

68. Phelps, 'Hitlers "grundlegende" Rede', pp. 411–12.

69. Speech on 6 July 1920, report in *VB*, 11 July 1920; see also speech on 17 April 1920, Phelps, 'Parteiredner', pp. 297–8.

70. Speech on 9 September, *MNN*, 11 September 1920.

71. Speech on 27 July 1920, Phelps, 'Parteiredner', p. 308; see also his speech on 20 September 1920, ibid., p. 318.

72. Speech on 10 December 1919, Deuerlein, 'Hitlers Eintritt', p. 209. See also the report in Phelps, 'Parteiredner', p. 291. For the Pan-German view, see Einhart, *Deutsche Geschichte*, p. 509.

73. Speech on 6 July 1920, Phelps, 'Parteiredner', p. 305.

finance her recovery provided plentiful ammunition for Hitler's attacks on 'interest-slavery'; on one occasion, he estimated that 'new loans from America, which are worth only 1300 milliard [marks], [would] devour 65 milliard in interest'.[74] Clearly, before the 'revelation' of Jewish manipulation of world affairs, Hitler — as a result of folkish propaganda before, during and immediately after the war — already imagined America to be a land dominated by considerations of high finance.

So initially at least, Hitler's view of the three powers whom he considered as Germany's most clear-cut opponents seemed to have been little affected by the adoption of a more conspiratorial anti-semitic worldview; their policies were, predictably, found to be compatible with those of the Jews. But what of the powers whom he considered to have become Germany's enemies only because of the failings of German diplomacy before the First World War?

Hitler still argued that Italy had joined the Entente powers against Germany only because of her hostility to Germany's ally, Austria–Hungary. Italy and Germany had no conflicting interests before the war and, after it, they shared an intense antipathy towards the Versailles Settlement. In 1920 at any rate, Hitler did not produce any ideological motive to justify his support for future Italo-German collaboration. The same applied to Japan; Hitler believed that, before the war, Japanese *Weltpolitik*, which consisted of establishing her own predominance in East Asia by excluding the white races, did not conflict with Germany's ambitions.[75] In 1920 he did not publicly advocate German-Japanese collaboration nor did he appear to relate the Jewish menace to Japanese affairs.

The situation is far more complex with regard to Hitler's appraisal of Russia, the other power in this category. His view seems to have undergone a very marked ideological revision in the course of 1920. His sympathetic treatment of Russian foreign policy has already been noted; in December 1919, he claimed that Germany and Russia ought to have been allies before the war: Russia's policy of Asiatic conquest did not infringe upon German interests and her search for an outlet to the sea ought not to have brought her into conflict with Germany if German diplomats had not shortsightedly discontinued Bismarck's Reinsurance Treaty with Russians. By April 1920, however, Hitler had 'uncovered' another force which had kept Germany and Russia apart: 'an understanding between us

74. Speech on 11 June 1920, ibid., p. 303.

75. Speech on 26 May, reported in *Süddeutsche Zeitung*, 29 May 1920, reprinted in Jäckel and Kuhn, *Hitler*, p. 135. For his views on Italy see above, pp. 60–1.

and Russia could not take place because the international Jewish press concern had prevented it'.[76]

This new 'insight' was, undoubtedly, the product of Hitler's introduction to the world conspiracy theory; Germany and Russia, as Alfred Rosenberg had 'revealed' in 1919, were the arch-enemies of the Jews and, therefore, as far as the Jews were concerned these natural allies had to be kept apart and indeed the two states had to be destroyed. The Jewish-led Bolshevik Revolution was an attempt to subjugate the Russian people, and the German people were about to face a similar threat. Armed with this 'knowledge' Hitler began to devote more and more time to descriptions of Russian conditions in his speeches. On 27 April 1920, he talked about a Russia 'which is economically destroyed, about the 12-hour-day there, about Jewish terrorism, about the mass murder of the intelligentsia'; the same things, Hitler predicted, were likely to happen in Germany.[77] In another speech, he claimed that Russia had fallen 'into the clutches not of the Russian proletariat but of capital'.[78] Hitler's revised view of Russia seemed to rest on the 'fact', constantly reiterated by Rosenberg, that the revolutionary Jews in Russia were secretly in league with the capitalist Jews in the West.[79]

There can be no doubt that this reflected a changed attitude towards Russia as a prospective alliance partner. When a brave Communist at a Nazi Party meeting on 6 July 1920 suggested that Germany should ally with Soviet Russia as England's arch-enemy in Asia, Hitler 'spoke against Soviet Russia where hunger and misery reigned'.[80] On 27 July, in an important speech, Hitler was even more explicit: 'an alliance between Russia and Germany can only come about when Jewry is removed.'[81] An alliance between the two states had, therefore, in the course of 1920 become conditional on the removal of 'Jewish' Bolshevism.

76. Speech on 17 April 1920, Phelps, 'Parteiredner', p. 297. For his earlier views, see above pp. 59–60.

77. Report in Phelps, 'Parteiredner', p. 299. See also speeches on 11 June, Deuerlein, 'Hitlers Eintritt', p. 214 and 20 September 1920, ibid., p. 216.

78. Speech on 22 September 1920, Phelps, 'Parteiredner', p. 321.

79. Rosenberg, *Die Spur des Juden*, pp. 151–8.

80. The communist was identified only as 'Branz' by the police observer present, Phelps, 'Parteiredner', p. 306. Folkish opinion was divided on issue of Russia at this time; the *Deutschsozialistische Partei* (DSP) favoured conciliation with Soviet Russia, feeling that Russian pressure on British colonies would force Britain to neglect her European duties, a situation from which Germany could only benefit, see *VB* (then still the DSP's paper) 28 February and 13 March 1920. However, Arnold Rechberg, a regular contributor to the *VB* and well-known francophile, did consistently warn his readers about Bolshevik Russia's commitment to worldwide revolution 'Bolschewismus in Russland', *VB*, 26 and 29 April 1920.

81. Report in Phelps, 'Parteiredner', p. 308.

However, whether this change was entirely the product of Hitler's adoption of the world conspiracy theory is difficult to say, since he also perceived in Russia in 1920 the resurgence of Pan-Slavism, which had, he believed, been revived by the Russo-Polish war of 1919–20. This might signify the launching of a phase of Russian expansion westwards, which would endanger German interests; Bolshevism, Hitler suspected was 'only a pretext for the construction of a great Russian Empire'.[82] He was clearly opposed to Russian imperialism in Eastern Europe; in a meeting on 19 November 1920, he answered a critic in the audience who blamed the absence of genuine reconstruction in Russia on the latter's continuing need to fight her enemies, by arguing that 'the Russians were responsible for the fact that they had not achieved peace. If they were to bother only about the purely Russian areas, then no Ukrainian, no Pole, no Latvian etc. would dare to take a stand against Russia'.[83] So it is possible that Hitler's caution about advocating German-Russian collaboration resulted from the perceived revitalisation of Russian imperialism and this was expressed in ideological terms solely for reasons of propaganda.

On the other hand, Hitler's comments on Pan-Slavism were rarely divorced from his ideological broadsides against Bolshevism. And it seems as if he welcomed its revival as a sign of the imminent collapse of Bolshevism; in other words, Pan-Slavism might accelerate the removal of the major obstacle to Russo-German collaboration. As Hitler argued on 27 July: 'The nationalistic wave will wash away Bolshevism. An alliance with Russia can be of use to us only when we are ourselves a single, strong, nationally aware nation.'[84] It is possible here that Hitler was postulating an alliance between a future Pan-Slavic Russia which would have liquidated Bolshevism, and a future National Socialist Germany able to resist the Russian trend towards westward expansion. Pan-Slavism was, therefore, a cause for concern in the short term but not in the long term.

What is clear is that a Russo-German alliance was not possible in the circumstances of 1920. Hitler left an audience in Nuremberg on 1 August 1920 in no doubt about this point: 'if we wanted today to conclude an alliance with Russia, England and France would come

82. Ibid. See also report in *MNN*, 29 July, BHStA I/1478.

83. Report in Phelps, 'Parteiredner', p. 329.

84. Report in *MNN*, 29 July 1920, BHStA I/1478. Another report of the same speech quotes Hitlers as saying that 'an alliance with Russia would be impossible without the precondition of complete national solidarity in Germany, *Bayerische Staatszeitung*, 29 July 1920, reprinted in Jäckel and Kuhn, *Hitler*, p. 166.

along and, with the utmost ease, we would be smashed. Germany must not be made into a battlefield.'[85] Here contemporary diplomatic alignments, the weakness of Russia and simple facts of geography seem to underlie Hitler's analysis, but it is important also to note the difference between what one might call an embryonic Nazi Party foreign policy *programme* and this comment on international affairs. A future Russian alliance was certainly conceived of as part of an emerging Nazi programme in 1920, but it was not a course recommended by Hitler to the diplomats of Weimar Germany.

Nevertheless, it has to be stressed that Hitler's view of Russia did alter in 1920. Several 'obstacles' had now emerged to hinder the collaboration between Germany and Russia which Hitler had favoured in his analysis of prewar diplomacy. It is impossible to ascertain whether the change was brought about solely by 'revelations' concerning the 'Jewish' nature of Bolshevism; but clearly this possibility cannot be ruled out. The revival of Pan-Slavism, which Hitler perceived in the Russo-Polish campaign, could have played a part, but then again he appeared to welcome resurgent Russian nationalism as a sign that Bolshevism was on the wane. This suggests that Russia's 'Judeo-Bolshevik' régime may indeed have been the main stumbling-block to future Russo-German collaboration.

Conclusion

By the end of 1920, therefore, Hitler's aspirations for Germany in foreign affairs and the policies of the major powers were, under the influence of Alfred Rosenberg, increasingly being portrayed in a wider context. The first three points of the party programme — the union of all Germans in one empire, the dismantling of the Versailles Settlement and the return of Germany's colonies — were now seen as essential stages in the conflict against the two arms of the Jewish world conspiracy — international high finance and revolutionary socialism. These were striving to keep Germans divided, to enslave the German economy through reparations and to deprive Germany of world-power status and the land to feed her population.

It must be stressed that the initial impact of an international antisemitic ideology seems to have been merely to reinforce Hitler's prior conceptions of the party's aims and his existing convictions

---

85. Account in H. Preiss (ed.), *Adolf Hitler in Franken*, p. 11.

about the major powers, with the exception of Russia. If ideology did revolutionise Hitler's outlook on foreign affairs, as Horn argues, then the transformation was incomplete in 1920. Indeed, it should be emphasised once again that Hitler's first priority in 1919–20 was the revival of Germany's internal fortunes. He did not want to be sidetracked into discussions of alliance policy; as he told his audience in Nuremberg in August 1920, 'a people which relies on foreign assistance is lost . . . . We Germans must decide whether we shall be slaves for ever or whether we want to be free. For freedom, we need, in the first instance, solidarity in our own land.'[86] In 1920, therefore, Hitler devoted little time to devising an alliance strategy.

86. Ibid.

4

Ideology and Alliance Policy, 1921–23

Between 1921 and 1923 Hitler's thoughts on foreign policy crystallised into a full-blown alliance strategy. Historians have been particularly interested in the role played by ideological considerations in this process and in the reaction of party colleagues to the decisions reached. Eberhard Jäckel, who has generally emphasised the importance of ideology in Hitler's *Weltanschauung*, believes, however, that 'the politics of alliance were to him always simple power politics'.[1] Axel Kuhn, in his study of Hitler's foreign policy programme, reaches a similar conclusion and maintains that the decisions to advocate an Anglo-German alliance and a campaign of expansion largely at Russia's expense were his alone. The choice of England as an ally, reversing the previously anglophobic trend in Nazi propaganda, was, according to Kuhn, made in the teeth of opposition within the party; the anti-Russian stance, though having vocal supporters within party ranks, was nevertheless also the result of 'Hitler's solitary decision'.[2]

The validity of these unequivocal interpretations has, however, to be queried. Did ideology have no effect on Hitler's choice of allies? Were the decisions really taken by Hitler in isolation? These questions, and indeed, the evolution of the Nazi Party's alliance policy as a whole needs re-examination since previous studies have tended to concentrate almost exclusively on the speeches and writings of Hitler himself. Hitler was never the party's sole spokesman on foreign affairs; after January 1921, when the *VB* became the official

1. E. Jäckel, *Hitlers Weltanschauung*, p. 34.
2. Kuhn, *Programm*, p. 155; on the role of ideology, ibid., p. 127; on opposition to the English alliance, ibid., pp. 87–8.

party newspaper, it provided a forum, in the absence of any clear 'party line' on foreign policy, for writers of varying points of view. Only by studying a range of party opinion, is it be possible to assess accurately the extent of support for any emergent alliance strategy as well as to chart exactly changes in Nazi attitudes. Furthermore, in order to explain how Hitler reached decisions on alliance policy and, indeed, to throw more light on some of the concepts underlying those decisions, it is necessary to investigate his response both to the ideas of the leading political theorists, with whom he came into contact at this time, and to the foreign policy of successive Weimar governments.

Finally, Hitler's ideas need to be examined within the context of Nazi ideology, which, as stressed above, did not constitute a static corpus of rational ideas but was essentially a way of looking at the world, a framework of reference, by which any event could be judged. So even if the party's antisemitic ideology did not determine the nature of Nazi foreign policy, but merely reinforced convictions based on other considerations, it would still *reflect* any changes of emphasis.

The study of the Nazi Party's ideological statements would be justified on these grounds alone. But that it is absolutely vital not to overlook them is made clear by Hitler's own comments in *Mein Kampf* on the evolution of the party's outlook on foreign affairs. Hitler admitted frankly that, apart from fulminations against the Versailles Settlement, foreign policy had been neglected by the party at first. He gave two reasons for this: firstly because as long as the party 'possessed only the scope of a small little-known club, problems of foreign policy could possess only a subordinate importance in the eyes of many adherents' and, secondly, because the Nazis believed that a successful foreign policy was conditional upon a position of internal strength: 'Only the elimination of the causes of our collapse, as well as the destruction of its beneficiaries, can create the premise for our outward fight for freedom.' Later, as the party grew in stature, Hitler went on, 'the necessity arose of taking a position on the questions pertaining to the developments in foreign affairs. It became necessary to lay down *guiding principles, which would not only not contradict the fundamental views of our world concept, but actually represent an emanation of this line of thought* [emphasis added].'[3] The inference is quite unmistakable: the foreign policy programme had to be compatible with the *Weltanschauung* of the party. This does not

3. Hitler, *MK*, pp. 555–6.

necessarily mean that Nazi foreign policy was merely an outgrowth of the ideology, for the latter was extremely flexible and could easily accommodate preconceived notions. What is certain, however, is that the Nazi Party's ideological pronouncements should not be neglected in an analysis of its alliance policy.

The Emergence of an English Alliance

In the early months of 1921 the Nazi attitude towards Britain remained unremittingly hostile. As we have seen, Hitler was fond of listing the crimes committed by the British Empire, usually in order to expose the hypocrisy of talk of British respect for the rights of smaller nations. On 3 February, he added persecution of the Irish and 'the extermination of half (of them)' and 'the crushing of the ancient state of India' to his catalogue of criminal acts perpetrated by the British against peaceful nations.[4] At this time, Hitler and other *VB* writers still believed that the overriding British aim was the 'enslavement' of Germany.[5] The Allies' occupation of three Rhine ports on 8 March and the ultimatum issued at the London conference on 5 May 1921, threatening occupation of the Ruhr district unless Germany accepted the recently produced reparations scheme and disarmed in accordance with the Versailles Treaty, were seen as attempts to do just this. On 22 May 1921, therefore, Hitler reproved the new German government of Dr. Wirth for having accepted the ultimatum and 'for courting the allegedly available favour of England and France'; it ought to have realised 'that one cannot negotiate with the force which has activated these Western democratic states'; the 'force' in question was the Jewish stock exchange, which he regarded as the ultimate recipient of German reparations payments.[6]

British efforts to find an equitable solution to another intractable problem, that of Upper Silesia, an area rich in mineral resources and vital to the economies of both claimants, Germany and Poland, initially met with a lack of appreciation in Nazi quarters. On 15 March 1921, Hitler predicted that the Entente — including 'per-

---

4. Report in *VB*, 6 February 1921.
5. Ibid. This line was reiterated in an article entitled 'Das Bündnis mit Sowjet-Russland', *VB*, 3 March 1921 (writer unidentified).
6. A. Hitler, 'Deutschlands letzte Hoffnung', *VB*, 22 May 1921. See also A. Rosenberg, 'Schicksalswende in London', *VB*, 15 March 1921.

fidious Albion' — intended to give Upper Silesia 'wholly or partly to Poland', irrespective of the results of the plebiscite to be held on 21 March and which was promised in the Versailles Treaty.[7] When disturbances occurred between Poles and Germans in Upper Silesia after the 'indecisive' plebiscite (roughly 60% of the vote went to Germany, 40% to Poland), he discounted reports of English protests to the Polish government.[8] France was of course trying to ensure that Poland, her ally since the treaty of 9 February 1921, gained possession of the disputed province; but Hitler gave no credence to news of British opposition to these plans. When the British Prime Minister Lloyd George delivered a speech criticising the Polish rebels, Hitler was concerned to correct both the impression gained by 'many Germans' that the attitude of the English had changed fundamentally and the belief that 'if we ourselves do not disturb our decent image, but remain respectable and well-behaved, and deliver all that is to be delivered, then England will become very shortly a "friend" of ours'. This was a deception; the Jews were behind 'Lloyd George's honey sweet words'.[9] However, when an army of German volunteers clashed for the first time with the Poles on 22 May 1921, Hitler admitted that the British troops in the area — far from turning on the Germans — appeared willing to collaborate with them.[10] Nevertheless, he did not take this as evidence of a genuine change of heart by the British government towards Germany but simply as proof of what he had been saying all along, namely that if Germany showed a fighting spirit and proved herself worthy of support, she would get it.

It is doubtful therefore, that evidence of sympathy for the German cause on this occasion had drastically altered Hitler's view of the British. In fact, further conciliatory moves by Lloyd George led Hitler to label him the new 'Pied Piper' enticing Germans to ruin; 'an intrinsic change in England's attitude towards Germany was impossible', Hitler explained, 'because the same society of Jewish press bandits directs the state there as it does here'.[11]

It is interesting to note here that Hitler resorted to an antisemitic slur to disparage Britain's pro-German stance on Upper Silesia. The

---

7. A. Hitler, 'Staatsmänner oder Nationalverbrecher', *VB*, 15 March 1921.

8. A. Hitler, 'Pollackenbüttengemeinheiten', *VB*, 15 March 1921; see also *VB*, 8 May and 12 May 1921.

9. A. Hitler, 'Der ewige Gimpel', *VB*, 22 May 1921; for further evidence of his distrust of Lloyd George, see his article, 'Rathenau und Sancho Pansa', *VB*, 13 March 1921.

10. A. Hitler, 'Lumpenrepublik', *VB*, 26 May 1921.

11. A. Hitler, 'Oberschlesiens Schicksal', *VB*, 29 May 1921.

Upper Silesian question obviously posed problems of interpretation
for the Nazis. For the first time a split had occurred in the ranks of
Germany's enemies and they were obliged to comment on pro-
German policies. However, the world conspiracy theory enabled
Hitler to discount Lloyd George's friendly words as a 'Jewish trick'
cruelly designed to raise the hopes of the German people, only to
dash them again later, thereby 'accelerating the internal destruction
of the final remnants of her ability to resist'.[12] Thus, if his comments
on contemporary diplomacy are to be taken seriously, Hitler remained fiercely opposed to the British. When necessary, he invoked
the spectre of the Jewish world conspiracy to discredit policies
apparently inconsistent with his previously established picture of a
hostile Britain.

Britain's role in the world Jewish conspiracy had already been
'revealed' by Alfred Rosenberg. Her interests were largely compatible with those of the Jews — for the moment at least. In Russia,
Britain's intermittent support for the White Russian forces against
the Bolsheviks ensured the continuation of a civil war from which
both the Jews (out to maximise the destruction of Russia) and
British (the opponents of Russian imperialism in Central Asia) drew
comfort. In the Near East, support for the creation of a Jewish state
in Palestine not only warmed the hearts of Zionists but offered
Britain the prospect of another strategic base in the area. All this, in
Rosenberg's eyes, made Britain the protector of World Jewry and
London the centre of Jewish activities.[13] By inference, Britain was
no friend to Germany at this time.

This basic scenario was often repeated in the *VB* during 1921. In
February 1921, the trade treaty signed by London and Moscow
provided Rosenberg with 'proof' that British industrialists were
working hand-in-glove with the Jewish Bolsheviks.[14] On 1 May 1921
he drew attention to the opening of a Bolshevik bank in London as
further evidence that the forces of world capitalism and world
revolution were actually in league.[15] Significantly, in a speech two
days later Hitler referred to Lenin as 'the mass murderer, who is
now turning towards England in order to establish trading relations
to ease the economic distress of Russia'.[16] Evidently he shared

12. Ibid. See also A. Hitler, 'Beginn der Judendiktatur', *VB*, 5 June 1921.

13. See above, pp. 22–4.

14. A. Rosenberg, 'Börsenjuden und Revolution', *VB*, 22 February 1921 (an unsigned article
but one referred to as his own by Rosenberg in 'Schicksalswende in London', *VB*, 6 March 1921).

15. A. Rosenberg, 'Weltbetrug', *VB*, 1 May 1921.

16. Hitler's speech on 3 May, report in *VB*, 8 May 1921.

Rosenberg's belief in the compatibility of British and Jewish policies in 1921. In preparing a speech entitled 'Workers and Peace Treaties' delivered on 31 May, he jotted down the following notes:

> England's goal   }
> Judah's goal   }
> The means
> Peace treaty of Versailles[17]

At this stage, therefore, the party's ideological world-view seems to mirror Hitler's continued hostility towards Britain.

However, this attitude began slowly to change, the first signs occurring during the continuing crisis over Upper Silesia, which may, indeed, have been the turning-point. Though Hitler continued to dismiss England's pro-German policy as Jewish trickery, Rosenberg reacted to it differently. On 18 August 1921 he wrote:

> There is now, without question, in England a strong group, who want to pursue only an English national policy. This can only consist of the European balance of power, not the creation of an absolute predominance of France or Germany . . . . These circles have already established multifarious trading relations with Germany, and however much they welcome the German Empire as a helpless victim they cannot in their own interests desire its complete destruction. Consideration of this English Realpolitik has, without doubt, caused Lloyd George to advocate officially and very forcefully a partly German Upper Silesia.[18]

Nationally-minded British politicians and businessmen — not the Jews — were now seen as the instigators of Lloyd George's pro-German policies. Such policies were evidently at odds with the interests of the Jews, but Rosenberg was cautious about the prospects for a decisive change of policy; World Jewry still wanted to destroy Germany and if Lloyd George were to act against the wishes of the London Stock Exchange, 'he would at that moment be a political corpse'.[19] Nevertheless, for the first time a basis for possible Anglo-German collaboration emerged (provided, of course, that Jewish influence in Britain was eradicated). It should be noted that it was the traditional British policy of maintaining a balance of

17. See Hitler's handwritten notes, NS 26/49. The report in *VB*, 5 June 1921 corresponds very closely to Hitler's notes but the reference to the identity of interest between the British and the Jews is not recorded.

18. 'Der Schurkenstreich des "Obersten Rates"', *VB*, 18 August 1921.

19. Ibid.

power in Europe which would provide the basis for Anglo-German cooperation, although the needs of the British economy were a secondary, if still significant, factor. For Rosenberg, evidence of Anglo-French dissension over Upper Silesia was of some importance; this was not to be dismissed as a Jewish trick but seen as a sign that the national interest was beginning to assert itself in England.

Rosenberg's conviction that true British interests could be reconciled with those of Germany appears in retrospect to have been the embryo from which the party's later support for an Anglo-German alliance grew; but at the time there was no question of a public endorsement of such a strategy. The only noticeable sign of a change was the henceforth ambivalent attitude towards Britain shown by Rosenberg and, occasionally, by other writers in the *VB*. On the one hand, they showed increasing sympathy with British needs and tended to explain away anti-German policies as the result of Jewish influence; on the other, they were markedly critical of the current British government and of past British diplomacy.

The first trend was evident in Rosenberg's interpretation of the Irish question in an article in September 1921. Whilst, like Hitler, he felt that the Irish were 'one of many oppressed peoples', whose folkish struggle for freedom ensured them the support of the Nazi Party, Rosenberg had grave doubts about their leader, Eamonn de Valera, who was, he claimed, 'laden with American money' and also 'half-Jewish'; moreover, his programme bore comparison with Bolshevism. Rosenberg concluded therefore that 'Ireland is the Jewish stock exchange's means of fashioning the policy of Great Britain'.[20] In other words, the Jews were manipulating the Irish question to make difficulties for the British and to maintain their own influence over British policy-making.

A further illustration of this trend was Rosenberg's suggestion that the centre of Jewish activities was shifting from London to New York. In January 1921 he 'identified' the base of the Jewish conspiracy against Germany as being in London but added '[and] recently perhaps in New York'.[21] By 26 November 1921 he was writing that 'today Washington has become the centre of this thieving world conspiracy'. The latter remark was undoubtedly prompted by the opening of the Washington Naval Conference on 21 November, but the conference itself confirmed to Rosenberg the gradual transfer of Jewish headquarters to the United States, which

20. A. Rosenberg, 'Das irische Problem', *VB*, 14 September 1921.
21. Rosenberg, 'Das Verbrechen der Freimaurerei', *Agd*, 15 January 1921.

he had been charting all year.[22] So whilst the Jews still controlled British policy-making, Britain was no longer, in his view, the main Jewish stronghold.

This barely discernible moderation of Rosenberg's anti-British stance was taken further in the 'Political Review' column of the *VB* on 21 January 1922, shortly after Eckart had taken over editorial control. The unidentified writer, presumably Eckart, wrote that *genuine* British interests were, in fact, in line with Germany's and required an anti-French posture: 'If the "England" ruled by the Hebrews were really Great Britain, then there would be reason for such hopes [those pinned on recent conferences]. Then the English representatives would give weight only to English national interests, which would have of necessity to consist of a vigorous cooking of the French goose.'

However, the same writer criticised the German government for expecting that the present British regime would follow such a policy.[23] This illustrates the second theme running through the paper's treatment of Britain — a marked scepticism about the prospect of a significant change in the policy of the current British government vis-à-vis France and Germany. On 14 August 1921, for example, Rosenberg wrote that 'we Germans have not the slightest hope that it could come to a final breach between the Entente powers in the foreseeable future'.[24] In February 1922 he criticised the *Frankfurter Zeitung* for welcoming the dissolution of the Anglo-Japanese alliance and the increase in Anglo-American collaboration, both of which resulted from the Washington Conference, because those moves laid the foundations for an 'Anglo-Saxon world-dominion', behind which stood, inevitably, the Jewish stock exchange.[25]

Hence the first sign of a moderation of Nazi hostility towards Britain was the slightly ambivalent attitude towards her in the *VB*, which Rosenberg appeared to foster. To the untrained eye, Rosenberg remained highly critical, particularly of Britain's past record and current policies, but isolated references to signs of life amongst

22. A. Rosenberg, 'Der Betrug von Washington', *VB*, 26 November 1921; see also 'Amerikanische Neuigkeiten', *Agd*, 15 February and 'Antisemitismus III', *VB*. 7 August 1921.

23. 'Politische Rundschau', *VB*, 21 January 1922. Eckart took over editorial control of the paper on 12 August 1921.

24. 'Eine Abrechnung', *VB*, 14 August 1921. Rosenberg criticised the German press for allowing Germans to pin hopes on Britain, 'Der deutsche Gedanke', *VB*, 22 October 1921.

25. A. Rosenberg, 'Wirth bleibt: Deutschland fault weiter', *VB*, 18 February 1922. Later he claimed that Britain was far from innocent of charges of 'war guilt', 'Ein Volksverräter', *VB*, 25 February 1922.

nationalist circles in the UK and to the compatibility of British and German national interests betrayed his belief in the feasibility of future Anglo-German cooperation. Since Britain's interests were increasingly out of step with those of the Jews, she became, in theory, as suitable an ally for Germany as Russia, once of course — a rider which applied to Russia also — Jewish influence had been removed. The question is, did Hitler's ideas undergo the same change at this time? Did he enjoy the same freedom of choice when he came to formulate an alliance policy?

On the whole this seems likely. It is true, however, that in his analyses of prewar German diplomacy during 1921, Hitler consistently favoured a Russo-German rather than an Anglo-German alliance; the failure to achieve the former was, in his opinion, the 'first huge error' made by Wilhelminian diplomats, whilst an alliance with England was considered to have been 'impossible in the long run'.[26] Admittedly, when Hitler discussed the projected Anglo-German alliance 'against Russia', mooted between 1898 and 1900, he did remark that 'that would have been the opportunity to achieve territorial expansion' but he went on to say that 'the other alternative would have been an alliance with Russia against England', which would have created 'unlimited possibilities for expansion eastwards'.[27] If in these retrospectives Hitler's own ideas on a future Nazi alliance policy may be discerned, then clearly in 1921 an English alliance was less attractive to him than a Russian one.[28] However, in fact, these observations on prewar diplomacy culled from Pan-German literature are perhaps more accurately regarded as substitutes for a Nazi alliance policy. In all probability Hitler had not yet formulated a foreign policy strategy to encompass postwar diplomatic realities. Foreign policy was still not the party's first priority.

What is certain, however, is that by the summer of 1922 Hitler had adopted the antisemitic world-view, popularised in the Nazi Party by Alfred Rosenberg. In a speech on 28 July 1922, he delivered his own account of the international menace of World Jewry:

> We all feel today that two worlds are struggling with one another and not only at home, but everywhere we look in the now oppressed Russia and in

26. Hitler's notes for a speech entitled 'Dummheit oder Verbrechen', NS 26/49, delivered on 4 January, report in *VB*, 9 January 1921.

27. Hitler's speech on 21 October, report in *Verlag Bayerisches Wochenblatt*, 22 October 1921; also in BHStA I/1480.

28. So Axel Kuhn perceives, *Programm*, pp. 66–7.

Italy, in France and in England etc. The poor struggle inexorably between the ideals of those who are nationally, folkishly minded and those of the intangible supra-state International. It is a struggle which today already stretches back about 120 years. It began at the moment when the Jew obtained the right of citizenship in European states.[29]

He believed that 'on the whole, England and France had already put on the chains of [Jewish] slavery' by allowing the Jews to become captains of industry and manipulate political parties, whilst the Jews had seized power in Russia by advocating socialist ideas.[30]

This world-view guaranteed Hitler complete flexibility when he decided to formulate a foreign policy programme. Since all these nations were already in varying degrees subject to Jewish control, all were potentially allies of a Nazi Germany in the struggle against World Jewry. Whichever power he chose as an ally could be given ideological sanction merely by citing evidence of its antisemitic inclinations. This antisemitic ideology did not necessarily determine his foreign policy strategy, but it did give Hitler and like-minded colleagues complete freedom to exercise their own inbuilt prejudices and preferences in foreign affairs. Thus Hitler may not yet have drawn up his 'guiding principles' for Nazi foreign policy, but, when he did, it was clear that they could be presented as an 'emanation' of the party's *Weltanschauung*.

In the winter of 1922–23 Hitler made two statements which did seem to commit him for the first time to a foreign policy programme of alliances with Britain and Italy. At a party discussion evening in Haidhausen on 14 November 1922, he talked about the creation of a nationalist regime in Germany on the Italian Fascist model; to survive, Hitler argued, it would need political success and in the political field there was only one possibility of achieving a real success for Germany: the Anschluss of Austria with Germany, but 'the precondition for this Anschluss would', according to him, 'be the agreement of England and Italy'.[31] Then at the party conference on 27 January 1923, in the wake of the Franco-Belgian invasion of the Ruhr which brought the reparations crisis to a head, Hitler asked his audience which powers had an interest in the further

29. The text of the speech is reprinted in E. Boepple (ed.), *Adolf Hitlers Reden* (Munich, 1925), p. 22; see also the report in *VB*, 6 August 1922. Rosenberg, like Hitler, traced the origins of the contemporary Jewish problem back to the ideals of the French Revolution; A. Rosenberg, '1789?–1517', *VB*, 22 February 1921.

30. Boepple, *Adolf Hitlers Reden*, pp. 23–36.

31. Report in *Münchener Post*, 20 December 1922; see also Kuhn, *Programm*, pp. 88–9 and Horn, 'Ein unbekannter Aufsatz', p. 291.

existence of the German state, answering his own question thus: 'Of course, not France and not Russia and not even America, who would like to look on Germany's internal conflicts with the impassioned partisan sympathy of a prospective bullfighter in order to learn the specific methods of combating Marxism and Bolshevism. England and Italy, however, probably.'[32] These two isolated remarks are usually taken as indicating the emergence of a pro-English strategy in Hitler's programme. If this was so, why did Hitler choose England (not Russia) as a prospective ally?

The most obvious explanation of Hitler's adoption of the English alliance is that the Ruhr crisis revealed once again that Britain could not support France's aggressive policy towards Germany. For although Hitler's first statement suggesting agreements with England and Italy was delivered before the actual invasion of the Ruhr on 11 January 1923, the French had of course been threatening to take this step since the Spa conference of July 1920 and Britain's opposition to it was well-known. The German-Russian agreement at Rapallo in April 1922 had resurrected French fears of a German revival and had made her more adamant that reparations should be paid in full. In mid-July 1922, Germany had requested a full moratorium on payments and Britain, fearing that this meant a genuine inability to pay, felt inclined to agree, unlike the French, who were afraid that, once stopped, payments would not be resumed. Besides, since the United States refused to consider cancelling allied war debts, France could not afford to waive the claim to German reparations.[33] Clearly, therefore, Hitler had adequate warning of the general thrust of French policy and the probability of British opposition to it before January 1923.

It is also true that Hitler's alliance strategy hinged on the existence of Anglo-French tension; in December 1922, he pointed out, in a private discussion of his strategy, that 'England has an interest in seeing that we do not go under because otherwise France would become the greatest continental power in Europe, whilst England would have to be content with the position of a third-rate power'.[34] The Ruhr crisis was, therefore, important to Hitler; in *Mein Kampf*,

32. Report in *Vorwärts*, 28 January 1923, in NS 26/386. Rosenberg recalled in his memoirs that Hitler asked himself 'who, in their own interests, could not wish for an annihilation of Central Europe?', *Letzte Aufzeichnungen*, p. 318.

33. On the background to the reparations issue, see S. Marks, *The Illusion of Peace. International Relations, 1918–1933* (London, 1976), pp. 45–9.

34. Report to Chancellor Cuno by E. A. Scharrer entitled 'Bericht nach Hitlers persönlichen Ausführungen. Ende Dezember 1922' in BAK R43I/2681.

he wrote that it 'for the first time really basically alienated England from France'.[35] However, it needs to be emphasised again that there were signs of Britain being rehabilitated in *VB* articles dating back to the middle of 1921; Rosenberg and others clearly perceived even then that Britain's real interests dictated opposition to French policies in Europe. It is more likely, therefore, that the culmination of the reparations crisis at the end of 1922 and beginning of 1923 merely reinforced the trend towards support for a future Anglo-German alliance.

In fact, during 1922 hints that Britain was about to come back into favour appear (in retrospect) to have strengthened. Certainly in Rosenberg's ideological diatribes against World Jewry, the softening of the earlier anti-British tone is quite marked. In his pamphlet, *Der staatsfeindliche Zionismus*, written between May and September 1922, several alleged changes in relations between the British and the Jews (some intimated earlier) are given with greater clarity. Firstly, Rosenberg now denied that the aims of World Jewry and British imperialism were compatible. For example, he quoted the Zionist leader, Chaim Weizmann, saying in March 1922 that Palestine was useless for England from the strategic and military point of view.[36] Furthermore, he said that the Jews were undermining British interests in India and Ireland; in India they were encouraging the articulation of anti-British sentiments, whilst in Ireland a Jewish threat to finance the Irish had 'induced the English to make many concessions'.[37] Secondly, Rosenberg noted that the anti-Jewish faction in England was growing larger and more vocal.[38] Thirdly, he argued that British foreign policy 'which was co-determined by Jewish bankers and journalists' was running counter to Britain's best interests; at the Washington Naval Conferece, Britain had, according to Rosenberg, abandoned her traditional naval policy; ' . . . for centuries, England had fought ruthlessly for her naval supremacy . . . and always realised the need to drive the strongest from the field. In Washington, this England gave up her position with a grand gesture and without a struggle and renounced the alliance with Japan and transferred the leadership of world politics to the United States'.[39] Hence the Jews were working to destroy

---

35. Hitler, *MK*, p. 617.

36. A. Rosenberg, *Staatsfeindlicher Zionismus auf Grund jüdischer Quellen erläutert* (Munich, 1922), reprinted in *Schriften*, vol. 2, p. 75.

37. Rosenberg, *Zionismus*, p. 53.

38. Ibid., p. 52.

39. Ibid., pp. 53, 8, 23. The final phrase about the United States and the leadership of world politics was omitted from the 1943 edition, *Schriften* vol. 2, p. 92.

Britain because they had acquired a new patron in the United States; the relocation of the centre of Jewish affairs was complete; America was now 'the newly chosen cherub of Israel'.[40]

The fall of the British prime minister Lloyd George in October 1922 led Rosenberg to speculate about whether recent trends in British foreign policy would now be reversed. 'Against all British traditions', he declared, 'Lloyd George had abandoned, or rather had had to abandon [because of Jewish pressure] the policy of a European balance of power', thereby playing into the hands of the Jewish stock exchange and the French. Lloyd George's resignation provided an opportunity for the British to stand up to the Jews, but he was not confident that it would be taken. In any case, Britain would soon face 'an invincible France' and 'in this situation' he concluded, 'assistance for Germany must, of necessity, result'.[41]

This account of the Jewish distortion of British foreign policy and the growing disenchantment between the British and the Jews heralded a more positive attitude towards Britain in Nazi circles. Rosenberg was not alone in noting that British and German national interests were not incompatible. An unidentified writer in the *VB* on 4 October 1922 wrote that 'if . . . England were ruled by the British, then the hostile stance towards Germany after Versailles would have had to have ended'.[42] Thus the way for the inclusion of an Anglo-German alliance in a Nazi foreign policy programme may have been prepared over a year before Hitler first referred publicly to it in November 1922. The Ruhr crisis of 1922–23, therefore, may not have been the reason for the conversion from his previous anti-British outlook. Possibly British support for German claims in the Upper Silesian crisis had been crucial. Perhaps also her very real difficulties in India and Ireland and abandonment of the 'two-power naval standard' at Washington, which prompted Rosenberg's revisions of his ideological world-view, encouraged Hitler to believe that Britain's attitude towards Europe could change. Other possible factors will be examined later.

However, what needs to be stressed is that Hitler's adoption of the English alliance is unlikely to have been a 'solitary decision contrary

40. Rosenberg, *Zionismus*, p. 50. 'North America is today another name for Israel' wrote Rosenberg in 'Der Antisemitismus', *Deutschlands Erneuerung*, vol. 6 (1922), p. 367. The main reason for Rosenberg's belief that the headquarters of World Jewry had moved to New York was probably America's refusal to write off Allied war debts which necessarily meant the continuance of German reparations payments; Cecil, *Myth of the Master Race*, pp. 73–4.

41. A. Rosenberg, 'Lloyd Georges Rücktritt', *VB*, 21 October 1922.

42. 'Jüdische Weltpolitik', *VB*, 4 October 1922. The unidentified writer acknowledged several quotes from Rosenberg's *Staatsfeindlicher Zionismus*.

to opinion in the party', as Axel Kuhn has argued.[43] He suggests that 'the party' was sceptical about the prospects of a transformation of British foreign policy. That is true, but it is also true that Hitler expressed similar doubts about current British diplomacy in public even after November 1922. Distinction must be made between comments about the emerging (and for the most part concealed) Nazi foreign policy programme and the party's commentary on current developments in the diplomatic arena. The adoption of an Anglo-German alliance as part of the NSDAP foreign policy programme did not mean that Nazi propaganda could suddenly abandon criticism of contemporary British diplomacy. Hence, when Rosenberg wrote in July 1923 that despite Anglo-French tensions over the invasion of the Ruhr 'England is not contemplating a serious break with France at all', this did not mean that he was questioning the assumptions behind Hitler's alliance strategy but merely commenting on the current state of Anglo-French relations.[44]

Indeed Rosenberg shared Hitler's assumptions. In July 1923, he stated that 'England was always the opponent of the strongest state on the European continent' and as a result bound at some time to challenge the emerging French hegemony in Europe, but he felt that 'under present conditions', with Germany so weak that she was not fit to enter an alliance (*bündnisfähig*), 'we can expect no advantages from the eventual breach in Anglo-French relations'.[45] This was precisely the same argument used repeatedly by Hitler in 1923; 'in view of our lack of energy', he pointed out on one occasion, 'England will not feel obliged to do anything for us, even if it is not at all in her interest that France attain predominance in Europe. The same goes for Italy'.[46] In short, therefore, both men argued that England and Italy would aid Germany only when she was worthy of assistance, in other words when a National Socialist government had taken over. Hence, criticism of current British policy would continue, despite the incorporation of an English alliance in the Nazi foreign policy programme.

This tactic was probably a deliberate attempt by the Nazi Party to camouflage its ambitions in foreign affairs. The need to comment

43. Kuhn, *Programm*, pp. 91, 84–8.

44. A. Rosenberg, 'Der neue Gimpelfang', *VB*, 14 July 1923. The same is true about an article which Kuhn cites, in which it was suggested that forthcoming elections in Britain would not bring about any decisive change: (unsigned) 'Politische Rundschau', *VB*, 15 November 1922.

45. A. Rosenberg, 'England, Frankreich und Alljudaan', *VB*, 5 July 1923; cf. 'Deutsche Aussenpolitik II', *VB*, 17 February 1923.

46. Hitler's speech on 20 March, reported in *VB* 22 March 1923; see also his speech on 25 July, reported in *VB*, 27 July 1923.

regularly on current events posed problems, as Rosenberg revealed
when he wrote in the *VB* that 'we want to hold back our positive
appraisal [of foreign affairs] for the time being . . . and we will wait
reservedly on events [and] not lapse into daily cackle over every
piece of news'.[47] The reasons why the Nazis were concerned to avoid
public disclosure of their long-term foreign policy schemes will
become clear later but this smokescreen, of course, makes it difficult
to gauge the extent of opposition within the party to Hitler's thinking on the English alliance; there is evidence, however, that Rosenberg and perhaps other writers in the *VB* supported him.

In view of the relative secrecy surrounding the emergent alliance
policy, one wonders why Hitler was tempted to make the remarks he
did in November 1922 and January 1923. On the first occasion, at a
local party discussion evening in Haidhausen, it was perhaps significant that he was discussing a National Socialist state on the Italian
Fascist model. It is important to acknowledge the impact of the
emergence of Fascist Italy in October 1922 on the Nazi Party; the
success of a movement with similar aims must have been an encouraging sign for the NSDAP but, coinciding as it did with the political
demise of Lloyd George, the last of the main architects of the hated
Versailles Settlement to lose office, it amounted to a considerable
diplomatic revolution.[48] This may have persuaded Hitler to speculate about the future in November 1922. His comments at the party
conference in January 1923, on the other hand, were in all probability a response to the Ruhr invasion and the renewed evidence of
Anglo-French tensions. It has to be stressed, though, that the
remarks on both occasions were not presented as part of a Nazi
Party alliance strategy; they were isolated comments, in which
historians have identified things to come. In other words, Hitler
probably did not take any conscious decision to reveal parts of his
emerging strategy for foreign affairs in public at this time.

To sum up, therefore, the emergence of an English alliance as part
of the NSDAP's foreign policy programme was not an isolated or a
sudden decision taken by Hitler late in 1922; the *Umwendung* with
regard to England had been evolving for over a year, as Rosenberg's
views on the Jewish world conspiracy indicate.[49] It is, of course,

47. Rosenberg did point out that by 'reading between the lines', the party's 'positive
appraisal' could be worked out; 'England, Frankreich und Alljudaan', *VB*, 5 July 1923.

48. It was a turning point in Hitler's own fortunes: 'a few weeks after the March on Rome I
was received by Minister Schweyer. That would never have happened otherwise', H. R. Trevor-
Roper (ed.), *Hitler's Table Talk 1941–1944* (London, 1953), p. 10. Hitler was immediately portrayed
in Nazi propaganda as the 'Bavarian Mussolini', see Tyrell, *Trommler*, p. 274.

49. This revises Schubert's view that the introduction of ideology into Hitler's foreign policy

difficult to accept that changes such as the alleged disparity between British and Jewish ambitions and gradual transfer of Jewish allegiance from London to New York could have determined Hitler's choice of alliance partner. However, this is not quite so implausible as it appears, in view of real developments which could have given rise to such fantasies: for example, Britain's imperial problems, her disagreement with France over reparations payments and the American insistence on full repayment of allied war debts. Nevertheless, a more likely reason for Hitler's choice of England would be the mounting evidence of British sympathy for Germany, which the Nazis interpreted as a sign of the resurgence of Britain's traditional balance of power strategy. However, one cannot rule out the possibility that Hitler turned to England as a direct result of his revaluation of Germany's other prospective ally, Russia, which will be examined shortly.

The Emergence of an Italian Alliance

It might be imagined that the rise to power of Mussolini's Fascists in summer and autumn of 1922 contributed to the evolution of Hitler's alliance strategy late in that year. Certainly the presence of a new regime ideologically akin to National Socialism in Italy could not be ignored by Hitler and his friends. However, historians are agreed that the origins of his interest in an Italian alliance date back to 1920 at least, and therefore did not depend on the success of the Fascists in 1922.[50] In 1920 Hitler had made it clear that Italy had not been one of Germany's 'deadly enemies' before the war and that her grievances had been directed against Austria–Hungary, not Germany. In August 1920 he argued for the exploitation of Franco-Italian differences over Fiume in order to win Italian support for the German campaign against the Versailles Settlement.

However, it needs to be stressed that, as in the case of England, it was never intended that an Italian alliance should be the immediate objective of Weimar diplomats. In the speech in 1920, in which he first called for Italo-German cooperation, Hitler criticised those who

---

'changed nothing at least for the period up to 1923', *Anfänge*, p. 36.

50. W. Pese, 'Hitler and Italien 1920–1926', *VfZG* vol. 3 (1955), pp. 113, 116; Kuhn, *Programm*, pp. 43, 72. Hitler recalled in a letter to Colonel von Reichenau on 4 December 1932 that he had argued for an Italian alliance for 'about the last twelve years'; on 1 July 1940 he told the Italian ambassador to Germany that he had foreseen the alliance 'as early as twenty years ago'; both recollections quoted in Jäckel, *Hitlers Weltanschauung*, p. 33.

suggested that Germany should ally with a strong state: 'for this plan it is now too late; our view would still be the same if we had not given up our weapons, but had continued to fight. We are mere cannon fodder and defenceless. We in Germany lack national solidarity.'[51] International agreements, therefore, were of no use *until* Germany had been revived internally. Since Hitler almost certainly associated the resurgence of Germany with the rise to power of the Nazis, the Italian alliance could only be implemented when the National Socialists were in power in Germany and the nationalists in Italy.

Because the alliance lay in the future, therefore, the policies of the present Italian government could still be criticised. Once again, there was the duality in approach to foreign nations noted above. So despite the talk of possible German-Italian collaboration in August 1920, leading members of the Nazi Party remained critical of Italian policy and indeed of Germany's conciliatory stand towards Italy. In November 1920, as has been shown, Hitler accused German foreign minister Walter Simons of lacking national feeling because of a statement on the South Tyrol, the Austrian province transferred to Italy by the Treaty of Saint-Germain, which held out no hope of its return to Germany.[56] Clearly, therefore, Hitler remained publicly committed to his Pan-German ambitions of uniting all Germans in one Reich. Furthermore, in February 1921 the *VB* published an article entitled 'Deutschland und Italien', which criticised those 'harmless souls who are still always dreaming of a reawakening of German-Italian friendship'. The unnamed writer stated forcefully that Italians were very much afraid of a German-Austrian *Anschluss* because they felt Germany would 'acquire an Austrian outlook with regard to Italy. Italy, therefore has no interest whatsoever in encouraging a union'.[53]

Whether Hitler shared this latter view is uncertain, but certainly some Nazi Party members expected Italy to oppose two of the party's most fervent demands: the return of German-speaking lands lost at Versailles and the *Anschluss*. Certainly, there would seem to have been an inherent contradiction between Hitler's support for an Italian alliance and his stated *grossdeutsch* ambitions for Germany. In all probability, he had not fully thought out his ideas at this stage; he merely had an instinctive feeling that Italy and Germany were

51. Speech on 1 August 1920 reprinted in H. Preiss (ed.), *Adolf Hitler in Franken*, pp. 9–10.

52. Speech on 19 November, reported in *VB*, 25 November 1920; see also A. Hitler, 'Irrtum oder Vebrechen', *VB*, 13 February 1921. See above, p. 61.

53. 'R. (Innsbruck)', 'Deutschland und Italien', *VB*, 17 February 1922.

compatible because of their mutual hostility towards 'Versailles'.

Perhaps surprisingly, the rising fortunes of Mussolini and his movement received a hostile reception in the *VB*. An unnamed writer on 29 July 1922 attacked the idea of building a party on Fascist lines in Germany because of Mussolini's background; he had wanted a war against Germany in 1914 and 'for this reason every folkish-minded German ought already to have most keenly shunned contact with the trickster Mussolini'. Worse than that, the Fascist movement had no antisemitic aims, indeed it had been founded with Jewish money; honourable Fascists had been seduced by Jewish capital, and the fault lay with their leader, Mussolini, who was 'a hired traitor'.[54] A further article on 2 August stressed the similarities between National Socialists and the best Fascists; the Fascists were believed to be in the front line of Italy's struggle against Bolshevism, but, once again, Mussolini was criticised because his struggle was not directed against 'the world's enemy'.[55] The absence of anti-semitism in his programme seemed to damn him in Nazi eyes until on 7 August, with his ultimate victory still far from certain, Hitler made it clear (without mentioning Mussolini) that the new Italy would be ideologically akin to National Socialism; he referred again to the struggle between nationalism and internationalism; 'the struggle, which up to today only the Italian state is willing to carry on, we also must fight and this struggle must emanate from Bavaria'. However, in the same speech, Hitler reasserted the need for *Anschluss* with German Austria, showing that he had still not seriously thought about the implications of a future German-Italian alliance.[56]

Hitler would undoubtedly have let the thorny issues of the South Tyrol and the *Anschluss* remain unresolved for the time being if the rapid success of the Fascists had not altered the situation drastically. And this is the sense in which the Italian alliance was ideologically *fashioned* (if not originally ideologically motivated). The presence of a nationalist leader in Italy, whose success the Nazi Party could emulate as well as exploit for propaganda purposes, and from whom, perhaps, direct aid might be forthcoming, brought Hitler's theoretical speculation about future allies down to earth. If Italian aid were to materialise, there could be no obstacles to Nazi–Fascist collaboration. It was this situation which moulded the Italian alliance in Hitler's programme.

54. Unsigned article, 'Wulle-Mussolini', *VB*, 29 July 1922.
55. Unsigned article, 'Faschismus und Nationalsozialismus', *VB*, 2 August 1922.
56. Report in *VB*, 19 August 1922.

At precisely this moment, a new face appeared in the ranks of the NSDAP: Kurt Lüdecke, the son of a chemical works manager in Oranienburg (Berlin), who had worked as a travelling salesman after the war.[57] Lüdecke's arrival in the party coincided not only with the emergence of Mussolini in Italy, but with Hitler's own maturing as a political leader, which Mussolini's success only accelerated. The summer of 1922 had seen Hitler conspiring with Heinrich Class and associates to launch a national revolution and he was clearly beginning to display 'the arrogance of the prima donna', which so offended his Pan-German associates. The newly self-confident 'Führer', according to Lüdecke, quickly agreed with his proposal to try to establish contact with Mussolini, for 'to have an ally who was succeeding, even though the alliance was purely one of mutual sympathy, would be encouraging'.[58] Hence Lüdecke set off for Paris (to test the strength of the antisemitic movement there) and for Italy, intending, if possible, to visit Mussolini. In the resulting interview, almost certainly in September 1922, Mussolini made quite plain his position on the South Tyrol: 'No discussion about that ever . . . . Alto Adige is Italian and must remain so'.[59]

So the South Tyrol was clearly revealed as the stumbling block to possible collaboration between the Fascists and the Nazis and also to Hitler's alliance plans for the future. On Lüdecke's return, a serious discussion of Mussolini and Italy took place, in which, in his view, 'for the first time Hitler was really considering the ultimate possibilities of his programme in relation to the rest of Europe'. Whether it was, in fact, the first time Hitler had spelt out his alliance plans is unknown. If so, it would suggest that Mussolini's rise was a major factor in the timing of the evolution of that policy. Lüdecke's account of the discussion is interesting for the light it sheds on Hitler's foreign policy as a whole.

The natural future alliance of our new Germany, we agreed, should be England and eventually the northern European states, therefore, our logical effort — when we had the power — would be to alienate England

---

57. Lüdecke heard Hitler speak on 11 August 1922 and, after meeting him, decided to join the movement; biographical details can be found in a report from the Munich police to the Ministry of the Interior, dated 5 February 1923, in BHStA I/1755 and also in a report from the German Foreign Office to the *Staatsministerium des Aussen*, dated 21 December 1923, reprinted in E. Deuerlein, *Der Hitlerputsch* (Stuttgart, 1962), pp. 543–7.

58. K. Lüdecke, *I Knew Hitler*, p. 63.

59. Ibid., p. 73. It is evident from Lüdecke's account that Mussolini was not yet in power, ibid., p. 80.

from France. As a corollary of our organic growth, a German–English alliance was imperative. Forces currently dominant in England were, and would indefinitely remain, opposed to Nazi Germany, that we envisioned. With France holding a military trump card, and Germany isolated politically and economically, we were in no position to bargain with England. If we had any hope of understanding amongst the major powers, we should find it in Italy — if Mussolini came to power.[60]

Hitler's argument clarifies a number of points. Firstly, it illustrates precisely the approach to alliance policy indicated above; namely that the alliances were meant for a future (Nazi) Germany and a future English or Italian government. The present government policy in England was opposed to this and would remain so for an indefinite period. Secondly, the English alliance was vital to the process of German expansion, but Hitler knew already that it would be difficult to obtain. Thirdly, the Italian alliance was the most practicable prospect but it too was dependent on Mussolini's rise to power. For this reason, therefore, Hitler decided, 'the Tyrol was not too great a price to pay for Mussolini's friendship'.[61]

It must be said that Lüdecke's recollection in his memoirs of discussions with Hitler some sixteen years earlier was remarkable, but, none the less, his account of Hitler's thinking does seem to be borne out by other evidence. When on 14 November 1922, following Mussolini's rise to power, Hitler argued that the only way to increase German power was by executing the *Anschluss* with Austria, he stressed that prior Italian (and English) agreement would be necessary and continued:

Germany must collaborate with Italy, which is experiencing her national rebirth and has a great future. For that, a clear and binding renunciation by Germany of the Germans in South Tyrol is necessary. The idle talk over South Tyrol, the empty protests against the Fascists, only harm us since they alienate Italy from us. In politics there is no sentiment, only coldbloodedness. Why should we suddenly get excited over the closure of a dozen German schools in South Tyrol, when the German press keeps quiet over the closure of a thousand German schools in Poland, Alsace-Lorraine, and Czechoslovakia?[62]

60. Ibid., pp. 80–1. The reference to the 'Northern European States' — presumably the Scandinavian countries — was not followed up at the time.

61. The alliance would also be favourably received in Hungary and Bulgaria, Hitler argued, because of its anti-French orientation; ibid., p. 81.

62. Speech by Hitler on 14 November 1922 reported in *Münchener Post*, 20 December 1922, BHStA I/1766.

Clearly Hitler believed that renunciation of the South Tyrol would make the *Anschluss* palatable to the Italians.

Though Hitler might still argue in private that 'the South Tyrol question will perhaps, be more simply solved later by means of compensation', there was no denying his public commitment to the renunciation of the province or the fact that it flatly contradicted his Pan-German outlook[63] It has to be admitted, though, that the ADV itself rather 'soft-pedalled' the issue even before Mussolini's take-over, announcing on 20 October 1922 that

> if the Italian government and Italian people wish to live honourably in peace with us and on good terms: we are ready. A precondition, however, is that the national life of our South Tyrolean fellow-countrymen is not disturbed further and that the damage so far done is made good and atoned for. Otherwise, consequences could arise which could cause a violent end, and not only for many of the Fascists . . . but also for many others in the decaying Italian states.[64]

The Pan-Germans were evidently not insisting on the return of the South Tyrol either. None the less, Hitler's outright public abandon-ment of the South Tyrol was markedly different and likely to attract rightwing criticism, so he had to have good reason to specify in advance the concessions which a National Socialist government would be prepared to make to secure alliance.

This, of course, was the possibility of direct financial assistance from Mussolini or, at least, of association of some kind with his government, which itself would greatly enhance the prestige of the Nazi movement. To this end, Lüdecke made further visits to Italy in 1922 and 1923.[65] Probably as a result, Mussolini commissioned Tedaldi, the Italian representative on the Inter-Allied Rhineland Commission, to report on the political situation in Bavaria. In November 1922, Tedaldi, having heard Hitler expound his ideas on the Italian alliance and place the South Tyrol in the context of oppressed German communities elsewhere, could tell Mussolini that

63. Scharrer to Cuno BAK R43I/2681. Hitler admitted to Scharrer that Italian aid to Germany would depend on the latter's attitude towards the *Anschluss* and the South Tyrol question.

64. *Alldeutscher Blätter*, 20 October 1922. See also *A.Bl.*, 31 January 1920; *A.Bl.*, 14 January 1922.

65. Unsigned article, 'Erwachende Erkenntnis in Italien. Interview der "L'Epoca" mit Herrn Lüdecke', *VB*, 1 November 1923; see also the reports of the German Embassy in Rome, Deuerlein, *Der Hitlerputsch*, pp. 543–4 and A. Cassels, 'Mussolini and German nationalism', *Journal of Modern History* 35 (1963), pp. 147–8.

only Hitler's party could be relied on not to lay claim to the South Tyrol.[66] In any event, as the German Embassy officials who were monitoring these events in Rome concluded, Mussolini was 'too clever to compromise himself by an agreement to lend money which is being sought openly by the Hitler people'.[67] But whilst the search for short-term pecuniary gain proved fruitless, Hitler's alliance policy was in no way impaired by Mussolini's refusal to commit himself; the Nazi Party's renunciation of South Tyrol did at least bring it to Mussolini's attention and provide a common link. That was all Hitler could reasonably hope for at the time.

It would seem, therefore, that the accession of Mussolini to power in many respects crystallised Hitler's thoughts on an alliance with Italy. Though he noted earlier the advantages of exploiting Italian dissatisfaction with the Treaty of Versailles against France, the prospect of Mussolini as leader of Italy forced him to relate his alliance theories to reality and to confront the South Tyrol issue. To suggest that the rise of Mussolini played little part in fashioning the Italian element in Hitler's alliance policy is therefore misleading. The presence of a Fascist government with a compatible ideology (albeit short of antisemitism) was something which Hitler could not ignore. The rise of Fascism was probably the crucial factor in the timing of the evolution of Hitler's alliances; it certainly forced him, as Lüdecke suggested, in the autumn of 1922 to relate his instinctive convictions to a real-life situation, perhaps for the first time.

The decision on the Italian alliance does seem to have been Hitler's alone. Rosenberg had little to say about Italy before 1923, though no doubt he, along with others, noted with regret the absence of antisemitism from the Fascist programme.[68] He may also have had qualms about the renunciation of the South Tyrol Germans; in a revealing article on Nazi attitudes towards Fascist Italy in June 1923, he implied that the South Tyroleans would not be abandoned in perpetuity. He made it quite clear that the final aim of Nazi policy was the unification of all Germans in one state but, in Germany's present parlous state, she needed allies, principally Italy, and sacrifices had to be made accordingly. Hence, he stressed, 'the South Tyrolean question is not to be allowed to become a *casus belli*

66. Tedaldi to Mussolini, 17 November 1922, published in *I Documenti Diplomatici Italiani. Settima Serie, 1922–35*, vol. I (Rome, 1953), p. 80. See also E. Rosen, 'Mussolini und Deutschland, 1922–23', *VfZG* vol. 5, (1957), pp. 21–4.

67. Report by Neurath as German Ambassador in Rome to the German Foreign Office, 29 March 1923, Deuerlein, *Der Hitlerputsch*, p. 543.

68. 'Politische Rundschau', *VB*, 15 November; 'Die Weltpolitische Lage Ende 1922', *VB*, 30 December 1922. Both articles appear anonymously.

between the German and Italian people'. However, once Germany had recovered her true diplomatic standing, then it might be possible 'to incorporate our separated brothers in the new German Empire. For there are many places whose possession would be more valuable to [Italy] than the possession of the South Tyrol'.[69] Clearly, whilst accepting Hitler's renunciation of the region as a temporary expedient, Rosenberg refused to abandon all hope. This may have been the result of his own genuine *grossdeutsch* convictions or an attempt to soften the blow of an abandonment of German-speaking people which so transparently contradicted the *grossdeutsch* orientation of party propaganda.[70] What does seem likely is that Hitler made the decision and the Party, with varying degrees of enthusiasm, concurred.

The Alienation from Russia

During 1921 Hitler continued to stress the prewar compatibility of Russia and Germany and to criticise the imperial government's failure to ally with her eastern neighbour before or during the First World War. He also claimed, of course, that Germany and Russia were the two greatest enemies of World Jewry and that the Jewish-led Bolshevik Revolution was the prelude to a similar onslaught on Germany. So, although Bolshevik rule prevented it at the time, a Russo-German alliance did seem likely in 1921 to form part of a National Socialist alliance programme for the future. By the time Hitler was writing *Mein Kampf* in 1924, however, Russia was no longer a prospective ally, but had been decisively relegated to the ranks of Germany's foes. When and why did this dramatic change occur?

The obvious answer would be that in 1921 or at the latest 1922, the Bolshevik government, having been victorious in the civil war, appeared unlikely to be overthrown, in the foreseeable future. Historians have generally been unwilling, however, to accept this explanation for Hitler's abandonment of the idea of a German-

69. He added that 'we do not want to go into this further today'; Rosenberg, 'Deutschland und Italien', *VB*, 17/18 June 1923. Rosenberg did imply in his memoirs that he disagreed with Hitler occasionally over foreign policy; but it is not clear that it was over the Italian question; Rosenberg, *Letzte Aufzeichnungen*, p. 318.

70. Hermann Göring later suggested that it would be possible to find a solution 'satisfactory to both sides' provided that the harassment of the South Tyroleans stopped; he hinted at compensation for Italy at Fiume; Göring, 'Zum deutsch-italienischen Konflikt', *VB*, 3 and 9 February 1926.

Russian alliance, mainly because unambiguous evidence to this effect is lacking. Another partial reason, one suspects, is their reluctance to take seriously the possibility that Hitler was genuinely motivated by an antisemitic and anti-Bolshevik ideology, in other words that the survival of 'Jewish' Bolshevism made a German-Russian alliance unthinkable to him as anything other than a temporary expedient. Instead it is argued that Hitler remained undecided as to his position on Russia until 1924 when, at his leisure in Landsberg gaol following the Munich putsch, he finally thought through his alliance strategy and saw that the Anglo-German and German-Italian alliances originally directed against France would be equally applicable against Russia.[71] This sounds less than convincing.

So too does the suggestion that in 1924 Hitler took a 'solitary' decision to relegate Russia.[72] Most contemporary witnesses assert that in this respect he primarily listened to Alfred Rosenberg's advice. So a re-examination of Hitler's growing disenchantment with Russia should begin with an analysis of Rosenberg's changing ideas on the Russian question and of the extent to which Hitler seemed to rely on them.

The degree to which Hitler's view of the Russian Revolution was coloured by Rosenberg's accounts has already been described. As time went by, Hitler, unable to read Russian, relied even more on information gleaned by Rosenberg from Russian sources. That Hitler fed upon others in this way was apparent at the time. Konrad Heiden wrote in the 1930s that Hitler 'sucked up information which he could use hurriedly and greedily, as a dry sponge sucks water'.[73] Ernst Hanfstängl, a close collaborator in the early 1920s, also recalled Hitler's receptivity: 'I had been feeding him ideas and items of news culled from the foreign press and had been agreeably surprised to find them cropping up in his speeches'.[74] Rosenberg must have had the same experience: indeed, Hanfstängl's reason for trying to enlighten Hitler, particularly with regard to America, was to counteract Rosenberg's influence on Hitler, which he considered too narrowly eurocentric.[75]

In 1921, with the appearance of the party newspaper, the unmistakable similarity between Rosenberg's and Hitler's views on Russia

71. Kuhn, *Programm*, pp. 99, 102–3; Horn, 'Ein unbekannter Aufsatz', p. 280; K. Hildebrand, *Vom Reich zum Weltreich*, p. 75. Only J. Düllfer has seriously questioned this scenario, *Weimar, Hitler und die Marine. Reichspolitik und Flottenbau, 1920–1939* (Düsseldorf, 1973), p. 207.

72. Kuhn, *Programm*, p. 115.

73. Heiden, *National Socialism*, p. 80.

74. Hanfstängl, *Missing Years*, p. 52.

75. Ibid., pp. 64, 43, 90, 121.

became more evident as the party leaders began to comment regularly on current events abroad. In 1920 Hitler's fear of Bolshevism seems to have been heightened by the belief that Pan-Slavism and Russia's expansionist ambitions in Western Europe had been revitalised by the Russo-Polish war. With the conclusion of the war, this primarily strategic consideration soon disappeared and in January 1921 Hitler wrote that 'the threatening Bolshevik flood is not so much to be feared as a consequence of Russian-Bolshevik victories on the battlefields as of a systematic destruction of our own people [by Bolshevik ideas]'.[76] Writing in the *VB* on 6 March 1921, he criticised those Germans who were calling for a Russian alliance to counterbalance Western pressure on the reparations issue, by arguing that contemporary Russia represented 'at least in power-political terms, little more than a cripple compared to the former Czarist state'.[77]

In the same issue of the *VB*, Rosenberg revealed the reason for Hitler's low estimate of the strength of Bolshevik Russia when he claimed that 'the whole of Russia is in revolt against the terror of the Jews. We do not know whether it will now be finally broken . . . [but] the days of Jewish Bolshevism in Russia are numbered'. On the other hand, if Germany were to accept a *Diktat* on reparations, then she too would face the same Jewish terror as in Russia but carried out by foreign troops; 'in Russia, it is the Latvians and Chinese who "pacify" the workers . . . with machine guns'. An alliance with the Bolsheviks, however, was not the solution; the Germans, according to Rosenberg, had to resist both the Jewish bankers in London (who were behind the reparations issue) and 'the enticements from the East'.[78]

Significantly, nine days after this article appeared on 6 March, Hitler repeated not only Rosenberg's general assessment of the situation in Russia but also many incidentals as well. 'After an unprecedented three years of bloody dictatorship', he wrote, 'the Bolshevik regime is beginning to totter.' The Russian worker was turning against 'the Jewish bloodhounds, who lay him low with knouts and machine guns' and against the torture administered by 'the Chinese and Latvian terror-guards'; finally the Russian proletariat was being moved to revolt against Bolshevism and in Russia

---

76. A. Hitler, 'Ist die Errichtung einer die breiten Massen erfassenden völkischen Zeitung eine nationale Notwendigkeit? II', *VB*, 30 January 1921.

77. A. Hitler, 'Deutschlands letzte Hoffnung', *VB*, 6 March 1921.

78. A. Rosenberg, 'Schicksalswende in London', *VB*, 6 March 1921.

this could only mean, in Hitler's view, 'the rooting out of the Jews'.[79] The close correlation between the two accounts, which interestingly linked ideology and power politics directly, is too striking to be coincidental.

The *VB* continued for some time to predict the downfall of Bolshevism and Hitler clearly seems to have taken his lead from Rosenberg and drawn snippets of information from the latter's articles attacking the Bolshevik government.[80] However, running alongside and complementing the day-to-day criticism of Bolshevik misdeeds, were frequent expressions of sympathy and support for the Russian people, especially for the nationalist forces working to overthrow Bolshevism. As Rosenberg had written on several occasions, if these (predictably 'antisemitic') forces were to succeed, then they would be the natural allies for Germany. In January 1921 he expressed the hope that his revelations about a Judeo-Masonic conspiracy against Czarist Russia would lead to 'a German-Russian national (that is, anti-Jewish) united front'.[81] Hitler seems to have accepted this ideological scenario, claiming in August 1921 that the only assistance which the German people could give the Russians lay in 'the annihilation of the present rulers of Russia'.[82]

These ideological comments appear to indicate that Hitler and Rosenberg, whilst condemning all suggestions of collaboration between Germany and Bolshevik Russia, still considered Russia as a possible ally in the future. This seems to be confirmed by their occasional references to prewar German diplomacy. On 6 March 1921 Hitler restated his conviction that an understanding between Germany and Russia (and with no-one else) in 1915 or 1916 would have been the former's salvation.[83] Interestingly, Rosenberg followed a similar line in a rare excursion into the field of pure power politics. He criticised German diplomats for maintaining a dialogue with Britain in the last years before the war and for 'counting on Great Britain's "magnanimity" instead of — as sound German interests dictated — uniting also with Russia, in my opinion at the

---

79. A. Hitler, 'Staatsmänner oder Nationalverbrecher', *VB*, 15 March 1921.

80. On 4 August 1921 Hitler spoke disapprovingly of attempts to collect food in Germany for starving Russians, arguing that all relief essentially aided the Jewish commissars. In this case he picked up a news item on relief aid in Russia published by Rosenberg that same day; 'Der Pogrom am deutschen und russischen Volke', *VB*, 4 August 1921; report on Hitler's speech in *VB*, 11 August 1921.

81. Rosenberg, 'Das Verbrechen', *Agd*, 15 January 1921, pp. 8–9.

82. Hitler's speech on 4 August, report in *VB*, 11 August 1921.

83. A. Hitler, 'Deutschlands letzte Hoffnung', *VB*, 6 March 1921.

expense of Austria–Hungary'.[84] It is not altogether clear whether Rosenberg was really suggesting German alliances with both Russia and England here; if so, then he evidently did not share Hitler's view that the two alliances were mutually exclusive alternatives.

Nevertheless, both men seemed to perceive Russo-German collaboration as dictated by the interests of both countries. There is no sign of the belief in Slav inferiority which was to underlie later anti-Russian policies. As has been seen, Rosenberg did make some critical remarks about the Russians in 1919 but, though he regarded the Russians as inferior to the Germans, he felt that the two peoples had a natural affinity; they were 'the noblest peoples of Europe', drawn to one another 'not only politically but also culturally'.[85]

Thus Hitler and Rosenberg were broadly in agreement on the Russian question, judging by their ideological commitment to the Russian people in the struggle against Bolshevism, their observations on prewar German diplomacy and the absence of any extreme racial elitism towards the Slavs. As in the case of Britain and Italy, they continued to criticise the actions of the current government in Russia, whilst retaining their belief in the possibility of collaboration with a future nationally-orientated government. On Russian affairs, Hitler seemed willing to accept Rosenberg's interpretation of events.

After the leadership crisis of July 1921, when Hitler's own contributions to the *VB* became fewer, and after Eckart took over editorial control of it in August, Rosenberg's influence on the party's interpretation of foreign affairs grew still more. He became the most regular contributor to the paper and did the bulk of the editorial work during Eckart's increasingly frequent bouts of indolence. As unofficial editor of the *VB*, Rosenberg was in a good position to sway opinion in the Party. The paper became preoccupied with Bolshevik Russia, as Ernst Hanfstängl discovered when he tried to arouse interest in some newspaper clippings; 'all Rosenberg wanted were articles and news items dealing with his particular anti-Bolshevist, anti-clerical, anti-semitic prejudices', he later complained.[86] Though Hanfstängl must be treated as a hostile witness, the substance of his criticism is borne out by reading the *VB* in 1921 and 1922. Rosenberg had established himself as the party authority on Russian affairs and was in a position to influence others. As the

84. A. Rosenberg, 'Die "Frankfurter Zeitung". Eine Abrechnung', *VB*, 14 August 1921.
85. Rosenberg, 'Das Verbrechen', *Agd* 28 February 1921, p. 120.
86. Hanfstängl, *Missing Years*, p. 71.

editor of a collection of his writings put it later, it was from his articles and speeches that 'the speakers and politicians of our movement collected material for their struggle, material indeed which was not only sharply honed but also true and incontrovertible'.[87]

The signing of the Treaty of Rapallo on 16 April 1922 by representatives of the Russian and German delegations to the Genoa economic conference provided a test of Nazi convictions on foreign affairs. As always, developments suggesting that Germany might have friends abroad posed problems of interpretation for Nazi audiences used to hearing that their country was surrounded by hostile conspiratorial powers. In December 1921 Rosenberg had typically explained the limited trade agreement of 6 May 1921 between Germany and the Soviet Union as a pretext for Bolshevik intervention in German internal affairs.[88] And, even before hearing of the Treaty of Rapallo signing, Hitler and Rosenberg had been suspicious of Russian offers of economic concessions to the capitalist West, fearing Western recognition of the Soviet Union.[89] As it happened, it was after all Germany who bestowed de facto recognition on the Soviet regime by signing the Rapallo treaty. How did the Nazis react?

The *VB*'s first reaction on 19 April was to denounce it as a 'great trick': 'Germany will be allowed to build up Soviet Russia with her technical science, her labour and her sweat, so that the stock exchange Jews from the rest of the world can take over the administration without risk . . . . The German–Russian treaty is the continuation of Pan-Jewish–Anglo-Saxon world policy and the exploitation of German impotence.'[90] On 21 April Hitler condemned the treaty because it furthered the destruction of the German as well as the Russian state, fulfilling the aim of the world stock exchange: 'in Russia', he declared, 'the Jews and their Chinese–Latvian security guards rule . . . . The same is being arranged for us. Genoa means the lasting enslavement of Germany.' And he concluded: 'Russia is not the last straw at which Germany, like a drowning man, can

---

87. Thilo von Trotha's introduction to A. Rosenberg, *Kampf um die Macht. Aufsätze von 1921–1932* (Munich, 1937), p. 13. He was referring to Rosenberg's articles between 1923 and 1925 but the comment was even more appropriate to his earlier writings.

88. A. Rosenberg, 'Regierungsbolschewismus im Reich', *VB*, 3 December 1921.

89. See Hitler's speech on 12 April 1922 in Boepple, *Adolf Hitler's Reden*, pp. 8–9; A. Rosenberg, 'Genua', *VB*, 19 April 1922.

90. Unsigned article, 'Genua', *VB*, 19 April 1922.

clutch, but a lead weight which instantly pulls us down into the depths.' The ideological nature of Hitler's rejection of the Rapallo treaty is quite apparent. An alliance with the Bolsheviks was to him anathema but, significantly, he reiterated his support for the Russian people. What could assist Germany, he argued, was not negotiations with those who were despoiling Russia, but German encouragement of the Russian people 'to shake off their tormentors in order then to draw nearer to them'.[91]

Hitler's response to the treaty does not appear to indicate any change in his attitude towards Russia. However, when Rosenberg gave his analysis of Rapallo on 3 May 1922, its real significance for the Nazis became clear. Rosenberg was very concerned about the Comintern's reaction to Rapallo- its call for a Russo-German alliance against France; this, as he admitted, inevitably found a ready echo in many German nationalist circles. Here was the test of the strength of Nazi convictions about Russia, for if the destruction of the arch-enemy France had been of paramount importance, then surely even a 'pact with the devil', the Soviet Union, would have been an acceptable short-term price to pay? Rosenberg did not think so; a military alliance with a decaying Soviet Russia against France, in his words, would be 'the greatest crime against the German people'. Germany was disarmed and certain to be defeated, but in any case the idea of such a conflict, which the Jewish press was also propagating in France, was evidently yet another attempt by the stock exchange and Soviet Jews to reduce Germany to a state of prostration.[92]

From Rosenberg, this was of course entirely predictable. More surprising, since he had said he would rather die in a Bolshevik Germany than live in a 'frenchified' Germany, was Hitler's repetition of precisely the same argument two days after the publication of Rosenberg's assessment. 'Whilst internationalism is being preached in Germany and, today, plans for a campaign against France are being worked out in communist lairs', he asserted, 'the same frivolous game is being played in France the other way round with extreme nationalism'. Only high finance, he concluded, could profit from inciting a Franco-German war.[93]

It is, of course, true that Hitler was unlikely to admit in public,

91. Hitler's speech on 21 April, report in *VB*, 26 April 1922.

92. A. Rosenberg, 'Frankreich in Genua', *VB*, 3 May 1922. The Pan-German press concurred, railing against a 'pact with the devil' and 'with an already decomposing corpse'; unsigned article, 'Zur Zeitgeschichte', *A.Bl.*, 22 April 1922.

93. Hitler's speech on 5 May, reported in *VB*, 13 May 1922.

even if he might have done so privately, that he supported an alliance with Russia against France. Nazi propaganda, as ever, required the sharpest condemnation of Weimar policies — in this case, the Treaty of Rapallo. So one cannot argue that Hitler's response to Rapallo necessarily showed that he was moving away from the concept of a future German-Russian alliance. What is significant is that the treaty seems to have brought home to him the central importance of Bolshevik Russia to his party's *Weltanschauung*. On 21 April, in the immediate aftermath of the news of the Rapallo agreement, he declared that 'the greatest task for our people still stands before it: to be leader in the coming struggle of the Aryans against the world-wide Jewish threat'.[94] For Hitler and the other party leaders such as Eckart and Hermann Esser, Rapallo seemed to symbolise the partnership between capitalism and revolutionary socialism; in a speech on 22 June, Hitler described the Soviet representatives and Western bankers walking arm-in-arm through the streets of Genoa and spoke of the need for a new *Weltanschauung*: 'Bolshevism is the final consequence of materialistic Marxism. To rise against this is the mission of the German people. The goal: the Germanic Empire of the German Nation. The deadly enemy: Jewry!'[95]

It must be stressed that, as yet, there was little apparent change in Hitler's view of foreign affairs; he still condemned collaboration with the Soviet Union, and promised support to the Russian people and a future nationalist government. However, he was now beginning to accept Soviet Russia as a permanent feature of the diplomatic scene and was making opposition to Bolshevism the pivot of Nazi ideology. The struggle against the Versailles Settlement (and the war of revenge against France) were only part of that ideology and no longer the main rationale of his outlook on foreign affairs. The Treaty of Rapallo may have helped to crystallise the change, but there is evidence that this had already been under way before the treaty was signed.

Early in 1922 Hitler went on a long tour of Germany trying to attract support from nationalist circles and, from reports of one of these private encounters, his assessment of the Russian question at

94. Hitler's speech on 21 April, reported in *VB*, 26 April 1922.
95. Report in *VB*, 24 June 1922. See also D. Eckart, 'Ein neuer Weltkrieg in Sicht', *VB*, 17 May 1922; the report on a speech by Hermann Esser in *VB*, 24 May 1922; and A. Rosenberg, 'Gegen die jüdische Bankenpest', *VB*, 31 May 1922.

that time can be determined. During the tour — probably in March 1922 — he delivered a speech to the *Juniklub*, named to commemorate the signing in June 1919 of the abhorred Treaty of Versailles, and met its leading light, Arthur Moeller van den Bruck.[96] Moeller was, by all accounts, a quiet serious man, a political writer and cultural historian; he was not a gifted public speaker, but wielded great influence over his associates through his prowess in discussion.[97] His major literary achievements were a new edition of Dostoevski's novels and *Das Dritte Reich*, the famous book often mistakenly assumed because of its title to anticipate the Nazi period.[98]

Hitler's usual beer-hall tirade on the 'Breaking of Interest-Slavery' left the intellectually sophisticated, and by the end somewhat depleted, audience at the *Juniklub* quite unmoved, but a private conversation then ensued between himself and Moeller. Hitler left this discussion greatly impressed by Moeller, according to Rudolf Pechel, the editor of *Deutsche Rundschau* and a member of the *Juniklub*; he is said to have told his host: 'You have everything I lack. You are creating the spiritual framework for Germany's reconstruction. I am but a drummer and an assembler. Let us work together.' Unfortunately, the admiration was not mutual: Moeller is reported to have commented after Hitler's departure that 'that fellow will never grasp it'.[99]

Hans Grimm, the poet, author of the influential novel *Volk ohne Raum* and a close friend and associate of Moeller, has related the latter's account of the encounter.[100] According to this, the two men quarrelled over foreign policy; 'it seemed to me', Grimm recalled,

96. Hitler's visit to the Juniklub must have occurred between the end of February, when he delivered his last speech before embarking on his tour, and 1 April 1922, when the *VB* announced his return to Munich. Rudolf Pechel, editor of *Deutsche Rundschau*, had learned about Hitler from geopolitician Karl Haushofer, and invited him to speak in Berlin; R. Pechel, *Deutscher Widerstand* (Zurich, 1947), pp. 277–80.

97. I rely here on the recollections of Moeller's friends; P. Fechter, *Menschen und Zeiten. Begegnungen aus fünf Jahrzehnten* (Gütersloh, 1949), pp. 329–33, and his *Moeller van den Bruck. Ein politisches Schicksal* (Berlin, 1934); H. Grimm, *Warum–Woher–Aber Wohin — vor, unter, und nach der geschichtlichen Erscheinung Hitlers* (Lippoldsberg, 1954), pp. 95–101, 108.

98. First published in 1923. On Moeller's influence see especially O. E. Schüddekopf, *Linke Leute von Rechts. Die nationalrevolutionären Minderheiten und der Kommunismus in der Weimarer Republik* (Stuttgart, 1960), p. 89 and H. J. Schwierskott, *Arthur Moeller van den Bruck und der revolutionäre Nationalismus in der Weimarer Republik* (Göttingen, 1962), pp. 103–14.

99. Pechel, *Deutscher Widerstand*, pp. 278–80.

100. Grimm suggests that the meeting between Moeller and Hitler took place in 1920; *Warum*, p. 108. It is possible that there had been a meeting in 1920 in which Hitler failed to impress Moeller; this might explain Moeller's anger at Pechel's arbitrary invitation to Hitler in 1922; Pechel, *Deutscher Widerstand*, p. 279. On the whole, this appears unlikely, however, as Grimm's account of the meeting in no way conflicts with Pechel's.

'that Russia and Bolshevism and its significance for Germany was touched upon by both men, and this had led to a basic difference of opinion'. Moeller saw in Bolshevism hope for Germany; he expected that Russian nationalism would of necessity emerge from Russian Bolshevism and that it would encourage Russo-German friendship. Hitler rejected this 'National Bolshevik' argument, fearing that such collaboration would lead to the influx of 'squadrons of Asiatic Bolsheviks' into Germany.[101]

The full implications of this disagreement can only be grasped within the context of Moeller's overall views on foreign policy. Central to his whole outlook was his belief in the existence of 'young' and 'old' nations. The distinction between these two groups, apparent as early as 1906 in his book *Die Deutschen*, was based principally on political longevity, cultural performance and population growth. The 'young nations' — Germany, Russia and America — were newly-formed states, culturally prolific and with expanding populations, whilst the 'old' nations — France, England and (perhaps surprisingly) Italy — were in cultural and demographic decline.[102] The similarity with Oswald Spengler's ideas on the decline of the West is obvious.[103] From this early stage Moeller argued that Germany should 'conquer a political share of the empire of the world'.[104] Such imperialistic expansion was justified in terms of geopolitics: 'as soon as the space has become too confined for a people', he wrote, 'it breaks over its borders and leads us to a point where we must adopt a world policy (*Weltpolitik*) in order to become a world people'.[105]

These ideas, first set out in 1906, underwent little modification over the years; Moeller's rejection of the Western European powers and his belief in the natural community of interest between the 'young nations', particularly Germany and Russia, survived the First World War, during which Russia and America were at odds with Germany. During the war, the direction of his proposed German expansion became evident; he declared that 'we must take a share of the East, to which we, in our own way, half belong and on which we

---

101. Grimm, *Warum*, p. 108. Hitler claimed to be quoting a remark by Karl Radek, a member of the Comintern's executive, to the effect that what the rightwing New Order in Germany needed was the addition of 'squadrons of Asiatic Bolsheviks'.

102. Moeller believed that the world was no longer divided into races but peoples; 'Die Deutschen', reprinted in H. Schwarz (ed.), *Das ewige Reich. Bd. 1: Die politischen Kräfte* (Breslau, 1933), pp. 331, 337–8.

103. Moeller described Spengler's work as 'the fateful book of our whole generation', cited in H. Schwarz (ed.), *Das Recht der jungen Völker* (Berlin, 1932), p. 13.

104. Moeller, 'Die Deutschen', p. 330.

105. Ibid., p. 336.

border, if we want to have a share in the future: air to breathe, space for movement, time for development'.[106] This expansion could only take place at the expense of Russia, so how could Moeller hope for Russo-German collaboration at the same time? The answer was that Russia would turn her back on Europe after her defeat and resume her proper role as an Asiatic eastward-looking power, abandoning her non-Russian land in the West. In the wake of the Treaty of Brest-Litovsk, he wrote in August 1918 that 'Russia is returning to her natural frontier, spatially as well as spiritually. That is the result for Russia, for Europe. It is signified by the reciprocal action which is not pushing Russia towards the West, but rather Europe towards the East.' For Moeller such expansion was not naked imperialism, but a resumption of the natural course of European development, which had been impeded only by Russia's attempt to become a European power. The areas to be acquired by the 'West' (that is, Germany) were 'the former Russian border areas, which, like the Baltic States, like Finland and Poland, have already been for a long time "culturally" part of Central Europe'. 'The same, however', he concluded ambiguously, 'applied to Russia herself'.[107]

After the war Moeller's attitude appears to have moderated. He produced what he called a 'socialistic foreign policy', which consisted primarily of 'adopting an association with Russia and playing off the revolutionary East against the capitalistic West'.[108] Historians have been unable to agree whether this 'Eastern orientation' meant that Moeller had now rejected expansion eastwards in favour of unconditional German-Russian collaboration in the creation of an Eastern European cultural community. Fritz Stern, for example, recognises the imperialistic streak in Moeller's ideas but feels that it was 'the vision of an aesthete' and not based on an objective appraisal of the political situation.[109] Others, on the contrary, have seen the old imperialistic ideas veiled by high-sounding talk of peaceful expansion, federations and so on; it was, according to one writer, simply the implementation of the Treaty of Brest-Litovsk by

106. A. Moeller, 'Unser Problem ist der Osten', first published on 10 May 1918, reprinted in H. Schwarz (ed.), *Rechenschaft über Russland*, (Berlin, 1933), p. 137.

107. A. Moeller, 'Die einzige Gewissheit', first published on 8 August 1918, reprinted in Schwarz, *Rechenschaft*, p. 175.

108. A. Moeller, 'Deutsche Grenzboten', first published on 19 May 1920, reprinted in H. Schwarz (ed.), *Sozialismus und Aussenpolitik* (Breslau, 1933), p. 65.

109. F. Stern, *The Politics of Cultural Despair*, pp. 202–9. Others who took a more charitable view of Moeller's 'imperialism' include R. Adam, *Moeller van den Bruck* (Königsberg, 1933), p. 11; K. von Klemperer, *Germany's New Conservatism* (Princeton, N.J., 1968), p. 159 and K. O. Paetel, 'Der deutsche Nationalbolschewismus 1918/1932: Ein Bericht', *Aussenpolitik* vol. 3 (1952), pp. 229, 232.

other methods, and there is surely some justification for this charge.[110] The whole trend of Moeller's writing before and during the First World War indicated a desire for German expansion eastwards; in the postwar period, he remained committed to the idea of imperialism, the only point still in doubt being the direction it would take. On the one occasion after the war when he was specific about his territorial ambitions for Germany in the east, Moeller showed that he had *grossdeutsch* ambitions at the very least; he wanted 'the frontiers of nationality' not the 'frontiers of the map'.[111] In all probability, his hopes were unchanged from those before the war: that Germany would expand eastwards and, with cooperation from an 'Asiatic Russia', would secure her spatial requirements at the expense of the newly independent states of Eastern Central Europe. What is certain is that, if there were cooperation between Germany and Russia, it was to be very much on German terms. As Moeller explained in August 1920: 'cooperation with Russia was only possible with independence from Russia'; the Russian revolutionaries, therefore, had to recognise that 'each land has its own socialism' and they were not to try to impose their socialism on Germany.[112] The Bolsheviks had to abandon their international aspirations: 'Bolshevism is Russian. And it is only Russian', declared Moeller in February 1920. If Lenin accepted this, then Russo-German cooperation against their common enemies, France and Britain, could begin.[113]

This was evidently the point over which Moeller and Hitler were at odds during their discussion. Hitler could not accept that the Bolsheviks would resist the temptation to extend Bolshevism to Germany. As a result, his verdict on the Treaty of Rapallo differed decisively from that of the older man. Whilst Hitler saw alliance with Soviet Russia as a fatal error, for Moeller it signified not a goal but 'a direction': 'the direct result of this decision is for Russia at the moment perhaps great, for Germany perhaps only small. But the

---

110. J. Petzold, 'Zur Funktion des Nationalsozialismus. Moeller van den Brucks Beitrag zur faschistischen Ideologie', *Zeitschrift für Geschichtswissenschaft* vol. 21, (1973), p. 1289.

111. A. Moeller, 'Deutsche Grenzpolitik', first published on 19 May 1920, reprinted in Schwarz, *Das Recht*, p. 70.

112. A. Moeller, 'Russland', first published on 4 August 1920, reprinted in Schwarz, *Das Recht*, pp. 65–7.

113. 'When Bolshevism pushed towards India, then it meant England. And when it pressed against Poland, then it meant France. It meant our enemies. That unites the Russian and the German socialism': A. Moeller, 'Sozialistische Aussenpolitik', first published on 11 February 1920, reprinted in Schwarz, *Sozialismus*, pp. 77–82. When, however, Karl Radek made a direct proposal in 1923 to German rightwing groups for collaboration against the West, Moeller ultimately avoided 'Radek's threatened embrace', Stern, *Politics*, p. 252. It may be that Radek's

indirect result is incalculable, because this decision is the first step on the way to a grouping of nations which want to live.'[114]

In fact, this dispute may reveal a change in Hitler's outlook during 1922. In October 1921, as has been seen, he had endorsed the view that a prewar German alliance with Russia would have allowed Germany to expand eastwards — precisely the argument with which Moeller (and the Pan-Germans) had been associated at the time of the Treaty of Brest-Litovsk in March 1918.[115] So it is likely that his disagreement with Moeller showed that he had abandoned the idea of eastward expansion in collaboration with Russia. This could mean either that Hitler was now taking very seriously the party's anti-Bolshevik ideology and would not consider collaboration with Soviet Russia against the newly independent states of Eastern Central Europe or that his territorial ambitions extended further than this, that is, into Russia itself (or, of course, both).

Hitler's response to the Treaty of Rapallo and to his encounter with Moeller van den Bruck shows that his attitude towards Russia had hardened. The increased virulence of his anti-Bolshevism and his rejection of 'National Bolshevism' may have been attributable to the influence of a more critical view of Russia propagated by Rosenberg during 1921–2 and perhaps also to Hitler's association with Dr. Max-Erwin von Scheubner-Richter, who had contacts with a group of Russian nationalists in exile in Southern Germany. The latter, not unnaturally, were opposed to any form of collaboration between Germany and the Bolshevik rulers of Russia. Certainly the changing views of Rosenberg on Russia and the influence of Scheubner-Richter on Hitler deserve closer examination.

Hitler's rejection of Moeller's arguments for Russo-German cooperation on the grounds that Germany would be subjected to the invasion of 'squadrons of Asiatic Bolsheviks' clearly seems to have been influenced by Rosenberg's interpretation of Bolshevism as an 'Asiatic pestilence'.[116] 'National Bolshevism' was impossible in Russia, according to Rosenberg, because Bolshevism was the product of an alien, non-Russian, culture. Rosenberg, by no means always a

---

concrete approach intruded awkwardly upon Moeller's purely intellectual russophilism. See also Schüddekopf, *Linke Leute*, p. 151.

114. A. Moeller, 'Politik der Willen', first published on 24 April 1922, reprinted in Schwarz, *Rechenschaft*, p. 190.

115. See above, p. 96.

116. The title of an article by Rosenberg in *Agd*, 12 December 1919.

Russophobe as some have suggested, had a great admiration for Russian culture, particularly for the works of Dostoevski and Tolstoy and at first he had denied that the Bolshevik leaders were Slavs at all and claimed that the Bolshevik regime had been destroying everything that was genuinely Russian.[117] However, as the Russian people proved incapable of overthrowing Bolshevism during the Russian civil war, his view of Bolshevism and the Russian people very gradually began to change.

The change was most apparent in his pamphlet, *Pest in Russland*, published in late June or early July 1922. Although Bolshevism was still regarded as a disease originating in the East, it was no longer considered totally alien to the Russian people. Rosenberg now identified a 'dormant anarchistic impulse' in the Russian character, which surfaced occasionally, as in the reign of Ivan the Terrible and the Strelzi rising in Peter the Great's time, for example, and which formed a direct link with the 'anarchism' of Bakunin, Trotsky and Zinoviev. Dostoevski, in his view, had shown that 'even the most genial Russian for no accountable reason can suddenly become a criminal and a murderer'.[118] For Rosenberg, *Crime and Punishment* evidently held the key to the Russian psyche! The anarchistic impulse which it revealed and which was responsible for the bloodletting, the rejection of Western values and indeed the denigration of past Russian achievements in the Bolshevik Revolution was ultimately, he believed, the result of 'a profound blood-mixture' during the period of Tartar domination of Russia. Ever since that time, the European and Asiatic elements in the Russian character had been at odds with one another. Bolshevism therefore represented a resurgence of Asiatic blood, Rosenberg claimed in 1922, 'a new deployment of the Near Eastern spirit against Europe'.[119] The Jews, of course, were orchestrating this new 'Mongol' advance.[120]

Nevertheless, though Rosenberg's view of Bolshevism and the Russians had changed, he had not abandoned the idea of a German alliance with a future non-Bolshevik Russia and, indeed, in the foreword to the second edition of *Pest in Russland*, he maintained that anti-Bolshevik forces were gaining in strength.[121] However, his

---

117. See above, p. 11, Laqueur, *Russia*, p. 70, R. C. Williams, *Culture in Exile. Russian Emigrés in Germany 1881–1941* (Ithaca and London, 1972), p. 168, and Horn, 'Ein unbekannter Aufsatz', pp. 392–3, all exaggerate Rosenberg's original hostility towards Russia. Boehm, 'Baltische Einflüsse', p. 64 presents a rather more accurate view.

118. Rosenberg, *Pest in Russland*, p. 38.

119. Ibid., pp. 93–94.

120. Ibid., p. 81.

121. Foreword to the second edition, dated March 1924, ibid., p. 6.

doubts about the purity of Russian blood represented a marked lowering of his estimation of Germany's would-be ally.

This change was also reflected in the appearance of a different attitude towards separatist movements inside Russia. In May 1921, Rosenberg had criticised the Berlin government at the time of the Treaty of Brest-Litovsk for having encouraged separatist movements inside Russia, instead of trying to unite all her peoples behind a nationalist regime representing a united Russian empire against the Bolsheviks.[122] But in 1922 he acknowledged the value of separatism, especially Ukrainian separatism, as a means of undermining the Bolshevik state.[123] Once again, the modification was slight but significant; Rosenberg still opposed the granting of independence to Poland and the Baltic states, which had contributed to Bolshevik success, but now he was beginning to recognise the usefulness of unsatisfied nationalism in the Ukraine to his own anti-Bolshevik crusade.

This had wider implications. Emerging in Rosenberg's mind at this time was a vision of a future Russia as a 'nation-state'. As explained in his memoirs, he had come to appreciate that the Russia of 1914 or 1917 was 'not a nation-state in the sense of Germany or France'. He went on:

> If one leaves aside the vexed question of the Ukraine or White Ruthenia, it was clear that Finland was not Russian. Neither the Balts, nor the Estonians, nor the Latvians, were Russians. All Caucasians were old peoples; Georgia was a state almost a thousand years old. The people of Turkistan were completely different from Russians. Russia was, therefore, despite the natural predominance of the Russians, a state of nationalities (Nationalitäten-Staat).[124]

Just when Rosenberg began to draw this distinction between the Russian Empire and nation-states in Europe is difficult to pinpoint. But in *Pest in Russland* he made it clear that one reason for the Russian Revolution of March 1917 was that Czarism constituted an obstacle to the emergence of a 'truly national Russia', since it repressed local autonomy.[125] So Rosenberg seems to have conceived the Russia of the future as a truncated Russia, a re-creation of pre-imperial Muscovite Russia.

122. A. Rosenberg, 'Von Brest-Litovsk nach Versailles', *VB*, 8 May 1921.
123. *Pest in Russland*, pp. 14, 56.
124. Rosenberg, *Letzte Aufzeichnungen*, p. 43.
125. *Pest in Russland*, p. 14.

If so, it was but a short step to argue that Germany might benefit territorially from the dismantling of the Russian empire. It has to be emphasised, however, that Rosenberg did not suggest this at that time. Nonetheless, he did criticise the Treaty of Brest-Litovsk for its moderation; German concern for the rights of Poland and the Baltic States had, in his words, 'undermined the possibility of a strong far-reaching policy in Russia'. The result was 'the historically un-natural and, in comparison to that of Versailles, positively mild peace of Brest-Litovsk'.[126] The implication here seems to be that a settlement more in tune with history would have led at least to German annexation of Russia's border states if not the splitting up of Russia into nation-states.

Further evidence of Rosenberg's interest in German annexations in Europe can be found in his commentary on the Party programme, *Wesen, Grundsätze und Ziele der NSDAP*, written early in 1923. There he criticised the democratic parties of prewar Germany, not only for 'preventing a systematic German colonial policy' which would have enabled Germany to absorb her growing population without the aid of emigration, but also for opposing 'every attempt at large-scale settlement in the east'. When he referred to 'settlement in the East', Rosenberg did not mean simply the settlement of the sparsely populated eastern provinces of Germany as he hinted: 'it is not possible under the present circumstances to indicate more clearly the European and extra-European areas in question which must come in consideration for colonisation. The imperialistic oppor-tunities of today can change in time.'[127] Despite the vagueness of this final comment, his elaboration of point three of the party pro-gramme — the demand for 'land and soil (colonies)' to feed the German people — revealed Rosenberg's support for territorial an-nexation within as well as outside Europe; no territory is specified, though there can be little doubt as to his ideas on the future of the Polish state, for which he had not the slightest respect.[128]

So all the indications are that Rosenberg's attitude towards Eastern Europe was changing: he was beginning to recognise the usefulness of the Ukrainian separatist movement; he seemed to envisage a 'decolonised' Russia reduced to its original Muscovite core; he felt that Germany should take advantage of this situation by annexing Poland and the Baltic States; and finally he believed that

126. Rosenberg, 'Von Brest-Litovsk nach Versailles', *VB*, 8 May 1921.

127. A. Rosenberg, 'Wesen, Grundsätze und Ziele der NSDAP', originally published in Munich in 1923 (the foreword is dated January 1923), reprinted in *Schriften*, pp. 135–6.

128. Ibid., p. 135.

Germany should establish a firm alliance with the truncated Russian state, when it had been liberated from Bolshevik leadership. It should be stressed that these changes occurred at a time when Rosenberg's influence on Hitler was probably at its greatest. Hitler seems, for example, to have used *Pest in Russland* as a sourcebook for his anti-Bolshevik tirades.[129] He also seems to have been pleased with the pamphlet *Wesen, Grundsätze und Ziele der NSDAP*, taking time at the party conference in January 1923 to thank Rosenberg publicly for 'his resolute collaboration and the theoretical amplification of the Party programme'.[130] So Hitler was fully aware of the development of Rosenberg's ideas, if indeed they did not merely reflect his own.

At the same time as these changes were occurring, the Nazi Party was in contact with Russian émigrés who had fled from the Bolsheviks in Russia and, as mentioned above, settled in Southern Germany. There can be no doubt that they too reinforced Hitler's more virulent anti-Bolshevism. The intermediary between Hitler and these émigrés was the Baltic German Max-Erwin von Scheubner-Richter, killed at Hitler's side at the Feldherrnhalle in the climax of the Munich putsch of 9 November 1923. Scheubner-Richter's political career and contribution to the Nazi Party is difficult to reconstruct, given his liking for backstage intrigue and secret negotiation; nevertheless an attempt must be made to investigate the background of the man of whom Hitler is reported to have said when referring to the 'martyrs of 9 November 1923', 'all are replaceable but not he'.[131]

Scheubner-Richter's expertise in Eastern European affairs was rooted in his wartime experiences with *Oberost*, the German government of occupation in Latvia. Early in 1918 he was in charge of *Oberost*'s press office in Riga and working closely with August Win-

129. Hitler had been in prison from 27 June until 26 July, during which time Rosenberg's book had been published. That he had read the work is clearly shown in his first speech after his release, given on 28 July; see the account of this speech in Boepple, *Adolf Hitlers Reden*, pp. 27–30, and *Pest in Russland*, pp. 30–1, pp. 18–20, p. 39 and pp. 46–9. The similarities in detail are too marked to be coincidental.

130. See the report of Hitler's speech at the party conference, *VB*, 31 January 1923. Lüdecke recalled Hitler expounding the party programme one evening, 'using Alfred Rosenberg's pamphlet, *Character, Principles and Aims of the Nazi Party*, fresh from the press . . .', *I Knew Hitler*, p. 98.

131. Quoted in W. Laqueur, 'Hitler and Russia, 1919–1923' *Survey* (October, 1962), p. 94. Born in Riga in 1884, the son of a German musician, Max-Erwin Richter grew up in Reval. In 1905 he married and acquired the aristocratic double-barrelled name 'von Scheubner-Richter'. In 1914 he joined a cavalry regiment of the German Army and served with Paul Leverkuehn, whose valedictory biography of Scheubner-Richter is the most valuable, if at times slightly suspect, source on his life; *Posten auf ewiger Wache. Aus dem abenteuerlichen Leben des Max von Scheubner-Richter* (Essen, 1938).

nig, the German commissioner in the Baltic provinces.[132] Scheubner-Richter saw his role clearly enough: to help to defend German interests in Latvia and, as the war continued to go badly for Germany, to help to defend Latvia against the advancing Red Army.[133]

At the end of 1918 he volunteered to remain in Latvia as the last German consular official to negotiate with the victorious Bolsheviks.[134] The experience can only have reinforced his anti-Bolshevik convictions. He witnessed the daily executions which took place during the Soviet occupation and was himself arrested on 14 January 1919 and sentenced to death, only to be reprieved in circumstances that are still far from clear.[135]

On his return to Germany in February 1919, he rejoined Winnig, by then *Reichskommissar* for East and West Prussia in Königsberg and organised the *Ostdeutscher Heimatsdienst* (OHD) to disseminate anti-Soviet propaganda and to work for economic cooperation between Germany and the border states.[136] This period in East Prussia made him aware of another danger to Germany other than that of Bolshevik Russia: the threat posed by the newly independent Polish state. During 1919 OHD organised mass protests against the transfer of West Prussia to Poland and the internationalisation of the port of Danzig.[137] By the end of 1919, therefore, Scheubner-Richter's anti-Bolshevik and anti-Polish prejudices had been well honed by bitter personal experience.

His activities in Königsberg were abruptly curtailed in March 1920 by the Kapp putsch in which Scheubner-Richter was implicated.[138] The ensuing decision to move to Munich was the turning-point in his life. It appears that he was attracted to a project devised by Alfred Rosenberg to establish trading links between Bavarian businessmen and the White Russian forces under General

132. C. Grimm, *Jahre deutscher Entscheidung im Baltikum 1918/19* (Essen, 1939), p. 284; Leverkuehn, *Posten*, pp. 165–7; A. Winnig, *Heimkehr*, (Hamburg, 1935), p. 18.

133. Leverkuehn. *Posten*, p. 173; Winnig, Heimkehr, pp. 60–71

134. Winnig, *Heimkehr*, p. 94. See also his report on his activities to the German Foreign Office, 'Bericht über die Tätigkeit der in Riga zurückgebliebenen Vertretung der deutschen Gesandtschaft bei den Republiken Livland und Estland', dated 3 February 1919, German Foreign Ministry (GFM) Weltkrieg Nr. 20d Nr. 1a Bd. 25 (Public Record Office microfilm GFM 21/426).

135. Scheubner-Richter himself offered no explanation for his last-minute reprieve. C. Grimm, *Jahre*, p. 296 and Winnig, *Heimkehr*, p. 130 refer to German Foreign Ministry intervention.

136. See Scheubner-Richter's report to the Foreign Office, 'Vom Kampf um die deutsche Ostmark. Tätigkeitsbericht des Obmanns des ostdeutschen Heimatdienstes für die Zeit von 1. Februar bis zum 1. Juni 1920' dated May 1920 (sic), reprinted in Leverkuehn, *Posten*, pp. 202–3.

137. Scheubner-Richter, 'Vom Kampf', pp. 200–8.

138. Winnig, *Heimkehr*, pp. 296–302; Leverkuehn, *Posten*, p. 183.

Wrangel in the Crimea. The commission which Scheubner-Richter eventually led in May 1920 convinced him that White Russian forces, if properly supported from Germany and under united leadership, could rid Russia of Bolshevism.[139]

Thereafter he set out to try to help secure both these preconditions. Firstly with his friend, Dr. Nemirovich-Danchenko, Wrangel's former press chief, he established the *Neue deutsch-russische Gesellschaft*, soon to be renamed *Aufbau*, with its own journal, *Wirtschaftspolitische Aufbau-Korrespondenz* (WPA), its aim being to advise German industrialists and unions on 'how reconstruction in the interests of Germany and Russia is possible'.[140] Secondly he established contact with the Russian émigrés in southern Germany and was soon entrusted with the organisation of the Russian monarchist conference at Bad Reichenhall in Bavaria in May 1921. The émigrés, however, were agreed only upon their opposition to Bolshevism and Scheubner-Richter made little progress at Bad Reichenhall towards his goal of uniting the monarchist movement.[141]

Meanwhile, of course, he had already established contact with the German Workers' Party. Through Alfred Rosenberg he met Adolf Hitler in October 1920, joined the party the following month and, according to the *VB*'s 1935 retrospective, he found himself 'in the following years, in ever closer collaboration with Adolf Hitler and his movement'.[142] In 1923 Scheubner-Richter was heavily involved in the planning before the Munich putsch.[143] He believed, as his involvement in the Kapp putsch showed, that only a national revolution in Germany could change governmental attitudes towards Russia and Bolshevism; and in Hitler he saw 'the new prophet' who could win over the masses to the idea of revolution.[144]

But did Scheubner-Richter exert any influence over Hitler's developing ideas on foreign policy? Contemporaries and historians

139. Leverkuehn, *Posten*, pp. 184–5. On the Crimean mission, see 'Max-Erwin von Scheubner-Richter', *VB*, 4 November 1935, HA 53/1263.

140. Scheubner-Richter's speech at Bad Reichenhall, reported in *Der Kampf*, 7 June 1921, HA 51/1197; on Nemirovich-Danchenko, see Williams, *Culture*, p. 217.

141. On the divisions between the monarchists, see Volkmann, *Emigration*, pp. 78–80. See also H. von Rimscha, *Russland jenseits der Grenzen 1921–26* (Jena, 1927), pp. 28–31.

142. 'Max-Erwin von Scheubner-Richter', *VB*, 4 November 1935.

143. W. Laqueur, 'Hitler and Russia', p. 102, calls this an unsubstantiated legend. In all probability Scheubner-Richter was involved in planning a putsch, which failed to materialise, earlier in November 1923 and it was Hitler who re-galvanised a disheartened Scheubner-Richter with a new scheme; see the interview with Scheubner-Richter's widow on 3 April 1936 in HA 53/1263 and the report of his adjutant, Johann Aigner, 'Als Ordonnanz bei Hochverrätern', HA 5/114II.

144. A. Scheubner-Richter, 'Bolschewisierung Deutschlands', *WPA*, 21 September 1923.

alike have tended to play down his contribution to Nazi ideology. But at least one contemporary, Arnold Rechberg, believed that in 1922 he was the 'foreign policy adviser of the National Socialist movement'.[145] Rechberg was a committed advocate of a Franco-German alliance and blamed Hitler's anti-Western stance on the influence of Scheubner-Richter, 'who represented the interests of a group of Russian emigrants'. The party leadership firmly denied these claims in the *VB*; 'it is not factually correct that Dr. von Scheubner-Richter, whose personality and work is of course known to the leadership of the party and who is valued because of this and for his anti-Bolshevik activities, is foreign policy adviser of our party'.[146] The party leadership also denied that Scheubner-Richter's *Aufbau* was exclusively a Russian organisation, but said it consisted of Germans 'who are working for the revival of Germany in coopera-tion with a future national Russia, and of Russians who see the rise of their fatherland in the future in cooperation with a national Germany'.[147] Though Scheubner-Richter also publicly denied being the party's adviser on foreign affairs, Rechberg refused to withdraw, claiming that he was 'considered as such'.[148]

Two things should be noted about this incident: firstly, the tact with which the party leadership managed to deny the role attributed to Scheubner-Richter whilst at the same time indicating how highly they valued him and the *Aufbau* organisation. Without doubt, Scheubner-Richter and his Russian émigré friends were important to the Nazis. The second notable aspect is the party's sensitivity on the issue of 'advisers'; 'the party has had no need so far of a foreign policy adviser', the *VB* commented.[149] The reason was that, in the wake of Mussolini's 'seizure of power' in Rome in October 1922, Hitler was being consciously groomed by the party as the 'German Mussolini'; the 'Führer-image' was already being cultivated and the party could not publicly acknowledge someone else's advice on foreign affairs. In view of all this, it is as well to treat the party's rejoinder to Rechberg's claims with some caution.

In fact, the views of Scheubner-Richter and his Russian émigrés

145. A. Rechberg in *Bayerische Staatszeitung*, 26 November 1922, in BHStA I/1474; Hanfstängl referred to Scheubner-Richter as 'a crony of Rosenberg's', *Missing Years*, p. 87, whilst Laqueur concludes that 'ideologically Scheubner-Richter's impact on Hitler was negligible; Rosenberg was a far greater influence during the early years', 'Hitler and Russia', p. 104.

146. 'Erklärung', *VB*, 6 December 1922.

147. Ibid.

148. Both Scheubner-Richter's denial and Rechberg's response were published in *Bayerische Staatszeitung*, 5 December 1922.

149. *VB* 6 December 1922.

can only have strengthened Hitler's anti-Bolshevism; they were devoted to the idea of a German alliance with a revitalised post-Bolshevik Russia, which Hitler's party was advocating in 1921–2. But did Scheubner-Richter also argue for the 'annexation of areas of Western Russia as the indispensable granary of Germany' as Ernst Hanfstängl suggests?[150] Did he, in other words, encourage Hitler's territorial ambitions in Russia? This is a crucial and difficult question to answer. Max Boehm, who met Scheubner-Richter in 1918, later claimed that 'in Baltic politics, we both represented a tolerant line against the Latvians and Estonians, and found ourselves at odds to a certain extent with the reactionary and Pan-German tendencies, especially in the Baltic aristocracy'.[151] On the other hand, during 1918 he tried to negotiate with the Latvian government an agreement by which German soldiers could acquire land for settlement. This idea of creating a militarised frontier zone to save Latvia from the Red Army certainly testifies to a desire to see Latvia remain in German hands.[152] However, when the German Army withdrew Scheubner-Richter did offer to recommend to the German Foreign Office on Latvian President Stutschka's behalf that Latvian independence be recognised, but since he was trying to seek protection for the Germans remaining in Latvia, the offer cannot be accepted at face value as a commitment in principle to Latvian independence.[153] His views on the fate of the Baltic Provinces are, in short, difficult to establish with any certainty since they seemed to change with successive stages in Germany's declining influence there.

As Scheubner-Richter became involved with the Russian émigrés, any annexationist designs which he may have had on the Baltic States had to be concealed. The Bad Reichenhall conference revealed how sensitive the émigrés were to the issue; opinions were so divided that discussion of the Baltic States was avoided, the conference lamely agreeing in principle that all states which took an active part in the rebuilding of Russia should have a right to join the Empire.[154] A majority at the conference wanted the Baltic States to

150. As did Rosenberg and Ludendorff, according to E. Hanfstängl, *Zwischen Weissem und Braunem Haus* (Munich, 1970), p. 122

151. Boehm, 'Baltische Einflüsse', p. 58. Leverkuehn, *Posten*, pp. 169–72 says that Scheubner-Richter felt that the Baltic provinces could not return to Russia, but with only a 9 per cent German population could they be retained by Germany?

152. A. Winnig, *Heimkehr* (Hamburg, 1935), p. 50. Heinrich Class discussed the idea of settling soldiers in insecure border regions in his war aims pamphlet: *Zum deutschen Kriegsziel*, pp. 39, 57–8.

153. Scheubner-Richter's reports to the Foreign Office on his interview with President Stutschka of Latvia, 3 February 1919, GFM 21/426.

154. Volkmann, *Emigration*, p. 81; von Rimscha, *Russland*, p. 61.

be part of Russia but enjoying a degree of autonomy. Whether this corresponded to Scheubner-Richter's own wishes is unknown; his stated aim certainly was to unite all Russian forces opposed to Bolshevism, and this included not only the Baltic States but also the other border regions, of whose separatist inclinations he was critical. The selfishness of Russia's border regions (the Ukraine, the Crimea, Armenia etc) had, in his view, been the fatal weakness in the anti-Bolshevik cause during the civil war and had accelerated Soviet victory.[155] So it would seem that Scheubner-Richter would have nothing to do with separatist ideas either.

Of course, even if he did think that Russia should be decolonised, he could not publicly express such views and still retain the support of his émigré friends. Indeed, the fact that he had amicable contacts not only with exiles from Greater Russia but also with Ukrainians such as General Biskupski and Colonel Poltawetz-Ostranitza, Hetman Skoropadski's former Chancellor, would suggest that Max Boehm's more charitable assessment of Scheubner-Richter's motives is closer to the truth than that of Ernst Hanfstängl; in sum, that in the 1920s he was genuinely concerned to overcome the many rivalries and intrigues in émigré circles and to unite the anti-Bolshevik forces abroad, rather than to encourage the fragmentation of the Russian Empire and German territorial expansion.[156]

All the evidence, of course, suggests that Scheubner-Richter sincerely desired a German alliance with a post-Bolshevik Russia. In September 1923, when reviewing his own career, he left no doubt about the consistent nature of his views on Russia. In 1918 he had criticised German diplomats for negotiating with the Bolsheviks at Brest-Litovsk: 'The one correct attitude towards the Eastern question would have been the installation of a Russian national government friendly to us.' Now the way forward for Germany was just as clear:

> In the future Germany and Russia, the German and Russian people, must go together. It is obvious because both people are assigned to each other and complement each other. But before this can happen, a struggle must first be fought between the people and the oppressors, the deputies or representatives of the International. And the outcome of this struggle will afford the opportunity of a partnership between the two peoples.[157]

155. M. Scheubner-Richter, 'Memento Mori', *WPA*, 26 July 1922.
156. Boehm, 'Baltische Einflüsse', p. 60. On Scheubner-Richter's contacts, see Williams, *Culture*, p. 174.
157. M. Scheubner-Richter, 'Bolschewisierung Deutschlands', *WPA*, 21 September and also in *VB* 21 September 1923.

One of the first tasks of such a partnership, of course, would be the revival of Russia; however, as Scheubner-Richter explained at the Bad Reichenhall conference, 'Russia can only be reconstructed by means of the surplus intellectual and technical power which we have in Germany', and to this end, Germany had to 'lead the streams of emigration to Russia'.[158] There is no evidence to suggest that he had in mind the idea of German settlement after territorial conquest, which Hitler was to discuss in *Mein Kampf*. What he wanted was to restore the dominant influence which German settlers had exerted in Russia in pre-revolutionary days. It was, one might argue, the natural dream of a Baltic German wanting to revive Germanic influence in Russia, rather than the desire of a Pan-German for conquest.[159]

So in public at least, Scheubner-Richter was a consistent supporter of a pro-Russian, anti-Bolshevik policy, untarnished by any dreams of German territorial expansion inside Russian territory. However, he certainly did have aggressive designs on Polish territory. In 1918–19, as has been seen, he opposed the transfer of West Prussia and the Polish Corridor to Poland and feared Polish aggression towards East Prussia. According to one source, the Bad Reichenhall conference had considered a German–Russian partnership whereby, in return for German assistance in the overthrow of Bolshevism, 'Russia [would] guarantee the revision of the Versailles treaty, the economic strangulation of Poland and economic concessions for Germany in Russia'.[160] In September 1923 when 'National Bolshevism' was being mooted, Scheubner-Richter indicated that the essential precondition of a German alliance with Bolshevik Russia against France would be a Soviet declaration of war on France's ally, Poland, and the latter's destruction and occupation by the Red Army.[161] That Russian and German nationalists should want to eliminate Poland should come as no surprise in view of the long-standing German and Russian attitudes towards her.

This outlook on foreign affairs could only confirm the Nazi Party's anti-Bolshevism and hostility towards Poland, whilst sustaining its interest in future Russo-German collaboration as opposed to an alliance with England. In February 1922, the *WPA* was arguing that Germany's condition was such that 'Russia signified for the German

158. Report in *Der Kampf*, 7 June 1921, HA 51/1197.
159. Williams, *Culture*, p. 175.
160. Discussion of the Bad Reichenhall resolutions by a group of Russian monarchists in Geneva on 16 June 1922, reported by 'Adolf Miller' of Berne to the German Foreign Office on 3 July 1922, AA IV Russland PO5A. bd. 2.
161. M. Scheubner-Richter, 'Moskauer Brandstifter', *WPA*, 29 September 1923.

Empire the only real chance of the restoration of her power', for in negotiations with England one always had to beware of her ally, France 'at our backs and behind her, the bayonets of Poland, Rumania and Czechoslovakia'.[162] Although Scheubner-Richter did recognise, like Hitler, that the British policy on reparations was more favourable to Germany than the French, he was unlikely to have endorsed Hitler's support for alliances with Britain and Italy as part of a future Nazi foreign policy.[163]

The two men did agree, however, that Bolshevik Russia was Germany's most dangerous enemy and it was on this subject that Scheubner-Richter's voice may have been influential. The Treaty of Rapallo, of course, gave substance to all the worst fears of the Russian émigrés for the future. Scheubner-Richter responded quickly on 21 April 1922, arguing that Russia and Germany were natural allies:

> ... Normally, a state in Germany's position would be grateful for any valuable ally but a partnership with a state [Bolshevik Russia] directed by such leaders would only be possible without danger for Germany, if the German people were led by a strong national government. Unfortunately this is still not the case, and one would have to be blind to ignore the dangers which a close partnership between Germany and Soviet Russia could at present occasion.[164]

This, of course, is precisely the same argument that Hitler used in a speech the same day and that Rosenberg was to use in *Pest in Russland*; Rosenberg felt that a future (that is, a National Socialist) Germany could ally with Bolshevik Russia; but for Weimar Germany this might be fatal. All three used the opportunity to condemn Rapallo, and urged Germans to consider an alliance only with a nationalist Russia.[165]

It cannot be said, however, that Hitler and Rosenberg followed Scheubner-Richter's lead; their response to Rapallo was entirely predictable in view of what they had already said and written, but certainly Scheubner-Richter's view must have reinforced their determination to reassert their support for a post-Bolshevik Russia. It is

162. M. Scheubner-Richter, 'Russlandhilfe', *WPA*, 24 February 1922.

163. On Britain, see M. Scheubner-Richter, 'Weltpolitische Möglichkeiten', *WPA*, 3 February 1922, and *WPA*, 9 and 30 August and 18 October 1922. He predicted 'difficult days' for the South Tyrolean Germans because of the Fascist takeover; 'Die Faszisten als Herren in Italien', *WPA*, 1 November 1922.

164. M. Scheubner-Richter, 'Deutsch-russischer Vortrag von Rapallo', *WPA* 21 April 1922.

165. M. Scheubner-Richter, 'Rapallo', *WPA*, 5 May 1922; for the views of Hitler and Rosenberg see above pp. 24–6; 115–7 and below, p. 179

also certain that Rosenberg utilised *Aufbau*'s resources. From the middle of 1921, articles on Russia from *WPA* began to appear in the *VB*. In *Pest in Russland* Rosenberg recommended *WPA* to those interested in reliable information on the Eastern question and cited it as the source of much of his information harmful to the Soviet image.[166] However, the *WPA* was only one of the several sources used by the Nazis and since Rosenberg worked on *Aufbau* it is difficult to be certain who influenced whom.[167] In the final analysis, however, Scheubner-Richter supplied the Nazis with ammunition which reinforced existing ideological convictions rather than exerting a formative influence upon Nazi ideology. Furthermore, he continued to stress the need for a partnership between a nationalist Germany and a nationalist Russia until his death in November 1923, by which time Hitler was already harbouring sweeping territorial designs on Russian territory; Scheubner-Richter could never have approved of these, not publicly at least, because of his commitment to the émigré cause.[168]

What made Scheubner-Richter such an 'irreplaceable' loss to Hitler after the Munich putsch was not so much his expertise on foreign affairs as his connections with leading figures in German political life as well as with Russian monarchists. 'He opened all doors for me', Hitler is supposed to have told Scheubner-Richter's widow.[169] The link with the Russian monarchists may have brought much-needed cash into the party coffers, but more important to Hitler's cause in 1922 was the respectability conferred by personal contact with General Ludendorff.[170] Although Scheubner-Richter had not introduced Hitler to Ludendorff, he was 'in close contact' with the German war hero throughout 1923 and acted as an intermediary; the two met several times at Scheubner-Richter's house to discuss the progress of the national revolution planned in 1923.[171]

166. The first article seems to have been 'Der kommunistische Kapitalismus', *VB*, 28 July 1921; the acronym AWP was referred to, though WAP became more usual; Rosenberg, *Pest in Russland*, pp. 29. Compare ibid. pp. 70, 49, 19–21 with 'Höchster Zynismus', *WPA*, 10 February, *WPA* 24 March and 'Kirchenplünderung', *WPA* 14 April 1922.

167. Rosenberg also cited 'ABC Korrespondenz', the journal of Eduard Stadtler's Anti-Bolshevik League in Berlin, *Pest in Russland*, pp. 29, 34, 46–9. Scheubner-Richter recommended Rosenberg's *Pest in Russland* very warmly to his readers, *WPA*, 26 July 1922.

168. See, for example, 'Die Bolshewisierung sprungbereet?' *WPA*, 29 September 1923.

169. Quoted in Boehm, 'Baltische Einflüsse', p. 57. The *VB* acknowledged that he had attracted several businessmen and politicians to the anti-Bolshevik cause, 'Herrn Rechbergs Selbstenthüllung', *VB*, 2 December 1922.

170. Franz-Willing believes that money from émigré sources was probably very intermittent; *Die Hitlerbewegung*, pp. 191–6.

171. E. Ludendorff, *Vom Feldherrn zum Weltrevolutionär und Wegbereiter deutscher Volksschöpfung,*

It is possible, of course, that contact with Ludendorff might also have affected Hitler's Russian policy. Indeed, the general had imposed on a reluctant German Foreign Office the extensive territorial demands eventually put to the Bolsheviks at Brest-Litovsk in March 1918. As Ludendorff revealed in his memoirs, he had decided that 'for the future of Germany it was all-important that the whole Eastern problem should be solved in a manner which satisfied the interests of Prussia and Germany and, as far as possible, removed the danger threatening from Poland'.[172] This meant that Germany had to secure a protective belt of agricultural land in Western Russia, to ensure her survival of any future blockade, as well as a union with the Baltic States of Courland and Lithuania, which would create a military buffer zone. In addition, Ludendorff wanted to weaken the Russian Empire by supporting separatist movements and so the German terms, eventually accepted in March 1918 by the reluctant but virtually impotent Bolshevik leadership, also included recognition of Estonian, Latvian, Ukrainian and Finnish independence.[173] He later claimed that 'it was no desire of mine to destroy Russia or to weaken her so that she could no longer exist' but there seems little doubt that his aim was to remove the threat from the East in any future war by reducing Russia to her Muscovite core by the establishment of a number of puppet states and by supporting demands by non-Russian nationalities for self-determination.[174] This, of course, was virtually identical to the concept of a future Russia which Alfred Rosenberg was cultivating in 1922. So it is possible that Ludendorff's presence added weight to Rosenberg's argument for creating a national Russia when he was brought into contact with the Nazi movement at the end of 1922.[175]

During 1922, therefore, Hitler's anti-Bolshevism was undoubtedly fed by his closest associates. Rosenberg argued that, whilst Bolshev-

---

Meine Lebenserinnerungen vom 1919 bis 1925 (Munich, 1940), p. 242. See also information from Scheubner-Richter's widow to the party archives, 3 April 1936, HA 53/2163.

172. E. Ludendorff, *My War Memories, 1914–18*, vol. 2 (London, n.d.), p. 544.

173. Ibid., pp. 534, 561.

174. 'I supported in all sincerity the formation of a Baltic littoral'; E. Ludendorff, *War Memories*, vol. 2, p. 562.

175. Otto Strasser claimed in 1926 that Ludendorff had popularised the idea of German settlement of the Baltic states with his wartime references to Courland; 'Fortschritte in der Bauernsiedlung', *Der nationale Sozialist*, 15 August 1926. This seems possible, Ludendorff wrote in 1922 that 'the peace should have brought Germany secured frontiers in the East, agricultural areas and, especially in Courland, areas of settlement for German soldiers'; *Kriegführung und Politik* (Berlin, 1922), p. 282.

ism was alien to Russia and therefore 'National Bolshevism' was a contradiction in terms, it did correspond to a weakness in Russian blood; Scheubner-Richter urged him to back the idea of collaboration with a 'post-Bolshevik' Russia, the dream of the Russian émigrés; and Rosenberg and Ludendorff from their different standpoints theorised about a truncated, decolonised Russian state. But what effects did they have on Hitler?

As has been indicated above, Hitler's views on Russia had begun to change during 1921 and 1922. In 1922, however, he still argued in public that a Russia purged of Bolshevism would be a suitable ally for Germany. But by the time he was writing *Mein Kampf* in 1924, Russia had of course been finally relegated to the ranks of Germany's foes and there was no mention of a future national Russian government. The vital questions therefore are when and why did this change occur?

In October 1921, as has been seen, Hitler had stressed that before the war, Germany had had the choice of allying with England or Russia; either would have, in his view, facilitated German expansion.[176] At that time, Hitler appeared to favour a Russo-German agreement as a 'natural alliance'.[177] These comments on prewar German diplomacy can be taken as reflections of his Pan-German schooling in foreign affairs but they also seem to suggest (in the absence of any other evidence) that he had not yet formulated an alliance strategy of his own for the postwar world.

In November 1922, however, Hitler publicly referred to the possibility of German alliances with England and Italy in order to implement the *Anschluss* with Austria. This was the first indication of a strategy to deal with postwar realities. It has been thought that Hitler did not make up his mind about the role of Russia in his foreign policy programme until 1924.[178] But, in fact, a secret report on the Nazi Party dating from the end of 1922 shows quite plainly that he had already abandoned all ideas of an alliance with Russia.

In December 1922, Eduard Scharrer, co-owner of the Munich daily *Münchener Neueste Nachrichten* and the rich proprietor of Schloss Bernried in Bavaria, submitted three reports on the Hitler move-

---

176. Report on speech by Hitler on 21 October in *Verlag Bayerisches Wochenblatt*, October 1921, See above, p. 96.

177. Speech on 4 August, report in *VB*, 11 August 1921. Hitler and Rosenberg believed that Germany had to choose to exploit either Britain against Russia or Russia against Britain because the two nations were such irreconcilable enemies: see, for example, the speech by Hitler on 13 April 1923, reprinted in Boepple, *Adolf Hitlers Reden*, p. 44 and Rosenberg, *Pest in Russland*, p. 63.

178. Kuhn, *Programm*, pp. 102–4.

ment to the chancellor of the day, Wilhelm Cuno.[179] One of the reports was Scharrer's account of an interview which he had arranged with Hitler earlier that month. During this interview, Hitler made it clear that he regarded England, above all others, as the power which was committed to the further existence of the German people: 'England has an interest in seeing that we do not go under, since, otherwise, France would become the greatest continental power in Europe, whilst England would have to be satisfied with the position of a third-rate power'. English assistance would be forthcoming, he told Scharrer, when Germany showed herself to be a viable economic proposition and an effective counterweight to France, and provided, of course, 'she posed no threat to England herself'. This meant, as far as Hitler was concerned, that Germany would have to avoid the overseas commercial and colonial rivalry with England which had caused problems before the First World War: 'Germany would have to adapt herself to a purely continental policy avoiding harm to English interests. The destruction of Russia with the help of England would have to be attempted. Russia would give Germany sufficient land for German settlers and a wide field of activity for German industry. Then England would not interrupt us in our reckoning with France.'[180]

Scharrer's account, whose authenticity there seems little reason to doubt,[181] shows that Hitler had fully thought out his alliance strategy in 1922: he felt that England could be enticed into an alliance against Bolshevik Russia as well as against France, though interestingly, he seemed to expect British non-intervention rather than active assistance in the campaign against France. Thus, despite his continued public commitment to a future nationalist regime in Russia, Hitler had already eliminated this as a serious consideration in his foreign policy programme.

179. BAK Reichskanzlei R43I/2681. Scharrer, who was also the Bulgarian consul in Munich, seems to have acted as a political agent for Cuno, though he was favourably disposed towards the Nazi Party, having apparently supported it financially; K. H. Harbeck (ed.), *Akten der Reichskanzlei: Das Kabinett Cuno* (Boppard a.Rh., 1968), p. 360. See also note 63 in this chapter.

180. Scharrer's report headed 'Bericht nach Hitlers persönlichen Ausführungen. Ende Dezember 1922', pp. 3–4, BAK R43I/2681, America and Italy, Hitler is reported to have said, would also be favourably disposed to Germany, but America was more interested in learning the methods of combating Bolshevism, and Italian aid depended on German attitudes towards the *Anschluss* and South Tyrol questions.

181. Scharrer may have requested a frank exchange of views as a condition of further financial aid; on another occasion, for example, he had asked for an assurance that Hitler would not attempt to overthrow the Bavarian government; G. Franz-Willing, *Krisenjahr der Hitlerbewegung*, p. 24. See also Hitler's comments on Scharrer and his wife on 21 February 1942, Trevor-Roper, *Table Talk*, pp. 325–6 and E. Matthias, 'The Western Powers in Hitler's World of Ideas', in A. J. Nicholls and E. Matthias, *German Democracy and the Triumph of Hitler* (London, 1971), p. 124.

Conclusion

To sum up Hitler's alliance policy, therefore, it must be said that the relegation of Russia to the ranks of Germany's foes cannot be seen as a belated afterthought a year or so after the decision to opt for an English alliance. Indeed, it is possible that Bolshevism's steadily increasing grip after 1921 persuaded Hitler to look to Russia's long-time imperial rival, Great Britain, as a future ally. In his eyes, British policy was beginning to assert its independence from France, criticising the latter's rigid stance on the question of Upper Silesia and of German reparations payments. This view probably encouraged Hitler to believe that Britain was once again following her traditional balance of power strategy towards Europe.

To return to the first of the two questions posed at the beginning of this chapter, what effect did ideology have on Hitler's alliance plans? It must be emphasised that, if the relegation of Russia to the ranks of Germany's enemies was fundamental to the development of Hitler's scheme, then more weight ought to be given to the influence of the party's antisemitic and anti-Bolshevik ideology; the success of 'Jewish' Bolshevism in the Russian civil war and the threat of the Bolshevisation of Germany were probably the decisive factors in persuading Hitler to abandon the idea of an alliance with Russia. It can be objected, of course, that he rejected Russia as an ally simply because he wanted territorial aggrandisement in Eastern Europe in a resurrection of the settlement reached at Brest-Litovsk in 1918. However, it should not be forgotten that in 1921 Hitler had been arguing, like Moeller van den Bruck, that an alliance with Russia before the war would have facilitated unlimited German expansion eastwards and that the Treaty of Brest-Litovsk itself would have provided a basis for Russo-German collaboration. So it is quite likely that an abhorrence of Bolshevism did help to alienate him from Russia, thereby helping to determine his alliance strategy.

It is also quite apparent (to return to the second question put earlier) that Hitler's decisions — apart from that on the Italian question (and even there Lüdecke's involvement seems likely) — were very probably not taken by him alone and in the teeth of party opposition. There were hints of a forthcoming realignment with Britain during 1921 and 1922 in Rosenberg's ideological diatribes, which showed that British national interests were increasingly at odds with those of the Jews and compatible with those of the Germans, while Russian interests were consistently shown to be fashioned by the Jews and directed against Germany. But, and this

must be stressed, neither Hitler nor Rosenberg made any unequivocal public statements about their anti-Russian, pro-English foreign policy at that time. The Scharrer interview was confidential;
in public Hitler often disguised his views by analyses of prewar
diplomacy, whilst changes in Rosenberg's views were barely discernible amidst the welter of accusations levelled at the Jews. The
reasons for these precautions will be investigated later, but they may
have included the desire to keep the support of influential and often
rich Russian émigrés, who would not look favourably on an anti-
Russian, as opposed to an anti-Bolshevik, Nazi foreign policy.

Finally, the exact point at which Hitler formulated his alliance
strategy is difficult to establish. If one believes Hitler's comments in
Mein Kampf and accepts the formulation of foreign policy guidelines
representing an emanation of the party's *Weltanschauung*, then a
Russian alliance was out of the question as soon as the Bolsheviks
were firmly entrenched in Russia and anti-Bolshevism clearly established as the keynote of Nazi ideology. The party's reaction to the
Treaty of Rapallo suggests that both preconditions had been ful-
filled; almost certainly, therefore, Hitler produced his blueprint for a
Nazi foreign policy in the autumn of 1922. Certainly the fall of Lloyd
George and the rise of Mussolini in October 1922, coupled with the
continuing tension between Britain and France, amounted to a
veritable diplomatic revolution which might, as Lüdecke suggests,
have prompted Hitler.

The formalisation of a party alliance strategy did not, however,
represent a sudden innovation, but merely confirmed changes that
had been evolving for some time. Nonetheless, as early as December
1922, the alliance scheme upon which Hitler was to elaborate in
Mein Kampf, and, some would say, to follow in the 1930s, had
already been determined.

5

Haushofer, Hitler, and Expansionism

Recently, historians have generally argued that Hitler's choice of allies determined the direction of German expansionism; in other words, the scheme of territorial aggrandisement outlined in *Mein Kampf* was primarily the result of his ruminations on alliance policy.[1] However, it must be doubted whether he really chose his allies — and indeed his enemies — without consideration of probable territorial implications. This is especially dubious when one remembers that, in his retrospective analyses of prewar German diplomacy, Hitler assessed the attractiveness of England and Russia as allies in terms of the territory which might be acquired as a result.[2] It is far more likely, therefore, that the choice of goal determined, or at least helped to determine, the selection of allies. So what then inspired the dreams of eastward expansion evident in *Mein Kampf*? Was the pursuit of living-space in Eastern Europe part of Hitler's Pan-German heritage? Was it the logical corollary of an ideological crusade against a 'Jewish-dominated' Soviet Russia? Or was Hitler influenced by the geopolitical theories of Karl Haushofer, the man so often blamed for feeding his territorial fantasies?[3] A great deal of rumour and speculation has clouded judgements about Haushofer over the years; it should now be possible with the aid of his private papers and other newly accessible sources to evaluate more accurately his likely contribution to Hitler's thinking.[4]

1. Kuhn, *Programm*, p. 21; cf. Hildebrand, *Vom Reich*, p. 75.
2. Speech by Hitler reported in *VB* 13 January 1921. See above, p. 96.
3. A. Dorpalen, 'Comment', *History of Childhood Quarterly. The Journal of Psychohistory*, vol. 1 (1973), p. 243. On wartime suspicions of Haushofer, see K. E. Russell, 'The Brains of the Nazi Party', *Daily Telegraph*, 5 August 1941, in the Wiener Library's file of newspaper clippings about Haushofer.
4. Most of Haushofer's papers are now housed at the Bundersarchiv in Coblenz (henceforth

Haushofer and the Nazi Party

At first sight, it is difficult to imagine a more unlikely ally for the Nazi Party than Karl Haushofer. Born in 1869 into an intellectually and artistically gifted family, his military and academic career placed him in the higher echelons of Bavarian society. After 21 years in the German army, Haushofer was sent in 1908 to study the Japanese army which had acquitted itself so well against the Russians in 1904–5. This mission, which took him through India, China and Korea as well as Japan between 1908 and 1910, seems to have been a crucial turning-point in his life; much of the undoubted expertise and interest in Far Eastern affairs which was to character-ise his later work was acquired during this visit.

This extensive tour also stimulated his enthusiasm for the new 'science' of geopolitics. This discipline studies the impact of the natural environment (the soil, population pressure, frontiers and waterways) on politics. His research on the tour provided the basis of a doctoral dissertation on Japan submitted in 1913.[5] During the First World War Haushofer maintained his interest in geopolitics by reading the works of the Swedish political scientist Rudolf Kjellen with whom he also corresponded. At one stage he contemplated undertaking research with Kjellen after the war was over.[6]

The outcome of the war changed all that. Though appointed as lecturer in geography at Munich University on his retirement from the army in 1919, Haushofer did not retreat into the ivory towers of academe. He identified the ignorance of geopolitical realities dis-played by the German people and especially its leaders as one of the main reasons for Germany's defeat and he set out to remedy that deficiency. As he put it in 1929: 'Out of this elementary craving for better scientific protection of the political unit and of the folkish and cultural base originated the challenge of geopolitics.'[7] After a brief

---

referred to as Haushofer Nachlass) but a somewhat smaller collection is housed at the family home at Hartschimmelhof bei Ammersee, Bavaria. Unfortunately, the present writer was unable to examine this collection as it was being arranged by Professor H.-A. Jacobsen; the latter's excellent two-volume biography, *Karl Haushofer — Leben und Werk* (Boppard, 1979), draws on both collections. I am extremely grateful to Professor Heinz Haushofer, Karl's son, for allowing me to view selected documents and to interview him on 16 August 1975.

5. S. Zweig, *Die Welt von Gestern*, (Stockholm, 1947), pp. 217–18. E. Obst, 'Karl Haushofer zum 60. Geburtstag', *ZfG*, vol. 6 (1929), p. 711. The thesis, 'Dai Nikon, Betrachtungen über Grossjapans Wehrmacht, Weltstellung und Zukunft' was accepted by Munich University in 1913.

6. Copy of letter from Haushofer to Kjellen, 10 October 1917, Haushofer Nachlass 955 (d).

7. K. Haushofer, 'Was ist Geopolitik?', unpublished manuscript, dated 28 May 1929, Haushofer Nachlass 834; see also, Obst, 'Haushofer', p. 711.

flirtation with the *Deutsche Volkspartei*, following the family's liberal traditions, he rejected the idea of involving himself in parliamentary politics.[8] Instead he decided to try through his own writing, lectures and through the pages of the journal *Zeitschrift fuer Geopolitik* which he helped to found in 1924 to make geopolitics 'the geographical conscience of the state'.[9]

Despite the overtly political purpose of his mission to educate Germany's masters, Haushofer's social and academic background made him an unlikely fellow-traveller for the politically and intellectually impoverished Nazi Party in the early 1920s. Two things, however, brought him to the attention of the Nazis: his opposition to the Versailles Settlement and his friendship with Rudolf Hess.

Haushofer refused to accept the postwar settlement as a *fait accompli* and he set out to expose the folly and injustice of the Versailles Treaty in the hope of bringing about its revision. For example, he delivered speeches regularly during the 1920s for the *Deutscher Kampfbund gegen die Kriegsschuldlüge* (DKK), the German League against the War Guilt Lie, and the *Akademischer Arbeitsausschuss gegen Friedensdiktat und Schuldlüge* (AA), the Academic Working Group against the Peace and Guilt Lie.[10] He also joined the *Verein fuer Deutschtum im Ausland* (VDA), the Association for Germandom Abroad, in an attempt to maintain contact between the areas lost in 1919 and the fatherland; in 1923 he was elected chairman of its Bavarian branch.[11] His appointment as head of the Practical Department of the new German Academy in May 1925 gave him further scope to help to sustain Germandom amongst Germans living abroad.[12]

8. Information from Heinz Haushofer. For further details of his involvement with the DVP see D. H. Norton, 'Karl Haushofer and his influence on Nazi ideology and German Foreign Policy, 1919–45', unpublished doctoral thesis, Clark University, Worcester, Mass., 1965 and Jacobsen, *Haushofer*, vol. 1, pp. 202–9.

9. K. Haushofer, E. Obst, H. Lautensach and O. Maull, 'Über die historische Entwicklung des Begriffs "Geopolitik"', *Bausteine zur Geopolitik*, (Berlin, 1928), p. 27.

10. The DKK was organised by Richard Graf du Moulin-Eckart, Professor of History at the Technische Hochschule in Munich; NS 26/1679. Details of Haushofer's involvement can be found in his correspondence with du Moulin-Eckart, Haushofer Nachlass 940 (b). The AA organised a series of regular lecture programmes at Munich University beginning in 1924; see *MNN*, 14 September, Haushofer took part in 1925, 1927 and 1928.

11. *VDA* circular, June 1923; Haushofer Nachlass 940 (b). The Nazis renamed it the *Volksbund für das Deutschtum im Ausland* in the 1930s; Haushofer was its president between 1938 and 1941.

12. See the report on the German Academy's activities in 1924–5 in Haushofer Nachlass 898. Haushofer became president of the Academy in 1934. Haushofer was also a member of the *Deutscher Schutzbund* which aimed to sustain the Germandom of Germans living in border areas or abroad, see 'Satzungen des Vereins Deutscher Schutzbund', Haushofer Nachlass 898.

The defeat of Germany in the First World War and the political disillusionment created by the Versailles Settlement cut across social, economic and academic barriers and it is likely that Haushofer's activities would have attracted the attention of the NSDAP even without his friendship with Rudolf Hess.[13] Haushofer's collaboration with *Bund 'Oberland'* (BO) — a pressure group headed by men well-known to the Nazi leadership — makes this almost certain.[14] Though he never became a member of BO, he was certainly an active supporter in the early 1920s, regularly attending its annual conference at Burg Hoheneck and writing in the association's periodical *Das Dritte Reich*.[15]

Under the leadership of Friedrich Weber, BO developed close links with the Nazi Party during 1922 and 1923; Weber in fact was implicated in the Munich putsch and was imprisoned alongside Hitler in Landsberg gaol in 1924. Though the membership of BO was undoubtedly of a different calibre socially and intellectually from the Nazi Party, as Weber admitted in 1927 'on the level of ideas, the National Socialist movement [stood] especially close to us'.[16]

However, it is clear that BO's increasing involvement with the Nazis was a matter of considerable embarrassment to Haushofer. This collaboration largely explains Haushofer's rejection of an executive position in BO in 1925. He told Weber that such a position was 'unsuitable' to one of his age and personality,[17] but this was not the real reason, as he confided privately to a friend: 'As you know I am completely absorbed in helping to establish in the German Academy a centre for Germandom . . . the success or failure of which depends very much on whether men take me seriously.'[18]

Evidently he felt his credibility would be impaired by close

13. The Nazis followed the VDA's activities with interest; see for example *VB* 26 May 1921 and the report on Haushofer's speech to the VDA, *VB* 20 October 1925.

14. *Bund 'Oberland'*, though avowedly nonpartisan, joined the *Kampfbund* in 1923 and took part in the Munich putsch, HA 32/642; see also H. J. Kuron, 'Freikorps und Bund "Oberland"', unpublished doctoral dissertation, Erlangen University, 1960.

15. Dr. Alois Alzheimer, Haushofer's friend and later vice-chairman of BO claims that Haushofer was never a member of BO but was attracted to its political orientation; letter from Dr. Alzheimer to the author, 22 October 1975. Haushofer contributed an essay to the fundamental statement of BO policy, *Oberland, Ziele und Wege des Bundes 'Oberland' e.V.* (Munich, 1926), pp. 5–10.

16. F. weber, 'Unsere Stellung zu anderen Gruppen und Bünden', *Das Dritte Reich*, 15 March 1927. An investigation by the German Ministry of the Interior in 1926 also concluded that the political goals of the two organisations were very similar; Ministry of the Interior to Dr. Schetter, director of the State Judiciary, 17 March 1926, HA 35/701.

17. Letter from Karl Haushofer to F. Weber, 19 April 1925. Haushofer Nachlass 940 (b).

18. Letter from K. Haushofer to A. Alzheimer, 8 March 1925. Haushofer Nachlass 945 (b).

association with a group who had been involved in the Munich putsch and who continued to collaborate with the newly re-formed Nazi Party. As Haushofer put it, 'the flag of Oberland by Hitler in the Bürgerbräukeller, the name of Friedrich Weber at the head: that signifies a programme that with the tongues of angels I could not argue away.'[19] Clearly he seems to have had little sympathy with the Nazi Party programme and he apparently 'opposed steadfastly the participation of the BO in the Kampfbund' before the Munich putsch.[20] This evidence hardly supports the view that Karl Haushofer was the *eminence grise* behind the Nazi Party at this time. In 1925, at least, his overriding concern was to avoid associating with rightwing extremists at a vital stage in his career.

As might be expected therefore, there is little solid evidence of close and continuous contact between Haushofer and the Nazi Party in the 1920s. What evidence there is revolves around his close friendship with Rudolf Hess. 'My friendship with Rudolf Hess', Haushofer wrote in 1945 in his own defence, 'began in 1918 and is, like his attendance at my lectures at the university, four years older [sic] than the foundation of the Nationalist Socialist Party'.[21] Whilst recognising that the younger man's 'heart and idealism were greater than his intellect',[22] Haushofer regarded Hess as his favourite student: he shielded him from the authorities after the Munich putsch; when Hess had been released from Landsberg gaol, Haushofer obtained a post for him at the German Academy. He was justifiably angry when his friend eventually decided to leave the Academy and become Hitler's secretary.[23]

When Haushofer first met Hitler is not certain; his memoirs state that he first saw Hitler in 1922. However, it seems from his pocket calendar that on 6 July 1920 he and Rudolf Hess attended a DAP discussion evening at which Hitler spoke. The calendar also suggests, however, that the first meeting probably did not take place until 24 July 1921.[24] From then on, it is clear that Haushofer was

19. Ibid.
20. Letter from Dr. Alzheimer to the author, 22 October 1975.
21. K. Haushofer, 'Defense of German Geopolitics' in E. A. Walsh, *Total Power. A Footnote to History* (New York, 1948), p. 351. Jacobsen believes that the first meeting with Hess occurred on 4 April 1919: *Haushofer*, vol. I, p. 22.
22. Quoted in Walsh, *Total Power*, p. 26.
23. Interview with Heinz Haushofer.
24. Jacobsen, *Haushofer*, vol. I, pp. 225–6; Haushofer, 'Defense', p. 351.

kept informed by Hess of developments within the party.[25] The *VB* began to take an interest in his activities in 1922; his lectures were thought to be instructive for party members and, according to one reporter, 'proved that knowledge is not for storing in books'; it also provided 'weapons in the struggle for the right to live'.[26] In 1924 Haushofer made regular visits to Landsberg gaol to see Rudolf Hess — at the very time when Hitler was dictating *Mein Kampf* to Hess — and it is commonly believed that Hitler's ideas received their geopolitical colouration as a result of these visits and Hess's own influence.[27]

It is difficult to establish what sort of relationship existed between Haushofer and Hitler; Haushofer later asserted that he had little to do with Hitler until the 1930s and this is probably true. However, two documents suggest that he was aware both that his ideas were attractive to Hitler and that the Nazis were willing to make use of them. In 1938, for example, Haushofer wrote a confidential letter to the Dean of Natural Science at Munich University, explaining his relationship with the Nazi Party. He had been, he said, 'well acquainted and friendly with significant personalities in the NSDAP since 1919' but he had not become a member of the party, he explained, 'for reasons of camouflage'. He also claimed that several books and articles had been written 'at the suggestion of the Führer's representative' (Hess), including two from the 1920s: an article, 'Nationaler Sozialismus und soziale Aristokratie', published in *ZfG* in 1924 and a book, *Grenzen in ihrer geographischen und politischen Bedeutung*, published in 1927.[28] It is a little hard to believe that these works were written simply at Hess's instigation; Haushofer had been studying the frontier problem for quite some time before he wrote *Grenzen*. Nevertheless, there is no obvious reason why he should invent such a story to impress the Dean and, even if there was, why did he choose to include 1920s titles? Possibly Hess did suggest the subjects in a private capacity; an article on National Socialism, though not dealing with the NSDAP, would obviously be of interest,

25. See for example Hess's account of party affairs in his letter to Haushofer, 6 October 1923, Haushofer Nachlass 955 (c).

26. Report by 'D' on Haushofer's lecture entitled 'The Thousand Year Struggle for the Rhine', *Völkischer Kurier* (VK), 4 June 1924 (the *VK* became the main Nazi paper when the VB was banned after the Munich putsch). For the first *VB* report on a Haushofer lecture see *VB*, 20 September 1922. For further details on Nazi coverage of Haushofer's lectures, see Stoakes, 'Evolution', pp. 389–90.

27. On 8 May 1934, Haushofer wrote to a friend that Hitler 'had not forgotten that I was at Landsberg every week', quoted in Norton, 'Haushofer', p. 83.

28. Letter from K. Haushofer to the Dean, 24 December 1938, Haushofer Nachlass 931 (a).

as would an analysis of the frontier problem, which loomed large in Nazi foreign policy discussions after 1924. At the very least, the letter shows that Haushofer had identified those writings which were of some relevance to the Nazi Party, and which perhaps conformed with Nazi thinking.

This impression is reinforced by a second document. In June 1924, the *Grossdeutsche Volksgemeinschaft* (GDVG), to which most of the former members of the then banned NSDAP belonged, issued a leaflet, urging its followers to attend an address on 'Living-space and the War Guilt Lies' to be delivered by Haushofer for the *Deutscher Kampfbund gegen die Kriegsschuldlüge*.[29] This was an unusual step, one perhaps partly explicable in terms of Hitler's own absence from the scene, but which nonetheless suggests that Haushofer's views were approved by Nazi leadership. The address, which the Nazi rank and file duly and noisily attended, certainly introduced them to the concept of *Lebensraum*, which was to be crucial to the foreign policy programme outlined by Hitler in *Mein Kampf*.[30]

Contacts between the leading geopolitician and the Nazi Party in the 1920s may have been 'camouflaged' because Haushofer wanted to conceal his relationship with rightwing extremists. But one should not exaggerate the significance of this; contact between Haushofer and the Nazi Party was probably very infrequent: he was a friend of Rudolf Hess, not of the party. He had no reason to take the party at all seriously in the mid-1920s; he could not have predicted Hitler's spectacular rise. Nevertheless, the fact remains that by the time Hitler did come to power in 1933, the Nazi Party had been paying lip-service at least to geopolitical ideas for several years and their impact on Nazi thinking must therefore be assessed.

Haushofer's Ideas on Foreign Policy

During the Second World War, it was claimed that Haushofer was the 'brains' behind the Nazi Party who had masterminded Hitler's foreign policy. Such exaggerated claims are not incomprehensible when his ideas are studied. It is difficult even now to accept that Haushofer believed his plans to be realisable without recourse to

29. GDVG leaflet in HA 42/857.

30. During the speech on 29 June there were shouts of 'Free Hitler' from the Nazi supporters; reports in *MNN* 30 June 1924. Haushofer told his audience: 'We must use everything in our fervent love of the fatherland in order to contradict the war-guilt lie and to fight to recover our living-space', report in *VK*, 1 July 1924.

war. His deep commitment to the redistribution of the world's living space, together with his pugnacious and often fairly opaque style, encouraged the conviction that geopolitics was synonymous with Nazi imperialism. But how justified was this belief? It is important to remember that geopolitics was not an individual *tour de force* from the pen of Karl Haushofer; it drew heavily on earlier work by political geographers and to understand its nature fully, its evolution must be studied.

Though Haushofer was greatly impressed by the works of the Americans A. T. Mahan and Brooks Adams, and by the British geographer, Halford J. Mackinder, his ideas on geopolitics were derived mainly from the German scholar Friedrich Ratzel, whose somewhat diffuse observations appear only to have been classified by Rudolf Kjellen, Haushofer's Swedish correspondent and mentor.[31] Ratzel was a distinguished political geographer who studied the dependence of a state on climate, geographical location, bodies of water, soil and physical resources, comparing the state to a living organism, capable of growth, stagnation and decline. States were always vying with each other for space. Hence, no people had originated in the land it now inhabited; nor would it remain on this land forever. Since a people expands, contracts or migrates, frontiers are only temporary phenomena. Therefore, nations had no natural rights to the land they inhabited.[32] Viewed out of context and bearing in mind German history since 1900, Ratzel's ideas can easily be interpreted as encouraging disregard for international frontiers and hence as a justification of aggression. However, though he was not averse to political polemic or immune to the germs of German nationalism, it would, on balance, be unfair to label him as the geographical sponsor of German imperialism. He was a serious scholar attempting to classify observations about the impact of the terrestrial environment on political decision-making.

Karl Haushofer, on the other hand, wanted to use the results obtained from exhaustive analyses of individual regions as the 'scientific' basis by which to forecast future developments and prescribe future policy.

The character of regions or areas of the world dealt with by geography provides the framework within which political events must take place if

31. This is the view of Kjellen put forward by leading geopoliticians, Otto Maull in *ZfG*, vol. 6 (1929), p. 617.

32. F. Ratzel, *Erdenmacht und Völkerschicksal* (edited and introduced by K. Haushofer) (Stüttgart, 1940), p. 33.

they are to have lasting success. Politicians will, of course, on occasion transcend the framework, but, sooner or later, the close tie with the soil will reassert itself. Recognising this fact, geopolitics desires to provide the tools for political action and to be a signpost in political life. In this way, it becomes an applied theory, capable of directing practical policies up to the necessary point of departure from firm ground.[33]

Hence, geopolitics was not so much concerned with the observation and classification of topographical information for its own sake, as to discover the geopolitical determinants of political action. Haushofer admitted that geopolitical forces constituted only twenty-five per cent of the historically-active forces determining political events: but this twenty-five per cent was worth knowing; the disaster of 1918 might have been averted by such knowledge.[34]

The assumption that scientific investigation could provide some insight into the mysterious workings of political destiny effectively marked the point of departure from political geography to geopolitics. Ratzel's comparison of the state to a living organism was treated as a fact of life by Haushofer and his colleagues and the state was considered to be 'a supra-individual living being'.[35] Once this 'leap of faith' had been taken, the line dividing objective analysis and political propaganda became very blurred. As Haushofer himself admitted later, 'The borderline between pure science and practical science is easily crossed in such times of tension. It happened, therefore, that I overstepped those borders occasionally.'[36] In reality, of course, Haushofer's 'practical science' was, in fact, pure propaganda. By trying to furnish the 'scientific' basis for successful government policy-making, he allowed his own political views to dictate his field of research; resenting the reorganisation of the frontiers of Central Europe at Versailles, he set out to assess the settlement by examining it in geopolitical terms. The verdict, of course, preceded and determined the analysis: Germany's living space was inadequate and the new frontiers were geographically unjustifiable.

At this point it would appear that Haushofer was very much on the same wavelength as Adolf Hitler and the other rightwing radicals determined to overthrow the Versailles Settlement. However,

33. Haushofer et al., 'Geopolitik', p. 27.

34. K. Haushofer, 'Grundlagen, Wegen und Ziele der Geopolitik', *Bausteine*, pp. 47–8.

35. K- H Harbeck 'Die Zeitschrift fuer Geopolitik. 1924–44', unpublished dissertation, Kiel University, 1963, p. 9.

36. Haushofer, 'Defense', p. 346.

he would have pointed to one significant difference between geopolitics and the outlook of the Nazi Party: namely, that geopolitics did not purport to be an ideology. It was not a 'secular religion', a system of beliefs designed to mobilise people into action, but an eclectic hotchpotch of principles drawn from social Darwinism and geographical determinism. Moreover, as geopolitics was free from party political bias, any politician, 'irrespective of his ideological or party background', could, in Haushofer's view, benefit from geopolitical knowledge.[37] Indeed the conscious aim of the German geopoliticians was to emancipate their political masters from too narrow a world-view. When asked for an unequivocal statement of a geopolitical foreign policy, Haushofer's son Albrecht replied that 'no-one brings ideological fanatics into an educational scheme just to let geopolitics provide them with a new pseudo-ideology'.[38] Geopolitics, then, did not provide a ready-made foreign policy programme for Germany's leaders.

But was this disclaimer true? Certainly the geopoliticians drew attention to the 'geographical foundations of foreign policy', the most important of which was the need for the state to extend its living-space — the land available to it — in order to keep pace with an increasing population. As Karl Haushofer put it:

> The main duty of foreign affairs is always at least to maintain and take care of the living-space bequeathed to it by past generations and to extend it when it has become too narrow, without creating a threat to the life and existence of the people, yet meeting any unavoidable danger with the full power of the nation, for the sake of the continued existence of the nation.[39]

This assessment, though written in 1926, effectively summarised the gist of Haushofer's thinking over several years and closely resembles, of course, Hitler's own analysis of a *völkisch* foreign policy in *Mein Kampf*.[40] Haushofer made use of up-to-date figures on population density to argue that only two advanced nations could prove

37. K. Haushofer, 'Was ist Geopolitik?', Haushofer Nachlass 834.

38. Letter from Albrecht Haushofer (on behalf of his father) to publisher Kurt Vowinckel, 22 February 1936, Haushofer Nachlass 955 (b).

39. K. Haushofer, 'Geographische Grundzüge auswärtiger Politik', *Süddeutsche Monatshefte*, (1927), p. 258.

40. Hitler wrote: 'The foreign policy of the folkish state must safeguard the existence on this planet of the race embodied in the state, by creating a healthy, viable, natural relation between the nation's population and growth, on the one hand, and the quantity and quality of its soil, on the other', *MK*, p. 587.

undeniably that they were overpopulated; 'only Germany and Japan have to settle, feed, and clothe more than 130 people on one square kilometer'.[41] Such arguments could certainly be seen as providing the framework of a foreign policy programme.

Haushofer also had a definite conception of the existing balance of world power. He believed that a gradual polarisation was taking place between, on the one hand, the 'oceanic' powers, the 'space-owning imperialists' of the western hemisphere (England, France and the United States) and, on the other, the oppressed 'continental' powers of 'Eastern Eurasia' (China, Japan, India and Russia).[42] The Germans were therefore not alone in 'striving for the right to self-determination and the freedom to move at will within our own living-space or, at least, to wander through the earth's unused spatial resources': 'three-fifths of the human race', he claimed, 'are striving for the same goal.'[43]

Germany could, therefore, find support against the 'space-owning' powers 'not just in the Far East, in the rising Pan-Asiatic movement, but also in Japan . . . and in the intelligent cooperation with the spatial requirements of the Russian homeland (*Volksboden*)'.[44] Germany had therefore to decide whether she belonged alongside the 'space-owning imperialists' or alongside the 'oppressed' nations. In 1925, the negotiation of the Locarno treaties and German entry into the League of Nations, Haushofer felt, brought matters to a head: 'it is up to us to decide whether we want to join the League of Nations in the only way possible today — burdened with the hatred of the suppressed, the deprived, the humiliated and the wronged, and with their curse'.[45] That Germany did so obviously disappointed Haushofer, but he continued to hope for German support for the nationalist movements of India and China. Common interests also drew Japan and Germany together; both had been threatened by the same powers (Britain and France) since the 1890s and 'more than once' Germany had rejected the proffered hand of Japanese friendship.[46] Furthermore, Japan had faced similar spatial

41. Haushofer, 'Geographische Grundzüge', p. 258.

42. K. Haushofer, 'Die geopolitishe Betrachtung grenzdeutscher Probleme' in K. von Loesch and A. H. Ziegfeld (eds.), *Volk unter Völkern* (Breslau, 1925), pp. 191–2. For more details on his views on Western imperialism, see Stoakes, 'Evolution', p. 391.

43. Haushofer, 'Geographische Grundzüge', p. 260. Japan's future lay as a 'continental' rather than 'oceanic' power according to Haushofer. 'Japan an der Schwelle des "Leuchtenden Friedens"', *MNN*, 1 January 1927.

44. Haushofer, 'Geographische Grundzüge', p. 260.

45. K. Haushofer, 'Weltpolitische Rundschau', *Das Dritte Reich*, 15 August 1925.

46. Haushofer, 'Geographische Grundzüge', p. 260.

problems to Germany, and had successfully extended her *Lebensraum* with the seizure of Korea after a press campaign had highlighted the country's shortage of space and mobilised public opinion. What is more, Haushofer had witnessed all this at first-hand and obviously hoped for similar success in Germany.[47]

Most interesting of all in Haushofer's outlook and that of the other geopoliticians was the position of Russia: she was neither economically exploited by the Western Powers nor short of space; nevertheless, she was to be the mainstay of the Eurasian alliance against the West. This is unlikely to have been because of the Soviet denunciations of Western imperialism, since Haushofer advocated spatial cooperation with the needs of the Russian homelands, 'irrespective of whether they are organised by the Soviets or any other power'. Nor did racial predilections influence his judgement of Russia: 'the worse the situation appears', he wrote, 'the more reason for a nation to think in global terms without regard for mistaken racial prejudices'.[48] Indeed, it is clear that Haushofer did not entirely trust the Russians; in 1925 he noted that they had not yet shown themselves to be reliable allies; and two years later, he was clearly disillusioned by the results of their collaboration with the Chinese nationalist forces.[49] Such disappointments did not, however, shake his conviction of the need to work with Russia because, as he explained, 'geopolitics judges daily events not according to their emotional value, but on the firm foundation of interests which arise with a degree of permanence from the land and living-space and are dictated by its broadness or narrowness and the stern demands of self-maintenance'.[50]

So what were these 'interests' which necessitated Russo-German collaboration? The key appears to lie in the ideas of the British geographer, Halford J. Mackinder, which seem to have made a great impression on Haushofer. Mackinder believed that the 'Heartland', roughly the area controlled by Russia at the time, was 'the pivot region of world politics'; it was potentially a vast economic world in itself and only a backward economy prevented it from dominating the rest of the world. A German alliance might tilt the balance of world power in favour of the 'Heartland' and then, Mackinder

---

47. A. Dorpalen, *The World of General Haushofer* (New York, 1942), pp. 11, 29; cf. K. Haushofer, *Grenzen in ihrer geographischen und politischen Bedeutung*, pp. 145–50.
48. Haushofer, 'Geographische Grundzüge', p. 260.
49. K. Haushofer, 'Politische Umschau', *Das Dritte Reich*, 15 October 1927.
50. K. Haushofer, 'Interessengemeinschaft der Selbsterhaltung', *MNN*, 1 February 1925.

argued, 'the empire of the world would be in sight'.[51] Whether Haushofer was intoxicated by this dream of a 'world-empire' is a question to which we shall return shortly, but clearly he was impressed by the general scenario; 'the greatest of all geographical world-views', he called it.[52] In particular, he picked up Mackinder's forecast of a confrontation between Russia and the 'oceanic powers' and made it the main rationale behind a Eurasian alliance between Germany, Russia, Japan and the emerging nationalist movements of India and China.[53] Spatial collaboration between these powers, for example concerning the disputed area of Manchuria, might, he thought, reduce diplomatic tensions around the world and in the long run help to 'alleviate the frightful position of Central Europe'.[54]

Just how this would assist Germany was never made clear. Perhaps Haushofer envisaged the transfer of Russian land to Germany. After all, he referred to Manchuria as part of 'the empty spaces of the Soviet Union' and on another occasion argued that Germany should be allowed 'the freedom to wander (*Wanderfreiheit*) through the unused reserves of space in the world'.[55] Certainly, the return of the overseas colonies lost at Versailles was not considered sufficient to correct the inbalance between the size of the population and the amount of land available: 'the old colonial area itself could only accommodate three to four million German settlers at most.' The European continent and in particular Germany's borderlands had more to offer: 'It is much more important to strive towards the borderlands . . . in which every German field is defended, even if it is for the time being under a foreign flag or under foreign control. We must place much more emphasis on a conscious widening and retention of our frontier area and on a strong balanced internal structure than on questionable overseas possessions.'[56]

However, Haushofer seemed reluctant to explain how such expansion was to occur and, more importantly, to specify which areas made up the 'borderlands'. Only very rarely did he tackle these questions. On one notable occasion in 1925, in an essay entitled *Die geopolitische Betrachtung grenzdeutscher Probleme*, he did point out several possible ways towards a peaceful devolution of the borderlands to

51. H. J. Mackinder, 'The Geographical Pivot of History', in Mackinder, *Democratic Ideals and Reality* (New York, 1962), pp. 260–2.

52. Quoted in F. W. Gilbert, *Mackinder's Scope and Methods of Geography and the Geopolitical Pivot of History* (London, 1951), introduction.

53. K. Haushofer, 'Bericht', *ZfG*, vol. 4 (1927), pp. 23–5.

54. K. Haushofer, 'Der Ostasiatische Zukunftsblock', *ZfG*, vol. 2. (1925), pp. 81–3.

55. Ibid; Haushofer, 'Geographische Grundzüge', p. 260.

56. Haushofer 'Das Dritte Reich' in '*Oberland*', pp. 8–9.

Germany. The first — a logical extension of his work with the VDA — was by maintaining contact 'between separated and endangered areas and the whole body of the larger unit . . . in cultural, economic and political affairs'. A second method was to sustain 'the strong awareness of regional unity, especially in those lands which our enemies are seeking, with good reason, to divide administratively, like Eupen-Malmédy, Alsace-Lorraine, Tyrol and the regions of the Vistula'. Thirdly, the publication of geopolitical studies revealing Germany to be overpopulated would create a 'community of feeling with all the people around the world who are oppressed like us'. Such methods, it was hoped, would prove successful in persuading world opinion of Germany's right to absorb these areas.

Haushofer made no mention of using force to achieve this goal and it is perhaps significant that the areas which he considered to be the 'borderlands' all had either sizeable German-speaking communities or historical ties with Germany; in this same revealing essay, he mentioned North Schleswig, Eupen-Malmédy, the Saar, the Palatinate, Lorraine, Alsace, Vorarlberg and Tyrol, Carinthia, Styria, Burgenland, Moravia, the Austro-Hungarian diaspora, the old duchies of Auschwitz and Zator, Eastern Upper Silesia, Austria (Ostmark), Danzig and Memelland.[57] These areas were all outside German control at that moment; however, Haushofer does not appear to have openly advocated the absorption of territories with no German connexion.

It is quite evident, therefore, that, whatever the geopoliticians might claim, Karl Haushofer, at least, had developed in broad outline a foreign policy programme of his own. However, whilst he constantly reiterated the need for Germany to expand her living-space, only rarely did he make plain his belief in peaceful persuasion and the peaceful transfer of territory to which Germany had some claim, whether on the basis of past history or of a linguistic or cultural identity. As a result, it is widely thought that he may have helped to fire Hitler's lust of expansion.[58]

---

57. Haushofer, 'Betrachtung', p. 189.

58. Norton argues that Haushofer 'never possessed' any influence over Hitler's thinking since the latter did not take him seriously until after 1933, 'Haushofer', p. 191. Laack-Michel admits that Haushofer took geopolitical literature to Landsberg but finds it difficult to reproach him for the fact that Hitler profited from it, *Albrecht Haushofer*, p. 12. Jacobsen concludes that Haushofer cannot be regarded as 'the spiritual father' of Nazi war aims, though he did do much to prepare the ground intellectually for the rise of the Nazi system, *Haushofer*, vol. 1, pp. 451–2, 464.

Haushofer and Hitler's Expansionism

How justifiable is the attribution of Hitler's expansionism to the influence of Haushofer and geopolitics? This is a complex question. In addition to the ever-present difficulty of ascribing one person's ideas to the influence of another, there is in this case uncertainty about the exact nature and frequency of contacts between the two men in the early 1920s. These problems are compounded by the fact that many of Haushofer's ideas were similar to those expressed in Pan-German propaganda before, during and after the First World War, and Hitler may already have absorbed these before he met Haushofer. As has been shown earlier, Hitler's awareness of the problem of Germany's overpopulation and the possible solutions to it — evident in his speeches in 1920 and 1921 — can be traced back to Pan-German literature. Hence, even when he claimed in a speech in 1921 that 'population increase implies increase in territory', this is no certain proof of geopolitical influence.[59]

In fact, it is impossible to derive the scheme of conquest and settlement of Russian territory explained in *Mein Kampf* (but evident as early as December 1922) from Haushofer's theories. Hitler's scheme of eastward expansion flatly contradicted Haushofer's conviction of the need for 'collaboration' with Russia over the question of space, which was to be the basis for his larger design of an 'East Eurasian' alliance. Indeed, Haushofer's views bore a strong resemblance to those of Moeller van den Bruck, with whom Hitler had clashed in 1922. Both argued that Germany's future lay in the East, but seemingly not as a result of conquest: both believed that Russia and Germany were somehow drawn together by destiny and that, together, they could solve each other's problems. Moeller put this somewhat ethereal relationship down to a cultural affinity, Haushofer to rather more concrete geographical realities. Accordingly, both refused to accept that political changes, such as the emergence of a Bolshevik government, could alter this destiny. By 1922, Hitler felt differently.

However, he may originally have shared the outlook of Haushofer and Moeller. It will be recalled that Hitler had argued that a Russo-German alliance before the war would have enabled Germany to expand eastwards at Russian expense, presumably by detaching the Baltic Provinces and the Polish lands. And again, he seemed to regard the Treaty of Brest-Litovsk as having implemented

59. Maser, *Hitler's Letters*, pp. 252–3.

this strategy; the treaty, he argued on 31 May 1921, had secured Germany's future 'by the acquisition of land and soil, by access to raw materials, and by *friendly relations between the two lands* [emphasis added]'.[60] However, Hitler's original enthusiasm for a Russo-German alliance was evidently based on a conviction far less rigid than that of Haushofer or Moeller: it seems to have been eroded during 1921 and 1922 by his growing aversion to Bolshevik Russia. By the end of 1922, Hitler was planning 'the *destruction of Russia* with the help of England [emphasis added]'.[61] This was quite a different matter and would not have received Haushofer's approval.

Haushofer's geopolitics, in short, provided neither the model nor the inspiration for Hitler's campaign of conquest and destruction at Russia's expense in Eastern Europe, and the disparity between the two men's political philosophies should not be underestimated.[62] Nevertheless the arguments of the geopoliticians were to be grist to Hitler's mill. The foreign policy sections of *Mein Kampf* leave little doubt that he found their theories highly useful. Although Haushofer later asserted that the Nazis had 'misused' and 'misinterpreted' geopolitics, does this claim stand examination?[63]

When interrogated by the Allies in 1945, Haushofer denied any part in the composition of *Mein Kampf*. It is perhaps significant, though, that he argued that 'a scientific comparison of my style of writing and the style of the book' would prove this. He was defending himself against the charge that he actually helped to *write* the work, thereby sidestepping the issue of whether he influenced the trend of its argument. In addition, given that the Allied interrogators knew that he had frequently visited Rudolf Hess in Landsberg gaol in 1923 and 1924 and that he had on occasion spoken with Hitler there, Haushofer contended that he had never seen Hitler 'alone'.[64] This was an attempt to conceal the fact that he had had discussions with Hitler and Hess, and the two prisoners had been reading Ratzel's *Politische Geographie* and other geopolitical literature

---

60. Hitler's speech on 31 May, report in *VB*, 5 June 1921. See above, p. 96.

61. Scharrer, 'Bericht', BAK R43I/2681.

62. Hitler was willing to sacrifice the interests of the Germans in the South Tyrol to attract Mussolini's support; Haushofer could not contemplate such a betrayal; Haushofer, 'Defense', p. 348.

63. Ibid., p. 351. Haushofer admitted that the Nazis had used the autarkic elements of the *Lebensraum* idea; Jacobsen, *Haushofer*, vol. 1, p. 336.

64. Haushofer, 'Defense', p. 350. According to Haushofer's own account of his interrogation by the Allies on 23 August 1945, he told them that he had not written 'even a line' of *Mein Kampf*; Jacobsen, *Haushofer*, vol. 1, p. 338.

supplied to them by Haushofer.[65] There can be no doubt that this exchange of ideas and information bore fruit in Hitler's autobiography and that Haushofer knew it.[66]

In chapter four of the first volume of *Mein Kampf*, published on 19 July 1925, Hitler reviewed prewar German diplomacy and four options open to it in dealing with Germany's growing population. He had discussed the same subject in a speech on 31 May 1921 and it is interesting to see how this essentially Pan-German analysis had developed in the intervening years.[67] Hitler rejected birth control — the first option — on pseudo-Darwinistic rather than geopolitical grounds, arguing that natural selection and the survival of the fittest was far more healthy than the artificial limitation of the birth rate.[68] His conclusion that 'anyone who wants to secure the existence of the German people by a self-limitation of its reproduction is robbing it of its future' is perfectly consistent not only with Ratzel's definition of *Realpolitik* as 'the policy which secures for a growing people the land indispensable for the future', but also with the ideas of Heinrich Class and the ADV, which, it should be remembered, Ratzel helped to found.[69] It is impossible, therefore, to distinguish between geopolitical and Pan-German influences here.

Evidence of the impact of geopolitical ideas is more easily traceable in Hitler's assessment of the usefulness of internal colonisation — the second option. Admittedly, Ratzel, Class and, in his turn, Hitler accepted that Germany should make maximum use of her own land before external colonisation was undertaken and all of them doubted whether this alone would be sufficient in the long term to feed a growing population.[70] However, in *Mein Kampf* Hitler developed one further argument against internal colonisation, and this seems clearly attributable to his reading of Ratzel's *Politische Geographie*. In the book, Ratzel stressed that one of the advantages of

65. Haushofer's introduction to Ratzel, *Erdenmacht*, p. xxvi. Jacobsen's research corroborates this; *Haushofer*, vol. 1, pp. 376, 239.

66. Heinz Haushofer quoted in 1946 the following remarks by his father 'I visited the Führer then in the Landsberg fortress on various occasions. In 1923 and 1924 the prisoner merely thumbed through what he found of geopolitical literature in the fortress. Now certainly I stimulated the people, counselled [them]. In certain parts of *Mein Kampf* there are strong traces of this. But then they popularised my train of thought falsely and for the purposes of propaganda', 'Ratgeber und Opfer des Dritten Reiches', *Schweizer Illustrierte Zeitung*, 26 June 1946, newspaper clippings file on Haushofer, Wiener Library.

67. *VB*, 5 June 1921, see above pp. 55–6.

68. Hitler, *MK*, p. 121.

69. Ratzel, *Politische Geographie* (3rd ed., Munich, 1923), p. 8. On Ratzel's relationship to the ADV, see K. Lange, 'Der Terminus "Lebensraum" in Hitler's *Mein Kampf*', *VfZG*, vol. 13 (1965), pp. 432, 429.

70. Ratzel, *Politische Geographie*, p. 90; Frymann, *Wenn ich*, p. 142; Hitler, *MK*, p. 122.

territorial expansion was that a larger area simplified foreign relations by reducing the number of possible neighbours.[71] Hitler
turned this argument around to suit his own purposes, suggesting
that the size of a state materially affected its security: 'The limitation
to a definite small area of soil, inherent in internal colonisation . . .
leads to an exceedingly unfavourable politico-military situation in
the nation in question. The size of the area inhabited by a people
constitutes in itself an essential factor for determining its outward
security. The greater the quantity of space at the disposal of a
people, the greater its natural protection.' Whilst a large amount of
territory acted as a deterrent against frivolous attack, a small
amount acted as 'a positive invitation to seizure', in Hitler's view.[72]
Ratzel's geo-military deliberations clearly proved useful in the
attempt to discredit the idea of internal colonisation.

Hitler's arguments concerning the third and favoured option —
the acquisition of new land for settlement of the excess population —
reflect a variety of influences. The first argument, namely that such
a policy would help to rectify the balance between the agricultural
and industrial sectors of the economy and make 'the subsistence of
the people as a whole more or less independent of foreign countries',
repeated almost verbatim the analysis of Heinrich Class in the
'Kaiserbuch'. However, these goals could not be met, in Hitler's
view, by overseas expansion but by aggrandisement 'almost exclusively in Europe'.[73] Writing before the First World War, Class
believed that expansion in Europe could only be achieved by resort-
ing to war; he therefore felt reluctant to advocate this course openly
and put great emphasis on overseas colonisation (this restraint
disappeared after 1914, however).[74] Hitler had decided to renounce
overseas colonies in order to avoid alienating Britain, but he had no
qualms about advocating the seizure of other nations' territory in
Europe; perhaps drawing on Ratzel's views as to the transient
nature of political frontiers, he argued 'we must not let political
boundaries obscure for us the boundaries of eternal justice'.[75] His
final argument in favour of territorial aggrandisement in Europe
seems to derive from Ratzel's observations on the fleeting success of
trading powers who acquire colonies, but whose homeland is too

71. Ratzel also pointed out the disadvantages of, for example, the consequent localisation of
authority and the danger of interracial clashes, *Politische Geographie*, pp. 272–5.
72. Hitler, *MK*, pp. 125–6.
73. Ibid., pp. 126–7; Frymann, *Wenn ich*, pp. 212–13.
74. Frymann, *Wenn ich*, p. 140.
75. Hitler, *MK*, p. 127.

small to warrant such an empire, for he asserted: 'Many European states are like pyramids stood on their heads. Their European area is absurdly small in comparison to their weight of colonies, foreign trade etc.' In order to avoid this fatal flaw, Germany, like the United States, needed a large territorial base on her own continent.[76]

Hitler dismissed the fourth alternative, that is, the policy of sustaining Germany by commercial exchange and overseas colonisation which had been followed by the imperial government before 1914, because it was based on two fallacies. The first was belief in the feasibility of the peaceful economic conquest of the world sought by German politicians; 'if we chose this road', Hitler wrote, 'England would some day inevitably become our enemy'.[77] The second was the conviction encouraged by Germany's successful technological and industrial revolution that 'the state itself primarily represented an economic institution . . . that its very existence depended on economics'. This heresy Hitler attributed to the insidious influence of the Jews: the state, in fact, was 'a national organism, not an economic organisation'.[78] In disparaging both attitudes as fallacies, he drew, consciously or otherwise, on the arguments of his precursors; Class for his critique on Imperial Germany's commercial policy and Ratzel for the biological view of statehood.[79]

In developing his analysis of prewar German foreign policy for *Mein Kampf*, Hitler therefore seems to have rifled Ratzel's *Politische Geographie* in search of 'scientific' justification for a campaign of conquest in Eastern Europe, already implied in his speech on 31 May 1921 by his support for the Treaty of Brest-Litovsk and probably inspired originally by Pan-German propaganda. It should be stressed that he used Ratzel's ideas out of context and conveniently overlooked the author's own political opinions.[80]

In the second volume of *Mein Kampf*, published on 11 December 1926 and presumably written after his release from Landsberg gaol, Hitler felt obliged to defend his views on eastward expansion, which had not received wholesale acceptance within the ranks of the Nazi Party. He now described the Russian question not only as probably 'the most decisive concern of all German foreign affairs', but also as

76. Ibid., pp. 127–8; Ratzel used Greece as an example on one occasion, but Britain on another, *Politische Geographie*, pp. 23–5, 252 (Hitler also used the British example, *MK*, p. 128).

77. Hitler, *MK*, pp. 131–2.

78. Ibid., pp. 137–8.

79. Frymann, *Wenn ich*, pp. 5, 19–24; Ratzel, *Politische Geographie*, p. 4.

80. Ratzel believed in some kind of European unity. The details remain vague but what is clear is his view that 'Europe's disunity can no longer be healed by conquest'; *Politische Geographie*, p. 308.

a test of the Nazi movement's ability 'to think clearly and act correctly'.[81] Faced with the challenge to his conception of a future German foreign policy, Hitler again looked to the ideas of the geopoliticians in search of positive reinforcement. His observations on the strategic and military significance of a larger territory and on the validity of Europe's frontiers seem to show a renewed pilfering of geopolitical ideas.

In particular, Hitler appears to have drawn on Karl Haushofer's developing views on military geography (*Wehrgeographie*). In an unpublished article in 1926 comparing Germany's living-space with that of her neighbours, Haushofer found that this had become 'highly unfavourable from a military-geographical standpoint'. Poland and Bohemia penetrated it deeply from the east and France from the west. To make matters worse, the population was mal-distributed, tending to accumulate in the 'exposed areas' of the Upper Rhine, Upper Silesia and Saxony. Furthermore 'over 160 km of coastline belongs to East Prussia, [which is now] cut off [from Germany], while the whole Baltic coast, unprotected as it is, is easily reached by sea, as shown by the appearance of the English fleet off Swinemünde before the war'. In total, Germany had '3,305 kilometers of wholly unprotected land frontier and 1,440 kilometers of open coastline'. In addition Haushofer stressed that Germany's shortage of raw materials, such as oil, copper, tin, zinc, not to mention coal and iron, added to the fact that her limited resources were situated in vulnerable areas, would detract from her ability to resist attack. Hence, he concluded gloomily, the German Empire is 'an over-industrialised industrial state without a chance of feeding its population from its own land, and therefore in its present form, mutilated and split into two, particularly susceptible to aggression'.[82]

Whilst there is no evidence to suggest that Hitler had access to this unpublished article or that he had discussed 'military geography' with Haushofer, it does seem probable that he was acquainted with the subject when he wrote the second volume of *Mein Kampf*. Though their ideas were not completely identical, Hitler shared Haushofer's concern for the 'extremely unfavourable situation of the Reich from the viewpoint of military geography'. 'The coastline especially', Hitler observed, 'was unfavourable from a military

---

81. Hitler, *MK*, p. 586. On opposition to Hitler's ideas, see chapter six.

82. K. Haushofer, 'Vergleich des Lebens-Raumes Deutschlands mit dem seiner Nachbarn unter besonderer Berücksichtigung der wehrgeographischen Lage der Vergleichs-Staaten', Jacobsen, *Haushofer*, vol. 1, pp. 524–6, 534, 536–7.

standpoint for a fight with England; it was short and cramped, and the land front, on the other hand, disproportionately long and open'.[83] Like Haushofer, he now considered access to food and raw materials to be a vital part of Germany's state security; his projected Anglo-German-Italian alliance would, he argued, free Germany from her 'unfavourable strategic position' by ensuring 'the most powerful protection on our flank on the one hand' and the 'complete guarantee of our food and raw materials on the other'.[84] These strategic arguments led to the foregone conclusion that 'only an adequately large space on this earth assures a nation of its freedom of existence'.[85]

If Haushofer's findings helped to justify Hitler's expansionist programme on the grounds of self-sufficiency and military security — and the similarity between their ideas is fairly remarkable — Ratzel's analysis of the geopolitical value of frontiers may also have proved attractive. Here again, Haushofer may have been an important intermediary, drawing attention in his own writings to the results of Ratzel's deliberations in order to cure what he saw as German ignorance of the 'true' nature of frontiers.[86]

In *Politische Geographie*, Ratzel argued that a frontier was 'organic' and subject to growth and contraction, according to the state of a particular nation. As a result, frontiers were 'by their nature inconstant'; 'the apparently rigid frontier' was, in fact, 'only the resting-point of a movement'; in short, there were 'no absolute frontiers'.[87] These views were echoed by Hitler in the second volume of *Mein Kampf*:

> Just as Germany's frontiers are fortuitous frontiers, momentary frontiers in the current political struggle of any period, so are the boundaries of other nations' living-space. And just as the shape of our earth's surface can seem immutable as granite only to the thoughtless soft-head, but in reality only represents at each period an apparent pause in a continuous development, created by the mighty forces of Nature in a process of continuous growth, only to be transformed or destroyed tomorrow by greater forces, likewise the boundaries of living-spaces in the life of nations.

83. Hitler, *MK*, p. 563. Hitler also argued that the 'mother country' was limited to an area of 500,000 square kilometers, ibid., p. 588; Haushofer cited the figure of 541,000 Jacobsen, *Haushofer*, p. 525.

84. Hitler, *MK*, p. 608.

85. Ibid., p. 587.

86. K. Haushofer, 'Das Wissen von der Grenze und die Grenzen der deutschen Volkes', *Deutsche Rundschau*, vol. 50 (1924), p. 233. See also *Grenzen*.

87. Ratzel, *Politische Geographie*, pp. 386–7, 434–8.

Hitler, however, used such arguments for his own ends, firstly to undermine respect for existing frontiers by arguing that no nation had any natural rights to certain territory and that 'state boundaries are made by man and changed by man' and secondly to discredit the idea of limiting German ambitions to the restoration of the frontiers of 1914. Those frontiers were, he wrote, 'neither complete in the sense of embracing the people of German nationality, nor sensible with regard to geopolitical expedience. They were not the result of considered political action, but momentary frontiers in a political struggle that was by no means concluded'.[88]

There seems little doubt, therefore, that in the second volume of his autobiography, Hitler marshalled both sets of reasoning: Haushofer's arguments concerning Germany's lack of self-sufficiency and military security to add greater conviction to his expansionist programme; and Ratzel's observations on the transient nature of frontiers to overcome any moralistic reservations among his followers towards such a programme. Though both themes were not without significance in the later foreign policy of the Third Reich, it must nevertheless be remembered that they were used to bolster a decision already made. They determined neither the decision to expand nor, more importantly, the direction which that expansion was to take. In *Mein Kampf*, geopolitics were harnessed to an antisemitic, anti-Bolshevik racial ideology, which reinforced Hitler's already evident interest in an eastward course of territorial aggrandisement.[89] Haushofer's claim that the Nazis 'misused' or 'misunderstood' geopolitics is, at best a half-truth. Hitler certainly misused geopolitical arguments; they were meant to convince world opinion of the need for a peaceful redistribution of territory in Europe; they were used to justify the resort to force in the pursuit of the same goal. Nevertheless, Haushofer's ideas (and to a lesser extent Ratzel's) were open to the interpretation which Hitler put on them. Haushofer's assertions of Germany's need for more living-space had obvious political implications, especially when, as so often, they were unaccompanied by a rider urging peaceful territorial change.

Hitler's 'Final Goals'

Some historians, of course, believe that the extension of Germany's

88. Hitler, *MK*, pp. 593, 596.
89. Ibid., pp. 595, 598, 604.

Lebensraum may not have been Hitler's ultimate goal. The conquest of territory in Eastern Europe may have been only the first of several 'stages' in the creation of a German 'world dominion' (*Weltherrschaft*). After the successful establishment of European hegemony with the defeat of France and the conquest of Russia, Germany would try, so the argument runs, to acquire a colonial empire bordering the Mediterranean and the Atlantic in preparation for a confrontation with the United States which would result in world domination by Germany.[90] But how convincing is the evidence that Hitler was mulling over such fantastic schemes in the early 1920s? At that time, he was a largely unknown orator and even the first step in the realisation of such ambitions — gaining power in Germany — appeared to be a pipedream. Lowly status does not, of course, preclude grandiose ideas and, if such notions were in his head, what inspired them?

Some historians have found evidence of Hitler's interest in German world dominion, and perhaps the inspiration behind it, in the antisemitic ideology which he adopted after 1919. The belief in an international Jewish conspiracy to take over the world instilled the idea that the Aryan race had a mission, a worldwide life-and-death struggle against the Jews; perhaps, therefore, Hitler conceived of an Aryan-dominated world when the Jews were defeated. Alternatively, it has been argued that, by accusing the Jews of pursuing world conquest, he was in fact revealing his own ambitions for Germany.[91] If this is true, then Hitler was dreaming of 'world dominion' as early as his speech of 13 August 1920, when he claimed that the Jew was trying to 'organise, build up and maintain his definitive world dominion (*Weltherrschaft*)'.[92] On the other hand, this interpretation is highly speculative. One can with equal justification argue, as shown above, that Hitler stressed the worldwide nature of the Jewish threat merely to provoke a national response. In the same speech in August 1920, for example, he declared that no-one could 'fight fire with fire' and the grip of international Jewish capitalism could only be broken 'by *national* strength'.[93] Indeed, the slogan of 'nationalism versus internationalism' was constantly reiterated in

90. See for example A. Hillgruber, *Hitlers Strategie*, and idem, 'England's Place in Hitler's Plans for World Dominion', *Journal of Contemporary History*, vol. 9 (1974), pp. 5–22; Hildebrand, *Vom Reich*. For a review of other literature see M. Michaelis, 'World Power Status or World Dominion?' *Historical Journal*, vol. 15 (1972), pp. 331–60 and M. Hauner, 'Did Hitler want a World Dominion?', *Journal of Contemporary History*, vol. 13 (1978), pp. 15–32.

91. J. Thies, *Architekt*, p. 44. See also G. Moltmann, 'Weltherrschaftsideen Hitlers'.

92. Phelps, 'Hitlers "grundlegende" Rede', p. 411.

93. Ibid., p. 410. See above, pp 69–70, 79–80.

Nazi proganda at the time and the party's main ideologues had since 1919 belaboured the institutions seen as having universal aspirations: the Catholic Church and the Freemasons, as well as the Communist Party.[94] So one wonders if a national revival was not the extent of Hitler's ambitions in 1920 and antisemitic propaganda was geared solely to that end.

It has been suggested, however, that by the time he wrote *Mein Kampf*, Hitler's antisemitism had 'hardened' or 'sharpened'; in 1920, it is pointed out, the Nazi Party was calling for the treatment of Jews in Germany as aliens and, at worst, for their expulsion; by 1924 Hitler was writing of the need to eradicate the Jewish bacteria from the German body.[95] One might, therefore, assume a causal connection between the increasing virulence of Hitler's antisemitism and an emerging preoccupation with the idea of German 'world dominion'. However, for several reasons this interpretation also has to be treated cautiously. Firstly, Hitler had, in fact, been using the violent language of *Mein Kampf* in private discussion of the problem since 1920; in a letter in July 1920, he referred to the Jews as 'bacilli', which must be combated 'by annihilation of the germs'.[96] In December 1922, he told Eduard Scharrer in a confidential interview that 'a solution to the question of the Jews has to come. If it is solved sensibly, this will be best for both parties.' He went on: 'If this is not achieved, then there are only two other possibilities, either the German people will become a nation like the Americans or the Levantines, or a bloody showdown will result'.[97] So it must be questioned whether there was any hardening of Hitler's attitude towards the Jews between 1920 and 1924 and hence any corresponding growth of his interest in German world dominion. Secondly, one should resist the temptation to take his talk of 'showdowns' and the 'annihilation of germs' too literally. It may have been pure rhetoric and certainly, as Hitler himself admitted, other more 'sensible' solutions, such as creating a national home for the Jews, were possible. Alfred Rosenberg suggested the resettlement of the Jews in Uganda: but Madagascar and even Southern Russia were mooted as possible locations.[98] So there are grounds for questioning the assumption that there was a connection between the

94. See chapters one and two above; cf. K. Lüdecke, 'Völkische Weltanschauung und völkische Weltpolitik', *Der Weltkampf*, vol. 2 (February 1925), p. 3.

95. Jäckel, *Hitlers Weltanschauung*, p. 66; cf. Thies, *Architekt*, pp. 42–3.

96. Letter from Hitler to Hierl, 3 July 1920, quoted in Tyrell, *Trommler*, pp. 214–15.

97. Scharrer, 'Bericht', BAK, R43I/2681.

98. A. Rosenberg, 'Die Raubvögel — Kongress in Budapest', *VB*, 20 October 1925; see also 'GJ', 'Weder Uganda noch Palastina sondern — Südrussland', *VB*, 27/28 October 1926.

increasing violence of Hitler's antisemitism and his interest in 'world dominion'.

On the other hand, Hitler's speculations in *Mein Kampf* on the long-term implicatons of a carefully considered racial policy do suggest a link with the idea of 'world dominion'. In the first volume he suggested that 'a racially pure people which is conscious of its blood can never be enslaved by the Jews'.[99] In the second volume he implied that such a people would actually come to dominate the world itself: 'A state which in this age of racial poisoning dedicates itself to the care of its best racial elements must some day become lord of the earth.'[100] Indeed, this might be a necessity: 'We all sense that in the distant future humanity must be faced by problems which only a highest race, become master people and supported by the means and possibilites of the entire globe, will be equipped to overcome.'[101] What he meant by all this, Hitler never made clear. In particular, it remains uncertain whether he was describing the political destiny of the German state or of the Aryan race. The evidence supports both interpretations.[102] So it is possible that talk of racial purity encouraged him to fantasise about an exalted destiny for either the Aryan race or the German state.

Signs of Hitler's interest in the concept of German 'world dominion' are not, however, to be found exclusively in his antisemitic and racial musings. The term *Weltherrschaft* crops up also in his discussions of prewar and postwar power politics. This has led some scholars to conclude that Hitler had a vague, but fairly concrete, long-term diplomatic and military scheme, by which Germany would come to dominate the world. However, the obliqueness of his occasional hints and a degree of confusion over the meaning of the terms he used, may have misled historians as to the actual goals envisaged. Three 'stages' can be identified in Hitler's foreign policy programme in *Mein Kampf*. Firstly, he sought to secure the continued existence of the German nation: 'Today we are not fighting for a position as a world power (*Weltmacht*); today, we must struggle for the existence of our fatherland, or the unity of our nation and the daily bread of our children.'[103] This was to be achieved in alliance with England and Italy against the French.

99. Hitler, *MK*, p. 295.
100. Ibid., p. 629.
101. Ibid., pp. 348–9.
102. On one occasion, he describes how the 'German Reich' could have been 'mistress of the globe', ibid., p. 360; on another, he called upon the 'Germanic states' to halt the bastardisation of the race, ibid., p. 365, cf. pp. 584–5.
103. Ibid., p. 565.

The second stage would see the establishment of Germany as a world power, primarily by the acquisition of more *Lebensraum* in Europe, largely at the expense of Russia. Though in 1914 Germany, with her far-flung imperial possessions, had 'supposedly' been a world power, she had not been so in reality; in Hitler's words: 'If the German nation in 1914 had had a different relation between area and population, Germany would really have been a world power (*Weltmacht*).'[104] What was needed, in the first instance, was not overseas colonies but 'exclusively . . . the acquisition of a territory for settlement, which will enhance the area of the mother country and hence not only keep the new settlers in the most intimate community with the land of their origin, but secure for the total area those advantages which lie in its unified magnitude . . . And for world power she needs that magnitude'.[105] Hitler hinted, though, that whilst overseas colonies had low priority at the moment, they might be valuable later; in a retrospective assessment of prewar German policy, he argued that the strengthening of Germany's continental power by territorial aggrandisement in Europe 'seemed to place a completion by later acquisitions of colonial territory within the realm of the naturally possible'.[106]

The third stage and — in the view of this writer — the ultimate ambition harboured by Hitler at this time was to make Germany the *dominant world power*. It is here that his looseness of language may have created confusion. He asserted that the lack of racial unity amongst Germans in the past had robbed them of 'world dominion' (*Weltherrschaft*); but for this, Germany would have been 'mistress of the globe' (*Herrin des Erdballs*); Germans would have enjoyed 'the right of masters' (*Herrenrecht*).[107] All three terms — *Weltherrschaft, Herrin des Erdballs* and *Herrenrecht* — seem to imply world conquest or world mastery by Germany.

But is this misleading? In *Mein Kampf*, Hitler referred to the 'reinforcement of British world dominion (*Weltherrschaft*)' as the goal of British foreign policy at the beginning of the twentieth century.[108] Clearly in this context *Weltherrschaft* did not mean world mastery; by no stretch of the imagination could Britain be said to have enjoyed such a position. She did have a worldwide empire, which gave her a

104. Ibid., p. 588.
105. Ibid., p. 597–8. Hence in the 1920s Germans should not advocate the restoration of Germany's 'sea power' before she was secure in Europe, ibid., p. 571.
106. Ibid., p. 558.
107. Ibid., pp. 360–1.
108. Ibid., pp. 561.

predominant influence in world affairs; she was, as Hitler put it elsewhere, 'the greatest world power on earth'.[109] On another occasion, he referred to a 'British world hegemony (*britische Welt-Hegemonie*)', one that had been challenged by a 'Germanic world hegemony' in 1914.[110] Therefore, he wanted for Germany what Britain currently enjoyed. Whether he called it *Weltherrschaft* or *Welt-Hegemonie*, it probably meant not actual world conquest, but a position of pre-eminence amongst other world powers.[111] Hitler seemed to believe that it was 'natural' for the world powers to vie with one another for predominance.[112]

This interpretation is necessarily speculative, given the paucity of the evidence and the ambiguous nature of Hitler's comments about his distant goals (nor does it necessarily mean that he did not seek world conquest later). Nevertheless, if one considers the origins of Hitler's fascination with the concept of 'world dominion', the existence of a limited *Stufenplan* seems more probable. His interest was almost certainly stimulated by the Pan-German literature which he had imbibed before the First World War. Heinrich Class, it will be recalled, had been fascinated by Britain's role as a world power and, indeed, he had described Britain after the signing of the Anglo-Japanese alliance as the 'master of world affairs' (*Herr der Weltlage*).[113]

But it was Class's predecessor as chairman of the ADV, Ernst Hasse, who, in a book entitled *Weltpolitik, Imperialismus und Kolonial-politik* and published in 1908, had defined most clearly the various types of imperial development: 'The world economy [*Weltwirtschaft*] can exist as a fact of life without world policy [*Weltpolitik*] and world policy can promote a world economy without leading to world power [*Weltmacht*]. World empires [*Weltreiche*] and world states [*Weltstaaten*] can exist without a world dominion [*Weltherrschaft*] being sought. Great powers [*Grosstaaten*] need not be world states. And an empire need not lead to world dominion.' In Hasse's view, the European balance of power of the mid-nineteenth century had

---

109. Ibid., p. 608.

110. Ibid., pp. 561, 563.

111. Hitler referred to America as potentially the new 'mistress of the world (*Herrin der Welt*)', ibid., p. 582. Again this seems to suggest that he was talking about her potential to become the foremost world power, not world conqueror.

112. He described the Jewish drive for *Weltherrschaft* as a 'process which is just as natural as the urge of the Anglo-Saxon to seize domination of the earth (*Herrschaft der Erde*)', ibid., pp. 604–5. Whether Hitler was drawing a qualitative and quantitative distinction between the two ambitions is not clear.

113. Class, *Deutsche Geschichte*, p. 301.

been replaced by an 'equality of status amongst world powers'. However, some world powers did not recognise this and strove for even greater eminence; these were 'world powers who demanded a dominion over the entire inhabited earth or over one or more continents [*Weltherrschaft*], as Russia does in Europe and Asia and the United States for the two Americas and Great Britain for all continents'.[114] Germany, Hasse made clear, would not try to establish an 'absolute dominion' (*Alleinherrschaft*), like that of Ancient Rome or Napoleon I; she wanted not to conquer the world but 'to be a world power next to other world powers of equal status'.[115]

Hitler's aim of a German 'world dominion' (*Weltherrschaft*) went beyond Hasse's vision of equal status for a German world power but fell short of the 'absolute dominion' attributed to the Romans and to Napoleon I. In fact, Hitler's ambition was precisely that which Hasse attributed to Britain, Russia and the United States. There is surely, therefore, a strong case for arguing that Hitler's *Stufenplan* derived primarily from his Pan-German political education, and not from his racial or antisemitic musings.[116]

However, it should be noted that his view of Germany's status in world politics before the war changed between 1920 and 1924. In 1919, like Hasse and Class before him, Hitler believed that Germany with her overseas empire, navy and growing commercial strength had been a 'world power' in 1914, indeed that she had been, as he put it 'in the process of emerging at the head of the world powers'.[117] In *Mein Kampf*, as has been seen, he denied that Germany had been a 'world power' because she did not have a better ratio of land to population. This change was evidently wrought by his growing conviction that to establish herself as a genuine 'world power' Germany needed a larger contiguous base in Europe rather than overseas colonies.

This conviction may have developed quite simply out of Hitler's renunciation of colonial expansion in favour of a campaign of conquest in Eastern Europe. But it is more likely that, having adopted this kind of *Ostpolitik*, he again sought arguments to justify it. It seems he may have found them again in Ratzel's *Politische Geographie*. Ratzel had identified two types of great powers — those with a large landed base, like Russia, and those with an imperial base, like Britain — and estimated that an area of five million square

114. E. Hasse, *Weltpolitik, Imperialismus und Kolonialpolitik* (Munich, 1908), pp. 2–3.
115. Ibid., pp. 64, 58.
116. Chickering agrees with this, *We Men*, p. 80.
117. Speech on 10 December 1919, report in Deuerlein, 'Hitlers Eintritt', p. 209.

kilometers provided an adequate foundation for genuine great-power status.[118] Size alone, however, did not, in Ratzel's view, assure a state real power; it had to have an adequate population as well: 'alongside the increase in the amount of space, the number of people must also grow, and it must be realised how the value of one determines the value of the other.'[119] Furthermore, to be of value, newly acquired land had to be settled.

Hitler's comments in the second volume of *Mein Kampf* seem to reflect this argument quite faithfully. He differentiated, like Ratzel, between the two types of great powers, identifying America, Russia and China as the 'giant states' and England and France as the imperial powers; all were 'power states, some of which not only far surpass the strength of our German nation in population, but whose area above all is the chief support of their political power'. Germany did not qualify as a world power, therefore, because the 'mother country is limited to the absurd area of five hundred thousand square kilometers'.[120] But to become a world power, Germany had not only to expand her territorial base but also, again in apparent conformity with Ratzel's views, to increase her population to settle the new land acquired. As Hitler wrote: 'This foreign policy will be acknowledged as correct only if, after scarcely a hundred years, there are two hundred and fifty million Germans on this continent, and not living penned in as factory coolies for the rest of the world, but as peasants and workers, who guarantee each other's livelihood by their labour.'[121]

So it seems possible that Ratzel's work may have provided Hitler with a doctrine of self-perpetuating expansionism, since any territorial expansion would require a population increase which, in turn, would necessitate further territorial expansion.[122]

Ratzel also wrote about *Weltmachtstellung*, a position of pre-eminence in world affairs; currently it was enjoyed by Britain but that would change in time: 'what England is today, Spain used to be, and Rome before that', wrote Ratzel.[123] Hitler's awareness of the idea of *Weltmachtstellung* (which is, in fact, broadly comparable with the idea of *Weltherrschaft*) perhaps helps to explain the confusion of terminology in

118. Ratzel, *Politische Geographie*, pp. 251–2.

119. Ibid., pp. 302–6.

120. Hitler, *MK*, pp. 588–9.

121. Ibid., p. 616.

122. On self-perpetuating expansionism, see M. Broszat, 'Betrachtungen zu "Hitlers Zweitem Buch"', *VfZG*, vol. 9 (1961), p. 423.

123. Ratzel, *Politische Geographie*, pp. 251–2. Haushofer referred to it as a *Wanderpokal* – a kind of trophy which passed from one nation to another; interview with Heinz Haushofer.

Mein Kampf. It must again be emphasised, though, that what Hitler had done was to rifle Ratzel's work in search of scientific arguments to make a preconceived policy of crude expansionism more respectable; he ignored much that did not suit his purpose.

All told, therefore, it seems likely that Hitler had in mind a rather ill-defined scheme by which Germany, in stages, would recover her strength and become a world power again, his ultimate ambition being to make Germany the predominant world power. His interest in this concept was, undoubtedly, initially aroused by Pan-German propaganda about the pre-eminence enjoyed by Great Britain at the end of the nineteenth century, but it was reinforced by geopolitical arguments, which he used to justify the creation of a large block of contiguous territory in Europe, rather than an overseas empire, as the basis of a German 'world dominion'.[124]

Conclusion

Two conclusions need, perhaps, to be reiterated here. Firstly, there is no substance in the claim that the geopoliticians helped, wittingly or unwittingly, to determine the goals of Hitlers foreign policy. Hitler merely utilized geopolitical arguments to reinforce his own predetermined schemes and remained quite immune to the *Weltanschauung* underlying much of German geopolitics. Ultimately, he found accounts of Russian racial inferiority and the invidious power of the Jews in Bolshevik Russia more convincing — or perhaps simply more useful in buttressing his own territorial ambitions — than geopolitical assessments of the value of future Russo-German collaboration.[125] Certainly it would seem that by 1925, racial questions were for Hitler of primary importance and geopolitical insights a secondary consideration; as he wrote in *Mein Kampf*:

124. It is possible that the geopoliticians taught Hitler to 'think in continents' — this was one of their catchphrases: Haushofer, 'Geographische Grundzüge', p. 260. Hitler may have picked up from them the idea of an eventual confrontation between Britain and America, which forms part of his speculations about the future. *MK*, p. 582. Certainly it was a common theme in geopolitical writing; for example, K. Haushofer 'Bericht', *ZfG*, vol. 2 (1925), p. 606; O. Maull, 'Bericht', *ZfG*, vol. 4 (1927), pp. 665–70; E. Obst, 'Berichterstattung aus Europa und Amerika, *ZfG*, vol. 5 (1928), pp. 711–12. It is quite possible, however, that Hitler gleaned the idea elsewhere.

125. 'If the importance of the American Union . . . lay in the size of the population alone, or else in the size of the territory, or in the relation in which this territory stands on the size of the population, then Russia would be at least as dangerous to Europe'. Racial impurity, however, made Russia weak (and racial purity made America strong) in Hitler's view: *Hitler's Secret Book*, pp. 104–5.

However much the soil, for example, can influence men, the result of the influence will always be different depending on the races in question. The low fertility of a living space may spur the one race to the highest achievements; in others it will only be the cause of the bitterest poverty and final undernourishment with all its consequences. The inner nature of peoples is always determining for the manner in which outward influences will be effective.[126]

This was the crux of the difference between Haushofer and Hitler. Haushofer's respect for other races prevented him from advocating large-scale annexations of alien territory. His solution to Germany's spatial problems was to develop her 'borderlands'. His geopolitical researches and his practical work for the German Academy and the VDA were designed to hasten the devolution of these areas to Germany by peaceful means. His long-term ambition was to see a mature Germany predominant amongst the great powers. Like so many Germans at time, Karl Haushofer shared the same dream as Hitler of a resurgent Germany as a leading world power, but not his ruthlessness in the pursuit of its realisation.

Nevertheless, a second conclusion is inescapable. Haushofer's ideas were a positive encouragement to Hitler. The popularisation and development of the concept of *Lebensraum* and, in particular, its emphasis on the pursuit of autarky as a military necessity was Haushofer's main legacy to the Nazis. It was to be of crucial importance in the formulation of and justification for Hitler's foreign and domestic policies in the 1930s. Hitler may already have been aware from Pan-German literature of the term *Lebensraum* and of the argument that the absence of self-sufficiency had been Germany's Achilles' heel in the First World War, but the geopolitical theorisation about *Lebensraum* elevated the problem to a pseudo-scientific level and, as a result, made his solution more palatable. That Hitler chose to pursue 'autarky by conquest' was not Haushofer's fault, but the latter does deserve a share of moral culpabilility for making — albeit inadvertently — Hitler's mission more respectable. Even so there is no reason to question the judgement of the Allied interrogators in 1945, who decided not to put Haushofer on trial at Nuremberg.

126. Hitler, *MK*, p. 262.

6

Hitler's Alliance Strategy — Opposition and Refinement, 1924–8

Hitler's alliance strategy was, as has been shown, formulated by the autumn of 1922 and discussed privately in party circles. However, during 1923 and 1924, apart from describing England and Italy as the only powers with an interest in the continued existence of the German state, he did not make public his convictions about a future Nazi foreign policy. Indeed, in an article published in April 1924, entitled *Warum musste ein 8. November kommen?*, he merely repeated what he considered to have been Germany's foreign policy options before the First World War, namely the acquisition of farm land at Russian expense, to be achieved by an Anglo-German alliance, or the pursuit of commercial and naval power at British expense by means of a German-Russian alliance.[1] Though there can be no doubt that he believed that postwar Germany faced the same choice, Hitler gave no clear indication in public of his preference for the conquest of *Lebensraum* in Eastern Europe until July 1925, when the first volume of *Mein Kampf* was published.[2] There he revealed his overall strategy but even then it was only implied. Such reticence clearly requires some explanation.

One possibility is that Hitler had not yet finally decided upon the goals of his foreign policy. Alfred Rosenberg argued in January 1923 that it was not possible to be specific about the party's foreign policy because 'the present conditions in world politics can change in time'

1. A. Hitler, 'Warum musste ein 8. November kommen?', *Deutschlands Erneuerung*, vol. 8 (1924), p. 199.
2. In April 1923 Hitler is supposed to have told Hanfstängl that 'in the next war the most important task will be to take possession of the grain-producing areas of Poland and the Ukraine'; Hanfstängl, *Zwischen Weissem und Braunem Haus*, p. 78.

and Nazi foreign policy would have to adjust to such changes.[3] Was
Rosenberg covering up the party's indecision in foreign affairs? Axel
Kuhn certainly believes that Hitler was still not certain about his
attitude towards Russia; indeed he cites the April 1924 article as
evidence of this. Evidently, Hitler still aimed at securing the return
of Germany's overseas colonies, a policy which, he admitted, England would oppose. In Kuhn's view, therefore, he had clearly not
resolved an inherent contradiction in his strategy. However, the
record of Hitler's conversation with Eduard Scharrer in December
1922 shows quite conclusively that Kuhn is mistaken; Hitler had
already decided to acquire land at Russia's expense and to abandon
colonial ambitions in order to 'avoid any damage to English interests'.[4]
So indecision is unlikely to have been the reason for Hitler's and
Rosenberg's reluctance to discuss Nazi foreign policy goals.

A more likely explanation is that disclosure of those goals would
antagonise supporters of the Nazi Party. The revelation of Hitler's
territorial ambitions in Russia would certainly alienate the support
of the fiercely nationalistic Russian émigrés, which Scheubner-
Richter had attracted to the Nazi movement between 1921 and
1923.[5] It was expedient, therefore, to continue a pay lip-service to
the idea of a future German alliance with a post-Bolshevik Russia,
for which Scheubner-Richter and the émigrés were working. On the
other hand, it could be argued that Scheubner-Richter's death
during the Munich putsch and Hitler's subsequent arrest and
imprisonment eliminated the prospect of further assistance from the
Russian nationalists; hence, after November 1923 the need for
caution on Hitler's part was removed. It is possible, however, that,
with the party in a state of collapse, he preferred to remain silent in
the faint hope of renewed émigré support; but a far more convincing
explanation is that his anti-Russian foreign policy and its presumed
architect, Alfred Rosenberg, were unpopular *inside* the Nazi Party.

It is difficult to asses the extent of the opposition in the party to
the anti-Bolshevik and anti-Russian line at this time; Ernst
Hanfstängl, an influential recruit from America, who figured prominently in Hitler's social life, may have been an isolated critic of this
outlook.[6] However, the personal animosity between Alfred Rosen-

3. Rosenberg, 'Wesen', p. 136.

4. Scharrer, 'Bericht', BAK R43I/2681, p. 4. Kuhn, *Programm*, pp. 97–9, 102–3, 113–14.
Horn disagrees; 'Ein unbekannter Aufsatz', p. 292.

5. In 1931 several Russian émigrés tried to enlist Göring in an attempt to change the party's
Ostpolitik, unsigned letter of 30 July 1931; NS8/121.

6. Hanfstängl, *Zwischen Weissem und Braunem Haus*, pp. 47–8, 78, 105.

berg and other leading Nazis jealous of his influence over Hitler was unmistakable and when Hitler selected Rosenberg to lead the party in his own absence after November 1923, the resentment towards him burst forth. Herman Esser and Julius Streicher accused Rosenberg of Jewish ancestry and of having spied for France during the war, and set about undermining his leadership of the Nazi Party rump.[7] Hitler refused to be drawn into this internecine conflict and it is conceivable, therefore, that he was unwilling to endorse publicly a russophobic foreign policy closely associated with Alfred Rosenberg, because it would compromise his studied impartiality in the party rivalries of 1924. In 1925, after his release from prison and the re-formation of the party under his own leadership, it would matter far less.

One final consideration deserves to be mentioned. The Franco-Belgian invasion of the Ruhr in January 1923 created a favourable environment for Hitler's anti-French strategy and gave it ample fuel. Indeed, British criticism of the invasion seemed to increase the credibility of his alliance strategy.[8] Hitler's programme of territorial conquest in Eastern Europe, on the other hand, would have seemed inappropriate in the circumstances. Nor could he then have produced the compelling argument for expansion in Europe rather than overseas which, given the opposition already evident within the party to this anti-Russian orientation, would have been necessary.

By the time he was writing the first volume of *Mein Kampf* in the summer of 1924,[9] Hitler had found the justification he needed in the arguments of the geopoliticians. In the fourth chapter he again set out the alternative solutions to prewar Germany's problem of overpopulation; 'either a territorial policy, or a colonial and commercial policy'. As has been seen, this time Hitler made it clear that the acquisition of soil in Europe would have been the 'healthier' policy for a number of reasons. An increase in the amount of land under cultivation would have made Germany virtually self-sufficient; a larger territorial base would also have increased Germany's national security for 'greater size meant greater depth of defence and deterrence against frivolous attack.'[10] Thus, expansion on the European continent was preferable to the acquisition of overseas colonies.

7. Lüdecke, *I Knew Hitler*, p. 211; Cecil, *The Myth of the Master Race*, pp. 45–8; W. Horn, *Führerideologie und Parteiorganisation*, pp. 172–89.

8. For his speech on 26 February 1924 at his trial, see *Der Hitlerprozess vor dem Volksgericht in München* (Munich, 1924), pp. 18–19; Hitler, 'Warum', pp. 203–4.

9. Hitler said he was writing with the tenth anniversary of the outbreak of the First World War approaching; *MK*, p. 150.

10. Hitler, *MK*, pp. 125–8.

Armed with those arguments culled from geopolitical literature, Hitler stated that such expansion could have been made only at the expense of Russia, and 'for such a policy there was but one ally in Europe: England'.[11] With England to protect her rear from attack, Germany could have taken on the Russians. There can be little doubt that Hitler's evaluation of Germany's prewar options revealed his own priorities for a future Nazi state; expansion in Europe was preferable because it offered 'gradual, yet solid, and continuous growth'.[12]

So it was only with the publication of the first volume of *Mein Kampf* on 19 July 1925 that the second phase of Hitler's foreign policy — the conquest of more *Lebensraum* in Eastern Europe with English assistance — was revealed in public for the first time, though only by implication in his analysis of prewar diplomacy. This strategy had been discussed in party circles at least as early as December 1922 but for several reasons — the party's reliance on support from Russian émigré sources and, later, internal party tensions which surfaced following the Munich putsch, perhaps also the absence of a rational and pseudo-scientific pretext for his advocacy of expansion in Europe rather than overseas — Hitler chose not to endorse it publicly before 1925.

The Challenge of the 'Strasser faction'

If there had been opposition within the Nazi Party before 1925 to the pro-English and anti-Bolshevik line advocated by Hitler and Rosenberg, it was largely subsumed within clashes of personality. However, the publication of the first volume of *Mein Kampf* and the diplomatic negotiations throughout the summer of 1925 which culminated in the signature of the Locarno treaties in October 1925 brought previously concealed differences of opinion within party circles to the surface. For if Gustav Stresemann's offer of security treaties, guaranteeing the Western European frontiers laid down by the Versailles Settlement, was accepted by the major powers, it was likely to be followed by Germany's entry into the Anglo-French dominated League of Nations. This would clearly lead to a 'Western orientation' of German foreign policy. To Gregor Strasser, his brother Otto and their associate Joseph Goebbels, this development

11. Ibid., pp. 128–9.
12. Ibid., pp. 130–1.

seemed like an unwarranted reversal of the trend established by the Treaty of Rapallo with the Soviet Union in 1922.

The emergence of this dissenting group reflected the growth in power and influence and, indeed, the relative independence of Gregor Strasser. Strasser, a pharmacist from Landshut in Bavaria, rose to prominence following the Munich putsch. He had organised and commanded the Landshut battalion of the SA, which secured the Wittelsbacher Bridge during the night of 8–9 November, marched back to Landshut and disbanded unmolested. On the strength of these exploits, it has been argued,[13] he was elected to the Bavarian Landtag in May 1924 as a member of the *Völkischer Block*, which represented members of the Nazi Party and of the North German-based conservative and antisemitic *Deutschvölkische Freiheitspartei* (DVFP). He soon became its chairman. Membership of the Landtag provided Strasser not only with a political platform but also free rail travel throughout Bavaria, an important asset which enabled him to keep in regular contact with the scattered local branches of the Nazi Party. During 1924 he attempted to mediate between the warring factions within the former party, principally between Rosenberg, head of the *Grossdeutsche Volksgemeinschaft*, the official rump of the party, and Herman Esser and Julius Streicher. With Ludendorff and Albrecht von Graefe, leader of the DVFP, Strasser established the *Nationalsozialistische Freiheitspartei* in an unsuccessful attempt to reunite the disintegrating movement.[14] In December 1924, he was elected to the Reichstag which gave him a national platform and, of more immediate and practical value, extended his free rail travel nationwide.

During the year and a half following Hitler's trial, Strasser was the most prominent spokesman of the Nazi hierarchy even after his leader's release in December 1924, since Hitler was banned from public speaking for over two years in many important *Länder*. In October 1925 the *VB* acknowledged Strasser's tireless devotion to the party, noting that he had addressed thirty meetings in the previous two months and a total of 216 meetings in the nineteen months since March 1924.[15] By October 1925, the re-formed Nazi Party was no longer merely a Bavarian pressure group; it now possessed an embryonic national organisation, due largely to Strasser's coordination of disparate Nazi groups in northern and western Germany. Hitler paid tribute to his efforts at a conference of party

13. U. Kissenkoetter, *Gregor Strasser und die NSDAP* (Stuttgart, 1978), p. 17.
14. Ibid.
15. Unattributed article in the 'Aus der Bewegung' column, *VB*, 8 October 1925.

representatives on 19 October 1925; 'it was', he said, 'thanks to the activities of Strasser that a wide area of Germany had been opened up for National Socialism'.[16]

What emerges from even a brief examination of Gregor Strasser's activities is that he had become an extremely valuable asset to the party and that, by virtue of his membership of the Reichstag and the freedom of movement which it gave him, he enjoyed a degree of independence from the Munich party headquarters. Whether he harboured dreams of leadership himself is very much open to debate.[17] The party chiefs did not appear to show any great alarm when he began to express opinions at variance with those of Hitler and Rosenberg. However when Rosenberg published controversial articles by Strasser and later by Goebbels in the *VB*, he usually did so with his own counter-arguments appended.[18] Hitler himself did not issue any immediate public refutation of Strasser's views, though they were clearly not in line with his own observations in the first volume of *Mein Kampf*. But how different were the ideas of the 'Strasser group' and what effect did the emergence of dissenting voices have on the development of Hitler's own ideas? It is to these questions that we must now turn.

It should be stressed at the outset that all the party's leading spokesmen condemned Stresemann's Locarno policy and for the same reasons. Firstly, they believed that the security treaties, by tying Germany more closely to the Western European powers would, as Strasser put it, 'complete what the Dawes Plan had introduced, the economic enslavement of Germany and the German working class to Jewish-international capitalism'. Secondly, the treaties would confirm the legitimacy of the territorial settlement in Western Europe effected at Versailles, which was, needless to say, totally unacceptable to the Nazis, who would, again in Strasser's words, 'never ever renounce Alsace-Lorraine, Eupen and Malmédy, the Saar and [Germany's] colonies'. Thirdly, the Nazis feared that since negotiations were being conducted concurrently with Poland

16. Report on Hitler's speech, *VB*, 27 October 1925.

17. Lüdecke did not think so; *I Knew Hitler*, p. 306; Strasser's latest biographer believes that he might have challenged Hitler's leadership if the circumstances had been right; P. D. Stachura, *Gregor Strasser and the Rise of Nazism* (London, 1983), pp. 45–6.

18. Rosenberg seemed to welcome the debate, commenting that 'through argument and counterargument, the viewpoints will be clarified'; Rosenberg's postscript to the article by von Nemirovich-Danchenko, a Russian émigré and friend of Scheubner-Richter, 'USSR, Deutschland und Russland', *VB*, 5 November 1925.

and Czechoslovakia, there was a danger that Germany's acceptance of the western frontiers imposed by the Versailles Settlement would be accompanied by a similar agreement about her eastern frontiers. Thus all hopes of reversing the postwar settlement by negotiation would be crushed.[19]

So Strasser agreed with Hitler and the rest of the party on the need to oppose Stresemann's policies and hold out for a revision of the Treaty of Versailles. Where he parted company with Hitler was, firstly, in his assessment of some of the major powers and, secondly, in the extent of his ambitions for German foreign policy.

The contrast between Strasser's and Hitler's evaluation of the major powers is most apparent in the appraisal of Britain, which as far as Strasser was concerned, was one of the 'moneyed' capitalist powers who had an interest in shackling Germany; as he put it:

> The profit economy of the moneyed powers, England and America, requires a pacified Europe; this pacified Europe is only to be secured when Germany can be moved to abjure the natural desire for vengeance against France produced by the agony of the Versailles Treaty, and comes to terms with the politico-military rule of France over Europe ... and by giving up all national political desires enrols in the huge profit business of world finance.[20]

Though Rosenberg had often written in similar vein about Western capitalism, he regarded such policies, when pursued by the English, as mere aberrations attributable to the distorting influence of the Jewish stock exchange; in May 1925, for example, he wrote that nine-tenths of the policies of 'England' (as well as 'France' and the 'United States') were 'determined today by the supra-state powers and in the first instance by international high finance'.[21] Rosenberg and Hitler, armed with this ideological corrective, could still present the English as suitable future allies for a National Socialist Germany, whilst condemning Stresemann's current collaboration with them. Strasser, it seems, had no time for such sophistry; for him, Britain remained one of the capitalist powers and a 'Western orientation' of German foreign policy was ruled out.

Furthermore, Strasser did not share Hitler's predilection and

---

19. G. Strasser, 'Die nationalsozialistische Abrechnung mit der Sicherheitspakt', *VB*, 23 May 1925; see also his article 'In letzter Stunde', *VB*, 22 September 1925. Rosenberg expressed very similar views in 'Deutsche Aussenpolitik und Stresemanns Unsicherheitspakt', *VB*, 9 May and 'Einkreisung von Westen und Osten', *VB*, 20 June 1925.

20. Strasser, 'Abrechnung', *VB*, 22 May 1925.

21. Rosenberg, 'Aussenpolitik', *VB*, 9 May 1925.

respect for the British Empire and certainly did not regard its interests as compatible with Germany's. 'English imperialism', he wrote in an article entitled 'Russia and ourselves' in October 1925, 'is not only indifferent to us — it is our enemy, which will always deny us every opportunity for activity around the world.'[22] Significantly, in his reply to this article, Rosenberg made no criticism of this comment on British imperialism.[23] The reason is obvious, Rosenberg (and Hitler) agreed with Strasser that the English would oppose Germany's overseas ambitions but, unlike him, they were prepared (at least for the foreseeable future) to sacrifice colonial aspirations for the sake of English friendship.

Essentially, the difference arose from the greater emphasis placed by Strasser on the 'socialistic' elements in National Socialism. The radicalism of the Strasser group has undoubtedly been exaggerated, in particular by Otto Strasser, in retrospective apologia. In fact, whilst Gregor Strasser campaigned for the abolition of large landholdings, the socialisation of large corporations and the nationalisation of parts of German industry, he also supported the 'maintenance of private enterprise' and 'regard for the rights of property'.[24] Nevertheless Strasser's 'radicalism', though more anticapitalist than genuinely socialist, coloured his outlook on foreign affairs.

In his view, the postwar world was characterised by a 'vertical division' between 'victor and vanquished, oppressor and oppressed, exploiter and exploited' and since all the 'oppressed nations' (he included India, Persia, Morocco and China, as well as Germany, in this category) had the same aim — the overthrow of the status quo created by the peace settlement — they should form a *League of Oppressed Nations* to confront the League of Nations and the capitalist world. Perhaps predictably, Strasser regarded Germany as 'the natural champion and ally' of the exploited in their struggle against 'French despotism, English imperialism and American financial exploitation'.[25] The concept of such a league was a pure abstraction

22. G. Strasser, 'Russland und wir', *VB*, 22 October 1925.

23. Rosenberg, 'USSR, Deutschland und Russland', *VB*, 5 November 1925.

24. 'Dispositionsentwurf eines umfassenden Programms des nationalen Sozialismus' NS 26/896. The programme, in fact, was not too different from the original programme of 1920, retaining its antisemitism and its anti-Marxism. Otto Strasser's attempt to distance himself and his brother from the Nazis is best illustrated in M. Geis (pseudonym of Otto Strasser), *Gregor Strasser* (Leipzig, 1933) and O. Strasser, *Hitler and I* (Oxford, 1940).

25. G. Strasser, 'Für einen Bund der unterdrückten Völker', *VB* 12/13, July 1925; see also Ulrich von Hutten (pseudonym of Otto Strasser), 'Deutschland und der ferne Osten', *VB*, 22 July 1925.

— Strasser presented no concrete proposals for making it a reality —
but it clearly reflected a profound distrust of the Western capitalist
powers. This outlook explains his hostility not only to Stresemann's
'Western orientation' in German foreign policy but also to Hitler's
projected Anglo-German alliance.

As if this were not a serious enough departure from the 'party
line', Strasser also believed that the best guarantee of Germany's
future lay in collaboration with a non-capitalist Russia. However, he
claimed to support such an understanding 'not out of love for
Russia, least of all out of love for Soviet Russia, but solely in the
interests of winning back German freedom'.[26] Securing this freedom
'determines our attitude to all foreign policy problems, to all forces
and constellations on the political stage' and, since the Versailles
Settlement was the greatest single obstacle to the realisation of this
goal, every power which opposed the settlement was Germany's
natural ally. On these grounds, Strasser concluded, Russia, even
Bolshevik Russia, could be an ally — provided that she refrained
from interference in Germany's domestic affairs.[27]

No matter how Strasser might qualify his support for an alliance
between Germany and the Soviet Union, it was impossible to
disguise the fact that his views flatly contradicted those of Hitler and
Rosenberg. It was precisely the danger of Soviet meddling in German affairs that eliminated Soviet Russia from their alliance considerations. Collaboration with the USSR might be conceivable,
Rosenberg admitted, for a strong National Socialist Germany but the
Soviets would not be interested in it because the spreading of Soviet
propaganda — the real purpose of such collusion from their standpoint — would be out of the question: in a National Socialist
Germany, Marxism would already have been eradicated.[28]

To counter such views, Strasser and his friends stressed that the
Soviets no longer wanted to export socialism; nationalism, not
internationalism, was now pervading the rank and file of the Bolshevik movement. The system had survived, in Goebbels' view, not
because it was Bolshevik, Marxist or internationalist, but 'because it
is nationalist, because it is Russian'.[29] These 'National Bolshevik'
ruminations must have had a familiar ring for Hitler; he had clashed

26. G. Strasser, 'Zu den aussenpolitischen Zielen des Jungdeutschen Ordens', *NS Briefe*, 15
January 1926.

27. Strasser, 'Russland und wir', *VB*, 22 October 1925.

28. A. Rosenberg, 'Ostorientierung' *VB*, 18/19 April 1926; cf. *Pest in Russland*, p. 86.

29. J. Goebbels, 'Nationalsozialismus oder Bolschewismus', *NS Briefe*, 15 October 1925; see
also Strasser, 'Zielen des Jungdeutschen Ordens', *NS Briefe*, 15 January 1926. Both pointed to

in 1922 with Moeller van den Bruck over the latter's prediction that Russian nationalism would eventually supersede the internationalism of Bolshevism, and there can be little doubt that the ideas of the 'Strasser group' owed a great deal to Moeller's inspiration.[30]

The significance of the challenge posed by the group's observations should not be underestimated. The concept of 'National Bolshevism' threatened to undermine the entire antisemitic and anti-Bolshevik ideology, pieced together principally by Alfred Rosenberg, by questioning one of its initial premises, namely, that Bolshevism was 'by its very nature anti-nationalist'.[31] Goebbels touched a very sensitive nerve when he suggested in an article entitled 'Nationalsocialism and Bolshevism' that 'the Jewish question, that is Bolshevism, is more complicated than one imagines. It is by no means certain that the capitalist and the Bolshevik Jew are one and the same thing. Perhaps in the last resort, but never in actual practice.'[32] Here Goebbels came close to challenging the conviction that Jewish capitalism and Jewish Bolshevism were two interrelated weapons in the Jewish conspiracy to take over the world. Rosenberg, replying in the *VB*, admitted that there had been 'differences of opinion' between the Jews in Moscow and those in New York and London but insisted that 'Russia's' policy remained 'Jewish' and that to talk of 'National-Bolshevism' was a 'nonsense', because Bolshevism combined Jewish Marxism and a 'Russian nihilism' derived from the intermixture of Nordic Russian with Tartar and Mongol blood.[33] Bolshevism, therefore, was essentially alien to Russia, and, even if the Soviet government did pursue a nationalistic and Pan-Slavic foreign policy, it was still in the hands of the Jews. This tortuous reply revealed the vulnerability of Rosenberg's central tenet when exposed to the thrust of the 'Strasser group's' argument.

---

evidence of Pan-Slavic policies as proof. Goebbels even talked of an emerging 'National Socialism' in Russia; open letter to Graf Reventlow (January 1925) quoted in W. Hess, 'Nationalsozialismus am Rhein und an der Ruhr', *VB*, 24/25 May 1925. See also J. Goebbels, 'Das russische Problem', *VB*, 15 November 1925 and *Lenin oder Hitler? Eine Rede* (Zwickau, 1926), p. 31.

30. Otto Strasser described Moeller as 'the purest of the pure' amongst right-wing writers; *Hitler and I*, pp. 38–9; whilst Goebbels described Moeller's *Das Dritte Reich* as 'shatteringly true' and wondered why he was 'not one of us', H. Heiber (ed.), *Goebbels Diaries*, pp. 55–7. Gregor Strasser adopted Moeller's central tenet that a growing population indicated a 'youthful' nation; 'Mehr Aussenpolitik', *NS Briefe*, 15 November 1926.

31. A. Rosenberg, '"Western" and "Osten"', *VB*, 29 March 1927.

32. J. Goebbels, 'Nationalsozialismus oder Bolschewismus', *NS Briefe*, 15 October 1925.

33. Rosenberg's postscript to Goebbels' 'Nationalsozialismus oder Bolschewismus; reprinted in *VB*, 14 November 1925.

So the 'Strasser group' favoured an 'Eastern orientation' in order to destroy the shackles of the Versailles Settlement and to free Germany from her enslavement to the capitalist West. Though Gregor Strasser reminded his readers that this policy was 'a temporary one and negative in terms of its objective',[34] the fact remains that his assessment of England and Russia quite clearly contradicted the ideological creed of Alfred Rosenberg and the alliance strategy outlined by Hitler in the first volume of *Mein Kampf*.

But how far did the foreign policy goals of the 'Strasser group' differ from those of Hitler? Their ambitions for Germany were most succinctly formulated at the end of 1925 in the programme produced for the *Arbeitsgemeinschaft* of North and West German Gauleiters of the NSDAP, set up in September 1925 under Strasser's leadership. The programme seems to have been the product of compromise; significantly the 'Eastern orientation' was soft-pedalled. Nevertheless, the four foreign policy objectives set out do seem to have reflected the views of Gregor and Otto Strasser and Joseph Goebbels.[35]

The first objective was the restoration of 'the frontiers of 1914, including colonies, and the unification of all the Germans of Central Europe in a Greater German Empire (including Austria, Sudetenland, South Tyrol)'.[36] As has been seen, Strasser objected to the Locarno treaties because they were based on acceptance of Germany's losses in Western Europe, and because he feared an 'Eastern Locarno'. He was prepared to contemplate forcible revision of Germany's eastern frontiers, since he considered hopes of peaceful revision, under the auspices of the League of Nations or by voluntary agreement (for example with the Poles), to be 'utopian' and, indeed, he believed that France had undertaken at Locarno to defend the frontiers of Poland and Czechoslovakia.[37] Revision of the Eastern settlement, therefore, in Gregor Strasser's view, meant conflict, first and foremost with Poland; as he declared bluntly on one occasion: 'Our Eastern enemy is Poland, not Russia on whom we do not even border.'[38]

Hitler and Rosenberg were unlikely to quibble with the idea of

---

34. Strasser, 'Zielen des Jungdeutschen Ordens', *NS Briefe*, 15 January 1926.

35. Goebbels certainly claimed a part in the writing of the programme; 'I am working on a new programme draft... Strasser's draft has flaws'; entry of 18 December 1925, Heiber, *Goebbels Diaries*, p. 55.

36. 'Dispositionsentwurf', NS 26/896.

37. G. Strasser, 'Immer wieder. Fort mit Locarno', *VB*, 18 November 1925.

38. Strasser, 'Mehr Aussenpolitik', *NS Briefe*, 15 November 1926.

such a confrontation; Hitler's *Ostpolitik* almost certainly envisaged the elimination of Poland and it had always been Rosenberg's first priority; he even conceded that a temporary Russo-German alliance against Poland might be necessary, although he insisted that only a National Socialist Germany could make 'pacts — albeit temporarily — with the Devil'.[39] Nevertheless, while the *grossdeutsch* aspirations of the 'Strasser programme' were largely compatible with the 'Munich line' on foreign affairs (the return of the South Tyrol excepted), the restoration of the frontiers of 1914 would be insufficient for Hitler's appetite.

The second goal of the North German Nazi programme was 'the establishment of a customs union with Switzerland, Hungary, Denmark, Holland and Luxembourg'. This concept was not elaborated upon but seems clearly linked to the programme's fourth goal, the creation of a 'United States of Europe', described in the programme as follows: 'A European league of nations with uniform measurement and coinage systems. Enlargement by tariff union with France and the other European states, otherwise complete reciprocal preference.'[40]

The idea of a 'United States of Europe' appears, at first sight, to be reminiscent of Richard Graf Coudenhove-Kalergi's *Pan-Europa* scheme, which had already been pilloried in the Nazi press as racially destructive and Jewish-inspired.[41] However, Strasser's dual conception, though never fully explained, appears to have differed in at least two important respects from *Pan-Europa*, and indeed to have owed more to Friedrich Naumann's *Mitteleuropa*.[42] Firstly, as has been seen, a precondition of Strasser's scheme was the restoration of the frontiers of 1914, whereas Coudenhove-Kalergi's *Pan-Europa* was to be based on the postwar territorial settlement.[43] Secondly, Gregor Strasser insisted that Germany should play a predominant role in the new Europe; a new 'organically arranged' and 'racially concentrated' Greater German Reich was to be 'the centre of gravity

39. Rosenberg, 'Ostorientierung', *VB*, 18/19 April 1926. On his preoccupation with Poland, see above, p. 124–6.

40. 'Dispositionsentwurf', NS 26/896.

41. See for example A. Rosenberg, 'Politische Persönlichkeiten — Coudenhove-Kalergi', *Der Weltkampf*, vol. 1 (1925), p. 88, and 'Edmund Stinnes und Pan-Europa', *VB*, 25/26 October 1925.

42. Friedrich Naumann's *Mitteleuropa* (Berlin, 1915) was one of the most widely read texts during the First World War. Naumann seemed to be interested in economic rather than political unity, but historians have puzzled over whether his ultimate aims were essentially expansionist or defensive. Klemperer, for example, favours the 'defensive' view, *Conservatism*, pp. 55–6; Fischer, *Germany's Aims*, p. 176 sees Naumann's objectives as 'expansionist'.

43. Coudenhove-Kalergi, R. N. Graf von, *Pan-Europa* (Vienna, 1923), pp. 114, 156; see also R. Frommelt, *Pan-Europa oder Mitteleuropa* (Stuttgart, 1977), p. 14.

for a Central European customs union and a dominant force (*Schwergewicht*) in the United States of Europe'.[44] Or, as he put it less ambiguously elsewhere: 'Central Europe under German leadership . . . From Memel to Strasburg, from Hamburg to Vienna the German Central Europe as heart and head, as supreme power and backbone of Europe.'

It is unclear whether Strasser envisaged unashamed German hegemony in Europe or merely a federated Europe, with Germany as *primus inter pares*, but even this second, less ambitious, design clearly differed from that of Coudenhove-Kalergi.[45] Otto Strasser, perhaps the author of this concept (he had a degree in national economy) argued that the aim of a united Europe was

> to achieve that political and economic consolidation, which alone enables it [Europe] to sustain itself economically against the great economic powers; such as the United States of America, the British Empire, Russia with Siberia, Japan with China and Mongolia, and which alone enables it to endure in face of the great political problems of the next century: defence of the white race against rejuvenated Asia, [and] awakening Africa.[46]

The concept of a 'United States of Europe' could not expect to meet with the approval of Hitler and his Munich clique. Indeed it was sharply criticised from within the ranks of the *Arbeitsgemeinschaft*, meeting on 26 January 1926 in Hanover to discuss the draft programme.[47] However, whether its begetters visualized outright German hegemony or not, the United Europe idea certainly aimed at restoring Germany's pre-eminence in Europe, and therefore avoided the internationalism which damned Coudenhove-Kalergi's conception in Nazi eyes. Furthermore, the racial animus apparently prompting it was not totally out of step with the views of Alfred Rosenberg, who admitted that he could conceive of a united Europe, provided it was united under the banner of National Socialism and organised in a defence against the yellow and black races.[48] So the 'Strasser group's' vision of a united Europe did, at least, have the

44. 'Dispositionsentwurf', NS 26/896.

45. G. Strasser, 'Ziele des Jungdeutschen Ordens', *NS Briefe*, 15 January 1926. Coudenhove-Kalergi wanted a Franco-German agreement to form the basis of Pan-Europa; Frommelt, *Pan-Europa*, p. 14.

46. O. Strasser, 'Aussenpolitische Rundschau', *VB* 3 October 1925.

47. See the memorandum by Ludolf Haase, one of the critics of the Strasser programme, 'Der Nationalsozialismus. Göttinger Antwort auf die Denkschrift von Herrn Strasser', HA 44/896; J. Noakes, *Nazi Party*, pp. 74–5.

48. A. Rosenberg, 'Vereinigte Staaten von Europa', *VB*, 13/14 September 1925.

virtues of a nationalistic inspiration and a racial principle.

The final foreign policy goal in the Strasser programme was the creation of 'a central African colonial empire (former German colonies, the Congo state, Portuguese colonies, in part French colonies)'.[49] This raises further doubts about the supposedly radical and socialistic nature of the group's outlook, and also about Otto Strasser's later claim that 'we had no territorial demands'.[50] It certainly seemed to contradict Gregor Strasser's expressed support for a League of Oppressed Nations against Anglo-French imperialism. This has led to suggestions that it was included to please Hitler, but in July 1925, at the very time he was advocating the league, Strasser had referred to colonies as 'a vital interest for a politically self-sufficient independent Germany'.[51] Furthermore, in the same month, Otto Strasser claimed that 'economic and political pressures' prevented Germany from aiding those nations suffering at the hands of Anglo-French imperialism.[52] So it would appear that the Strasser brothers did, indeed, support colonialism in the pursuit of autarky and would even consider a German seizure of Belgian, Portuguese and French colonies in Central Africa.[53]

An analysis of the outlook and goals of the 'Strasser group' in foreign policy, therefore, confirms that it was not as radical and socialistic as was once thought. Its approach to foreign policy was not as selfless or so lacking in national chauvinism and imperialistic designs as Otto Strasser would have liked posterity to believe. However, its commitment to overseas empire and a federated Europe under German leadership, as well as to an alignment, however temporary, with Soviet Russia against the Western Powers, did amount to a serious alternative to the programme briefly sketched by Hitler in the first volume of *Mein Kampf*.

Hitler's Response

The relationship between the Strasser circle and Hitler and his

---

49. 'Dispositionsentwurf', NS 26/896.

50. O. Strasser, *Hitler and I*, p. 93. The colonial facet of their programme was dropped in 1929; Hildebrand, *Foreign Policy*, pp. 16–17.

51. G. Strasser, 'Instinktloser Geschäftemacher', *VB*, 10 July 1925. Stachura suggests that he may have been trying to appease Hitler; *Gregor Strasser*, p. 47.

52. Ulrich von Hutten, 'Deutschland und der ferne Osten', *VB*, 22 July 1925.

53. On autarky, see G. Strasser, 'Immer wieder', *VB*, 18 November 1925; Heinz Seibert, a regular contributor to the Strasser newspapers, also argued for the seizure of French coastal possessions in West Africa; 'Fragen der Dritten Reich-Kolonialpolitik', *NS Briefe*, 1 October 1926.

Munich acolytes is a fascinating example of factional opposition in a party otherwise seemingly characterised by authoritarian control and rigid ideological conformity. Not surprisingly, some historians have suggested that what was at issue was not so much differing opinions as 'the principle of absolute leadership'.[54] In other words, Hitler was more concerned that party members were loyal to his leadership than that they conformed absolutely to his ideas. Hence, the *Arbeitsgemeinschaft* of the North and West German Gauleiter and its journal, the *Nationalsozialistische Briefe*, could receive Hitler's 'express approval' despite the views they expounded.[55] It was only when the Strasser group inside the *Arbeitsgemeinschaft* produced an alternative to the party programme of 1920 and directly challenged Hitler's status as the party's chief *Programmatiker* that he was stung into action: he summoned the dissenters to a meeting in Bamberg on 14 February 1926 and forced them to withdraw their draft programme. That Hitler did not discuss the alternative programme seems to lend weight to the view that he was disturbed not so much by its contents as by its very existence.[56] Now it may well be argued that it was the challenge to his leadership which caused Hitler to confront the 'Strasser group'; nevertheless several pieces of evidence suggest that it would be wrong to conclude that he was relatively unconcerned about the views being expressed by the group in speeches and articles.

Firstly, the foreign policy section of the second volume of *Mein Kampf*, written (as Hitler said himself) in August 1925,[57] reveals his awareness of opposition within the party to his proposed alliance policy, as well as his attempt to defend himself against criticism. He admitted, for example, that 'even for us, of course, it is hard to represent England as a possible future ally in the ranks of our movement'. This, in his view, was due to agitation about the loss of Germany's colonies and the destruction of German seapower by the British, which prevented Germans from recognising that 'what we have to fight for today is not "sea power", etc.'[58] What Germany

54. J. L. Nyomarkay, 'Factionalism in the National Socialist German Workers' Party 1925–26: The Myth and Reality of the "Northern Faction"', *Political Science Quarterly*, vol. 80 (1965), p. 29.

55. Report by Goebbels on the meeting of 22 November in *NS Briefe*, 1 December 1925. See also the party circular to local party branches dated 11 December 1925 and signed by Rudolf Hess; Tyrell, *Führer befiehl, ... Selbstzeugnisse aus der 'Kampfzeit' der NSDAP* (Düsseldorf, 1969), pp. 116–17.

56. Nyomarkay, 'Factionalism, p. 36; cf. Noakes, *Nazi Party*, pp. 78–9; Lane and Rupp, *Nazi Ideology*, p. xxvii.

57. A. Hitler, *Hitler's Secret Book*, introduced by Telford Taylor (New York, 1961), p. 1.

58. Hitler, *MK*, p. 570–1.

needed to do first was to re-establish her position on the European continent and, for that, English support was vital. Hitler also tried to discredit Gregor Strasser's idea of supporting 'oppressed nations' against the British; as he commented:

> It just so happens to be impossible to overwhelm with a coalition of cripples a powerful state that is determined to stake, if necessary, its last drop of blood for its existence. As a folkish man, who appraises the value of men on a racial basis, I am prevented by mere knowledge of the racial inferiority of these so-called 'oppressed nations' from linking the destiny of my people with theirs.

The idea was not simply unrealistic, it was also 'catastrophic' because it distracted the German people 'again and again from the practical possibilities, making them devote themselves to imaginative, yet fruitless, hopes and illusions'.[59]

Turning to the Russian question, which he described as 'the touchstone for the political capacity of the young National Socialist movements to think clearly and to act correctly',[60] Hitler restated his case for the conquest of more *Lebensraum* at Russian expense, but again admitted that 'not only in German-National but even in folkish circles, the idea of such an Eastern policy is violently attacked'.[61] This was, in all possibility, another reference to the Strasser circle. Similarly, when Hitler criticised the restoration of the frontiers of 1914 as a suitable goal for German foreign policy, he was again attacking views expressed 'even in so-called folkish circles'. The restoration of prewar frontiers was not enough to warrant a further letting of German blood. Only a policy which aimed 'to secure for the German people the land and soil to which they are entitled on this earth' — that is, the conquest of more *Lebensraum* — would justify that.[62]

Hitler also considered the idea of a Russo-German alliance against the West, but found it wanting in several respects. Firstly, it would mean that the ensuing war would be fought on German soil. Secondly, Russia would have to subdue Poland before giving Germany assistance; Germany, in other words, would have to begin fighting the war almost single-handed. Finally, there was the unre-

---

59. Ibid., pp. 600–2.
60. Ibid., p. 586.
61. Ibid., pp. 598–9.
62. Ibid., pp. 593–8. Hitler's comments were, of course, not directed exclusively at members of the Strasser group; he had other critics.

liability of the Bolshevik leadership and the risk that such an alliance would spread the debilitating influence of Bolshevism inside Germany.[63]

In short, therefore, it appears as if Hitler wrote the foreign policy section in chapters thirteen and fourteen of the second volume of *Mein Kampf*, in part at least to refute the arguments mainly, but not exclusively, originating from the Strasser faction. Since this was written in August 1925 — months before the 'Strasser programme' was formulated — it provides unmistakable proof that Hitler was perturbed by the dissenting views of the North German group even before they openly challenged his authority by producing an alternative party programme.

A second piece of evidence concerning Hitler's reaction to the emergence of dissent in the party is his speech at Bamberg on 14 February 1926. The speech was devoted to three issues: the defence of his alliance strategy; the question of whether the land of the German princes, confiscated in 1918, should be returned to them or expropriated; and, finally, the inadvisability of public discussion by National Socialists on religious issues.[64]

Hitler was concerned primarily to reiterate his own views on Germany's alliance strategy and to discredit the 'Eastern orientation' propagated by the 'Strasser group' in the Nazi press but omitted from the draft programme. This once more seems to suggest that he was worried by the general outlook of the group as well as the content of their programme. Gottfried Feder, who attended the meeting of the *Arbeitsgemeinschaft* on 26 January which discussed the 'Strasser programme', shared this concern; he wrote later of his 'increasing astonishment' at the outspokenly pro-Russian and pro-Soviet line in the *Nationalsozialistische Briefe* and said of Joseph Goebbels that 'even a communist agitator could speak no differently'.[65] In discussing expropriation of the princes' land, Hitler overruled the resolution favouring this course passed by the *Arbeitsgemeinschaft* on 26 January. He argued that the princes 'should have nothing that they do not own, and lose nothing that they do own'.[66] This second rebuke probably reflected his growing fear that the

63. Ibid., pp. 602–4.

64. For the record of his speech, see 'Die Bamberger Tagung', *VB*, 25 February 1926.

65. Feder's letter to the party leadership dated 2 May 1926; reprinted in Tyrell, *Führer befiehl*, pp. 124–5.

66. 'Die Bamberger Tagung', *VB*, 25 February 1926. For Otto Strasser's view of this dispute, see his letter to Goebbels on 26 January 1926, reprinted in Jochmann, *Nationalsozialismus*, pp. 221–2.

socialistic stance of the North German faction, and in particular its questioning of the sanctity of property, could well jeopardise the support already enjoyed by the party in conservative circles, as well as his hopes of attracting future support in business quarters. Hitler was also determined to avoid getting the party embroiled in religious controversy, which he argued would 'undermine its political effectiveness'. The latter remarks may have been directed at the anticlerical propaganda which his former associate Ludendorff had drummed up after 1924, though they are as likely to have been made against Alfred Rosenberg.[67] What linked all three elements in Hitler's speech was his disquiet over the ideas being expressed within the party. And his speech represented, as the *VB*'s report emphasised, 'directives on the position which National Socialism takes on the most important issues of the day'.[68] So, whilst Hitler's appearance at Bamberg was probably prompted by the production of a draft party programme, he was nevertheless very concerned about the ideas expressed both in the programme and in articles and speeches by Strasser and his friends.

This interpretation is confirmed by a third piece of evidence: Hitler's decision in February 1926 to publish a pamphlet, *Die Südtiroler Frage und das deutsche Bündnisproblem*. He had originally written this in August 1925 as chapter thirteen of the second volume of *Mein Kampf*, but had, he explained later, been 'forced to have this part . . . published as a special edition'.[69] It is true that the South Tyrol problem was again in the news following the Bavarian Minister-President Held's public condemnation in January 1926 of Italy's oppressive measures in the province, coupled with talk of a possible retaliatory economic boycott against Italy.[70] However, there can be little doubt that the decision to publish the pamphlet at this time was affected by the controversy within the party. The 'Strasser group' had, of course, called for the return of the South Tyrol as part of a Greater Germany, but the pamphlet had a purpose beyond a simple refutation of this anti-Italian stance among North German Nazis and many other German nationalists. It was intended to re-establish Hitler's reputation as the party's leading spokesman on foreign affairs: 'Mussolini has spoken! Stresemann

---

67. 'Die Bamberger Tagung', *VB*, 25 February 1926. For Ludendorff's anticlericalism, see Parkinson, *Tormented Warrior*, p. 223; on Rosenberg's, see above pp. 76.
68. 'Die Bamberger Tagung', *VB*, 25 February 1926.
69. *Hitler's Secret Book*, p. 1.
70. See Rosenberg's coverage in 'Krisenstimmung' *VB*, 9 February 1926.

has also spoken./ The League of Nations is in confusion!'[71] So ran the advertisement of the pamphlet in the *VB*, the implication clearly being that where other statesmen had tried and failed, Hitler had the solution to the thorny problem of the South Tyrol.

These arguments are not intended to deny the fact — confirmed by Goebbels — that Hitler was enraged by the formulation of a new party programme.[72] But the foreign policy sections for the second volume of *Mein Kampf*, Hitler's speech at Bamberg and the publication of his pamphlet, taken together do imply that he was already very disturbed at the opinions being voiced at meetings and in the Nazi press. He was certainly not 'indifferent' to ideological questions, as some have suggested.[73] The publication of an alternative party programme simply brought matters to a head and he determined to lay down an official party line on current issues. However, once this had been done and the draft programme withdrawn, Hitler did not force his followers to speak with one voice. To have done so might have forced Gregor Strasser and Joseph Goebbels to leave the party, which was clearly not in its best interests; the organisation of the NSDAP in North and West Germany was the most, and perhaps the only, encouraging development in the gloomy year following its re-formation in February 1925. So Hitler tried instead to heal the wounds of the conflict by wooing Strasser and Goebbels over to his side in long discussions and by invitations to Munich. This strategy produced dividends with Goebbels, who was soon doubting — if the entries in his diaries are to be believed — his previous convictions about Russia; the 'National Bolshevik' line disappeared from his speeches and articles, and in March 1926, apparently impressed by Hitler's 'amazingly lucid' pamphlet on the South Tyrol, he wrote an article advocating the sacrifice of the Germans in the area to the needs of an Italian-German alliance.[74]

Gregor Strasser proved less willing to compromise his ideals. When the Treaty of Berlin was signed by Russia and Germany in April 1926, for example, he admitted that he 'more than any other circles in the party had emphasised the need for Germany to look eastwards'.[75] On occasion, he continued to express views at odds with the alliance strategy favoured by Hitler; it was a mistake, he

71. *VB*, 19 February 1926.

72. Heiber, *Goebbels Diaries*, p. 65, entry of 6 February 1926.

73. Stachura, *Gregor Strasser*, p. 49.

74. Heiber, *Goebbels Diaries*, p. 72, 74–9, 93; see his article 'Der Apfelsinenkrieg', *NS Briefe*, 15 March 1926.

75. G. Strasser, 'Die politische Lage', *Der nationale Sozialist*, 9 May 1926.

insisted in November 1926, 'to keep Russia in a state of impotence, for Russia sits on the flank of Poland and our Eastern enemy is Poland not Russia'. Following what he described as a 'geopolitical' maxim of 'always choosing one's friends so that they sit on the flanks of the next enemy', Strasser added that he could approve a German alliance with Italy because Italy was situated on the French flank. Though he admitted that 'geopolitically, this also applied to England', he added that 'here limitations of another kind come into play'.[76] He was not alone in his views, for Count Ernst zu Reventlow, who joined the NSDAP in February 1927, also proved to be a vocal and influential critic of British foriegn policy.[77]

Thus Gregor Strasser adhered to his vision of a *Grossdeutschland* based on Central Europe as the most sensible goal of the future Nazi foreign policy, whilst his brother Otto continued to expound the notion of *Mitteleuropa* with Germany as 'the leader of Europe, not the ruler', rejecting a Pan-European solution in favour of an exclusively German one.[78]

Despite these displays of heterodoxy, Gregor Strasser continued to control the party's propaganda department until January 1928 when he was appointed Reich Organisation Leader, a very influential post which he retained until 1932; Reventlow became the party's leading spokesman on foreign affairs in the Reichstag and was asked to address the 1927 party rally on the subject. Both were invited regularly to speak in Bavaria, in all probability refraining on these occasions from overt criticism of Hitler's foreign policy programme. Rosenberg certainly sought to avoid 'unpleasant debates' by refusing to publish a number of Gregor Strasser's articles.[79] Nevertheless their continued defiance of the party's guidelines was well-known to observers within the party and outside.[80] That Hitler was prepared to tolerate and even to promote members of this dissenting group, was probably due to three considerations: firstly, he considered these men to be useful in attracting support to the movement;

76. G. Strasser, 'Mehr Aussenpolitik' *NS Briefe*, 15 November 1926. He did not, as Stachura claims, abandon his pro-Russian stand, *Gregor Strasser*, p. 42, or his views on the South Tyrol; *VB*, 15/16 April 1927.

77. See Reventlow's articles in *VB*, 6/7 March, and *NS Briefe*, 15 September 1927, and his speech in the Reichstag, report in *VB*, 2 July 1927.

78. G. Strasser, *Kampf um Deutschland* (Munich, 1932), pp. 141–3. Ulrich von Hutten, 'Wir und "Paneuropa"', *Der nationale Sozialist*, 23 October 1927.

79. Rosenberg's letter to Gregor Strasser, 24 February 1927, NS 8/143; *VB*, 23 August 1927.

80. There were complaints about Reventlow's views; see letter from Dr. Henry Grohé to Rudolf Hess, 13 April 1930, Sammlung Schumacher, Bundesarchiv Koblenz, 260. In 1931 it would appear that several Russian émigrés decided to use Göring and Reventlow to try to effect a change in Hitler's Ostpolitik; unsigned letter dated 30 July 1931; NS 8/121.

secondly, he recognised that their views, though heterodox, were basically moderate and inspired by the spirit of German nationalism. Finally, he decided to ignore differences of opinion within the movement, provided that they were not 'fought out' in public.[81]

It would seem, therefore, that the confrontation at Bamberg occurred partly because of the production of the 'Strasser programme' and partly because the Nazi leadership had not yet published clear guidelines on foreign affairs. In 1925 Hitler began to fear that party members and potential supporters would be confused by the conflicting opinions being expressed in the Nazi press. He therefore sought in *Mein Kampf*, in his foreign policy pamphlet and in his speech at Bamberg, to establish the party's official line. Once that was firmly established, dissent was not welcome but could at least be recognised for what it was. It was therefore probably concern about the 'Strasser group' which forced Hitler to include the first serious rationalisation of a future Nazi foreign policy in the second volume of *Mein Kampf*.[82]

The Elaboration of Hitler's Outlook

Hitler's foreign affairs programme was virtually complete when he finished the second volume of his autobiography in 1926. However, he was not satisfied with its elaboration in *Mein Kampf*, which he admitted later had been 'structured on general national socialist insights as a premise'; in the time and space available, it had not been possible to give 'a real fundamental proof of the soundness of our national socialist conception of foreign policy'. For this reason he chose to write a second book between May and July 1928, but eventually decided not to publish it.[83] Between 1926 and 1928, however, the foreign policy programme had been amplified and its main assertions substantiated. An analysis of these changes serves to

81. On 17 September 1928 Hitler warned the editors of the *NS Briefe* not to get involved in 'the fighting out of any kind of clashes of opinion inside the movement' Sammlung Schumacher 260. Rosenberg told Gregor Strasser in a letter dated 24 February 1927 that he had avoided beginning a polemic with him personally in the *VB* over the last few years, 'although this would have been natural in view of your outlook on the Russian question and perhaps also many other foreign policy matters'; NS 8/143.

82. Rosenberg, reviewing the second volume of *Mein Kampf*, urged every National Socialist to draw it to the attention of 'the people who reproach us with the lack of a foreign policy programme'; 'Der Zweite Bund: Adolf Hitler: Mein Kampf', *VB*, 10 December 1926.

83. *Hitler's Secret Book*, p. 2. On the dating of the book see Taylor's introduction, ibid., pp. xvi-xviii.

highlight the hidden assumptions behind Hitler's approach to the major foreign powers.

Italy

The question of the South Tyrol continued to pose difficulties for Hitler's Italian policy. In February 1928 it was again in the forefront of political debate after the revelation that the Italian language was to be used in religious instruction in its schools. The Austrian chancellor Ignaz Seipel had declared that there could be no question of friendly relations between Austria and Italy until the problems of the province had been resolved. Mussolini responded on 4 March by threatening to use force against the Austrians if they continued their agitation in the South Tyrol.

In his pamphlet on this issue, Hitler had argued that the regaining of lost German territories was less important than the restoration of the political power and independence of the mother country and, therefore, since Germany's recovery required Italian collaboration, in his view the South Tyrol had to be sacrificed.[84] This argument may have impressed Joseph Goebbels but Hitler, Rosenberg and even Hermann Göring, in a rare series of articles, attempted to justify this sacrifice further. They were not prepared, of course, to condone Mussolini's oppressive measures in the province, but they questioned why the South Tyrolean Germans should be singled out for special commiseration from the millions of oppressed Germans under French, Polish and Czech rule, and also why the South Tyrol should become the sole determinant of German foreign policy.[85] In his second or *Secret Book*, Hitler argued that, since two-thirds of the inhabitants of the province were Italian, if it were to become a German territory then an even greater injustice would have been done to Italy.[86] This rare concern for justice only serves to emphasise Hitler's commitment to an Italian alliance at any cost.

Judging by the pamphlet on Germany's postwar alliance policy and by *Mein Kampf*, the case for Italo-German collaboration rested on two premises: the continuation of the rivalry between Italy and France, and the supposed compatibility between Italian and German ambitions. As evidence for the first claim, Hitler referred briefly in *Mein Kampf* to Franco-Italian competition in the Adriatic; in his

84. Hitler, *MK*, p. 557, 571–5.

85. *Hitler's Secret Book*, pp. 180–1, 189–90; Rosenberg, 'Mussolinis Südtiroler Rede', *VB*, 6 March 1928; H. Göring, 'Zum deutsch-italienischen Konflikt', *VB*, 3, 6, 9 March 1926.

86. *Hitler's Secret Book*, p. 179.

speech at Bamberg on 14 February 1926 he also noted Italo-French tensions concerning the Riviera.[87] These rivalries were more fully documented by Alfred Rosenberg in articles in the *VB* and later in his book *Zukunftsweg einer deutschen Aussenpolitik*, published in the autumn of 1927. Rosenberg not only pinpointed the causes of the troubles on the Riviera as the Frenchifying of 500,000 Italian immigrants in the Toulouse–Nice area added to the changes in statehood experienced by the region and by Corsica in previous centuries, but also stressed Franco-Italian rivalry in North Africa.[88] In the *VB* he also chronicled the evolution of France's relations with the 'Little Entente'; he felt that Franco-Yugoslav cooperation was particularly menacing for Italy, given her Adriatic ambitions. Significantly, this point was reiterated in Hitler's *Secret Book*.[89]

In *Mein Kampf*, Hitler had failed to elaborate upon the assertion that Italian interests did not conflict with those of Germany, 'not in the most essential points, at least'.[90] However by 1927–8, he and Alfred Rosenberg were making it plain that they accepted that Italy, like Germany, was overpopulated and needed to expand her living-space and that the land available to the two countries meant expansion in quite different directions: 'Italy to the south, widening to the south-west and the south-east, Germany to the east and north-east' was how Rosenberg put it.[91] The two countries need not become rivals as they had separate spheres of interest; in Hitler's words: 'the east coasts of the Baltic Sea are for Germany what the Mediterranean sea is for Italy.'[92]

By 1927, Hitler and Rosenberg were also showing a fuller appreciation of the strategic realities of the Italian position. In a speech on 30 March of that year, Hitler explained that Italy could not afford to take on the British because of her exposed coastline and the latter's naval strength, whilst for the same reasons Rosenberg later cautioned the Italians against risking conflict with the British by expanding along the North African coast towards Egypt.[93] Hitler concluded in the *Secret Book* that Italy had, of necessity, to favour collaboration with the English; this, and not her unreliability as an

87. Hitler, *MK*, pp. 566–7; 'Die Bamberger Tagung', *VB*, 25 February 1926.

88. A. Rosenberg, 'Die Reise nach Tripoli', *VB*, 10 April 1926; *Der Zukunftsweg einer deutschen Aussenpolitik* (Munich, 1927), p. 51.

89. *Hitler's Secret Book*, pp. 161–4; Rosenberg, *Zukunftsweg*, pp. 55–6.

90. Hitler, *MK*, p. 566.

91. Rosenberg, *Zukunftsweg*, p. 57 and cf. pp. 50–3.

92. *Hitler's Secret Book*, p. 195, and cf. p. 164.

93. Hitler's speech on 30 March, report in *VB*, 1 April 1927; Rosenberg, *Zukunftsweg*, pp. 55–6.

ally, explained her withdrawal from the Triple Alliance when Austro-Hungarian policy provoked conflict with Britain in 1914.[94]

Mussolini's opposition to the *Anschluss* with German Austria was the only real bone of contention. Whilst Hitler thought the Duce should recognise the advantage of having a smaller Austria on his frontier, Rosenberg could appreciate Mussolini's resistance to the scheme as long as a pro-French government held power in Berlin; but a folkish goverment might make the prospect more appealing.[95] Both Hitler and Rosenberg seemed to have been curiously blind to the fact that Italy might well be apprehensive about exchanging Austria for Germany as her northern neighbour.

Hitler's support for an Italian alliance (dating back to 1920, as he repeatedly mentioned in the *Secret Book*) was based primarily on Italy's dissatisfaction with the territorial settlement of 1919–20 and her consequent hostility towards France, its main defender.[96] This, together with the rise of Mussolini, convinced Hitler long before he wrote *Mein Kampf* that he should abandon all hope of freeing the South Tyrol from Italian rule and that he should tread warily on the issue of the *Anschluss*. Further consideration up to 1928 merely yielded more evidence to suggest that Italy would be inclined to work with Germany and Britain against France.

France

The 'spirit of Locarno' sparked off considerable discussion in some right-wing circles in Germany about the possibility of Franco-German collaboration. Arnold Rechberg (already referred to in chapter four), a sculptor and member of a wealthy family of indus-trialists, who had long been a passionate opponent of Bolshevism and ardent advocate of an understanding between the two countries, was profoundly disappointed with the Locarno treaties. He urged the signing of Franco-German economic treaty, to be followed by a military alliance, provided France agreed to a rapid withdrawal from the occupied territories and the revision of Germany's eastern frontier.[97] These ideas were adopted as a foreign policy programme by the *Jungdeutscher Orden*, an anti-Bolshevik and antiparliamenta-

---

94. *Hitler's Secret Book*, p. 68 and cf. pp. 48–9.

95. Rosenberg, *Zukunftsweg*, pp. 55–56; *Hitler's Secret Book*, pp. 196–7.

96. *Hitler's Secret Book*, pp. 166, 167, 173, 176.

97. See Rechberg's articles in *Éclair*, 6 and 8 August 1925; see also E. von Vietsch, *Arnold Rechberg und das Problem der politischen West-Orientierung Deutschlands nach dem ersten Weltkrieg* (Co-blenz, 1958), p. 98.

rian pressure group under the leadership of Arthur Mahraun.[98] This programme soon came to the attention of the Nazi Party and was discussed at a meeting of the *Arbeitsgemeinschaft* of North and West German Gauleiters on 22 November 1925. Later Gregor Strasser published an article criticising it on the grounds that France (along with Britain) had a 'vital interest in keeping Germany politically and economically weak'.[99]

The signing of an international steel agreement by Germany, France, Belgium and Luxembourg on 26 September 1926 and of a Franco-German commercial treaty a week later naturally revived interest both in the idea of Franco-German cooperation and in the *Jungdeutscher Orden* programme. In November 1926 Rosenberg published a series of articles, later issued in a pamphlet entitled *National-sozialismus und Jungdeutscher Orden*, in which he listed the reasons why such a collaboration was out of the question. Firstly, the French were 'a nation in racial decay' because of the onset of democratic ideals since the French Revolution and the 'mulattoization' of the population through immigration from her African Empire. Secondly, the French, despite Mahraun's optimism, had not abandoned their 'thousand-year ambition' of making the Rhine their frontier; in Rosenberg's view, because of her 'immutable geographical position', bounded to the north and west by the Atlantic Ocean and to the south by the mountains of Spain, France could only expand eastwards. Thirdly, she would never accept German military equality as the basis for an agreement; she was preoccupied with security, as shown by her alliances with Poland and Czechoslovakia. The fourth and most serious fault which Rosenberg saw in Mahraun's proposals was that they ruled out any solution to the problem of overpopulation in Germany. A Franco-German agreement would alienate the British and thus rule out the acquisition of overseas colonies, whilst the other option, expansion eastwards, was 'feasible only after a confrontation with the Poles and Czechs', who were, of course, also France's allies.[100] Rosenberg concluded, therefore, that it was not the duty of a German foreign minister to negotiate an agreement with the French but rather 'to strengthen the prevailing French *angoisse* by all diplomatic means, by stirring up

98. For more on the Jungdeutschen Orden, see K. D. Bracher, *Die Auflösung der Weimarer Republic* (Berlin, 1965), pp. 139–42.

99. G. Strasser, 'Zielen des Jungdeutschen Ordens', *NS Briefe*, 15 January 1926. See also *NS Briefe*, 1 December 1925.

100. A. Rosenberg 'Jungdeutsche "Franzosenpolitik"', *VB*, 18, 21/22, 23 November 1926; idem, *Nationalsozialismus und Jungdeutscher Orden. Eine Abrechnung mit Arthur Mahraun* (Munich, 1927), pp. 18–22.

Spanish-French, Italian-French and British-French tension'.[101]

The Nazis evidently were more impressed by the France's construction of an alliance system in Eastern and South-Eastern Europe than by the 'spirit of Locarno'. France's alliances with Poland (1921) and Czechoslovakia (1924) and later with Romania (1926) and Yugoslavia (1927) served to reinforce Nazi convictions about French opposition to any revival of German power, even prompting consideration of other potential allies. In September 1926, in another article on Arthur Mahraun, Rosenberg included Spain as one of the powers (along with Britain and Italy) interested in 'hindering the growth of French power'.[102] Soon Hitler, too, was talking about a possible alliance between Germany, England, Italy and Spain 'to encircle France'.[103] The same reasons also brought Hungary into the reckoning. The 'Little Entente' of Czechoslovakia, Yugoslavia and Romania had originally been formed to resist Hungarian revisionism: French support for these three powers in 1926 and 1927 persuaded the Hungarians to negotiate a ten-year treaty of friendship with Mussolini in April 1927. The Nazis welcomed this development and reiterated their call for Germany to join the emerging anti-French coalition. Hitler put it quite succinctly in his *Secret Book*: 'That already today probably Spain and Hungary are also to be reckoned as belonging to this [anti-French] community of interests, even if only tacitly, lies grounded in Spain's aversion to French colonial activity in North Africa as well as in Hungary's hostility to Yugoslavia, which is at the same time supported by France.'[104]

Though Spain and Hungary can, at best, be described as potential junior partners in Hitler's projected alliance system, their inclusion does show that, on this occasion at least, Hitler's selection of allies against France was determined primarily by consideration of power politics unaffected by racial prejudice or personal predilection. It also seems to confirm Alfred Rosenberg's continuing influence on the development of policy; as editor of the *VB* and so obliged to comment every day on current events, he was ideally placed to help shape Nazi attitudes on foreign affairs. In the case of France, of course, Nazi hostility, largely on the basis of French

---

101. Rosenberg, *Jungdeutscher Orden*, p. 29.

102. A. Rosenberg, 'Abrechnung mit Mahraun', *VB*, 14 September 1926. He preferred Spanish rather than French control of Morocco; see his postscript to an article by Dr. Herbert Albrecht, 'Tanger auch eine deutsche Frage', *VB*, 1 October 1926.

103. Hitler's speech on 13 April, report in *VB* (Sondernummer), 15/16 April 1927.

104. *Hitler's Secret Book*, p. 209. See also the unsigned article, 'Der italienisch-ungarische Vertrag', *VB*, 9 April 1927.

defence of the Versailles Settlement, was already well established.

Britain

The case for an Anglo-German alliance was, perhaps, the weakest part of Hitler's programme. In the second volume of *Mein Kampf*, he claimed that England had opposed and still opposed the French bid for hegemony in Europe and would therefore be amenable to a revival of German power to counter this threat. He also asserted that England would nevertheless allow Germany to dominate the European continent, provided that the latter renounced the ambitions of being a worldwide colonial and commercial power. As proof of the first statement, Hitler had been able to point in *Mein Kampf* to British opposition to the Franco-Belgian invasion of the Ruhr;[105] for the second, he had offered no proof whatsoever. On the face of it, one could be forgiven for wondering whether an England striving against French hegemony in Europe might not also combat German hegemony. Not surprisingly, therefore, Hitler and Rosenberg looked around for further evidence of these two claims: in its absence, the case for collaboration with Russia against the Western European powers might seem more attractive and tangible.

The further evidence of alleged British interest in a German revival produced by Hitler and Rosenberg arose out of what they saw as the growing threat to the security of Britain and her Empire, and her relative impotence to deal with it. In a five-part series called *Englands Schicksalsstunden* published in the *VB* in June 1927 and later reproduced as part of the *Zukunftsweg einer deutschen Aussenpolitik*, Rosenberg catalogued Britain's difficulties. First and foremost, he assured his readers, England was on the verge of war with the Soviet Union following the deterioration of relations over the Zinoviev Letter, Russian meddling in various parts of the Empire (particularly in India) and Russian support for the anti-imperialist movement in China, developments which culminated in the breaking-off of diplomatic relations in 1927. Britain, therefore, needed allies. She faced a second difficulty in her worldwide competition for oil resources with the American oil industry. This was also causing friction between British diplomats and the 'Jewish' City, but Rosenberg regarded this as an encouraging sign that British foreign policy was beginning to reflect real British interests as opposed to those of the Jews. A third and more serious weakness was that financial stringen-

105. Hitler, *MK*, pp. 614–18.

cy had compelled Britain to abandon 'the two-fleet standard' and to accept naval parity with the United States, to whom she was heavily indebted. Rosenberg concluded in *Zukunftsweg* that, looked at realistically, Britain was in no position to mount a military campaign against the Soviet Union on her own; to defeat the Moscow regime, she would have to rely either on 'anti-Bolshevik elements in Russia itself, be they nationalistic Greater Russians or peoples with separatist inclinations', or else on the Baltic nations.[106] But even then, as Rosenberg had written earlier in 1927, success was not assured; England needed German support for such a venture and this would require 'a change in the previous policies of both sides: a rejection of all ties with France on the part of England as well as Germany'.[107]

Hitler had already noted in *Mein Kampf* the vulnerability of the British Isles to air attacks from France and of her shipping lanes to a submarine campaign orchestrated by the French in the Atlantic and Mediterranean. In his *Secret Book*, he repeated those observations, referring also to the abandonment of the two-power standard, and concluded that France was 'the state that is most dangerous to England'. He also acknowledged the Russian threat to India and Russia's possession of vital oil resources.[108] Hitler devoted less attention than Rosenberg to 'ideological' evidence of Britain's growing need for German support but towards the end of the *Secret Book* he suggested that an Anglo-German rapprochement depended on whether World Jewry's 'decisive influence' in England were eliminated: 'If the Jew were to triumph in England, British interests would recede into the background . . . . On the other hand, if the Briton triumphs then a shift of England's attitude vis-à-vis Germany can still take place.'[109] This ideological rider is almost certain to have been a mere afterthought.

Rosenberg, predictably, also placed Anglo-German relations in an apocalyptic racial context. The threat to the British Empire from national self-determination was only part of a more widespread challenge from the 'coloured nations' to white Nordic supremacy. In his view there was only one solution: England had to 'undertake, along with Germany, the protection of the white race: England on the sea, Germany on the continent'.[110] In Rosenberg's scenario,

106. Rosenberg, *Zukunftsweg*, pp. 71–8; 'Englands Schicksalsstunden' *VB*, 18, 21, 23, 24, 26/27 June 1927.

107. A. Rosenberg, 'England, Deutschland, und Russland', *VB*, 9 February 1927.

108. *Hitler's Secret Book*, pp. 156–7; *MK*, p. 563.

109. *Hitler's Secret Book*, p. 215, 159.

110. A. Rosenberg, 'Erpressungen an England', *VB*, 25 February 1927.

England was to protect the white race in Africa, India and Australia; North America would protect it on the American continent and Germany — in alliance with Italy who would control the Adriatic — was to isolate France and defeat her attempt to lead black Africa against a white Europe.[111] Thus he saw racial considerations as also driving England and Germany together.

Hitler did not resort to racial theories to illustrate this argument; in fact, in the *Secret Book*, he was more concerned to prove his second assertion that England would allow domination of Europe by a Germany who had abandoned hopes of becoming a major commercial and colonial power. It looks as if his attention had been drawn to the contradiction in his alliance strategy, for at one point he remarked that:

> There is a very erroneous and widespread notion, especially in Germany, according to which England would immediately fight against any European hegemony. As a matter of fact this is not correct. England actually concerns herself very little with the European conditions as long as no threatening world competitor arose from them, so that she always viewed the threat as lying in a development which must one day cut across her dominion over the seas and the colonies.[112]

Hitler pointed out that England had fought Spain, Holland and later Napoleonic France only because they were, or aspired to be, overseas powers. Furthermore, England's friendly relations with Prussia in the eighteenth century, he felt, proved that she did not automatically oppose the pre-eminence of a military power in Europe, as long as 'the foreign policy aims of this power are manifestly of a purely continental character'. When Germany began to build a fleet and to conquer overseas territories, the English attitude altered dramatically and the result was the First World War.[113] This rather strained argument did not convince the doubters.[114]

What all this suggests is that Hitler and Rosenberg were trying retrospectively to rationalise a concept of Anglo-German friendship which was based either on a personal predilection, or on a misreading of British history, or even perhaps on a prior decision to seize

111. Rosenberg, *Zukunftsweg*, p. 85.
112. *Hitler's Secret Book*, p. 149.
113. Ibid., pp. 151–6.
114. Graf Reventlow felt that this argument overlooked the fact that 'Great Britain has for 100 years always taken the most serious offence at Germany's expansion into continental markets'. 'Besides', he added, 'a revived Germany is seen in London as more dangerous than present day France'; 'Nationalsozialismus und Umwelt', *NS Briefe*, 1 January 1929.

Russian territory which seemed to require Germany to find an ally in Western Europe.

Russia

Hitler had still some way to go before all opposition to his Russian policy was also overcome. Whether his russophobia was inspired primarily by the belief that the Bolshevik government was controlled by Jews or by the conviction that Germany needed to annex Russian territory is still uncertain. What is certain is that both premises, as seen earlier, had been questioned by the 'Strasser group'. Not surprisingly, therefore, after 1926 the Nazi leadership sought to discredit the group's pro-Russian and anti-Western stance and its accompanying limited territorial demands.

In the *Secret Book*, Hitler again discussed the possibility of a German-Russian understanding, but repeated that it would be folly 'as long as a regime rules in Russia which is permeated by one aim: to extend into Germany the Bolshevik poison'.[115] He devoted more time to showing how 'incomprehensible' it was to consider waging a war against the capitalist West in alliance with this Russia: 'present day Russia', he argued, 'is anything but an anti-capitalist state'; though the Bolsheviks might have destroyed Russia's national economy, it was only in order to place the country in the hands of international finance capitalism. Hitler admitted that it was conceivable, as the 'Strasser group' suggested, that nationalist elements were 'crowding out' the Jews and turning Russia into a genuinely anti-capitalist state, but he believed that, if this did happen, it would provoke an attack by the capitalist nations of Western Europe. In such circumstances, a German-Russian alliance would be 'complete insanity', for two main reasons. Firstly, the alliance could not be kept secret and Germany would not be allowed time to rearm for this conflict; secondly, strategically Russia would have to defeat Poland before she could aid Germany: Russian troops could not bypass Poland and land troops in Germany from the sea, because of Anglo-French naval control of the Baltic.[116]

Over and above this, of course, was Hitler's fervent belief that any kind of Russo-German alliance was incompatible with his solution to Germany's problem of overpopulation. He now firmly ruled out the idea of settling Germany's surplus population in overseas colonies, since, unless they could be kept in a 'close political and

115. *Hitler's Secret Book*, p. 132.
116. Ibid., pp. 132-3.

governmental relation with the mother country', this was equivalent to allowing Germans to emigrate.[117] Since colonies had no longer been available even in the late nineteenth century, a solution had to be found in Europe. In *Mein Kampf*, Hitler had made it clear that this meant the acquisition of Russian territory; in the *Secret Book*, he was more explicit: 'The thinly settled western border regions which already had once received German colonists as bringers of culture could likewise be considered for the new territorial policy of the German nation.'[118] No Russian government would ever concede this territory voluntarily as the price of German friendship. Indeed, Hitler was in any case convinced that the dream of creating a Pan-Slavic empire was a perpetual enticement for all Russian governments to pursue expansion westwards.[119] In short, Russia and Germany were irreversibly set on a collision course.

Hitler's arguments in his *Secret Book* were designed to make his anti-Russia stance unassailable, irrespective of any change in the political complexion of Russia's rulers. In view of this, one wonders whether in the 1920s he and his associates in the Nazi Party would ever have seriously considered an alliance with Russia even if Bolshevism had been overthrown. Was talk in 1922 and 1923 of an alliance with a future nationalist Russia merely designed to solicit support under false pretences from the Russian émigrés? In Hitler's case, the revelation of his lust for Russian territory to Eduard Scharrer in December 1922 makes this extremely likely. But can the same be said of Alfred Rosenberg, the chief advocate of an alliance with a post-Bolshevik Russia?

It has long been assumed that Rosenberg was in full accord with Hitler's territorial ambitions.[120] However, this is not substantiated by his books, pamphlets or articles. In fact Rosenberg, in all his comments on the settlement of Germans in the East, with notable consistency declared that the land necessary was to be acquired 'from the Poles and the Czechs'.[121] Furthermore, in a significant article entitled 'Deutschland und der Osten' in September 1926, he cautioned Germany against the cultivation of 'utopian plans of conquest', remarking that: 'We had no cause to spin out plans

117. Ibid., p. 71.

118. Ibid., p. 74.

119. Hitler's speech on 30 March, reported in *VB*, 1 April 1927; cf. *Hitler's Secret Book*, pp. 136–7.

120. Hanfstängl, *Zwischen Weissem und Braunem Haus*, p. 78; Cecil, *The Myth of the Master Race*, pp. 163–8. Horn, *Führerideologie* p. 270 has, however, questioned this.

121. Rosenberg, 'Englands Schicksalsstunden', *VB*, 26/27 June 1927, 'Wesen', pp. 135–6; 'Der freigebige Rechberg', *VB*, 12 May 1926.

beyond the essentials as if there were an empty *Lebensraum* in the east. The direction of this impulse is towards the Poles and the Czechs. Beyond that we can, in no sense, reflect in any practical way.' Since he did not suggest that Russian land should be settled by the Germans, he could argue (without self-contradiction) in favour of a future alliance between Germany and a nationalist Russia. As he saw it, Germany needed Polish territory, a fact which 'in no way hinders friendship with Russia, who likewise can have no interest in a strong Poland'. However, he added, 'this necessity must be recognised as absolutely legitimate by nationalist Russia'.[122] If not, then Russia could expect German hostility. Rosenberg's public utterances, therefore, sustained the idea of a 'national Russian alliance' long after the prospect of support from the Russian émigrés had disappeared. Perhaps, therefore, in his case the notion was based on genuine conviction.

Rosenberg's attitude towards the separatist movements inside Russia reinforces this impression. He believed that one day the Russian empire would disintegrate into its component parts; it was already being torn apart by separatist movements in the Ukraine and the Caucasus.[123] If Germany were to assist the Ukrainians actively, she would not simply weaken the Soviet Union, she would also acquire an ally against the Poles since the Ukrainians were 'the deadly enemies of Poland'.[124] Rosenberg summed up his strategy in *Zukunftsweg* as follows: 'If we now accept that the removal of the Polish state is Germany's first priority, then an alliance between Kiev and Berlin and the creation of a common frontier becomes a folkish and a national necessity for a future German policy.' So it would seem again that Rosenberg's main goal was the removal of Poland; he was apparently not interested in annexation of the Ukraine. Hitler, on the other hand, is supposed to have been fascinated by the prospect of acquiring this vital grain-producing area.[125]

Rosenberg continued to refer to a future 'nationalist Russia' until the publication of *Zukunftsweg einer deutschen Aussenpolitik*, when he

122. Rosenberg, 'Deutschland und der Osten', *VB*, 22 September 1926.

123. A. Rosenberg, 'Aufkläricht [sic] und deutsche Aussenpolitik', *VB*, 29 March 1927; cf. 'Bolschewistischer Judenbluff', *VB*, 15/16 April 1927.

124. Rosenberg's editorial commment on an unsigned article, 'Die ukrainischen Kosaken und ihre politischen Bestrebungen', *VB*, 9 September 1927; 'Englands Schicksalsstunden', *VB*, 26/27 June 1927.

125. Rosenberg thought that the Ukrainian agreement would open up export possibilities for German industrial products; *Zukunftsweg*, p. 97; Hitler supported annexation, according to Hanfstängl, *Zwischen Weissem und Braunem Haus*, p. 122.

reluctantly admitted that this was not a realistic prospect,' at least not in the foreseeable future, which comes into consideration for a practical German foreign policy' and that, in any case, such a Russia would be unlikely to accede to Germany's wishes concerning the settlement of the East (*Ostsiedlung*).[126] This change may mean that Hitler had finally brow-beaten Rosenberg into accepting his own *Ostpolitik*, or alternatively that the idea of seizing Russian territory had always been Rosenberg's secret dream. However, it is more likely that Rosenberg had entertained unrealistic hopes that a future nationalist Russia would prove amenable to Germany's territorial requirements; in 1927 he had written that if nationalist Russia were prepared 'to give up her right to land in the struggle against the Czechs and the Poles, so that 100,000,000 Germans could feed themselves well', then 'nothing would stand in the way of good political relations'.[127] These illusions were abruptly shattered by the publication in July 1927 of Archduke Cyril Vladimirovich's book, *Mit oder gegen Moskau*. Archduke Cyril, a descendant of the Czar and the choice of most Russian émigrés as leader of a post-Bolshevik Russia, recognised that Germany was overpopulated but was interested only in attracting German technicians to help rebuild Russia; though he urged Russo-German collaboration, he had no intention, as Rosenberg recognised when reviewing the book, of allowing Germany to expand eastwards.[128] Thus the main rationale for Rosenberg's highly theoretical German alliance with a post-Bolshevik Russia had been eliminated.

Whether Rosenberg thereafter came to accept Hitler's version of *Ostsiedlung* is open to debate. His continued calls for aid to the Ukrainian separatists suggests that he remained primarily more interested in eliminating Poland than annexing Russian territory.[129] What should be fully recognised, however, is that before 1927 Rosenberg's published views on Eastern Europe differed markedly from those of Hitler. He hoped for the annexation of the whole of Poland and Czechoslovakia by Germany with Ukrainian assistance and, if possible, with Russian neutrality. His ambitions were therefore not as limited as the revisionist policy favoured by the 'Strasser group', nor as extensive as the *Ostpolitik* favoured by Hitler.

126. Rosenberg, *Zukunftsweg*, pp. 89–90.
127. Rosenberg, 'Aufkläricht', *VB*, 29 March 1927.
128. Rosenberg, 'Eine nationalrussische Annäherung', *VB*, 17/18 August 1927. The article is unsigned but whole sections were repeated verbatim in *Zukunftsweg*.
129. Rosenberg, *Zukunftsweg*, p. 97.

The United States

In general, the United States continued to be rather neglected in Nazi appraisals of foreign affairs between 1926 and 1928. This was hardly surprising in view of the limited American involvement in European affairs in the 1920s and the Eurocentric conception of a Nazi foreign policy geared in the first instance to removing the Versailles Settlement. Hitler had begun, however, to appreciate the enormous potential of the United States in geopolitical terms; in *Mein Kampf*, he had described America as 'a giant state' with a very favourable ratio of land to population size. He felt that she was now beginning to challenge the pre-eminence of Great Britain in both the naval and the economic spheres.[130]

In his *Secret Book*, Hitler added a racial dimension; the Americans, he said, were 'a young and racially select people', who had 'for centuries received the best Nordic forces of Europe by way of immigration'. Furthermore, they were conscious of the need for racial purity, having already introduced selective immigration control.[131] He did, however, see one cloud on the horizon; the second wave of immigrants from south-eastern Europe and the Far East were not assimilating so easily as the first, racially compatible wave.[132]

Nevertheless, Hitler identified in America a threat, albeit in the long term, to the economic well being of Europe and to the established balance of world power. He believed that 'England', provided she remained 'true to her great world-political aim', would join the 'new association of nations', which would eventually stand up to the threat of US world domination.[133] However, though Hitler did show some awareness of America's potential, he clearly did not consider her likely to be an active opponent of the re-establishment of German power in Europe — his first goal.

Alfred Rosenberg also largely omitted America from his foreign policy deliberations. He certainly noticed the signs of increasing Anglo-American competition in naval and economic affairs, but tended to see the hand of the 'Jewish' financiers of Wall Street behind the machinations of US foreign policy.[134] In fact, Rosenberg regarded 'Nordic' America as a valuable ally in the racial confront-

130. See above, p. 169 note 125; *Hitler's Secret Book*, p. 19.
131. *Hitler's Secret Book*, pp. 100–1.
132. Ibid., pp. 107–8.
133. Ibid., p. 209 and cf. pp. 93, 98.
134. Rosenberg, *Zukunftsweg*, pp. 73–4; see also his article 'Der Abrüstungsbetrug', *VB*, 13/14 February 1927.

ations of the future; in the First World War, America and Britain had been on the wrong side and had aided France, 'the champion of the black racial pestilence'; but in future America, along with Britain and Germany, would defend the white race against the emerging challenge from Africa.[135]

So Rosenberg, like Hitler, did not expect the United States to play an important part in the restoration of Germany's position in Europe. However, unlike Hitler, he did not appear to appreciate fully the danger which North America would present in the future to the established balance of world power. He seems also to have had fewer doubts about the racial purity of 'Nordic' America or about her willingness to orchestrate the defence of the white race on the American continent.

Japan

Japan also received relatively short shrift from the National Socialists. She did not feature prominently in the alliance systems of the Strasser circle or of Hitler and Rosenberg. Nevertheless, she was not overlooked entirely. Indeed, Ernst Hanfstängl said that, during a discussion with Hitler in Landsberg gaol 'late in 1924', Hitler had insisted that 'only in alliance with that hard-working, martially aware and racially unspoiled people, the Japanese, which is "without space" just like the German people and consequently our natural partner in the struggle against Bolshevik Muscovitism, can we lead Germany into a new future'.[136] If this story is true, the background to Hitler's judgement comes into question, and why he chose not to reiterate it in *Mein Kampf* or even in his unpublished second book.

Hanfstängl at once attributed Hitler's statement to the influence of Karl Haushofer, who, through Rudolf Hess, had the ear of Hitler during his imprisonment. This seems quite likely, as Haushofer, a keen advocate of German-Japanese cooperation, considered Japan to be the rising Asiatic power and frequently compared her demographic and spatial predicament with Germany's. Significantly, Rosenberg's appraisal was based on same criteria. In June 1926 he welcomed the emergence of Japan at the head of a Pan-Asiatic movement and hoped she would succeed in pushing the Russians out of China.[137] He also noted her surplus population and consequent

135. Rosenberg, *Zukunftsweg*, pp. 84–5.
136. Hanfstängl, *Zwischen Weissem und Braunem Haus*, pp. 167–8.
137. A. Rosenberg, 'Pan-Asien', *VB*, 26 June 1926.

need to expand and find an outlet in East Asia.[138] He recognised that Japan's 'folkish imperialism' pursued in China had incurred the hostility of America and Britain; as a result, she had been driven to look to the distrusted Bolsheviks for support.[139] Rosenberg's admiration for the Japanese was obvious; he described Japan as 'almost the only nation state opposed to the international stock exchange' — from Rosenberg, this was quite a compliment![140] However, even though Japan's and Germany's interests and outlook were evidently compatible, he stopped short of advocating an alliance.

Hitler showed similar restraint. In *Mein Kampf*, he argued that the Jews were determined to destroy the Japanese nation state, but were unable 'to mimic' the 'yellow Asiatic races', or to assimilate with them and undermine them from within, as they had done in Europe and America; the Jews were therefore forced to incite other powers against Japanese militarism and imperialism. Hitler also commented on the strained relationship between Japan and the United States.[141] Nevertheless, though he had established both an ideological and a strategic precondition for German-Japanese collaboration, he did not go on to advocate it outright. It is possible that racial antipathy towards the Asiatics prevented him; however, there is no evidence to support this view and it is even unlikely, since Alfred Rosenberg, the party's racial theorist, found the Japanese unobjectionable on racial grounds. It is more probable that British abandonment of the Anglo-Japanese alliance in 1922 and signs of increasing disenchantment between the two powers, blamed by Hitler in *Mein Kampf* on the 'British-Jewish press', prevented him from including Japan alongside Britain as Germany's allies in the future campaign against the Russians.[142] Since he usually invoked the Jewish menace to explain away evidence which did not fit his preconceived scenario, it seems very likely that Hitler decided that, at that time, the case for a German-Japanese alliance would lack conviction. But it would appear nevertheless as if he recognised Japan's strategic value on the Russian front.

138. A. Rosenberg, 'Weltpolitische Rundschau: Europäische Aussenpolitik', *Der Weltkampf*, vol. 2 (15 April 1925), p. 261.

139. On 'folkish imperialism', see Rosenberg, 'Verwirrung der Begriffe. 2. Imperialismus', *VB*, 8 June 1927; on Japanese tensions with Britain and America, see 'Weltpolitische Rundschau', *Der Weltkampf*, vol. 2 (15 January 1925), p. 178.

140. Rosenberg, 'Pan-Asien', *VB*, 26 June 1926.

141. Hitler, *MK*, pp. 582–4.

142. Ibid., p. 584.

Conclusion

What emerges from an analysis of Nazi literature during the years 1924–8 is that the Nazi Party, despite the virulence of its francophobic and anti-Bolshevik propaganda, had not publicly and unequivocally delineated a coherent programme on foreign affairs before the publication of Hitler's pamphlet on the South Tyrol question in February 1926. This omission reveals, not the absence of such a programme in the mind of its leaders — Hitler certainly had a fairly concrete scheme in mind — but a reluctance to publicise it, a reticence initially dictated by the need to avoid alienating party support by the Russian émigrés. Later, there may have been a fear that the programme would stir up opposition within an already disrupted party; there was also no really convincing argument for its projected campaign of territorial conquests in Europe. There was, in short, little to be gained from a public exposé of Hitler's grandiose schemes.

In 1925–6 the 'Strasser group' challenged the assumptions, still largely concealed from the public, behind Hitler's alliance strategy, forcing him to reveal in February 1926 his foreign policy programme, by this time embellished by the pseudo-scientific reasoning culled from geopolitical literature. However, he established the authority of his proposals, primarily by relating them to the ideological tenets of the Nazi movement and offering very little objective data to confirm his analysis. Consequently, after the publication of the second volume of *Mein Kampf* in December 1926, Hitler and Rosenberg, who sympathised with the broad outline of Hitler's proposals, set about finding the necessary corroborative evidence. In 1927, in his *Zukunftsweg einer deutschen Aussenpolitik*, Alfred Rosenberg published findings accumulated in his day-to-day editorial work for the *VB*, while Hitler planned to produce his own version in a second book. Why he ultimately chose not to publish this is uncertain. It could be, as has been suggested, that *Mein Kampf* was not selling well and he did not want to produce a rival work, particularly one concentrating almost entirely on foreign affairs; or it may be that his developing association with the orthodox rightwing in the 1929 campaign against the Young Plan compelled him to reconsider publishing an embittered attack on bourgeois politicians.[143] Perhaps, also, Hitler decided that issuing a more detailed analysis of

---

143. See G. L. Weinberg's introduction to *Hitlers Zweites Buch. Ein Dokument aus dem Jahr 1928* (Stuttgart, 1961), pp. 36–7 and Taylor's introduction to Hitler's *Secret Book*, pp. xix–xx.

foreign policy — like the publication of an expanded party programme — would only encourage more debate within the party and
expose him to harmful counter-attacks.

The observations of Hitler and Rosenberg were intended to
establish the immutability of Franco-German and Russo-German
hostility, irrespective of changes in the political complexion of the
respective governments. They were also designed to convince the
Nazi rank and file that England and Italy were likely to collaborate
with a Nazi Germany, in the first instance against the French (in
such a campaign Germany might also be aided by Spain and
Hungary); next, England at least might be prepared to give help
against the Russians and finally, if need be, also against the distant
threat of American world hegemony. To bolster these arguments,
Hitler and Rosenberg resorted to racial and geopolitical theories,
observations on power politics and, in the last resort, ideological
claptrap. Whatever the intentions of the 'Strasser group', the effect
of their challenge to Hitler was to force him to defend his published
views, especially on England and Russia, rigidly and inflexibly.

Conclusion

This study has examined the evolution of Nazi ideas on foreign policy between 1919 and 1928 by considering the views of Adolf Hitler within the context of other opinions, both of the Nazi Party as a whole and of the political circles in which its leaders moved. Four broad issues have emerged: firstly, who or what influenced the party's, and more especially Hitler's, emerging outlook on foreign affairs? Secondly, how important was racist and antisemitic ideology in fashioning that outlook? Thirdly, what was the full extent of Hitler's territorial ambitions? Finally, how uniform was the Nazi Party's outlook on foreign affairs in the 1920s? The threads can now be drawn together and some answers to these questions formulated.

Who or What Influenced Hitler?

When Hitler first encountered the infant German Workers' Party in September 1919, his political standpoint had largely been formed by Pan-German literature, probably absorbed over many years. The resentment which he felt towards the former Austro-Hungarian empire suggests that it was the Austrian Pan-German Movement under Georg von Schönerer, rather than the Berlin-based Alldeutscher Verband, which first left its imprint on his mind. However, it also seems quite clear that by 1919 Hitler had read and absorbed much of the literature produced by the ADV in Germany, especially items written by its long-serving chairman Heinrich Class. The similarities between Hitler's comments on foreign policy between the years 1919 and 1921 and the views expressed in Class's books *Wenn ich der Kaiser wär* and *Deutsche Geschichte* are too similar to be entirely coincidental.

To make a glib attribution of all Hitler's ideas to Pan-German inspiration is, of course, all too easy. On the other hand, in some cases, the cryptic records of his early speeches are fully intelligible only by reference to prewar Pan-German propaganda. Furthermore, in his early speeches about Germany's need to expand because of population pressure, Hitler's discussion of the relative merits of overseas expansion and aggrandisement in Europe is so reminiscent of Class's earlier analysis in the 'Kaiserbuch' that one might legitimately suspect plagiarism. Both men favoured overseas colonisation on the grounds of practicality but secretly harboured designs on territory in Eastern Europe. Both felt also that the Treaty of Brest-Litovsk in March 1918 had provided all that Germany needed; both were drawn towards the idea of a Russo-German alliance since, they argued, the two powers had few conflicting interests. It may seem remarkable that they believed that Russia would accept a future transfer of territory on the lines of Brest-Litovsk, while remaining well disposed towards Germany; but, as has been seen, Hitler and Class were not alone in sharing this pipe-dream. Finally, both considered Britain, France and America to be Germany's irreconcilable enemies.

Though the personal relations between Class and Hitler became embittered after the Munich putsch of 1923 and though Hitler became increasingly critical of the ADV's inability to translate words into action, he never entirely outgrew his Pan-German mentality.[1] In addition to his preoccupation with the defence of the German *Volk*, Hitler's interest in notions of 'world power', 'world empire' and 'world dominion', which some would say amounted to a *Stufenplan*, a stage-by-stage plan of world domination, may well be directly attributable to his Pan-German 'education'. However, he did not carry out the Pan-German creed to the letter, as his renunciation of the South Tyrol showed: it was a move which made him unpopular in rightwing circles. Hitler's alliance strategy also revealed that he had, consciously or unconsciously, abandoned an established Pan-German frame of reference. Nevertheless, it seems likely that the goals of his projected foreign policy owed more to Pan-Germanism than to any other influence.

In terms of Hitler's ideological development, Class's influence had already been supplanted in 1920 by that of Dietrich Eckart and,

---

1. For his sympathy for the Pan-Germans, see *Hitler's Secret Book*, pp. 36–8.

more especially, Alfred Rosenberg. Whilst Eckart's relationship
with Hitler and the German Worker's Party should not be overlooked — his early support was instrumental in attracting larger
audiences and his ideas on the 'Jewish-materialistic spirit in and
around us' stimulated discussion and found their way into the party
programme of February 1920 — it did not contribute as much in
terms of the development of ideological and foreign policy tenets as
the collaboration between Hitler and Alfred Rosenberg.

Rosenberg was largely responsible for providing Hitler and the
NSDAP with an international perspective on the Jewish question.
The idea of the existence of a worldwide Jewish conspiracy to
overthrow established nation-states, which Rosenberg continually
postulated, was of tremendous value to the party, for it explained
not only Germany's remarkable internal collapse in 1918, but also
the hostile international environment which she then faced. The
threat of left-wing revolution inside Germany after 1918, the menacing power of Bolshevik Russia and the danger of Germany's economic enslavement to the victorious capitalist nations of the West
were all traceable to the same source. This scenario (by no means
Rosenberg's own creation) had the effect of reducing a very complex
national and international scene to a delightfully simple and in-
finitely adaptable formula. As such, it provided the framework for
instant interpretation of events in international affairs; if foreign
governments took any step which seemed likely to harm Germany,
this could be presented as carrying out the plans of world Jewry; all
developments abroad which favoured Germany could be used as
evidence either of Jewish trickery or of the existence in the respective
country of nationalistic groups concerned to combat the prevailing
tide of Jewish influence there. This antisemitic ideology, therefore,
served as an essential sheet anchor for Nazi analyses of foreign
affairs.

It is tempting to conclude that Hitler cynically used this ideological claptrap for his own ends — to argue away events which did
not tally with his own forecasts. However, it seems possible that he
moderated his early support for the idea of a Russo-German alliance
because of Rosenberg's revelations about 'Jewish' Bolshevism. From
September 1920 onwards, Hitler argued that such an alliance would
only come about when Jewry was deposed in Russia. To what extent
this ideological transformation was the direct source of his eventual
plan for conquest of Russian territory will be considered more fully
below. Here it is necessary to determine exactly how far Rosenberg's

ideas on foreign, affairs resembled those of Hitler. There were, perhaps, two main areas of disagreement, which were largely hidden from contemporaries.

Firstly, some disparity is evident on the question of policy towards Russia. Rosenberg's real attitude towards Russia has been the subject of much debate. Walter Laqueur regards Rosenberg as being distinctly anti-Russian because of his Baltic German heritage, whilst Ernst Hanfstängl (quoting Eckart) described Rosenberg as a 'National Bolshevik' — that is, one who favoured a Russo-German alignment once concern for national interests superseded the internationalist aspirations of early Bolshevism; Wolfgang Horn also tends to this latter opinion.[2] Both interpretations fail to understand fully Rosenberg's perception of Russia. Laqueur's view is based on Rosenberg's comments on the racial inferiority of Slavs to Germans; but, as has been shown, he nonetheless did regard Russians and Germans as compatible in some ways: the Slavs were not the equals of the Germans but they were not subhumans either. Horn's view of Rosenberg as a 'National Bolshevik' is rooted in a misunderstanding of his consistent avowal of support for a 'national Russia': but this was to be not a 'National Bolshevik' Russia, but a *post-Bolshevik* Russia; freed from her 'Jewish' Bolshevik government, she would be an attractive ally for Germany.

Rosenberg remained publicly committed to this line long after the Bolshevik victory over the nationalist forces in the Russian civil war eliminated all realistic hope of the overthrow of Bolshevism in the near future. So, at least on the basis of his public statements, he can be considered as neither virulently russophobic, nor Slav-hating nor a supporter of 'National Bolshevism'. In the first instance, he simply opposed a Bolshevik-led Russia.

However, Rosenberg was violently opposed to the existence of the Polish and Czechoslovak states created at Versailles out of the ruins of the Russian, Austro-Hungarian and German empires. From the outset, he was determined that Germany should destroy these states. It seems likely, however, that this revisionist impulse was overtaken by a growing preoccupation with the need for Germany to expand her *Lebensraum* in Eastern Europe.[3] While this may have been the result of Hitler's impact on him, it did not produce, in the period under review, an identical Eastern policy. Nowhere did Rosenberg, at the time express his support for a campaign of territorial expansion at Russian expense. Poland was for him the main enemy and he hoped that a future German foreign policy would eliminate Poland and Czechoslovakia and incorporate their lands within a German Empire, so furnishing necessary *Lebensraum*. Russia, of course, would not be easily persuaded to accept this German annexation of what was, in part, formerly Russian territory; therefore Rosenberg wanted Germany to support the separatist movements, especially that of the Ukrainians, inside Russia. The separatists could tear Russia apart and ensure her inability to oppose German plans. He also foresaw the shrinkage of the Russian Empire, as a result of the establishment of a new nation-states by the separatist movements, to its former Muscovite core; Hitler envisaged a similar outcome — at least in Western Russia — but by different means: that is, as the result of German territorial aggrandisement.

The second area in which some difference may have existed between the views of Rosenberg and Hitler related to the role of England. Both, though initially hostile to England, were by the end of 1922 advocating an Anglo-German alliance as part of a future National Socialist strategy designed to defeat first France, then Russia. The reasons for this volte-face will be examined below; the important point at issue here is the level of commitment of each man to the proposed alliance. Klaus Hildebrand has argued that Hitler's attachment to an English alliance was fundamentally grounded in power politics, whilst Rosenberg's was mainly based on racial grounds; hence Hitler believed in long-term, but not indefinite, Anglo-German cooperation, whilst Rosenberg believed in an eternal alliance.[4]

This interpretation may be slightly misleading. Essentially, for Rosenberg, the English alliance would serve both a short-term and a long-term purpose, as he explained in *Der Zukunftsweg einer deutschen Aussenpolitik*. In the short run, it would facilitate German acquisition of land in 'an easterly — Polish — direction' — that is, the acquisition of *Lebensraum*. Significantly, the reason for England's willingness to cooperate in this action was explained by Rosenberg — admittedly unconvincingly — in terms of power politics. England wanted to combat the Russian threat to her empire and would therefore support Germany, the Baltic States and the Russian separatist movements against Moscow; this might initially only produce 'interim solutions' (*Zwischenlösungen*) to Germany's problems, but would eventually ensure her acquisition of living-space.[5]

---

4. Hildebrand, *Vom Reich zum Weltreich*, p. 85.
5. Rosenberg, *Zukunftsweg*, pp. 78–80.

Rosenberg's short-term alliance strategy was, therefore, a combination of Germany, England, Italy and the Ukrainian separatists in opposition to France and Russia. The same combination, he made clear, was capable also of destroying 'the Jewish world state': evidently he had not abandoned his ideological frame of reference.[6] In the longer term, he was horrified by the spectre of the rising challenge of the black races to white supremacy; he wanted England and America to join Germany as 'stalwarts against the black racial pestilence'; England was to protect the white race in Africa, India and Australia, while America defended it on the American continent, and Germany and Italy were to play their part in Europe.[7] So, whilst Rosenberg's long-term vision of Anglo-German cooperation was based on racial considerations, and there is perhaps the implication that these were immutable, his short-term strategy owed much to calculations based on political and strategic realities capable of change.[8]

So clearly Rosenberg's conception of foreign affairs was identical only in broad outline to that of Hitler. The differences in their policies towards England and Russia do not, of course, preclude Rosenberg having exerted considerable influence over Hitler's thinking on foreign affairs, not merely on the Russian question but perhaps on the whole issue of alliance strategy. He did not allow his differences of opinion with Hitler to surface in public and, after the publication of the second volume of *Mein Kampf*, he strove hard to substantiate the foreign policy programme endorsed by Hitler.

The fact that Rosenberg failed in his ambition to become German Foreign Minister after 1933 and that he was later given the unpleasant job of Commissioner for the Eastern European Regions should not in any way be allowed to diminish his early contribution to Nazi ideology. If (and this has yet to be proved) he was relatively overlooked in the 1930s and 1940s, it was partly because he had powerful enemies within the party; jealous of the high esteem in which Rosenberg was held by Hitler, they had been working for some time to undermine his standing.[9] It has to be admitted, though, that Rosenberg's main asset to Hitler and the party was his ability to uncover useful antisemitic propaganda and to comment on

6. Ibid., p. 143.
7. Ibid., pp. 84–5.
8. Rosenberg argued consistently that 'foreign policy can never be dogmatic' because of changing world conditions; see his postscript to Nemirovich-Danchenko's 'USSR, Deutschland und Russland', *VB*, 5 November 1925.
9. For details of the opposition to Göring, Hanfstängl and Otto Strasser in the 1920s, see HA 53/1259.

current events, especially in the field of foreign policy. Once a foreign policy programme had been constructed and the conduct of foreign policy was largely in the hands of career diplomats, Rosenberg, a poor public speaker and a rather withdrawn character, could not seriously claim a place amongst the foremost party officials on merit or personality.

In 1922 and 1923 Hitler came into contact with a number of political theorists enjoying either established political or academic reputations in foreign affairs or practical experience in that field. Whether these encounters left any indelible imprint on his approach to foreign policy is debatable. His meeting with Moeller van den Bruck in March 1922 forced him to come to terms with the concept of 'National Bolshevism'. However, Hitler's rejection of this was probably not a turning-point in the refinement of his programme, but showed the apparent firmness of his anti-Bolshevik convictions at this fairly early stage in the construction of his alliance strategy.

Hitler's increasingly close association with Max-Erwin von Scheubner-Richter in 1922 and 1923 reflected his desire to attract the support of the nationalist Russian émigrés with whom Scheubner-Richter was in regular contact, and provided substance for his claim to support an alignment of Germany with a future post-Bolshevik Russia. Hitler and Scheubner-Richter became fairly close friends, so it is possible that the latter's early career in the Baltic States in 1918 (as mentioned earlier, he was engaged in negotiations with the Latvian government in the hope of obtaining the right for German soldiers to acquire land for settlement in the area) may have revitalised Hitler's interest in a policy of conquest in Eastern Europe along these lines. It is curious, for example, that in his second book he should write that the sole aim which would justify the horrific slaughter of a world war, 'could consist only in the assurance to German soldiers of so and so many hundred thousand square kilometers to be allotted to front-line fighters as property, or to be placed at the disposal of a general consolidation by Germans'.[10] It is more than likely, however, that Hitler had already reached this conclusion before he grew particularly fond of Scheubner-Richter. The idea of creating a militarised frontier zone by settling soldiers there had, for example, been discussed by the ADV during the First World War; and Hitler's scheme to annex not just Latvia but also large areas of Western Russia would, of course, cut across the type of Russo-German collaboration for which

10. *Hitler's Secret Book*, p. 78.

Scheubner-Richter was working with the Russian émigrés in the early 1920s.

A great deal of attention has been devoted to the part played by Professor Karl Haushofer's geopolitical theories in the formulation of Hitler's foreign policy schemes. Klaus Hildebrand has argued, for example, that although in 1923 Hitler's alliance strategy was evolving, one ingredient was missing — a spatial policy; this Hitler acquired through his contact with Karl Haushofer, especially during his imprisonment in Landsberg gaol between November 1923 and December 1924. This analysis cannot now be accepted. Hitler had already adopted a spatial policy involving expansion at Russian expense by December 1922, as he revealed to Eduard Scharrer.[11] Haushofer's role is likely, therefore, to have been far less crucial than has been hitherto imagined, since Hitler's original scheme of conquest in Eastern Europe probably predates any substantial contact with Haushofer, whose own views on the need for Russo-German collaboration were in any case totally out of step with Hitler's after 1922.

Nevertheless, Hitler's introduction to geopolitics proved extremely fruitful in the sense that it furnished a pseudo-scientific justification of his nakedly imperialistic impulses. The second volume of *Mein Kampf* and *Hitler's Secret Book* drew heavily on the geopolitician's strategic, autarkic and demographic arguments in favour of larger living-space. In fairness, it has to be stressed that, whilst Haushofer's continued talk of the need to expand German living-space was irresponsible and open to misuse, Hitler did deliberately pervert and exploit his theories. In Hitler's hands — and it does seem to have been his own concoction — *Lebensraum* became the key concept in Nazi philosophy. An increase in Germany's living-space would ensure a healthy *Volk* and, hence, as Hitler put it in his *Secret Book*: 'A healthy foreign policy therefore will always keep the winning of the basis of a people's sustenance immovably in sight as its ultimate goal.'[12] Greater space would also secure for Germany a larger supply of food and raw materials, thus making her less dependent on foreign trade and more self-sufficient.[13] It would also guarantee greater strategic security for the German state.[14] Since such space was, in Hitler's view, to be acquired primarily at Russian expense, the pursuit of *Lebensraum* also dovetailed neatly with the anti-Bolshevik stance which had been developed since 1920. The racial

11. Hildebrand, *Vom Reich zum Weltreich*, p. 75.
12. *Hitler's Secret Book*, p. 34.
13. Ibid., pp. 20–4.
14. Ibid., pp. 49–50 and cf. pp. 72–5.

and Russophobic connotations later acquired by the term *Lebensraum* were certainly not of Haushofer's creation. The one concrete piece of advice on foreign affairs which he undoubtedly proffered — that is, a careful appraisal of the rising power of a Japan with, allegedly, similar problems and appetites to Germany — was taken up but, in the short-term at least, not to great effect as far as the party's alliance strategy was concerned.

Such were the main influences on Hitler's emerging *Weltanschauung*. The youthful ingestion of Pan-German propaganda and the example of the treaty of Brest-Litovsk almost certainly explains his interest in eastward expansion. Rosenberg's revelations about Jewish Bolshevism probably explains the rejection of any idea of Russo-German collaboration. Though Hitler was certainly not ignorant of postwar Germany's economic dilemmas, the idea of expanding her *Lebensraum* was inspired less by an awareness of the country's economic dilemmas than by the slogans of prewar Pan-German coinage, albeit updated by fashionable geopolitical studies. It was he, however, who was responsible for assimilating these disparate elements into what appeared to him to be a coherent foreign policy scheme.

How Important was Racist and Antisemitic Ideology in Fashioning Hitler's Programme?

Attempting to unravel the process by which Hitler's foreign policy programme evolved is particularly difficult. The central question is: which came first — *a decision about the goals* of a Nazi foreign policy which determined the selection of suitable allies, or *the selection of allies* which determined those goals which might be attained? According to Hitler, prewar Germany could have expanded either overseas or into Eastern Europe; however an overseas empire could only have been achieved in alliance with Russia against Britain, while the acquisition of territory in the east would have been possible only by an Anglo-German alliance against Russia. After 1922, he believed that Germany had the same options. Hence the choice of one ally or one territorial goal would automatically determine the rest of the programme.[15] So which was the decisive selection? The answer to this question will largely determine the part which the Nazi Party's racist or antisemitic ideology played in the fashioning of Hitler's programme.

15. Hitler, 'Warum', p. 119.

Axel Kuhn attempted to answer this question in a study published in 1970. He decided that Hitler had espoused the concept of
an Anglo-German alliance in order to be able to fight a revisionist
war against the arch-defender of the Versailles Settlement, France.
Hitler had noted England's emerging distaste for French pre-
eminence in Europe, as shown by her increasing disengagement
from France's harsh policy towards Germany, which culminated in
the disagreements over the Ruhr invasion in January 1923. Hence
his decision, according to Kuhn, was based on strategic considerations and had nothing to do with Nazi ideology. Having taken the
crucial first decision and opted for an *alliance* with England, Hitler
belatedly — two years later in fact — produced a corresponding set
of foreign policy *goals*: the conquest of territory in Eastern Europe at
Russian expense.[16] Leaving aside the question of the two-year
period of gestation following the initial decision (which Kuhn does
not adequately explain), his interpretation does not stand up to close
scrutiny.

It must be doubted, firstly, whether the desire to fight a revisionist
war against France was, by itself, sufficient cause of Hitler to abandon his previous view of England as one of Germany's 'deadly
enemies' on the grounds of the prewar naval, colonial and commercial rivalry. Secondly, his argument that England opposed French
pre-eminence in Europe and would therefore help Germany to destroy it, without objecting to the resulting German hegemony, is at
best tenuous, if that was its full extent. In fact, as Eduard Scharrer
revealed in the record of his interview with Hitler in December 1922,
Hitler's projected Anglo-German alliance aimed not merely at re-
vising the Versailles Settlement, but also at the conquest of Russian
territory and, furthermore, he evidently hoped that Germany's
express renunciation of an overseas colonial policy would prevent
England from opposing German ambitions in Eastern Europe.[17]
Viewed from one perspective, Scharrer's evidence appears to lend
plausibility to the argument by Kuhn that Hitler's choice of England
determined his attitude towards Russia; it makes it quite clear that
Hitler was fully aware of the implications in Eastern Europe of
deciding for an English alliance and that he envisaged a way to avert
British hostility to German hegemony in Europe. From another
aspect, however, Scharrer's evidence suggests an entirely different
interpretation to that of Kuhn: namely, that the projected English

16. Kuhn, *Program*, pp. 102–4; 94–5.
17. See above, p. 137.

alliance was merely a *response* to a prior decision about Russia; this may have been negative, that is, the rejection of a Russo-German alliance, or positive, that is, the adoption of a plan for aggrandisement at Russian expense.[18]

Each of these explanations of the original motivation behind Hitler's alliance strategy fits the available evidence and is worth considering. The first — rejection of Russia as a prospective ally — is understandable in terms of Hitler's progressive disillusionment concerning Russia, following the revelations about 'Jewish' Bolshevism and the increasing likelihood of a Bolshevik victory in the Russian civil war. This interpretation is supported by his qualification in 1920 of his previous approval of a Russo-German alliance (that it could only come about after Jewry had been removed). Later, it is true, Hitler argued that the westward ambitions of Pan-Slavism put Russia on a collision course with Germany, but since only a few months earlier he had declared that the two countries had no conflicting interests, this is unlikely to explain his altered stance on the Russian question.[19] It is possible, therefore, that Hitler did take seriously the anti-Bolshevik and antisemitic propaganda of his party and that, as the Soviet regime looked increasingly likely to remain in power, so he was encouraged to take an increasingly virulent anti-Russian line.

The fact that, from the beginning of 1921, Rosenberg was subtly rehabilitating England could be seen as strengthening this case. Whereas in 1919 and 1920 England had been portrayed as the 'patron' of World Jewry, Rosenberg began to identify signs of English resistance to Jewish plans and to argue that the centre of Jewish activity had moved from London to New York. Whilst this might be explained as a response to the more lenient attitude of the British government towards Germany, it is equally possible that it was a result of Hitler's emergent anti-Russian policy. It could have been designed to prepare the way for the announcement of an Anglo-German alliance as part of an anti-Russian strategy. This view would, of course, suggest that the party's anti-Bolshevik or antisemitic ideology was of crucial importance in Hitler's decision-making.

The second alternative to Kuhn's interpretation is also plausible: namely, that Hitler's alliance strategy was primarily motivated by

18. Henke also noticed this; *England*, pp. 28–9, note 46.
19. See above p. 85. Later Hitler argued that Slav inferiority made a Russo-German alliance unthinkable, but this is unlikely to have been the main reason; *Hitler's Secret Book*, pp. 134–5.

his adoption of a plan of territorial conquest at Russian expense. It is known that he approved of Germany's *Ostpolitik* in 1918; and in June 1921 he declared that her requirements would have been met by the Treaty of Brest-Litovsk (signed by Russia and Germany in March 1918) and the consequent land transfers to Germany. As has been seen, in 1921 he apparently believed that a German-Russian *alliance* before the war would have allowed Germany to expand eastwards and that the Treaty of Brest-Litovsk could have been followed by Russo-German *collaboration*.[20] Thus, up to 1922, Hitler seems to have thought that his territorial ambitions for Germany in Eastern Europe could be realised without the need for an alliance with England. In that year, he abandoned the idea of Russo-German collaboration in solving Germany's spatial problems in favour of the conquest of *Lebensraum* and the destruction of Russia.

This change almost certainly indicated that Hitler's annexationist ambitions now extended beyond the seizure of the Baltic States and Poland — the goals he derived from the Pan-Germans and the German *Otspolitik* of 1918 — to include areas of Western Russia such as the Ukraine. The conquest of *Lebensraum* in the East now involved the 'destruction' of Russia. The reason for his enlarged 'appetite' could be that he now perceived the possession of the Ukraine — the granary of Europe — as the key to Germany's survival in any future war and/or that the acceptance of Russia as the ideological arch-enemy fired his imagination for an anti-Bolshevik 'crusade', a campaign for which British assistance would be necessary.

Both these interpretations would suggest that, whilst Hitler may have been attracted towards England (and Italy) by their increasing opposition to French policies, what determined his eventual alliance strategy was his decision either to abandon a Russo-German alliance or to conquer Russian territory. It has to be admitted, however, that the available evidence does offer convincing proof of any one of these interpretations (Kuhn's included). What it does show, however, is that in 1922 Hitler considered all the implications of the choice of an English ally for a campaign of conquest in Eastern Europe — there was no 'period of gestation' as implied by Kuhn. The most persuasive conclusion to be drawn from this is that the signs of growing British distaste with French policies towards Germany coincided with Hitler's alienation from Russia under its Bolshevik leadership and with his preoccupation with dreams of even greater conquest in Eastern Europe. This interpretation serves

20. See above, pp. 96, 154–5.

to demonstrate with some force the possibility that Hitler's schemes were inspired, in part at least, by genuine anti-Bolshevik convictions. The role of the party's antisemitic ideology in the development of Hitler's alienation from Russia under its Bolshevik leadership and in his preoccupation with dreams of even greater conquest in Eastern Europe should not, therefore be overlooked.

What Was the Full Extent of Hitler's Territorial Ambitions?

Hitler's entire foreign policy programme was, of course, justified in terms of race. The ultimate goal was, supposedly, the survival of the Aryan race and in the last resort the racial value and not the geopolitical situation of a people would, Hitler believed, determine its fate.[21] For this reason, preservation of the race's quality was absolutely vital and, to ensure this, the pursuit of larger living-space was crucial; as Hitler wrote in his second book: 'the compulsion to engage in the struggle for existence lies in the limitations of the living-space; but in the life struggle for this space lies also the basis for evolution.'[22] A healthy people would secure the necessities of life by expanding its living-space; a healthy people would also continually increase in number. Hence the acquisition of more space would permit further population growth, which would in time and in turn necessitate further territorial expansion. The heady mixture of race and *Lebensraum* produced, as Martin Broszat has argued, a doctrine of apparently self-perpetuating expansionism.[23]

But did Hitler seriously envisage a future global conquest by Germany? It is certainly true that implicit in his racist theorising is the idea that one race, the Aryan race, could eventually dominate the planet; it can be argued that his attribution to the Jews of schemes of world conquest merely disguised his own. But it has to be borne in mind that Aryan world domination was not necessarily synonymous with *German world conquest*. The Aryan race extended beyond Germany's frontiers and was likely so to remain indefinitely. Furthermore, though Hitler might talk of defeating the mighty American Union in some future epic confrontation, this did not necessarily entail the physical conquest of the United States by Germany. Perhaps what he initially envisaged for Germany was the

---

21. *Hitler's Secret Book*, p. 104.
22. Ibid., p. 6.
23. M. Broszat, 'Betrachtungen zu "Hitler's Zweitem Buch"'; p. 423; see *Hitler's Secret Book*, pp. 13–5.

securing of a position of pre-eminence as the *leading world power*, a position which, like his Pan-German mentors before him, he thought Britain had enjoyed at the turn of the century.

These ambitions probably still stopped short of the physical conquest of the world and the complete elimination of other world powers; Britain, for example, would be offered partnership in the confrontation with the United States. Uncontested world dominion, possibly shared with Britain, but shopping short of global conquest, may very well have represented the extent of Hitler's distant fantasies in the 1920s about his new Germany.

How Uniform was the Party's 1920s Outlook on Foreign Affairs?

Klaus Hildebrand in *The Foreign Policy of the Third Reich* has identified four different positions on foreign affairs within the Nazi Party during the Weimar Republic.[24] Two groups, the 'Wilhelmine imperialists', represented by Franz Xavier Ritter von Epp and Hermann Göring, and the Agrarian Radicals, led by Walter Darré, are outside the chronological scope of this study. The former, however, were solidly in the Pan-German tradition, looking to the restoration of Germany's 1914 frontiers by gaining territory in Europe and recovering the former overseas colonies; the latter criticised colonial aspirations overseas because the future of the race lay in the acquisition of more farming land in Eastern Europe. The remaining two sets of opinion, those of the 'revolutionary "Socialists"' of the Strasser group and of Hitler himself, have here, it is hoped, been adequately explored. It should now be clear, however, that there were more than four conceptions represented within the Nazi Party. The differing ideas of Alfred Rosenberg, Max-Erwin von Scheubner-Richter, Karl Haushofer (shared by Rudolf Hess before he fell finally under Hitler's spell), Ernst Hanfstängl and Kurt Lüdecke all found expression in the NSDAP at one time or another in the 1920s. There was, in short, a wide range of viewpoints represented within the party, which Hitler largely tolerated because, with the notable exception of the controversy in January and February 1926, the groups or individuals concerned were either not sufficiently organised to pose a threat to his authority or were unwilling to risk a public confrontation with him over foreign affairs.

24. Hildebrand, *Foreign Policy*, pp. 13–23.

The clash with the Strasser group probably convinced him of the need to assert more clearly the 'official' party line in *Mein Kampf*, but thereafter the same laissez-faire attitude towards dissenting voices reasserted itself. The clash forced Hitler to establish his authority in the field of foreign affairs, but nevertheless the Nazi Pary could not afford to alienate its most able and articulate propagandists by insisting on strict conformity on all issues.[25] Hence the competition between different individuals to influence the making of Nazi foreign policy in the 1930s was almost certainly in part the result of earlier unresolved differences of opinion and of Hitler's failure to lay down a rigid line on foreign affairs in the 1920s.[26]

25. J. Hiden points out that few historians have 'seriously disputed that when it came to foreign policy, Hitler's role was supreme'; 'National Socialism and Foreign Policy, 1919–33' in P. Stachura (ed.), *The Nazi Machtergreifung*, p. 154.

26. On this view, see W. Michalka, 'Die nationalsozialistische Aussenpolitik im Zeichen eines "Konzeptionen-Pluralismus"' in M. Funke (ed.), *Hitler, Deutschland und die Mächte*, p. 58.

Postscript

Nazi Foreign Policy —
The Programme Implemented,
1933–41

This is not the place either for a detailed narrative of Nazi foreign policy between 1933 and 1941 or even for a concise historiographical review of recent interpretations of that policy.[1] However, it does seem important that the significance of findings about the 1920s Nazi outlook on foreign affairs should be evaluated in relation to the continuing debates about Nazi policies, in particular the current controversy between the so-called 'intentionalist' and 'functionalist' schools of thought. The 'intentionalists' are, of course, in direct line of descent from those historians of the 1950s and 1960s who regarded Nazi foreign policy as a product of long-term planning by Hitler. The research of Andreas Hillgruber and Klaus Hildebrand suggests that there was even more consistency in Hitler's thinking on foreign affairs than had been earlier suspected. They also confirm what the 'planning' school had always thought, namely that Nazi foreign policy was essentially Hitler's foreign policy. The 'functionalists', on the other hand, are more distantly related to those historians who, following the lead of A. J. P. Taylor, have argued that Hitler was primarily an opportunist responding to situations and circumstances created by others. Hans Mommsen has questioned whether Nazi foreign policy was, in fact, 'an unchanging pursuit of established priorities'. Nazi expansionism was not an attempt, after long-term planning, to realise Hitler's long-cherished ambitions, but rather a matter of 'expansion without object'.[2] It was the product

---

1. For recent reviews of the historiography of the subject see P. Aycoberry, *The Nazi Question* (London and Henley, 1981); J. Hiden and J. Farquharson, *Explaining Hitler's Germany* (London, 1983); I. Kershaw, *The Nazi Dictatorship* (London, 1985).

2. H. Mommsen, 'National Socialism: Continuity and Change' in W. Laqueur (ed.), *Fascism. A Reader's Guide* (Hardmondsworth, 1979), p. 177.

both of the 'internal dynamics' of the Nazi regime — the pressures generated by competing authorities with an interest in foreign affairs such as the German Foreign Office, the 'Rosenberg Office', the Four Year Plan Office, by still powerful traditional elites like the Wehrmacht and industry, and by the economic and social tensions stimulated by rapid rearmament — and of developments in the international arena.[3] Nazi foreign policy, therefore, can no longer, in the view of the 'functionalists', be reduced to the mere exercise of Hitler's dictatorial will.

Critics of the 'intentionalist' school have not been slow to point out the pitfalls of studying Hitler's views on foreign policy expressed in the 1920s. There is the danger of reading history backwards and discovering prophetic statements by Hitler which magically explain every twist and turn of Nazi foreign policy in the 1930s. Mommsen has put it very bluntly: 'the regime's foreign policy ambitions were many and varied ... hindsight alone gives them some air of consistency.'[4] It is also possible to underestimate or even overlook the very real discrepancies between Hitler's outlook before the *Machtergreifung* and the international situation after 1933. Hans Koch has very recently argued that Hitler's vision of Soviet Russia in the early 1920s as a state destined to disintegrate because of its Jewish-Bolshevik leadership 'hardly corresponded with reality' by the time he came to power.[5] Tim Mason has also pointed out that 'the wars which the Third Reich actually fought bore very little relation to the wars which [Hitler] appears to have wanted to fight'.[6]

However, it would be equally wrong to allow reasonable qualms about the use of hindsight to blind one to real evidence of consistency in Hitler's thinking in the 1920s and 1930s on foreign affairs. Equally one should not expect 'an impossibly exact relationship between the ideas of Hitler in the 1920s and the actions of the 1930s'.[7] His views before 1933 may reveal what he intended to do, and what he attempted once in power; they do not, in the main, reveal what he might do if he failed in those intentions: but they are in no way invalidated as evidence by that failure. Thus his misread-

---

3. M. Broszat, *The Hitler State* (Harlow, 1981), pp. 294–327; T. Mason, *Sozialpolitik im Dritten Reich* (Opladen, 1977), p. 40.

4. Mommsen in Laqueur, *Fascism*, p. 177.

5. H. Koch, 'Introduction to Part II' in H. Koch (ed.), *Aspects of the Third Reich* (London, 1985), pp. 182–3.

6. T. Mason, 'Intention and Explanation: A Current Controversy about the Interpretation of National Socialism' in G. Hirschfeld and L. Kettenacker (eds.), *Der 'Führerstaat': Mythos und Realität* (Stuttgart, 1981), p. 39.

7. J. Hiden in Stachura, *Machtergreifung*, p. 153.

ing of the Russian situation (if indeed he did misread it as Koch suggests) and the fact that Germany had to fight wars which he had not foreseen, proves that Hitler was not an infallible twentieth-century prophet but it does not prove that the 'programme' developed in the 1920s is irrelevant to the study of Nazi foreign policy.

The key debates about Hitler's supposed 'programme' concern: (1) the question of consistency in his policies on alliances and German expansionism; (2) the ultimate scope of that expansionism; and (3) the extent to which Nazi foreign policy was essentially 'Hitlerist'.

1. Consistency in Hitler's Foreign Policy Programme

Some historians have suggested that there was an 'inner consistency' in Hitler's foreign policy, primarily determined by his ideological beliefs.[8] This study has shown that, whilst his original thoughts on an Anglo-Italian–British alliance may have been inspired by the desire to revise the Versailles Settlement against French opposition, a fully-fledged alliance scheme may have been the result of his adoption of an anti-Bolshevik ideology. In this way Hitler's early thoughts of a Russo-German alliance may have been dispelled. Since he believed that Germany both before and after the First World War had to choose between England and Russia as allies — an English alliance committing Germany to territorial expansion at Russian expense, a Russian alliance to overseas expansion — the relegation of Bolshevik Russia automatically promoted the English alliance and the pursuit of living-space in Eastern Europe. If this was so — in other words, if Hitler was motivated by a genuine antipathy towards Bolshevism — it would greatly strengthen the case for continuity in his thinking on foreign policy from the 1920s to Operation Barbarossa.

However, the available evidence cannot put this beyond doubt. It is also possible, for example, that Hitler's alliance strategy was dictated by the desire for territorial aggrandisement in Eastern Europe. His imagination may have been fired by imperialistic wartime Pan-German propaganda or by the actual annexation of Russian territory authorised by the Treaty of Brest-Litovsk in March 1918. The prospect of re-creating this empire may ultimately have prompted him into advocating an alliance with Britain. The

8. K. Hildebrand, *The Third Reich* (London, 1984), p. 27.

movement's anti-Bolshevik convictions, in this case, would merely be of secondary importance, reaffirming that strategy.[9]

However, what is at issue here is not so much the question of ideological or power political inspiration, as whether or not Hitler's alliance policy was consistent. The evidence from the 1920s certainly suggests that it was. In discussions of a prospective Nazi foreign policy, the Anglo-Italian-German alignment against first France and then Russia and the concomitant renunciation of overseas colonisation in favour of expansion in Europe was consistently advocated by Hitler — in private with Eduard Scharrer in 1922, publicly in the second volume of *Mein Kampf* and, at greater length, in his unpublished second book. He even seemed proud of his consistency; he wrote in 1928 that 'since the year 1920 I have tried with all means and most persistently to accustom the National Socialist movement to the idea of an alliance with Germany, Italy and England'.[10] Also his response to the alternative pro-Russian and colonial strategy put forward by the 'Strasser group' seems to suggest that his alliance policy was not a matter for debate.

Hitler's basic scenario left some scope for flexibility or opportunism, as *Hitler's Secret Book* makes clear. There, he included Spain and Hungary as potential junior partners in the anti-French coalition — Spain because of emerging Franco-Spanish tensions around the Mediterranean, Hungary because of her hostility to France's *Little Entente* partners in Central Europe.[11] Rosenberg even conceded that an alliance between Nazi Germany and the Soviet Union was conceivable on a short-term basis; but Hitler would have none of this: such a future alliance would make 'no sense for Germany', not even 'from the standpoint of sober expediency'.[12]

Evidence from the period after 1933 seems to suggest that Hitler did attempt to implement his alliance strategy and that his convictions dating from the 1920s about international relations continued to provide his terms of reference. The signing of the Anglo-German Naval Treaty on 18 June 1935 was seen by Hitler and Ribbentrop as the first step towards a 'general accommodation' with Britain, though they were already aware that it would be difficult to secure.[13] In March 1935 Hitler had already raised the demand for the return

9. See above, pp. 135–9.
10. *Hitler's Secret Book*, pp. 166–7, cf. pp. 173, 176.
11. Ibid., p. 209.
12. See above p. 179; *Hitler's Secret Book*, pp. 134–9.
13. Hildebrand, *Third Reich*, p. 19.

of Germany's colonies in order to 'compel' Britain into an alliance.[14] The very use of this threat shows the consistency of his thinking about England — it was meant to 'remind' the British that German expansion in Eastern Europe was preferable to Germany's re-emergence as a colonial rival.

However, despite this and despite Ribbentrop's celebrated mission as ambassador to Britain 'to bring back England', the British were not to be enticed or intimidated into a bilateral agreement with Germany. It was almost certainly the anticipated failure of Hitler's attempt to realise the key feature of his alliance strategy that led him on 13 September 1937 to assert that 'neither Britain nor France wanted to see any favourable readjustments of power in Europe in favour of Germany or Italy' and two months later to refer in the famous 'Hossbach meeting' on 5 November to Britain as a 'hate-inspired antagonist'.[15]

Hitler's actions and statements, thereafter, should not be taken as evidence of inconsistency. His call in October 1938 for a new programme of Luftwaffe expansion, Ribbentrop's attempt to turn the Anti-Comintern Pact into a military alliance against Britain and his own approval in January 1939 of the so-called 'Z Plan' — the construction of a large surface fleet — were Hitler's response to the increasing likelihood of something he had not foreseen — a future war with Britain. This is not to imply that he expected that war which broke out in September 1939; indeed, Hitler's comment at the Führer conference on 23 May 1939 that 'it must not come to a simultaneous showdown with the West' suggests that he was still determined to persuade Britain to remain neutral. The Nazi-Soviet Pact was evidently meant to clinch this.[16] When it failed to do so, Hitler hoped to sign an early peace settlement with Britain in 1940; when his hopes were again dashed, on 11 June 1940 he reactivated the 'Z Plan', which had been shelved at the outbreak of war.

It would appear that Hitler also sought to achieve the Italo-German alliance which he had advocated since 1920. Once again, however, developments did not go as he had envisaged. Italy did not initially support Germany's attempts to revise the Treaty of Versailles. Moreover, in the case of Italian opposition to the Austrian Nazi putsch of 25 July 1934, he failed to obey his own self-denying ordinance, namely, to secure prior Italian agreement to any move

14. Henke, *England in Hitlers politischem Kalkül 1935–39* (Boppard a.Rh.), p. 38.

15. Kuhn, *Programm*, p. 209.

16. See Hitler's speech to his Commanders-in-Chief on 22 August 1939, *Documents on German Foreign Policy*, D, vol. VII, pp. 200–4; for his speech on 23 May 1939, *DGFP*, D, vol. VI, p. 576.

towards the *Anschluss*.[17] In April 1935, in the wake of Hitler's reintroduction of conscription — another infringement of Versailles — Italy joined Britain and France in the Stresa Front. It was only Mussolini's alienation from these two countries following the Italian invasion of Abyssinia that in January 1936 persuaded him to remove his unconditional guarantee of Austrian sovereignty, allowing Germany to negotiate the inappropriately named 'Gentleman's Agreement' with the Austrian government, which brought Austrian foreign policy into line with Germany's. By the time Mussolini approved the *Anschluss* on 11 March 1938, Italy (as a member of the Anti-Comintern Pact) was already being used by Hitler in an almost unforeseen war of nerves against Britain.[18]

Nevertheless the division of Eastern and Central Europe into separate German and Italian spheres of influence, which Hitler had described in his second book as the basis of an Italo-German alliance, had been realised in the Rome-Berlin Axis. Italy was to penetrate the countries bordering the Mediterranean, Germany the eastern coasts of the Baltic.[19] Also Hitler was as good as his word on the subject of the South Tyrol. Though occasionally mentioning the vexed subject of the Germans there in order to put pressure on Mussolini, in the same way as he played the colonial card with Britain, he never made a serious issue of it. Göring may have promised the eventual evacuation of the German population during his visit to Rome in January 1937 and Hitler certainly endeavoured to reassure Mussolini about an eventual settlement during his own visit to Rome in May 1938.[20]

Thus it would appear that, in the case of England and Italy, not only did Hitler attempt to carry out his intentions as stated in the 1920s, but he also seems to have been guided, in part at least, by his preconceived ideas about the tactical preconditions for Anglo-German and German-Italian collaboration in the approach to negotiations with those countries.

The relationship between Hitler's early views on Russia and actual Nazi policy is especially interesting. 'Intentionalists', of course, detect a clear ideological thread connecting Hitler's adoption of an expansionist and anti-Bolshevik ideology in the 1920s and

17. Indeed Hitler had been aware in 1922 of the need to avoid antagonising Italy over the *Anschluss* and the South Tyrol; Scharrer, 'Bericht', BAK, R43I/2681.

18. G. L. Weinberg, *The Foreign Policy of Hitler's Germany. Starting World War II* (Chicago/ London 1980), p. 299.

19. *Hitler's Secret Book*, p. 195; cf. p. 164; D. M. Smith, *Mussolini's Roman Empire* (Harmondsworth, 1979), p. 96.

20. Weinberg, *Starting World War II*, pp. 270-1 and cf. p. 307.

the launching of Operation Barbarossa in 1941. Some of the 'functionalists', on the other hand, deny that his conception of Russia in the 1920s informed his policy after 1933; they point to his ratification on 5 May 1933 of the Treaty of Berlin and, of course, to the Nazi-Soviet Pact as evidence that anti-Bolshevik ideology was 'largely left in limbo' after 1933. Though theory and practice seemed to coincide in Operation Barbarossa, it was not the final execution of Hitler's 'programme' but the result of his inability to control Soviet aggression in South-Eastern and North-Eastern Europe and to 'harness Russia into a common front against Great Britain'.[21]

Koch has recently criticised the 'intentionalists' for spending 'little or no time' examining the 'genesis' of *Mein Kampf*. This, he implies, would have revealed to them that Hitler's vision of Soviet Russia (much influenced by Rosenberg and Scheubner-Richter), as a state doomed to disintegrate because of its essentially Jewish leadership, was totally inappropriate when he came to power, because the Soviet Union was by then an established political fact.[22] This criticism is misconceived on at least three levels. Firstly, Hitler's alliance policy as developed in *Mein Kampf* and *Hitler's Secret Book* accepted that Soviet Russia was not going to collapse immediately. He thought it impossible for the Russians by themselves to overthrow Bolshevism, and he did not advocate, as Rosenberg did, a German alliance with a future nationalist Russia, but rather an Anglo-German-Italian alignment against the Soviet Union.[23] Secondly, one conviction remained firm: that Russia would ultimately disintegrate because of its Jewish leadership *and* because of the centrifugal force of various separatist movements. On 22 July 1936, Hitler told the Japanese military attaché, General Oshima, of his determination 'to split up once more the gigantic block of Russia into its original historical components'.[24] The same conviction probably explains why Hitler believed in 1941 that Russia would collapse 'like a house of cards' under a German assault.

The third point to make about Koch's arguments is, of course, that the survival of the Soviet Union reaffirmed the central importance of anti-Bolshevism to the Nazi *Weltanschauung* in the 1930s. The economic and military revival of Russia under the Soviet regime

21. H. Koch, 'Hitler's Programme and the Genesis of Operation "Barbarossa"' in Koch, *Aspects*, p. 321.

22. Koch, 'Introduction to Part II' in Koch, *Aspects*, pp. 182–3.

23. Hitler told Scharrer in December 1922 that 'the development of Russia is to be carefully watched. She could be the power to turn against us as soon as she has recovered internally', Scharrer, 'Bericht', BAK R43I/2681; cf. *MK*, pp. 598–9; *Hitler's Secret Book*, p. 135.

24. Quoted in Hildebrand, *Third Reich*, p. 25.

increased the need for vigilance. It should be noted that Hitler's continuation of the 1926 Treaty of Berlin did not long delay the launching of an anti-Bolshevik campaign. His decision to aid Franco's forces against the Spanish Popular Front government is likely to have been prompted by the emergence of socialist regimes in both Spain and France, even though Göring may well have been more impressed by possible economic gains.[25] The signing of the Anti-Comintern Pact by Germany and Japan on 25 November 1936 (and by Italy a year later) was the most obvious illustration of anti-Soviet prejudices in action. Furthermore, in the memorandum launching the Four Year Plan in August 1936, Hitler stated that it was Germany's inescapable 'mission' to be 'the focus of the Western world against the attacks of Bolshevism' and the strength of the Red Army was evidently giving him cause for concern.[26]

The available evidence tends to suggest that the attempt in 1938–9 to convert the Anti-Comintern Pact into an anti-British alignment, as well as the signing of the Nazi-Soviet Pact in August 1939, were desperate attempts to secure British neutrality during the planned campaign against Poland. They did not reflect a fundamental change in attitude towards Russia; on 11 August Hitler told Carl Jacob Burckhardt, the League of Nations High Commissioner in Danzig: 'Everything I do is directed against Russia. If the West is too blind and stupid to understand that, I shall have to come to terms with the Russians, defeat the West and then turn with all my forces against the Soviet Union.'[27]

The fact that this comment was intended to dissuade the British from interfering in the Polish campaign does not preclude its being a faithful reflection of Hitler's outlook. There is a strong case for arguing that this was precisely what he tried to do after 1939. However, when despite the defeat of Western Europe the British refused to make peace, as another means of forcing them to do so, Hitler decided to attack Russia; as he told army leaders on 31 July 1941, 'if Britain's hope in Russia is destroyed, her hope in America will disappear also, because the elimination of Russia will enormously increase Japanese power in the Far East'.[28] This strategic reasoning, of course, was not incompatible with his intention to eliminate Bolshevism.

---

25. Ibid., pp. 25–6.
26. J. Noakes and G. Pridham, *Nazism 1919–45, vol. 2: State, Economy and Society, 1933–39* (Exeter, 1984), pp. 281–2.
27. Quoted in Hildebrand, *Third Reich*, p. 37.
28. Ibid., p. 54.

It is, in short, quite possible that, despite the vicissitudes of international relations in the 1930s and the early 1940s forcing him reluctantly to abandon the alliance strategy devised in the 1920s to facilitate the defeat of Russia, Hitler's determination on this point remained constant.

The 'functionalists', have however, also raised doubts about the consistency with which the Nazi regime is supposed to have pursued clearly established goals. Mommsen describes Hitler's foreign policy aims as 'purely dynamic in nature', preferring the label 'expansion without object'.[29] Few historians would go this far. Broszat, however, presents a rather more subtle view that there was a fairly consistent direction to Hitler's expansionism, but that 'the aim of winning *Lebensraum* in the East had until 1939/40 largely the function of an ideological metaphor, of a symbol for the initiation of ever new foreign policy activity'. In other words, it did not represent carrying out a 'rational plan of action' to secure a concrete goal, but rather a 'fanatical adherence to an active, dynamic movement'. However, the need to satisfy this 'movement' eventually forced Hitler to turn metaphor into reality.[30]

This is a persuasive argument, which at first sight seems to be supported by research. As Broszat suggests, in the 1920s Hitler was vague about the location of the new living-space to be acquired ('Russia and her vassal border states').[31] He said very little about the fate of Poland, which would geographically be of crucial importance in the realisation of such 'plans'. He barely indicated how *Lebensraum* would ensure German self-sufficiency beyond asserting that 'Russia would give Germany sufficient land for German settlers and a wide field of activity for German industry'.[32] Indeed, one suspects that Hitler was merely trotting out Pan-German clichés gleaned before and during the First World War.

However, this seemingly ritualistic use of the term *Lebensraum* does not necessarily mean that it lacked all specific meaning for Hitler. It was almost certainly inspired by clearly defined Pan-German war aims and the Treaty of Brest-Litovsk in March 1918, which suggests that he probably had a fairly precise idea of the territory to be annexed. In his second book, Hitler referred to the eastern coasts of the Baltic and the 'thinly settled western border regions' of Russia.[33]

29. Mommsen in Laqueur, *Fascism*, p. 177.

30. M. Broszat, 'Soziale Motivation und Führer-Bindung des Nationalsozialismus', *VfZG*, vol. 18 (1970), pp. 407–8.

31. Hitler, *MK*, p. 598.

32. Scharrer, 'Bericht', BAK, R43I/2681.

33. *Hitler's Secret Book*, pp. 195, 74.

This, undoubtedly, meant not only the Baltic States but also the rich agricultural land of the Ukraine, which, as has been shown, he coveted.

Significantly these goals seem to have remained firmly in his mind. In the midst of the Polish crisis Hitler told leading members of the Wehrmacht that 'it is not Danzig that is at stake. For us it is a matter of expanding our living space in the East and making food supplies secure and also solving the problem of the Baltic States'.[34] In 1939 he also clashed with Rosenberg over the latter's continued support for the idea of German assistance to the Ukrainian separatists as a way of accelerating the disintegration of the Soviet Union.[35] Hitler had other plans for the Ukraine, as he revealed to Burckhardt on 11 August 1939: 'I need the Ukraine so that we can never again be starved out as we were in the last war.'[36]

Although Hitler made no mention in the 1920s of Poland in connection with the pursuit of *Lebensraum*, this is not necessarily a proof that he had no rational thoughts on the subject. Hitler so consistently 'disguised' his own territorial ambitions by discussing prewar Germany's foreign policy options, or, perhaps better put, his ambitions were so deeply rooted in the re-creation of German *Ostpolitik* of 1918 that, not surprisingly, he spoke as if Poland did not exist. Almost certainly, he was determined that, as Rosenberg put it in his pamphlet on the party programme in 1923, Poland would not be allowed to obstruct the settlement of the East.[37] Neither this conviction nor the fact that Poland contained former German territory, as Hitler revealed in his second book, rule out the possibility of an alliance in the short run.[38] Hence the signing of the Ten-year Non-Aggression Pact in 1934 and the negotiations in 1938–9 do not mean that he had changed his mind about Poland. The pursuit of *Lebensraum* could not override vital short-term strategic considerations.

So, whilst Hitler gave little serious thought in the 1920s or the 1930s to the details of the execution and the economic implications of extending German living-space, and indeed whilst the idea of a *Grossraumwirtschaft* — the creation of a huge German-controlled market economy in Central and South-Eastern Europe — appeared

34. *DGFP*, Series D, vol. VI, p. 575.

35. Weinberg, *Starting World War II*, p. 475.

36. Quoted in Hildebrand, *Third Reich*, p. 37; see also Goebbels' diary entry on 16 June 1941: 'The rich lands of the Ukraine beckon', F. Taylor (ed.), *The Goebbels Diaries 1939–41* (London, 1982), p. 415.

37. Rosenberg 'Wesen' in *Schriften und Reden*, p. 135; cf. *Zukunftsweg*, pp. 20–1, 97.

38. *Hitler's Secret Book*, pp. 174–75.

to replace *Lebensraum* in Nazi literature for a time, it still seems likely that Hitler's aim was always to extend Germany's frontiers through Central Europe and into Western Russia.[39] '*Lebensraum* in the East' was more a convenient shorthand for his territorial ambitions than an 'ideological metaphor'. It did stand for real and tangible aspirations: for the revival of the halcyon days of the German Empire in Eastern Europe in 1918: and ultimately it meant war with the Soviet Union.

The evidence of the 1920s, therefore, strongly supports the view that Hitler's stated intentions cannot be ignored when analysing Nazi foreign policy in the 1930s. This is not to say that every word which Hitler is recorded as having uttered should be taken literally or regarded as truthful. Nor can it be suggested that Hitler had in mind any timetable of aggression; nor denied that the internal dynamics of the Nazi regime and the international response to Hitler's aggressive policies did influence the course of Nazi foreign policy. What it does mean is that Nazi foreign policy set out to realise the goals chosen by Hitler in the 1920s and attempted to utilise the alliance strategy which he elaborated after 1922. The thinking behind that strategy continued to provide his basic frame of reference in foreign affairs at least until 1937–8, when it became clear that his predictions about Britain were unlikely to be realised. Even though this meant abandoning his preferred strategy — securing Germany's western frontiers before expanding eastwards — in favour of a series of improvised campaigns, Hitler remained committed to the pursuit of *Lebensraum*, in the last instance at Russia's expense.

2. Hitler's 'Ultimate Goals'

The debate within the 'intentionalist' school of thought has been discussed above: the main argument is between those who see Hitler's ambitions as going no further than the expansion of Germany's living-space in Europe (the 'continentalists'), and the 'globalists', who believe that he seriously contemplated the establishment by stages of a German 'world dominion'. Here, the rele-

---

39. For a summary of Hitler's comments on *Lebensraum* and *Grossraumwirtschaft* see W. Carr, *Hitler: A Study in Personality and Politics* (London, 1978), pp. 127–30.

vance for the 1930s of findings relating to the 1920s are worth a brief elaboration.

There can be no doubt that Hitler was acquainted with Pan-German discussions of 'world power status' and 'world dominion'. It is also clear that, ideally, he would have liked Germany to expand both in Europe and overseas, but believed that this would provoke an Anglo-Russian alliance against Germany and the danger of repeating the disastrous 1914–18 two-front war. He therefore decided to acquire territory in Europe first, being convinced, partly perhaps by geopolitical arguments, that a large base of contiguous territory was the best foundation for a revitalised German 'world power'. This, Hitler felt, would leave the way open for later development of an overseas empire.[40]

However, having said that, a number of doubts then arise about the 'globalist' case. Firstly, it has to be remembered that Hitler never clearly laid out any stage-by-stage plan by which Germany would become first a 'world power', then acquire overseas colonies and then establish a German 'world dominion' by taking on the United States in an apocalyptic confrontation. The 'globalists' *Stufenplan* must be regarded, therefore, as possibly 'over-schematic'.[41] Secondly, it cannot be stated with absolute confidence what Hitler meant by 'world dominion'. He certainly gave the impression at one stage that what he wanted for Germany was what Britain enjoyed at the turn of the century; in other words, a position of pre-eminence amongst the other world powers, but certainly not, on this basis, world mastery or world conquest. A third qualm concerns Hitler's comments about America. There was much discussion in the 1920s, especially in geopolitical literature of the emerging challenge of the United States to British and European predominant influence in world affairs.[42] It seems probable, therefore, that Hitler's talk of a distant confrontation between the United States and Germany, the latter possibly allied to Britain, really concerned the probable competition between the North American and European continents. There are certainly no grounds for interpreting this confrontation as a 'last stage' in which Germany would conquer the world.[43] Finally, Hitler's prediction that one race, the purest, would ultimately come to dominate all the earth should not be taken as evidence of his

---

40. Hitler, *MK*, pp. 558, 571.
41. Hiden in Stachura, *Machtergreifung*, p. 153.
42. See above, pp. 166 note 111; Stoakes, 'Evolution', pp. 261–2.
43. Aigner has reached similar conclusions; J. Aigner, 'Hitler's Ultimate Aims — A Programme of World Dominion?' in Koch, *Aspects*, p. 261.

belief in German world supremacy. The Aryan race was never perceived by the Nazis as synonymous, or likely to be synonymous, with the German state.

Even if all these doubts about the *Stufenplan* are misconceived and Hitler really did have far-off global ambitions, the question would still remain whether his distant visions affected the formulation of Nazi foreign policy in the 1930s and 1940s. Hildebrand has argued that about 1938 the Nazi leadership began to consider the execution of plans to make Germany a global world power 'in the later 1940s'. He points to the 'Z Plan' as evidence that 'while still preparing the continental stage of his programme, [Hitler] also had an eye to the future overseas phase'.[44] However, the construction of a large surface fleet could, as Hildebrand himself admits, equally be regarded as evidence of Hitler's preparation for a possible conflict with Britain over his continental aspirations. The colonial propaganda revived at that same time is again, perhaps, more plausibly interpreted as another attempt to persuade Britain not to intervene, rather than as further evidence of an approaching 'overseas phase'.

Hitler's references to conflict with America and the acquisition of colonies in Africa during 1940 and 1941 are also seen by the 'globalists' as evidence that his *Stufenplan* had been telescoped.[45] However, it is far more likely that he was considering the possibility of American intervention in the war in Europe; colonial bases would clearly be of benefit in that case. Hildebrand fails to make the distinction between urgent strategic considerations and Hitler's fantasies about a distant showdown between *Europe* and America. This project was not 'postponed' after German setbacks in Russia; it was always intended for a future in which Germany and Britain would defend the European continent against North America.[46]

In the absence of more concrete evidence — for Hitler's architectural plans, however grandiose, cannot be taken as decisive proof of global aspirations[47] — it must be concluded that in all probability Hitler did not seriously contemplate German world conquest. What he did hope was that Germany would replace Britain as the pre-eminent world power and the way to achieve this was to acquire *Lebensraum* in Eastern Europe and to become master of continental Europe.

44. Hildebrand, *Third Reich*, pp. 32–3.
45. Ibid., p. 58; A. Hillgruber, *Hitler's Strategie*, pp. 316–88.
46. See Hildebrand, *Third Reich*, p. 58.
47. See Thies, *Architekt der Weltherrschaft*.

3. *Hitler's* **Foreign Policy?**

As Tim Mason has written, the central thrust of the 'functionalist' position is 'an insistence upon the fact that the way in which decisions are reached in modern politics is vital to their specific outcomes and thus vital to the historian for an understanding of their meaning'.[48] Historians have in the past too glibly assumed that Hitler made all the important decisions in foreign affairs. A careful examination of the role of various organisations and individuals inside the Nazi state with an interest in foreign policy is now being undertaken.

The present study has shown that Hitler's was by no means the only 'programme' on foreign affairs developed by the Nazi Party in the 1920s. The 'Strasser programme' was the most fullly developed alternative: nor should one overlook Göring's support for a policy akin to Wilhelmine imperialism (strongly criticised by Darré), or the variants by Scheubner-Richter and Rosenberg on Hitler's *Ostpolitik*. Despite the fact that Hitler ensured the primacy of his own views in Nazi propaganda at Bamberg in 1926, the differences of opinion within the party remained unresolved and, arguably, became institutionalised in the Third Reich.[49]

However, the significance of these differences of opinion should not be exaggerated, especially once Gregor Strasser had left the party. Nevertheless, they did lead on occasion to tensions within the Nazi leadership. Goering, having worked hard to secure an Italo-German alliance in 1936 and 1937, clearly had doubts about the risks Hitler was taking in the Czech and Polish crises and together with moderates in the German Foreign office, evidently sought to advance the idea of overseas colonisation and so to avert the danger of European war.[50] Somewhat less well-known are the tensions generated by Rosenberg's commitment to Ukrainian independence: in the short term, his views were at odds with Hitler's offer of 24 October 1938, under which Poland should receive Ukrainian land in return for joining the Anti-Comintern Pact; in the long term, they contradicted Hitler's own ambitions for the area.[51] Hitler's 'go-ahead' for the Hungarians to invade the Carpatho-Ukraine in March 1939 must have irritated Rosenberg's *Aussenpolitisches Amt*,

---

48. Mason in Hirschfeld and Kettenacker, *Führerstaat*, p. 27.

49. As W. Michalka suggests; 'Die nationalsozialistische Aussenpolitik im Zeichen eines "Konzeptionen-Pluralismus"' in M. Funke (ed.), *Hitler, Deutschland und die Mächte*, p. 58.

50. Hildebrand, *Third Reich*, p. 31.

51. Ibid., p. 35.

which was still in contact with representatives of the Ukrainian separatists.[52] Göring, too, may have helped to persuade Hitler to avoid war over the Sudetenland. However, there can be little doubt that in each case Hitler ultimately got his own way.

The role of Joachim von Ribbentrop as Nazi Foreign Minister after February 1938 has attracted a great deal of recent interest. W. Michalka has argued that German foreign policy was 'fundamentally determined' by Ribbentrop after February 1938 and that the Anti-Comintern Pact was the realisation of a conception of foreign policy developed before 1937 'in complete contrast to Hitler's foreign policy programme'.[53] However, it has to be stressed that Ribbentrop's policy of turning the Anti-Comintern Pact into a military alliance against Britain was adopted, as Michalka readily admits,[54] only because of Britain's failure to act as Hitler expected and only in order to facilitate the attainment of Hitler's goals in Eastern Europe. His alternative vision of a Eurasian alliance of Germany, Italy, Russia and Japan did not supplant Hitler's own 'programme', but his tireless negotiations with the Italians and the Japanese between 1937 and 1941 were very much a part of Hitler's flexible response to the 'loss' of Britain.

It would appear therefore that, despite what has been called the 'pluralism' of foreign policy conceptions inside the Nazi state, the chief author of policy remained Hitler. This does mean that he was in complete control of foreign policy-making or able to follow his own whims. SS machinations probably caused the ill-timed Austrian Nazi putsch of 25 July 1934, which was a considerable embarassment to Hitler.[55] Certainly the reaction of the Western Powers to his revisionist policies after 1936 put pressure on him to accelerate preparations for war. Many documents of the time suggest that British rearmament, in particular, convinced him that time was running out for Germany. It is, however, difficult to say whether this alone determined the timing or direction of Hitler's policy initiatives.

52. Weinberg, *Starting World War II*, p. 475.
53. W. Michalka, 'From the Anti-Comintern Pact to the Euro-Asiatic Bloc: Ribbentrop's Alternative Concept of Hitler's Foreign Policy Programme' in Koch, *Aspects*, p. 268.
54. Ibid., p. 284.
55. Hildebrand, *Third Reich*, p. 19.

Conclusion

Research into Nazi attitudes on foreign affairs in the 1920s would therefore tend to point to the following conclusions. Firstly, one cannot overlook the remarkable degree of consistency between Hitler's declared aims in the 1920s and the course of Nazi foreign policy after 1933. This suggests that Nazi diplomacy, whilst by no means impervious to 'structural' pressures from within Germany and from outside, was largely determined by Hitler's convictions about Bolshevism and the pursuit of living-space in the East. This is, of course, not to ignore the considerable degree of opportunism evident in the conduct of that policy, especially after Hitler's preferred alliance strategy proved elusive. Secondly, Hitler's style of leadership (or lack of it) encouraged others in the Nazi movement in the 1920s and in Nazi government after 1933 to develop their own ideas on foreign policy and to pursue them, provided that they did not affect the implementation of Hitler's own strategy. Thirdly, Hitler's territorial ambitions were, in all probability, limited primarily to the European continent. The securing of *Lebensraum* in the East (even if followed by the acquisition of overseas colonies) was not to be the springboard for a later campaign aimed at global conquest. The pursuit of '*Lebensraum* in the East' was not an 'ideological metaphor' but it certainly was a fanatical obsession. Only this could explain why Hitler's final message to the Armed Forces, written on 29 April 1945 with the Third Reich in ruins around him, could end with the exhortation 'to win territory for the German people in the East'.[56]

---

56. Quoted in H. R. Trevor-Roper, 'The Mind of Adolf Hitler' in *Hitler's Table Talk*, p. xxxii.

Bibliography

Unpublished Primary Sources

Bayerisches Hauptstaatsarchiv, Munich, Abteilung I (Allgemeines Staatsarchiv)

i. Sonderabgabe I: Munich police reports on meetings of the NSDAP State Ministry of the Interior: 1474–80; 1738–66.
ii. Akten des Staats-Ministeriums des Innern: M. Inn. 71624–26. Aufenthalt von Russen in Deutschland

Bundesarchiv, Coblenz

i. Nachlass Heinrich Class: Wider den Strom Vol. 2. (Manuscript). Untitled manuscript referred to in the text as 'Class und die NSDAP'.
ii. Nachlass Karl Haushofer: HC 832–955d.
iii. NS 26 Hauptarchiv der NSDAP: 49–50; 81–2; 95–7; 386; 899.
iv. NS 8 Kanzlei Rosenberg: 3; 20; 21; 120; 121; 143; 177; 213.
v. R 43I Reichskanzlei: 558; 760; 2681–8.
vi. Sammlung Schumacher: NSDAP Parteikorrespondenz 1925–33: files 200–208II; 260.

Foreign Office Library, London

i. German Foreign Ministry Files and Microfilms, 1867–1920: AAI Politik 2 — Baltikum F.O. K1752
AA IV-Russland: PO 5A: Innere Politik, russische Emigranten und Monarchisten im Russland: K1865 Vols. 1–7; K 1647.
AA IV-Russland PO5: Innere Politik Parlaments- und Parteiwesen in Russland: K1865, vols. 1–6.
ii. Correspondence between Albrecht and Karl Haushofer (August-September 1940).

Haushofer Family Archive, Hartschimmelhof, Bavaria

Unpublished collection of Karl Haushofer's articles.

Institut für Zeitgeschichte, Munich

National Archives — German Records Microfilmed at Alexandria, Virginia: Microcopy No. T–253. Records of private individuals (Karl Haushofer): Reel/file 46/829–34; 51/919–56/940.

Public Record Office, London

i. German Foreign Ministry Files and Microfilms, 1867–1920:
   Weltkrieg 20d No. 1: Die Zukunft der baltischen Provinzen Kurland, Livland und Estland: vols. 25–47 (21.9.18–25.11.19)
   Weltkrieg 20d Nr. la: vols. 25–6 (24.1.19–28.2.19). (Microfilm G. F. M. 14/27; 21/430–2; 21/426)

Wiener Library, Institute of Contemporary History, London

i. Hauptarchiv der NSDAP (microfilm): Reel/folder number 2/46–50; 4/107–11; 5/139, 114II, 33/636–42; 35/698–704; 41–43/821–72; 44/893–6; 51/1197; 53/1242–63; 56/1370; 68/1495–7A; 80/1604; 83/1662–79; 92/1893; 96/1923II
ii. Newspaper cuttings files: Karl Haushofer

Published Primary Sources

(a) Journals and Newspapers

Alldeutsche Blätter (1918–24)
Der Angriff (1927–8)
Arminius (1926–7)
Auf gut deutsch (1919–21)
Deutsche Zeitung (1923–24)
Das Dritte Reich (1924–6)
Gewissen (1921–4)
Grossdeutsche Zeitung (1924)
Münchner Neueste Nachrichten (1921–8)
Der nationale Sozialist (1926–8)
Nationalsozialistische Briefe (1925–7)
Völkischer Beobachter (1920–8)
Völkischer Kurier (1924–5)
Der Weltkampf. Monatsschrift fuer die Judenfrage aller Laender (1924–8)
Wirtschaftspolitische Aufbau (1922–3)
Zeitschrift für Geopolitik (1924–9)

(b) Contemporary Publications

Alter, Junius (pseud. of Sontag, F.), *Nationalisten. Deutschlands nationales Führertum der Nachkriegszeit* (Leipzig, 1930)

Class, H., *Zum deutschen Kriegsziel* (Munich, 1917)

Coudenhove-Kalergi, R. N. Graf von, *Pan-Europa* (Vienna, 1923)

Drexler, A., *Mein politisches Erwachen* (Munich, 1919)

Eckart, D., *Bolschewismus von Moses bis Lenin. Zwiegespräch zwischen Adolf Hitler und mir* (Munich, 1924)

——, *Totengräber Russlands* (Munich 1921)

Einhart (pseud. of Class, H.), *Deutsche Geschichte* (Leipzig, 1921)

Fechter, P., *Moeller van den Bruck. Ein politisches Schicksal* (Berlin, 1934).

Feder, G., *Der deutsche Staat auf nationaler und sozialer Grundlage* (Munich, 1933), 15th ed.

——, *Das Manifest zur Brechung der Zinsknechtschaft des Geldes* (Munich, 1919)

Frymann, D. (pseud. of Classs, H.), *Wenn ich der Kaiser wär. Politische Wahrheiten und Notwendigkeiten* (Leipzig, 1913)

Goebbels, J., *Lenin Oder Hitler? Eine Rede (19.2.26)* (Zwickau, 1926)

——, *Die zweite Revolution. Briefe an Zeitgenossen* (Zwickau, 1927)

Grimm, H., 'Übervölkerung und Kolonialproblem' in: A. Moeller van den Bruck (ed.), *Die Neue Front* (Berlin, 1922), pp. 329–51.

——, *Volk ohne Raum* (Munich, 1931)

Hasse, E., *Weltpolitik, Imperialismus und Kolonialpolitik* (Munich, 1908)

Haushofer, K., Obst, E., Maull, O., Lautensach, H., *Bausteine zur Geopolitik* (Berlin, 1928)

Haushofer, K. 'Das erwachende Asien', *Süddeutsche Monatshefte*, vol. 24 (1926), pp. 97–121.

——, 'Geographische Grundzüge auswärtiger Politik', *Süddeutsche Monatshefte*, vol. 25 (1927), pp. 258–61.

——, 'Zur Geopolitik des fernen Ostens', *Wissen und Wehr*, (1920), pp. 333–45.

——, *Geopolitik des pazifischen Ozeans* (Berlin, 1925)

——, 'Die geopolitische Betrachtung grenzdeutscher Probleme', K. von Loesch and A. H. Ziegfeld (eds.), *Volk unter Völkern* (Breslau, 1925), pp. 188–92.

——, 'Die geopolitische Tragweite der Rheinfrage', *Deutsche Rundschau*, vol. 48 (1922), pp. 113–19.

——, *Grenzen in ihrer geographischen und politischen Bedeutung* (Berlin, 1927)

——, *Der nationalsozialistische Gedanke in der Welt* (Munich, 1933)

——, 'Die Weichsel — eine gefährdete Wirtschaftsstrasse', *Deutsche Rundschau*, vol. 49 (1923), pp. 113–20.

——, 'Das Wissen von der Grenze und die Grenzen des deutschen Volkes', *Deutsche Rundschau*, vol. 50 (1924), pp. 233–9.

Hitler, A., *Mein Kampf* (London, 1969)

——, 'Warum musste ein 8 November kommen?', *Deutschlands Erneuerung*, vol. 8 (1924), pp. 199–207.

Mackinder, H. J., *Democratic Ideals and Reality, with additional papers* (ed. A. J. Pearce) (New York, 1962)

Manteuffel-Katzdangen, Baron, *Deutschland und der Osten* (Munich, 1926)

Moeller van den Bruck, A., *Das Dritte Reich* (Hamburg, 1931), 3rd ed.

——, *Das ewige Reich*, 3 vols. (ed. H. Schwarz) (Breslau, 1933–35)

——, *Der politische Mensch* (ed. H. Schwarz) (Breslau, 1933)

——, *Rechenschaft über Russland* (ed. H. Schwarz) (Berlin, 1933)

——, *Das Recht der jungen Völker* (ed. H. Schwarz) (Berlin, 1932)

——, *Sozialismus und Aussenpolitik*, (ed. H. Schwarz) (Breslau, 1933)

'Oberland'. *Ziele und Wege des Bundes 'Oberland' e.V.* (Munich, 1926)

Ratzel, F., *Erdenmacht und Völkerschicksal* (ed. Karl Haushofer) (Stuttgart, 1940)

——, *Politische Geographie* (Munich, 1923), 3rd ed.

Rosenberg, A. 'Der Antisemitismus', *Deutschlands Erneuerung*, vol. 6 (1922), pp. 361–70.

——, *Blut und Ehre. Reden und Aufsätze von 1919–1923* (Munich, 1937)

——, *Börse und Marxismus oder der Herr und Knecht* (Munich, 1924)

——, *Dietrich Eckart. Ein Vermächtnis* (Munich, 1935), 3rd ed.

——, *Kampf um die Macht. Aufsätze von 1921–1932* (Munich, 1937)

——, *Nationalsozialismus und Jungdeutscher Orden. Eine Abrechnung mit Arthur Mahraun* (Munich, 1927)

——, *Pest in Russland* (Munich, 1922)

——, *Die Protokolle der Weisen von Zion und die jüdische Weltpolitik* (Munich, 1923)

——, *Schriften und Reden* (Munich 1943)

——, *Dr. Simons, der Anthroposoph in London* (Munich, 1921)

——, *Die Spur des Juden im Wandel der Zeiten* (Munich, 1920)

——, *Der staatsfeindliche Zionismus auf Grund jüdischer Quellen erläutert* (Munich, 1922)

——, *Unmoral im Talmud* (Munich, 1920)

——, *Der völkische Staatsgedanke* (Munich, 1924), 2nd ed.

——, *Das Verbrechen der Freimaurerei* (Munich, 1921)

——, *Der Weltverschwörerkongress zu Basel. Um die Echtheit der zionistischen Protokolle* (Munich, 1927).

——, *Der Zukunftsweg einer deutscher Aussenpolitik* (Munich 1927)

Strasser, G., *Kampf um Deutschland. Reden und Aufsätze eines Nationalsozialisten* (Munich, 1932)

Tafel, P. (ed.), *Das neue Deutschland. Ein Rätestaat auf nationaler Grundlage* (Munich, 1920)

(c) Memoirs

Class, H., *Wider den Strom. Vom Werden und Wachsen der nationalen Opposition im alten Reich.* (Leipzig, 1932)

Fechter, P., *An der Wende der Zeit* (Gütersloh, 1949)

——, *Menschen und Zeiten* (Gütersloh, 1949)

Geis, M. (pseud. of O. Strasser), *Gregor Strasser* (Leipzig, 1933)

Goltz, Graf Rüdiger von der, *Meine Sendung in Finnland und im Baltikum* (Leipzig, 1920)

Grimm. H., *Rückblick* (Göttingen, 1960)

——, *Suchen und Hoffen. Aus meinem Leben 1928 bis 1934* (Lippoldsberg, 1960)

——, *Warum–Woher–Aber Wohin — vor, unter und nach der geschichtlichen Erscheinung Hitlers* (Lippoldsberg, 1954)

Hanfstängl, E., *The Missing Years* (London, 1957)

——, *Zwischen Weissem und Braunem Haus. Memoiren eines politischen Aussenseiters* (Munich, 1970)

Kubizek, August, *The Young Hitler I Knew* (New York, no date)

Lüdecke, K. W., *I Knew Hitler* (London, 1938)

Ludendorff, E., *Auf dem Wege zur Feldherrnhalle* (Munich, 1937)

——, *Kriegführung und Politik* (Berlin, 1922)

——, *My War Memories, 1914–1918*, vol. 2 (London, no date)

——, *Vom Feldherrn zum Weltrevolutionär und Wegbereiter deutscher Volkschöpfung. Meine Lebenserinnerungen von 1919 bis 1925* (Munich, 1940)

Müller, K. A. von, *Im Wandel einer Welt. Erinnerungen. Bd. 3. 1919–32* (Munich, 1966)

Pechel, R. *Deutscher Widerstand* (Zurich, 1947)

Röhm, E., *Die Geschichte eines Hochverräters* (Munich, 1934)

Rosenberg, A., *Grossdeutschland: Traum und Tragödie* (ed. H. Härtle) (Munich, 1970)

——, *Letzte Aufzeichnungen. Ideale und Idole der nationalsozialistischen Revolution* (Göttingen, 1955)

——, *Memoirs of Alfred Rosenberg*, with commentaries by S. Lang and E. von Schenck (New York, 1949)

Speer, A., *Spandau. The Secret Diaries* (London, 1977)

Strasser, O., *Hitler and I* (Oxford, 1940)

Winnig, A., *Heimkehr* (Hamburg, 1935)

Zweig, S., *Die Welt von Gestern* (Stockholm, 1947)

(d) Published Documents

Boepple, E., (ed.), *Adolf Hitlers Reden* (Munich, 1925)

Bonnin, G. (ed.), *Le putsch de Hitler à Munich en 1923* (Les Sables-d'Olonne, 1966)

Deuerlein, E., *Der Aufstieg der NSDAP in Augenzeugenberichten* (Düsseldorf, 1968)

——, 'Hitlers Eintritt in die Politik und die Reichswehr', *VfZG*, vol. 7 (1959), pp. 177–227.

——, '(ed)., *Der Hitler-Putsch. Bayerische Dokumente zum 8/9 November 1923* (Stuttgart, 1962)

I Documenti Diplomatici Italiani. Settima Serie 1922–35, vol. 1 (Rome, 1953)

Documents on German Foreign Policy, 1918–1945, Series D (London, 1949–64)

Harbeck, K. H., (ed.), *Akten der Reichskanzlei. Das Kabinett Cuno* (Boppard am Rhein, 1968)

Haushofer, K., 'Defense of German Geopolitics' in E. A. Walsh, *Total Power. A Footnote to History* (New York, 1948)

Heiber, H., (ed.), *The Early Goebbels Diaries. The Journal of Joseph Goebbels from 1925–26* (London, 1962)

Der Hitler-Prozess vor dem Volksgericht in München (Munich, 1924)

Hofer, W., (ed.), *Der Nationalsozialismus. Dokumente 1933–1945* (Frankfurt/ Main, 1957).

Jäckel, E. with Kuhn, A., (eds.), *Hitler. Sämtliche Aufzeichnungen 1905–1924* (Stuttgart, 1980)

Jacobsen, H. A. and Jochmann, W. (eds.), *Ausgewählte Dokumente zur Geschichte des Nationalsozialismus 1933–1945. Kommentar* (Bielefeld, 1966)

Jochmann, W., (ed.), *Nationalsozialismus und Revolution. Ursprung und Geschichte der NSDAP in Hamburg, 1922–1933. Dokumente* (Frankfurt, 1963)

Kühnl, R., 'Zur Programmatik der nationalsozialistischen Linken: Das Strasser-Programme von 1925/26', *VfZG*, vol. 14 (1966), pp. 317–33.

Lane, B. M. and Rupp, L. J. (eds.), *Nazi Ideology before 1933. A Documentation* (Manchester, 1978)

Maser, W., (ed.), *Hitler's Letters and Notes* (New York, 1976)

Noakes, J. and Pridham, G., *Nazism 1919–45*, vol. 2: *State, Economy and Society, 1933–39* (Exeter, 1984)

Phelps, R. H., 'Hitlers "grundlegende" Rede über den Antisemitismus', *VfZG*, vol. 16 (1968), pp. 390–420.

——, 'Hitler als Parteiredner im Jahre 1920', *VfZG*, vol. 11, (1963), pp. 274–330.

Prange, G. (ed.), *Hitler's Words* (Washington, 1944)

Preiss, H., (ed.), *Adolf Hitler in Franken. Reden aus der Kampfzeit* (Nuremberg, 1939)

Schlabrendorff, F. von, *The Secret War Against Hitler* (Appendix I. Class's autobiographical notes) (London, 1965)

Taylor, F. (ed.), *The Goebbels Diaries 1939–41* (London, 1982)

Taylor, T. (ed.), *Hitler's Secret Book* (New York, 1961)

Trevor-Roper, H. R. (ed.), *Hitler's Table Talk 1941–44* (London, 1953)

Tyrell, A (ed.), *Führer befiehl . . . Selbstzeugnisse aus der 'Kampfzeit' der NSDAP* (Düsseldorf, 1969)

Weinberg, G. L. (ed.). *Hitlers Zweites Buch. Ein Dokument aus dem Jahr 1928* (Stuttgart, 1961)

Secondary Sources

Adam, R., *Moeller van den Bruck* (Königsberg, 1933)

Aigner, D., *Das Ringen um England. Das deutsch-britische Verhältnis*, (Munich, 1969)

Auerbach, H., 'Hitlers' politische Lehrjahre und die Münchener Gessell-schaft 1919–1923', *VfZG*, vol. 25 (1977), pp. 1–45.

Aycoberry, P., *The Nazi Question. An Essay on the Interpretations of National Socialism (1922–1975)* (London and Henley, 1981)

Binion, R., 'Hitler's Concept of Lebensraum: The Psychological Basis', *History of Childhood Quarterly*, vol. 1 (1973), pp. 187–258.

Boehm, M. H., 'Baltische Einflüsse auf die Anfänge des Nationalsozialis-mus', *Jahrbuch des Baltischen Deutschtums*, vol. 14 (1967), pp. 56–69.

Boog, H., 'Graf Ernst zu Reventlow (1869–1943). Eine Studie zur Krise der deutschen Geschichte seit dem Ende des 19. Jahrhunderts', doctoral dissertation, University of Heidelberg, 1970.

Bracher, K. D., *Die Auflösung der Weimarer Republik* (Berlin, 1965)

Broszat, M., 'Betrachtungen zu "Hitlers Zweitem Buch"'; *VfZG*, vol. 9 (1961), pp. 417–29.

——, *The Hitler State* (Harlow, 1981)

——, 'Soziale Motivation und Führer-Bindung des Nationalsozialismus', *VfZG*, vol. 18 (1970)

Bullock, A., *Hitler: A Study in Tyranny* (Hardmondsworth, 1962)

Carr, W., *Arms, Autarky and Aggression* (London, 1972)

——, *Hitler: A Study in Personality and Politics* (London, 1978)

Cecil, R., *The Myth of the Master Race: Alfred Rosenberg and Nazi Ideology* (London, 1972)

Chamberlin, B. S., 'The Enemy on the Right. The Alldeutsche Verband in the Weimar Republic, 1918–1926', doctoral dissertation, University of Maryland, 1972.

Chickering, R., *We Men Who Feel Most German. A Cultural Study of the Pan-German League, 1886–1914* (London, 1984)

Cohn, N., *Warrant for Genocide. Myth of the Jewish World Conspiracy and the Protocols of the Elders of Zion* (London, 1967)

Daim, W., *Der Mann, der Hitler die Ideen gab* (Munich, 1958)

Deist, W., *The Wehrmacht and German Rearmament* (London, 1981)

Deuerlein, E., *Hitler. Eine politische Biographie* (Munich, 1969)

Dickmann, F., 'Machtwille und Ideologie in Hitlers aussenpolitischen Zielsetzungen vor 1933', in K. Repgen and St. Skalweit (eds.), *Spiegel der Geschichte*. (Münster, 1964), pp. 915–40.

Dorpalen, A., 'Comment', *History of Childhood Quarterly. The Journal of Psychohistory*, vol. 1 (1973), pp. 239–45.

——, *The World of General Haushofer* (New York, 1942)

Düllfer, J., *Weimar, Hitler und die Marine. Reichspolitik und Flottenbau, 1920–1939* (Düsseldorf, 1973)

Fest, J., *The Face of the Third Reich* (London, 1972)

——, *Hitler. Eine Biographie* (Frankfurt am Main, 1973)

Fischer, F., *Germany's Aims in the First World War* (London, 1967)

——, *War of Illusions. German Policies from 1911 to 1914* (London, 1975)

Franz-Willing, G., *Die Hitlerbewegung: der Ursprung, 1919–22* (Hamburg, 1962)

——, *Krisenjahr der Hitlerbewegung 1923* (Oldendorf, 1975)

Frommelt, R., *Paneuropa oder Mitteleuropa* (Stuttgart, 1977)

Funke, M. (ed.), *Hitler, Deutschland und die Mächte. Materialien zur Aussenpolitik des Dritten Reiches* (Düsseldorf, 1978)

Gilbert, F. W., *Mackinder's Scope and Methods of Geography and the Geopolitical Pivot of History* (London, 1951)

Görlitz, W. and Quint, H., *Adolf Hitler. Eine Biographie* (Stuttgart, 1952)

Grimm, Claus, *Jahre deutscher Entscheidung in Baltikum 1918/19* (Essen 1939)

Harbeck, K.-H., *'Zeitschrift für Geopolitik, 1924–44'*, doctoral dissertation, University of Kiel, 1963.

Hart, F. T., *Alfred Rosenberg. Der Mann und sein Werk* (Berlin, 1939)

Hartwig, E., 'Der Alldeutsche Verband, 1890–1939' in D. Fricke et al. (eds.), *Die bürgerlichen Parteien in Deutschland 1830–1945* (Leipzig, 1968)

Hasse, E., *Weltpolitik, Imperialismus und Kolonialpolitik* (Munich, 1908)

Hasselbach, U. von, 'Die Entstehung der Nationalsozialistischen Deutschen Arbeiterpartei 1919–1923', doctoral dissertation, University of Leipzig, 1931.

Hauner, M., 'Did Hitler want a World Dominion?', *Journal of Contemporary History*, vol. 13 (1978), pp. 15–32.

Heiden, K., *Der Fuehrer. Hitler's Rise to Power* (London, 1944)

——, *A History of National Socialism* (London, 1971)

Henke, J., *England in Hitlers politischem Kalkül 1935–39* (Boppard am Rhein, 1973)

Hiden, J. and Farquharson, J., *Explaining Hitler's Germany. Historians and the Third Reich* (London, 1983)

Hildebrand, K., *The Foreign Policy of the Third Reich* (London, 1973)

——, *Vom Reich zum Weltreich. Hitler, NSDAP und koloniale Fragen, 1919–45* (Munich, 1969)

——, *The Third Reich* (London, 1984)

Hillgruber, A., 'Die "Endlösung" und das deutsche Ostimperium als Kernstück des rassenideologischen Programms des Nationalsozialismus', *VfZG*, vol. 20 (1972), pp. 133–51.

——, 'England's place in Hitler's plans for world dominion', *Journal of Contemporary History*, vol. 9 (1974), pp. 5–22.

——, *Hitlers Strategie. Politik und Kriegführung, 1940–1941* (Frankfurt am Main, 1965)

Hirschfeld, G. and Kettenacker, L. (eds.), *Der 'Führerstaat': Mythos und Realität* (Stuttgart, 1981)

Horn, W., *Führerideologie und Parteiorganisation in der NSDAP* (Düsseldorf, 1972)

——, 'Ein unbekannter Aufsatz Hitlers aus dem Frühjahr 1924', *VfZG*, vol. 16 (1968), pp. 280–94.

Jäckel, E., *Hitlers Weltanschauung. Entwurf einer Herrschaft* (Tübingen, 1969)

Jacobsen, H.-A., *Karl Haushofer — Leben und Work*, 2 vols. (Boppard am Rhein, 1979)

——, *Nationalsozialistische Aussenpolitik 1933–8* (Frankfurt, 1968)

Jenks, W. A., *Vienna and the Young Hitler* (New York, 1960)

Jetzinger, F., *Hitler's Youth* (London, 1958)

Kershaw, I., *The Nazi Dictatorship. Problems and Perspectives of Interpretation* (London, 1985)

Kissenkoetter, U., *Gregor Strasser und die NSDAP* (Stuttgart, 1978)

Klemperer, K. von, *Germany's New Conservativism* (Princeton, N.J., 1968)

Koch, H. W., (ed.), *Aspects of the Third Reich* (London, 1985)

Krebs, W., 'Der Alldeutsche Verband in den Jahren 1918 bis 1939', unpublished Dr. Phil. thesis, Humboldt Universität zu Berlin, 1970

Kruck, A., *Geschichte des Alldeutschen Verbandes, 1890–1939* (Wiesbaden, 1954)

Kuhn, A., *Hitlers aussenpolitisches Programm. Entstehung und Entwicklung 1919–1939* (Stuttgart, 1970)

Kuron, H. J., 'Freikorps und Bund "Oberland"', unpublished dissertation, Erlangen University, 1960.

Laack-Michel, U., *Albrecht Haushofer und der Nationalsozialismus* (Stuttgart, 1970)

Lane, B. M., 'Nazi Ideology: Some Unfinished Business', *Central European History*, vol. 7 (1974), pp. 3–30.

Lange, K., 'Der Terminus "Lebensraum" in Hitlers Mein Kampf', *VfZG*, vol. 13 (1965), pp. 426–37.

Laqueur, W. (ed.), *Fascism. A Reader's Guide* (Harmondsworth, 1979)

——, 'Hitler and Russia 1919–23', *Survey*, (October 1962), pp. 89–113.

——, 'Russia and Germany', *Survey*, (October 1962), pp. 3–12.

——, *Russia and Germany. A Century of Conflict* (London, 1965)

Leopold, M. A., *Alfred Hugenberg. The Radical Nationalist Campaign against the Weimar Republic* (Yale, 1977)

Leverkuehn, P., *Posten auf ewiger Wache. Aus dem abendteuerlichen Leben des Max von Scheubner-Richter* (Essen, 1938)

Lohalm, U., *Völkischer Radikalismus. Die Geschichte des Deutschvölkischen Schutz- und Trutzbundes 1919–1923* (Hamburg, 1970)

Maser, W., *Adolf Hitler* (London, 1974)

——, *Die Frühgeschichte der NSDAP* (Frankfurt, 1965)

——, *Hitler's 'Mein Kampf' — An Analysis* (London, 1966)

Marks, S., *The Illusion of Peace. International Relations, 1918–1933* (London, 1976)

Matthias, E., 'The Western Powers in Hitler's World of Ideas' in A. J. Nicholls and E. Matthias (eds.), *German Democracy and the Triumph of Hitler* (London, 1971), pp. 161–74.

Michalka, W., *Ribbentrop und die deutsche Weltpolitik, 1933–40* (Munich, 1980)

Michaelis, M., 'World Power Status or World Dominion?' *Historical Journal*, vol. 15 (1972), pp. 331–60.

Moltmann, G., 'Weltherrschaftsideen Hitlers' in O. Brunner and D. Gerhard, *Europa and Übersee. Festschrift für Egmont Zechlin* (Hamburg, 1961), pp. 197–240.

Mosse, G., *The Crisis of German Ideology* (New York, 1964)

Neurohr, J., *Der Mythos vom Dritten Reich. Zur Geistesgeschichte des Nationalso-*

zialismus (Stuttgart, 1957)

Noakes, J., *The Nazi Party in Lower Saxony, 1921–33* (Oxford, 1971)

Norton, D. H., 'Karl Haushofer and the German Academy, 1925–45', *Central European History'* 1 (1968), pp. 80–100.

——, 'Karl Haushofer and his influence on Nazi Ideology and German Foreign Policy, 1919–45', doctoral dissertation, Clark University, Worcester, Mass., 1965.

Nyomarkay, J., 'Factionalism in the National Socialist German Workers' Party, 1925–26: the Myth and Reality of the "Northern Faction"', *Political Science Quarterly*, vol. 80 (1965), pp. 22–47.

Overy, R. J., *Göring. 'The Iron Man'* (London, 1985)

Paetel, K. O., 'Der deutsche Nationalbolschewismus, 1918/32: Ein Bericht', *Aussenpolitik*, vol. 3 (1952), pp. 229–41.

Parkinson, R., *Tormented Warrior. Ludendorff and the Supreme Command* (London, 1978)

Pese, W. W., 'Hitler und Italien 1920–26', *VfZG*, vol. 3 (1955), pp. 113–25.

Petzold, J., 'Zur Funktion des Nationalismus. Moeller van den Brucks Beitrag zur faschistischen Ideologie', *Zeitschrift für Geschichtswissenschaft*, vol. 21 (1973), pp. 1285–300.

Phelps, R. H., 'Anton Drexler — Der Gründer der NSDAP', *Deutsche Rundschau*, vol. 87 (1961), pp. 1134–43.

——, 'Before Hitler Came: The Thule Society and Germanen Orden', *Journal of Modern History*, vol. 35 (1963), pp. 245–61.

——, 'Hitler and the Deutsche Arbeiterpartei', *American Historical Review*, vol. 68 (1962–3), pp. 974–86.

——, 'Theodor Fritsch und der Antisemitismus', *Deutsche Rundschau*, vol. 87 (1961), pp. 442–9.

Plewnia, M., *Auf dem Weg zu Hitler. Der 'völkische' Publizist Dietrich Eckart* (Bremen, 1970)

Rich, N., *Hitler's War Aims* (London, 1973)

Rimscha, H. von, *Russland jenseits der Grenzen 1921–26* (Jena, 1927)

Robertson, E. (ed.), *The Origins of the Second World War* (London, 1971)

Rosen, E., 'Mussolini und Deutschland 1922–23', *VfZG*, vol. 5 (1957), pp. 17–41.

Schilling, A., *Dr. Walter Riehl und die Geschichte des Nationalsozialismus* (Leipzig, 1933)

Schubert, G., *Anfänge nationalsozialistischer Aussenpolitik* (Cologne, 1963)

Schüddekopf, O. E., *Linke Leute von rechts. Die nationalrevolutionären Minderheiten und der Kommunismus in der Weimarer Republik* (Stuttgart, 1960)

Schwierskott, H. J., *Arthur Moeller van den Bruck und der revolutionäre Nationalismus in der Weimarer Republik* (Göttingen, 1962)

Smith, B. F., *Adolf Hitler: His Family, Childhood and Youth* (Standford, 1967)

Smith, D. M., *Mussolini's Roman Empire* (Harmondsworth, 1979)

Stachura, P. D., *Gregor Strasser and the Rise of Nazism* (London, 1983)

——, (ed.), *The Nazi Machtergreifung* (London, 1983)

——, (ed.), *The Shaping of the Nazi State* (London, 1978)

Stoakes, G., 'The Evolution of Nazi Ideas on Foreign Policy, 1919–1928', doctoral dissertation, University of Sheffield, 1984.

Stern, F., *The Politics of Cultural Despair* (Berkeley, 1961)

Thies, J., *Architekt der Weltherrschaft. Die 'Endziele' Hitlers* (Düsseldorf, 1976),

Tyrell, A., *Vom 'Trommler' zum 'Führer'* (Munich, 1975)

Vietsch, E. von, *Arnold Rechberg und das Problem der politischen West-Orientierung Deutschlands nach dem I. Weltkrieg* (Coblenz, 1958)

Volkmann, H. E., *Die russische Emigration in Deutschland 1919–29* (Würzburg, 1966)

Weinberg, G. L., *The Foreign Policy of Hitler's Germany. Diplomatic Revolution in Europe, 1933–36* (Chicago/London, 1970)

——, *The Foreign Policy of Hitler's Germany. Starting World War II* (Chicago/London, 1980)

——, 'National Socialist Organisation and Foreign Policy Aims in 1927', *Journal of Modern History*, vol. 36 (1964), pp. 428–33.

Whiteside, A. G., *The Socialism of Fools. Georg Ritter von Schönerer and Austrian Pan-Germanism* (Berkeley, 1975)

Williams, R. C., *Culture in Exile. Russian Émigrés in Germany 1881–1941* (Ithaca and London, 1972)

Woerden, A. V. N. van, 'Hitler faces England: Theories, Images, and Policies', *Acta Historiae Neerlandica* vol. 3 (1968), pp. 141–59.

Index

APR 2 4 1988

DEC 0 4 1988